SELF-KNOWLEDGE
AN ESSAY IN AUTOBIOGRAPHY

NIKOLAI BERDYAEV

Self-Knowledge
An Essay in Autobiography

⊕

Translated by
Katharine Lampert

Foreword by
Boris Jakim

SEMANTRON PRESS

Philmont NY

First Edition, Geoffrey Bles, Ltd., London, 1950
Second, enlarged edition © Semantron Press 2009
Semantron is an imprint of Sophia Perennis LLC
Foreword and Biography © Sophia Perennis 2009
Translated by Katharine Lampert

For information, address:
Sophia Perennis, P.O. Box 931
Philmont NY 12565

Library of Congress Cataloging-in-Publication Data

Berdyaev, Nikolai, 1874–1948.
[Samopoznanie. English]
Self-knowledge: an essay in autobiography / Nikolai Berdyaev;
2nd, enl. ed.

p. cm.
ISBN 978 1 59731 258 5 (pbk: alk. paper)
ISBN 978 1 59731 191 5 (hbk: alk. paper)

1. Berdyaev, Nikolai. 2. Philosophers—Soviet
Union—Biography. I. Title.
B4238.B44A33 2009
197—dc22   2009022490

Cover design: Michael Schrauzer

I DEDICATE THIS BOOK
TO MY DEAREST FRIEND
EUGENIE RAPP

CONTENTS

FOREWORD TO NEW EDITION

The Russian title of the present work is *"Samopoznanie,"*[1] self-knowledge, self-knowing. This implies a Socratic exercise of plumbing one's own depths and rising back to the surface with a philosophical understanding and justification of one's life. Nikolai[2] Berdyaev describes his book as "a philosophical autobiography or a history of spirit and self-knowledge" (p. ix, present work). The book is not tied to any systematic plan; it contains reminiscence, but that is not what is important in it. He states that this book is openly egocentric—but egocentric in the sense that he subjects his self and his life to critical inquiry. By design, this book is philosophical and is devoted to the problems of philosophy. Berdyaev's aim is to understand himself, to discover his "own image and ultimate destiny" (p. x, present volume). By plumbing the depths of his soul, he felt that he could help formulate and resolve certain problems concerning human destiny and contribute to the understanding of our era. He also felt the need to explain the apparent inconsistencies and contradictions which have been ascribed to his philosophical outlook.

This idea of exploring man's destiny in the present era is tied to Berdyaev's realization that it has been his lot to live in an age of catastrophe both for his nation and for the whole world. He writes: "Before my eyes, old worlds have collapsed and new ones have arisen, I was able to observe the extraordinary vicissitudes of the destiny of man. . . . In the trials which I have

---

1. Published in Russian in 1949. The original translation into English (1950) was entitled: *Dream and Reality. An Essay in Autobiography.*

2. "Nikolai" is the more correct form of Berdyaev's first name. The original translations of Berdyaev's works into English used "Nicolas"; in order to avoid confusion this spelling is retained on the cover and title page.

iii

undergone, I have come to believe in a higher power which has guided me and probably saved me from my own undoing" (p. xi, present volume).

One of Berdyaev's underlying motives in writing this book was to express the hidden tragedy of life, of which he was so intensely aware. His sense of the tragedy of life was connected with the fact that he was a member of the Russian nation and also a Russian philosopher. He was a member of the Russian intelligentsia, which was characterized by a search for the truth and by a yearning for universality, for the community of brotherhood. He inherited the tradition of the Slavophiles and of the Westernizers, of both Khomiakov and Herzen. This is how he characterizes himself: "I am above all an heir of Dostoevsky and Tolstoy, as well as of Vladimir Solovyov. . . . I am a Russian, and I regard my universality, my very hostility to nationalism, as Russian" (p. xiv, present volume). Thus, the sense of tragedy and the sense of universality, two characteristics of the Russian soul, formed an integral part of Berdyaev's life and cried out to be expressed.

He speaks of a distinct rhythm of ebb and flow in his life, marked by moments of creative inspiration and by moments of weariness and lassitude. He was never able to attain a lasting equilibrium of mind, and all his thinking was accompanied by continual tension and inner conflict. This is how he puts it: "Sometimes I was moved in my thinking by anger, by a spirit of opposition to or dissension from this or that, and by other passionate emotions, thereby often falling into extremes, without, however, ever allowing my consciousness to be wholly obscured or my inmost vision to be troubled" (p. 104, present volume).

Berdyaev characterizes his relationship with the world as one of alienation: everyday life always seemed repellent to him, and this realization of the alien character of the world resulted in an inability to acquire a firm footing in it. But it would be erroneous to infer that he was a solipsist; on the contrary, the movement of self-transcendence was a matter of intense concern to him: "Always and everywhere, I am allured by and drawn towards the transcendent, the Other, which reaches out beyond all boundaries and limitations and holds within itself the mystery of life" (p. 47, present volume). Related to this is the fact that Berdyaev always experienced a profound sense of anguish. Anguish never left him and was more or less intense at different stages of his inner development. For him, anguish meant a longing for another world, for that which is beyond the boundaries of our finite world. "Anguish can awake my awareness of God, but it can also signify my God-forsakenness. It intervenes, as it were, between the transcendent and the abyss of non-being" (p. 50, present volume).

Some have called Berdyaev the philosopher of freedom; when he was young he was called "the free son of the ether." He says about himself: "the war for freedom which I waged all my life was for me the thing of the greatest value and importance" (p. 57, present volume). He fought not just for political freedom (although he did that too); for him, freedom was a primordial source and condition of existence; and he put Freedom, rather than Being, at the basis of his philosophy. According to Berdyaev, "God desired freedom and freedom gave rise to tragedy in the world" (p. 56, present volume). Part and parcel of this yearning for freedom was his rebelliousness. He tells us that rebellion marked not a phase in his intellectual development, but an innate quality of his thinking and living. He was easily moved to revolt, and injustice and violence done to the dignity and freedom of man evoked angry protests in him. Did he revolt against God? If he did, it was in the name of God. He writes: "I have often rebelled against the ideas and beliefs about God framed by men, that is to say, against false gods rather than God himself" (p. 64, present volume).

The sufferings of man roused Berdyaev to pity and compassion. It was always difficult for him to accept anything that degrades the dignity of man, even for a single individual; yet he was aware that the struggle for the dignity of man involves a readiness to accept suffering and affliction on the part of those who join the cause. This is an excruciating antinomy: man is called upon to be compassionate to all living things, but at the same time he must assent to the suffering that is implied in the recognition of and struggle for the dignity and freedom of man. Berdyaev's rejection of traditional eschatology is connected to the value he attached to pity and compassion: he was unable to conceive of any joy or bliss in the face of the immeasurable suffering and agony of the world, and he was disgusted by and rejected the traditional notion of the torments of hell. He writes: "I could never admit that there is less compassion and pity in God than in myself, imperfect and sinful as I am" (p. 73, present volume).

Alienation, anguish, pity, wrestlings of the spirit—this is the soil out of which Berdyaev's philosophy grew, so it is obvious that he could not limit philosophical knowledge to logic and epistemology as so many of his contemporaries did. He writes that true philosophical knowledge "appeared to him as creative understanding, involving a movement of the spirit, a direction of will, a sensitivity, a search for meaning, where one is shaken, elated, disillusioned, and imbued with hope" (p. 94, present volume). For Berdyaev, philosophy truly signifies love of wisdom; it is rooted in emotion and passion. Philosophical knowledge springs from the integral life of the spirit; it is pre-eminently spiritual knowledge.

He regards his philosophy as "existentialist" in the sense that he believes in the priority of the subject over the object. He is an "existentialist" because he sees the life of man and of the world torn by contraries, which must be confronted and maintained in their tension, and which no intellectual system of a closed and complete totality can resolve. Here is what he writes: "I have always desired that philosophy should be not *about* something or somebody but should be that very something or somebody, in other words, that it should be the revela-

tion of the original nature and character of the subject itself"
(p. 97, present volume).

Berdyaev is often considered a "religious philosopher."
What is his religious belief or religious worldview? He asserts
that he is not a theologian, is not bound by the dogmas of any
church, but rather speaks with "the voice of free religious
thought" (p. 176, present volume). He says about himself that,
although he considers himself a Christian, he was never particularly drawn to the sacramental and liturgical element in the
religious life, and no intense experiences are associated in his
memory with that side of the Church. His original religious
impulse was bound up with a bitter sense of discontent with
and dissent from the world with its evil and corruption. This
led to the subsequent conviction that "the existence of evil is
not so much an obstacle to faith in God as a proof of God's
existence, a challenge to turn inward toward that in which love
triumphs over hatred, union over division, and eternal life over
death" (p. 173, present volume). For Berdyaev, God does not
dominate this fallen and dejected world; God's revelation to
the world and to man is eschatological in character; in other
words, it is a revelation of a kingdom that is not of this world.
Berdyaev cannot apply to God the categories of power and government, or of anger, jealousy, vengeance, and even justice. He
thinks of divine love in terms of sacrificial love, of an eternal
movement toward the loved one; and for Berdyaev "this relative anthropomorphism is bound up with a recognition of the
central place of man in the world" (p. 174, present volume). He
tells us that when he became conscious of himself as a Christian, he came to a belief in Divine Humanity[1]; "that is, in
becoming a believer in God, I did not cease to believe in man

1. The doctrine—first formulated in the Nicaeno-Constantinopolitan
Creed and later developed by Russian religious philosophers, notably
Vladimir Solovyov—that man shares in God's divinity and is destined to be
God's creative collaborator in the world.

and in man's dignity and creative freedom.[1] I became a Christian because I was seeking for a deeper and truer foundation for belief in man" (p. 178, present volume).

This belief in Divine Humanity is directly linked with Berdyaev's ideas about the creative vocation of man. For Berdyaev, human creativity is not a claim or a right on the part of man, but God's claim on and call to man. God awaits man's creative act, which is the response to the creative act of God. "Man awaits the birth of God in himself, and God awaits the birth of man in Himself. It is at this level that the question of creativity arises, and it is from this point of view that it should be approached" (p. 204, present volume). Creativity is a flight into the infinite, an activity that transcends the finite towards the infinite. The creative act is an "ecstasy," a breaking through to eternity.[2] The evils that man caused in the 20th century did not shake Berdyaev's faith in him, in the divine image and the divine idea of man. For Berdyaev, life is the mystery of the spirit, a drama in which man strives in a constant but often futile effort to embody the creative vision of his spirit. Here is what Berdyaev writes: "The meaning of life lies in a return to the mystery of the spirit in which God is born in man and man is born in God. However, the return is not a relapse into some primal innocence, but a process of creation which contains in some sense all the experiences, trials, and ordeals which attend the destiny of man" (p. 292, present volume).

BORIS JAKIM
2009

---

1. Berdyaev calls himself a "modernist" in the sense that he recognized the possibility of a creative process of Christianity, of the emergence of ever new realities within the latter. He was one of the representatives of Russian religious thought at the beginning of the 20th century who yearned for a continued revelation in Christianity, for a new outpouring of the Holy Spirit.

2. These ideas receive a profound and comprehensive development in Berdyaev's book *The Meaning of the Creative Act*.

PREFACE

The idea of this book has been in my mind for a long time. I conceived it as something quite new. Books written about oneself are avowedly egocentric. The reading of reminiscences leaves a feeling of discomfort: the writer recalls people and events and is yet, in fact, throughout concerned with his own person. There are several kinds of autobiographical books. There is, in the first place, the diary, written year by year and day by day. This represents a very free form of literature, extremely popular to-day in France. Amiel's diary is an outstanding example; and, among more recent diaries, André Gide's *Journal*. Then there is the confession, of which St. Augustine and Jean-Jacques Rousseau have given the most celebrated examples. Further, there are reminiscences. Alexander Herzen's *Past Events and Thoughts*, for which a maze of historical data serves as material, is one of the most brilliant works of this kind ever written. Finally, there is the autobiography strictly so called, which recounts the events, both outward and inward, of a life in chronological order. All these types of books achieve, with more or less accuracy and candour, a record or recapitulation of the past. The thoughts and feelings expressed by the writer are concerned with the past.

The present book does not belong wholly to any one of these types. I have never kept a diary. I do not intend to confess my deeds and misdeeds in public. I do not want to write reminiscences about the happenings which occurred in the course of my life: at any rate this is not my chief concern. I do not even propose to write an autobiography in the current sense of the word, or to tell the story of my life in chronological order. Inasmuch as my book is autobiographical in character, it may be described as a philosophical autobiography or a history of spirit and self-knowledge.

Remembrance of the past can never remain a passive attitude; it cannot be a mere objective record of past events. It is not surprising, therefore, that autobiographies are usually regarded as lacking in candour. But memory must needs be active: it is characterized by a creative, transfiguring power inherent in it, and involves individual emphasis, partiality and, therefore, prejudice. Memory is selective; it draws out or chooses certain things, both consciously and unconsciously, while leaving others in the background of oblivion. The remembrance of my life in its varied manifestations is for me an avowedly active remembrance, that is to say, a creative effort of my mind apprehending my past in my present. Between the facts of my life and their record in this book there intervenes a creative cognitive activity, whereby these facts acquire significance; and it is this that interests me above everything else.

Goethe wrote a book about himself which bears the significant title, *The Poetry and Truth of my Life*. It contains not merely a factual record of his life but reflects also the creative imagination of the poet. I am not a poet; I am a philosopher. The book I have written contains no fictional material, but it reflects a process of cognitive activity and an endeavour to discover the meaning in my life. Such a cognitive process is not a mere remembering or recapitulation of the past: it is a creative act performed at the present moment. The value of this act is determined by the degree to which it rises above time and is united with 'existential' time, that is to say, with eternity. The conquest of the deadly flux of time has always been the chief concern of my life.

This book is frankly and openly egocentric. But egocentricity, repulsive though it is, may be redeemed by the fact that I call my self and my life into question and make them the object of critical enquiry. That is what I am trying to do in this book. I do not want to lay bare my soul or to wash my linen in public. This book is philosophical in conception and it is devoted to the problems of philosophy. It is concerned with knowledge of self and with the need to understand oneself, to discover one's own image and ultimate destiny.

So-called existentialist philosophy (the novelty of which, by the way, has been greatly exaggerated) regards philosophy as the knowledge of reality through human existence and its concrete manifestations. Now it is a fact that my own existence is the most 'existential' of all. In knowing himself man is initiated into mysteries unknown to him through his knowledge of others. I have experienced the world around me and all the historical processes and events of my time as part of myself, as my spiritual biography. At the deepest mystical level everything that has happened to the world happened to me. And here I come up against the fundamental conflict inherent in me. On the one hand, I experience the events of my age and the destiny of the world in which I live as events happening to me, as my own destiny; but, on the other hand, I am conscious of, and tormented by, the fact that the world is utterly alien and divorced from me. If I had written a diary it would have borne the legend: *nothing is my own and all things are mine.*

It has been my lot to live in an age catastrophic alike for my own country and the whole world. Before my eyes old worlds have collapsed and new ones have arisen. I was able to observe the extraordinary vicissitudes of the destiny of man. I have seen people transformed by their experiences; I have seen them adapt and betray themselves in the course of these experiences. Such betrayal is, perhaps, what is hardest to bear in life. In the trials which I have undergone I have come to believe in a higher power which has guided me and probably saved me from my own undoing.

It is usual to consider epochs crowded with events and changes as 'interesting' and 'exciting'. In point of fact, they bring extreme unhappiness and suffering both to individual human beings and to whole generations. History does not spare man and does not even take notice of him. I have lived through three wars, of which two were world-wars, and two revolutions in Russia, that of 1905 and of 1917; I have lived through the spiritual renascence in Russia at the beginning of the twentieth century, through Russian communism, through the crisis of a whole civilization, through the upheavals in Central Europe, through the collapse of France and her occupation by the German armies; I have lived in exile and my exile has not come to an end. The devastating war on Russian soil was a source of agony for me. And I do not know how all these turmoils and ordeals of the world will end. My life as a philosopher was under the constant impact of this torrent of events. I have been in prison four times—twice under the old *régime* in Russia and twice under the new; I was exiled to the north of Russia; I was brought to trial and threatened with permanent deportation to Siberia;

I was banished from my mother country and shall probably end my life in exile. But I have never actively engaged in political activities. I have been deeply involved in many things, yet have not belonged entirely to any one of them. I have never surrendered myself to anything, except my creative calling, to which alone the core of my being owes allegiance. Far from having ever been indifferent to social questions, I have, indeed, suffered deeply from their impact on me, and my 'social conscience' seemed never at rest. But in the last analysis and in a still deeper sense, I have been non-social. Social movements have never been able to claim my wholehearted allegiance. I have always been a spiritual 'anarchist' and 'individualist'.

This book is not tied to any systematic plan. It contains reminiscences, but they are not what is of most importance in it. Memories of events and people alternate with reflections, and the reflections are of more consequence. I have not divided the chapters, as is usual in autobiographies, in strict chronological order, but according to the themes and problems which have been of particular concern to me all my life. Still, the sequence of events is not without significance. The reader may have difficulty in following my repetitive manner. My only justification is that I see the same theme arising in different contexts.

I decided to make this study of myself not only because I feel the need of expressing and communicating myself (a reason for which I cannot possibly claim the attention of the reader), but also because this may help to raise and resolve certain problems concerning man and his destiny and contribute to the understanding of our age. I also feel the necessity of explaining the apparent inconsistencies and contradictions which have been ascribed to my philosophical outlook.

The writing of this kind of book implies the exercise of the most mysterious power in man: that of memory. Memory and oblivion alternate in human life. I forget many things for a time; many things disappear from my consciousness and are yet preserved at a deeper level. Oblivion has always been a source of profound disquiet to me. I have sometimes forgotten not only significant events but even people who have played a great part in my life. I always regarded this as a failing and a kind of betrayal. There is a life-giving power in memory: memory seeks to conquer death. But the time came when I remembered

once more what I had forgotten. This remembrance had a truly transfiguring power.

I am not one of those who look towards the past: I look towards
the future. The past is significant to me inasmuch as it is pregnant with
the future. I am not subject to moods of disillusionment: these are
characteristic rather of people who look to the past. But I know the
pain of longing, which is quite a different matter. There is more in me
of the dramatic than of the lyrical, and this is bound to leave its mark
on my autobiography.

When I think about my life I am led to the conclusion that it has not
been the life of a philosopher in the current sense of the word. It has
been too passionate and too full of dramatic events, both individual and
social. I have sought for the truth, but my life has not been ruled by
wisdom and reasonableness: I was always more aware of its irrational
and unpredictable nature. Periods of joy have alternated in my life with
periods of darkness and anguish; periods of exaltation were followed
by periods of depression. But never at any time have I ceased to think
and to seek intensively.

I should like above all to bring out the more luminous and creative
periods of my life. I should like memory to overcome oblivion in regard to all that is of value in it. One thing only I consciously leave aside:
I shall speak little of those personal relationships which have affected
my private life. Memory must hold these above all things for eternity.

Marcel Proust, who devoted his whole creative imagination to the
problem of Time, wrote in his principal work, *Le Temps Retrouvé*:
'*J'avais trop expérimenté l'impossibilité d'atteindre dans la réalité ce qui était
au fond de moi même.*' I could have used these words as the epigraph to this
book, for they express the underlying experience of my whole life.

The impulse which informs the book issues from a series of conflicts
in me. I am by nature extremely reserved, and yet I want to try to communicate myself. I have, therefore, set myself a very difficult task. Dis-
cretion forbids me to speak of much that has very definitely affected me
both inwardly and outwardly. It is particularly difficult to express the
enrichment derived from communion with another person. It is equally
difficult to express the hidden tragedy of life, of which I am so intensely
aware. Despite the Western element which is active in me, I belong to

the Russian intelligentsia whose characteristic attitude is a perennial search for truth. I inherit the tradition of the Slavophils and the Westerners, of Chaadayev and Khomyakov, of Herzen and Belinsky, and even of Bakunin and Chernishevsky, despite the differences in our respective attitudes to life. I am above all an heir of the tradition of Dostoevsky and Tolstoy, as well as of Vladimir Solovyev and Nicolas Fyodorov. I am a Russian, and I regard my universalism, my very hostility to nationalism, as Russian. I am also conscious of being an aristocratic thinker who has come to acknowledge the truth of socialism. Some have said of me that I speak for the aristocratic meaning of socialism.

I have endeavoured to write this book with the utmost simplicity and frankness and without any embellishment. The biographical sections are bare and matter of fact. These sections are necessary to bring out more concretely the atmosphere which marked the various stages in the history of my mind. But the main emphasis of this autobiography is on self-knowledge, on the way in which I came to know and apprehend my own mind and my spiritual quest. I am interested not so much in the nature of my environment as in the way I have reacted to it.

CHAPTER I

ORIGINS. ENVIRONMENT. FIRST INFLUENCES.
THE RUSSIAN GENTRY

The origin of man is only partially susceptible of rationalization. No one can fully comprehend the mystery and unique character of personality. Man's personality is infinitely more mysterious than the world in which he lives, for it is, indeed, a whole world to itself. Man is a microcosmos and contains all things within himself; but of these only what is distinctly individual and characteristic acquires tangible form. He is, moreover, a being who lives in many dimensions, and I have always been conscious of this within myself.

The first response to the world of a creature who is born into it is of immense significance. I cannot remember my first cry on encountering the world, but I know for certain that from the very beginning I was aware of having fallen into an alien realm. I felt this as much on the first day of my conscious life as I do at the present time. I have always been a pilgrim. Christians ought to feel that they have no abiding city on earth, and they should be seekers of the city to come. But I have never regarded such feeling and seeking as a virtue or achievement. In fact, it has even seemed to me to reveal a rift in my attitude to the world and to life. The consciousness of being rooted in the earth was alien to me, and I was strongly attracted by the Orphic myth concerning the origin of the human soul, which speaks of a falling away of man's spirit from a higher world into a lower.

> The music of heaven she heard at her birth
> Still drowned the sad songs of the earth.[1]

I was never conscious of 'belonging' to my parents; and the relations of kindred, the ties of blood, the 'generic', evoked a strange aversion in me. I am unable to entertain a liking for the principles of family life

[1] From the poem *The Angel* by Lermontov, translated by Patrick Thompson. (Tr.)

I

and domesticity, and the attachment to these principles prevalent in Western society astonishes me. Some of my friends used to call me in fun 'the enemy of the human kind'—and yet I have an intense love for man. I was always repelled by family resemblances, as between parents and children, brothers and sisters: family likenesses have always struck me as a challenge to the dignity of the human person. I only held dear the distinctly individual, the particular in man.

Yet it would be a mistake to infer that I was not fond of my parents. On the contrary, I loved and esteemed them; but my attitude was rather that of a father than of a son. I cared for them, I was anxious lest they should fall ill, and the thought of their death was a source of continual torment to me. My feeling of sonship, on the other hand, was always weak. I could never see why people attached such importance to the principle of motherhood, or even to so-called 'mother earth'. My own mother was strikingly beautiful, but I was never able to discover the relevance of anything remotely approaching the Oedipus complex, of which Freud has created a universal myth. It seemed to me, in fact, that blood relationship must needs exclude any experience of erotic love. The object of love must be distant, transcendent, over against myself: this, indeed, characterises the romantic cult of the 'fair lady'; and I am a Russian romantic of the early twentieth century.

I am by origin a member of the Russian gentry: this is not, I believe, mere chance, for it has left its mark on my mental make-up. My parents belonged to 'society', not simply to the gentry. At home we generally talked French. My parents had many connections with the nobility, especially during the first half of their married life; some of these were ties of blood kinship, and others came about as a result of my father's service in the Horse Guards. During my childhood my parents were friends of the Chief Lady-in-Waiting, Princess Kochoubey, who had a great influence on Alexander III. The Commandant of the Palace, Cherevin, also a close friend of Alexander III, was my father's colleague in the regiment. On my father's side I came of a military family. All my forbears were generals and Knights of the Order of St. George, and they all began their military career by serving in the Guards. My grandfather, M. N. Berdyaev, was *ataman* of the Don Cossacks. My great-grandfather, N. M. Berdyaev, was Governor-General of Novorossyisk, and his correspondence with Paul I was published in *Old Russia*.

My father was an officer in the Guards, but he retired early and went to live on his estate, Oboukhovo on the banks of the Dnieper, where he was made Marshal of the Nobility. During the Turkish war he rejoined the army; but subsequently he became managing chairman of the south-west regional Agrarian Bank, and held the post for twenty-five years. He had no inclination to make a career, and he even refused a title which was his due for having been an honorary Justice of the Peace for more than twenty-five years. As a child I was enrolled in the special so-called Military Cadet Corps of Pages, on account of my family's services to the nation. But as my parents lived in Kiev I entered the Corps there, though I had the right to be moved to the Corps of Pages in the capital at any moment.

My mother was born Princess Kudashev. She was half-French, and her mother, my grandmother, was Countess Choiseul. At heart my mother was more French than Russian: she received a French education, and in early youth she lived in Paris; she wrote letters exclusively in French and never learnt to write correct Russian. Though she was born an Orthodox, she felt herself to be more of a Roman Catholic, and always prayed from her mother's French Catholic prayer-book. I used to make fun of her and tell her that she was not on terms of 'Thou' with God. It may be of interest that one of my grandmothers and one of my great-grandmothers were nuns. My father's mother, *née* Bakhmeteva, took the veil secretly, while my grandfather was still alive. She had a close connection with the Kievo-Pechersky monastery. The celebrated *starets* Parfeny was her spiritual father and friend, and her life was entirely under his guidance. In this connection I have the following impression as a child. When my grandmother died and I was taken to her funeral (I was six years old at the time) I was amazed to see that she lay in her coffin dressed as a nun, and was buried according to the monastic rite. The nuns came and said that she belonged to them. My mother's grandmother, Princess Kudashev, became a nun after her husband's death. Even under the Soviet *régime* a large oil-painting of her in a monastic habit, with a very forbidding expression, hung in my room.

My grandmother on my father's side lived in her own house with a garden in the old upper part of Kiev, called Pechersk. Pechersk had a special atmosphere combining monastic and martial elements. The Kievo-Pechersky monastery, the Nikolsky monastery and many other churches were situated here. Monks were continually to be met in the streets. The tomb of Askold was in the cemetery on the hill over the Dnieper, where my grandmother and other members of my family were buried. At the same time Pechersk was a military fortress, inhabited by a large number of soldiers. It was old, fighting, monastic Russia, which had successfully opposed all attempts at modernization. Kiev is one of the most beautiful cities in Russia and indeed in the whole of Europe. It stands high up in the hills on the banks of the Dnieper; its height commands an almost infinite view, and it has wonderful gardens; its Cathedral of St. Sophia is one of the finest examples of Russian Church architecture. Adjoining Pechersk was Lipki, also in the upper part of the town. This was the quarter inhabited by the nobility and principal government officers; it consisted of large houses with gardens. It was here that my parents always lived; they had a house which was sold while I was still a boy. I remember that our garden adjoined another very big one belonging to a Dr. Mering, which occupied the central part of Kiev. All my life I have had an affection for gardens. But I had a sense of having been born in a forest; I was particularly fascinated by forests, which were to me nature's symbol of the primeval mystery of life. My childhood and boyhood were associated with Lipki. It was a world rather different from that of Pechersk, a world open to the influences of European civilization; a world inclined to gaiety, which was not admitted in Pechersk. On the other side of Kreschatik, the main street with big shops, which lay between two hills, lived the lower middle-class, i.e. the trading population. Right down beside the Dnieper lay Podal, inhabited mostly by Jews, but the Kiev Theological Academy was also there. Our family, though of Muscovite origin, belonged to the aristocracy of the south-west, which was subject to strong Western influences, and these were always very conspicuous in Kiev. My mother's family was of a distinctly Western type, with recognizable Polish and French features. Kiev, throughout her chequered history, always showed signs of intercourse with Western Europe. From childhood onwards I frequently went abroad. I was seven when I first travelled with my mother to Karlsbad, where she underwent a cure. The first impression I had of a foreign country was of Vienna, which greatly aroused my interest.

Among my forbears the most vivid and interesting figure was my grandfather, M. N. Berdyaev. I used to hear many stories about him. My father was fond of telling the story of how my grandfather 'conquered' Napoleon. In 1814 in the battle of Kulmsk Napoleon beat the Russian and German armies. My grandfather was in a part of the army where all the commanding officers, including the general, were killed. He was only a young lieutenant in the Guards at that time, but he had to take command of a whole brigade. He went over to the offensive and fiercely attacked the French positions. The French thought that their opponents had received reinforcements. Napoleon's army was shaken and lost the battle of Kulmsk. My grandfather was awarded the Cross of St. George and the Prussian Iron Cross. I was told another story. My grandfather was in command of a regiment. He treated his men extremely well, and for a soldier of the time of Nicholas I he was very humane. My father used to say that he was always revolted by serfdom and was ashamed of it. When he was made a general and left for the war, the men of his regiment presented him with a medal in the form of a heart, with the inscription: 'God preserve you for your goodness to us.' This medal always hung in my father's study and he was especially proud of it. Here is another story. My grandfather was *ataman* of the Don Cossacks. Nicholas I arrived and wanted to abolish the Cossacks' special liberties as part of the policy of military and political centralization. There was a parade in Novocherkask and Nicholas I asked my grandfather, as commander of the district, to see that his order concerning the abolition of the Cossacks' liberties was brought into force. My grandfather said that he considered the abolition of these liberties would be detrimental to the life of the whole district, and asked to be allowed to proffer his resignation. Everyone was terrified and expected Nicholas I, who was frowning, to punish him. But, unexpectedly, Nicholas's mood changed; he kissed my grandfather and countermanded his order. Another thing I remember is that in his old age my grandfather was in the habit of expressing his dislike of monks, although he was a member of the Orthodox Church.

It may be fitting at this point to speak of certain traits of character which seem to be hereditary in our family. I am quick-tempered and inclined to outbursts of anger. My father was a very good and kind man, but he was extremely impetuous, and he had many conflicts and quarrels in life on this account. My brother was at times overpowered by real paroxysms of rage. I myself inherited a hot and irascible temper, a tendency not uncommon among the Russian gentry. As a small boy I used to strike out in anger. These characteristics bred wilfulness in my behaviour and attitude to life. Despite all my father's good qualities he was inclined to be wilful and obstinate. I am also conscious of these defects in myself; and I believe they are shared by the Russian gentry as a whole. I have sometimes even been aware of this wilfulness in my thinking and mental attitude. However true it may be—and I believe it is profoundly true—that the real spirit of man, his creative spirit and achievement, surpasses his natural, hereditary dispositions, nevertheless his character, his psycho-physical qualities, are profoundly affected. When I was in exile in Vologda I struck a man, a local government official, because he pursued a young lady of my acquaintance in the street. When I had hit him I threatened him with dismissal from his job. On such occasions 'the blood of my ancestors' rushed to my head. I have even known real ecstasies of rage. While calling these things to remembrance, I cannot help thinking that I was able to display my temper with impunity because I enjoyed a privileged position. We were still living in a patriarchal age. My father, who in the latter half of his life entertained very liberal views, could not imagine life except in a patriarchal or semi-patriarchal society, where established family traditions and family ties play the decisive rôle. When I was arrested and searched, the gendarmes walked about on tip-toe and spoke in a whisper in order not to disturb my father. They and the police knew that my father was on intimate terms with the Governor, that he was a friend of exalted personages and had connections in Petersburg. I myself, even while engaged in revolutionary activity and a convinced social-democrat, never ceased to be fundamentally, though unconsciously, a nobleman. It was so in my very repudiation of the world to which I belonged by birth and upbringing. I resented this, especially when I noticed that my origin produced a feeling of inferiority in my comrades.

Of the people among whom I lived as a child, my nurse, Anna Ivanovna Katamenkov, made a most enduring impression on me. *Nyanya*, the Russian for nurse, was a peculiar and remarkable type, characteristic of old Russia and immortalized by Pushkin. It is astonishing that this type should have been produced in conditions of serfdom. My own *nyanya* was my grandfather's serf. She was nurse to two generations of Berdyaevs, that of my father and myself. My father had a very great affection and esteem for her. She was a classical *nyanya* of ardent Orthodox faith, of extraordinary kindness and tenderness, and possessing a sense of dignity which raised her above the position of a servant and made her a member of the family. Nurses in Russia had altogether a special position, which was distinct from, and in a sense above, all the established social classes. For many of the Russian gentry their *nyanya* was the only close link with the people. My own *nyanya* died in extreme old age, when I was about fourteen years old. My very first recollection of childhood is associated with her: I remember walking by her side, at the age of four or so, down an alley in the garden, in my father's family estate, Obukhovo.

In fact, I am not aware of any previous recollections, and there is a long gap after that before I can remember anything else. Subsequent memories are already associated with our house in Kiev. My father's family estate was sold when I was still a child, and in its place my father bought the house in Kiev with a garden. My father always had a tendency to wild spending. Throughout his whole life he wistfully looked back to life on the estate and felt homesick for it. But my mother was fonder of the town, and I remember arguments between them on this count. I myself always dreamt of the country and hoped that my father would buy a new estate, even if it were a smaller one. I often pictured in my imagination what kind of a country-house I would like to live in: of course, I wanted it to be near a forest, which had always exercised my imagination. But this never came true. My father also owned an entailed estate in the extreme west of Poland, which was presented to my grandfather in recognition of his services; but we never lived there and it was occupied by a tenant. I went there only once in my life, as a boy, on the way back from Germany to Russia. As it was entailed, it could neither be sold nor mortgaged, which, however, turned out to be a blessing, since it saved us from complete ruin.

I always had a peculiar attitude to property. I was never able to perceive anything even remotely sacrosanct about it; in fact, I was beset by a sense of its fundamental sinfulness. I had, nevertheless, a feeling of ownership towards objects of immediate personal use, such as books, my writing-table, my clothes, etc. Money necessary for existence always seemed to me to be sent 'from above', so that I might devote myself entirely to my creative work. Indeed, I counted on this in a strangely calculating manner, though in other respects I was extremely unpractical. Apart from my childhood and adolescence, all my life was passed in straitened financial circumstances, and sometimes I experienced positive hardship. As a boy I generally spent the summer on the magnificent estate of my aunt J. N. Gudimov-Levkovich. We were closely connected with this family, which was one of the centres of Kiev society. Whereas there was something deeply, even if intangibly, sad and weary about the atmosphere in our own family, the Gudimov-Levkovich's house was at all times full of young people, and the atmosphere there was cheerful and gay. I was much attached to my cousins, particularly to Natasha, with whom I continued to be on friendly terms later on in Paris until her tragic death. It was indeed a happy family. At home, on the other hand, everything seemed different: there was a sense of some affliction and of maladjustment to life; there was absence of true concord, with the result that susceptibilities and sensibilities were easily aroused. Our family had already abandoned the old-established order of a semi-feudal society and had not as yet succeeded in adapting itself to a new and more 'democratic' way of life. My father's convictions underwent a crisis and he made liberal ideas more and more his own. He gradually broke with established traditions and often came into conflict with the society in which he lived. There also occurred a rift in our family on account of profound disagreements between my parents, on the one hand, and my brother (who was fifteen years older than me) and his family, on the other. My brother was endowed with great talents, though in quite a different line from my own; but he was rather unstable, neurotic, lacking in character, and very unhappy because he was not able to realize his gifts in life. When I look back I cannot help thinking that all these circumstances are, for better or for worse, faintly reminiscent of the families described in Dostoevsky's novels.

As a child and as a boy I lived, through my mother's Polish family connections, in the sphere of a semi-feudal aristocratic society. Countess Maria Branitskaya and her husband were my mother's cousins. She was à close friend of my mother's and in my childhood we often went to stay with the Branitskys. There was even a wing in their house especially kept for our family. My aunt owned the town Belaya Tserkov, about a hundred and fifty thousand acres of land in the district of Kiev, and palaces in Warsaw, Paris, Nice and Rome. The Branitskys were related to the royal family. Alexandria, their summer residence, on the outskirts of Belaya Tserkov, had a magnificent park laid out in a baroque manner and, together with the town, it represented something like a feudal duchy, with a court attended by a host of people, with huge stables of pedigree horses, with shoots for which the whole nobility of the south-west assembled. Meals were glittering and sumptuous. While at the Branitskys, I was always provided with a gig and two ponies which I used to drive myself into the woods to gather mushrooms; the coachman, in Polish livery, sat behind. I also had a donkey on which I rode about the park. But visits to Alexandria continued even in later years, when I was a student and professed social-democratic convictions. Sometimes I went also to the Branitskys' winter residence for a month or so of quiet study. Nevertheless, I never liked this world and rebelled against it even as a child. I always felt a great incongruity, indeed an impassable gulf, between myself and that world's way of life, although Countess Branitskaya remained, in her worldly and charming way, always kind to me, even when I became a Marxist and used to go to see her hot from discussions with Lunacharsky. I made a point, however, of being elegantly dressed. On such and on many other occasions I was even somewhat inclined to dandyism and was very particular about my appearance. I have, typically enough, always been fond of scent and good cigars.

I liked to wander about by myself in the wonderful park of Alexandria, dreaming of another world, very different from that in which I found myself. In the heat of the Revolution all these magnificent grounds were devastated and the mansion burnt down. Countess Branitskaya, a remarkable woman in her way, had to flee and died soon after. When, as a Marxist, I sat in the Branitskys' drawing-room, I did not foresee that Marxism would spell the destruction of this beautiful and yet, in a sense, so unreal world. Later on, in exile, in Paris, I used to meet Countess Branitskaya's daughter Princess Bichette Radzivil.

To the feudal world, which I remember as something almost prehistoric, also belonged Princess Lopukhine-Demidov, another cousin of my mother's. Her husband, a fellow-officer of my father's in the Guards, was my godfather. Olga Lopukhine-Demidov was a *grande dame*, stately proud, imperious, and very beautiful. My father was at loggerheads with her and refused to join us whenever we went to see her at her estate Khorsun. There was a curious rivalry for pre-eminence between the Branitskys and the Lopukhine-Demidovs. The latter were inclined to live extravagantly and the royal family lent them money from time to time. I used to meet my aunt Lopukhine-Demidov in exile, in Berlin, a short while before her death. She never failed to express her contempt for the Russian monarchists and right-wing politicians: she recognized in them a complete lack of the true aristocratic spirit and a pronounced tendency to the plebeian. The so-called 'Union of the Russian People',[1] for example, always had a plebeian character and was shunned by most of the nobility. I remember my aunt as always knitting something for the Empress Maria Feodorovna, with whom she was on intimate terms. But she despised the Russian monarchists and refused to admit even their leaders into her house.

As I have already said, I was educated at a military Academy, in the Kiev Cadet Corps. But I lived at home and attended daily, which was a rather exceptional case. To qualify for the University I had, therefore, to pass the external entrance examination. I did not like the Corps or the army; I disliked all things military, and I rebelled from childhood against regimentation. When I entered the second form of the Cadet Corps, and whenever I found myself in the intervals between lessons amongst a crowd of my fellow-cadets, I felt extremely miserable and

[1] An extreme reactionary and monarchist movement, prominent during the reign of Nicholas II, which was largely responsible for anti-Semitic pogroms in Russia. (Tr.)

forlorn. I never enjoyed the company of the boys of my own age and always avoided mixing in their society: I was able to get on only with girls. The society of boys always seemed to me very coarse, and their talk low and stupid. To this day I consider that there are few things more revolting than the kind of conversation which goes on among young boys: it is a source of corruption. The cadets seemed to me particularly uncouth, commonplace and intellectually callow. Moreover, my comrades sometimes laughed at the nervous tic from which I had suffered since childhood. I did not develop any feelings of comradeship, and this affected my whole life. The only boy with whom I was friends in childhood was N. M. (a sailor), whom my father helped financially with his education. I was warmly attached to him and we remained friends for the whole of our lives: he became just like a member of our family. In later life he served with distinction in the navy and was sent on various naval expeditions. We were together in exile, in Vologda. But in the collective atmosphere of a military Academy I tended to be a violent individualist, very much cut off from the rest. The boys regarded me as a snob, a son of the nobility and a future Guards officer, whereas most of the others were to be officers of the line. But my divergence from the cadets and the whole atmosphere of the Corps had still deeper roots. In very early years there awoke in me an interest in philosophical problems, and already as a boy I became conscious of my philosophical vocation.

At school I was a mediocre pupil, and was always made to feel my ineptitude. At one time I had a coach at home who came to my father and said that it was difficult for him to work with such a stupid pupil. By then I had already read a great deal and begun to meditate on the meaning of life; yet I could not solve a single mathematical problem, or learn four lines of poetry by heart, or write a page of dictation without making a host of mistakes. If I had not known French and German from childhood, I should probably have acquired them only with great difficulty or not at all. As it was, my knowledge of languages gave me a certain advantage over the other cadets. I knew the theory of mathematics passably well, and so was able to get along somehow; but I could not solve practical mathematical tasks. I wrote fairly good essays, despite my inability to spell. My best subjects were history and natural

history. The syllabus of the Cadet Corps was very similar to that of
the secondary schools. Mathematics had, naturally, a preponderant place
in the curriculum, and in the higher forms analytical trigonometry and
the differential calculus were taught. Natural science included botany,
zoology, mineralogy, physics, chemistry and cosmology. When I became a student and joined the faculty of science at the University I was
able to find my bearings in scientific subjects better than my colleagues.
Considerable importance was attached to modern languages, but Greek
and Latin I learnt only for two years, while preparing for the University entrance examination. The teaching in the Kiev Cadet Corps was
fairly good, and the staff comprised some lecturers from the University.
The headmaster, General A., was a fine man, and was always friendly
towards me.

But fundamentally I was unable to reconcile myself with any insti-
tutional education, even that of the University. This is, perhaps, partly
due to the fact that I never managed to succeed at school, even though,
or because, I began to develop intellectually earlier than is usual, and
liked to read books which no other boy of my own age would dream
of reading. When I took the examination in logic I had already read
Kant's *Critique of Pure Reason* and Mill's *Logic*. My abilities betrayed
themselves only when I took the initiative in my thinking, when my
mind became consciously active and creative: they remained hidden
and unknown to myself while my mind was passive, merely assimi-
lating or memorizing something that was external to me. In point of
fact, I could never 'assimilate' knowledge, learn by heart and commit
to memory; I could not, so to say, put myself in the position of someone
who is set a task. For this reason I found examinations quite unbearable.
I am incapable of retorting, echoing in a passive way: I instantly want
to develop my own line of thought. At an examination in divinity I
once got one out of twelve marks—an unheard of event in the history
of the Cadet Corps. I have never succeeded in making a summary of
a single book, and had I been asked at an examination to summarize
one of my own books I should probably have failed to do so.

All my life I have read much and widely; I read with ease and rapidity.
I am instantly at home in the thought of any given book and very soon
discern its purport and implication. But I never remain passive in the

process of reading; while I read I am engaged in a constant creative activity, which leads me to remember not so much the actual matter of the book as the thoughts evoked in my mind by it, directly or indirectly. I have, likewise, never been able to submit my mind to external direction or to be instructed by others: I am self-taught and my methods are autodidactic. I have never acquired knowledge and truth by way of instruction and education, rather I struggled for them. I was, therefore, always obliged to draw up my own plan of enquiry.

Nobody ever suggested that I should study philosophy: the impulse came entirely from within me. I never belonged, or indeed could belong, to any 'school 'of thought. I have been a learner all my life and I continue to learn, but I make truth, which is universal, my own from within, through the exercise of my freedom, and my knowledge of truth is my own relation to truth. It has always been a great joy to me to acquire books. I remember how I used to go to the large book-shop 'Ogloblin' on the Kreschatik; I went there almost every day to look at the new books, and to this day I can spend hours in a book-shop.

As I have already said, I come of military stock and had a military training. But I had an innate antipathy to men of war and to soldiery: all my life I was conscious of a feeling of irritation on meeting a soldier in the street. I respected soldiers in war-time, but disliked them in peace-time. As a cadet I used to look at students with envy because, instead of marching, they were engaged in intellectual pursuits. I served in the ranks for about six years. The Cadet Corps was the only educational place with opportunities for physical training and sport, though these opportunities were used, of course, according to the somewhat elementary ideas of the time. Gymnastics were compulsory, and so was dancing. My own aversion from all things military produced in me a dislike of physical exercise. Gymnastics bored me to distraction, and only in later life I formed, for reasons of health, the habit of taking physical exercise in the morning. I did not like dancing and danced badly: balls seemed to me exceedingly dull.

There were only two things outside my intellectual preoccupations at which I excelled: riding and target-shooting. I was very fond of riding on horseback. When I was about nine years old a Cossack used to come and teach me to ride; we would ride outside the town. I could ride both in Cossack fashion and as was customary in the cavalry. Galloping fast was a source of particular delight to me. It was one of the few things in which I surpassed my comrades in the Cadet Corps. I was sorry when later on circumstances did not allow me to indulge in this activity. I was equally good at shooting and seldom missed a bull's eye.

I believe that there must be a profound link between the activities of the body, such as physical labour and physical exercise, and the fact that man is a microcosmos, a potential universe, who is given the task of mastering his own body and thereby the body of the created universe, to which he belongs and which belongs to him. As a small boy I was very keen on handicrafts: I was a carpenter, and I used to paint and plaster. I learnt carpentry in a workshop and was particularly fond of this craft. I made a number of frames and chairs and was very proud of my performance, and even now a carpenter's workshop gives me a sense of delight. At one time I even took to gardening and grew vegetables. But this proved to be the limit of my physical achievements, and, I am afraid, on the whole I was singularly clumsy in this respect.

My limited artistic gifts expressed themselves in various attempts at painting. I had a considerable gift for drawing, and I was one of the most competent art pupils at the Corps. I even went to an art school, where I took a three years course in drawing. I had begun to paint in oils; but, in all probability, I did not possess any real talent, though I may have had a certain facility. As soon, however, as I began to be seriously preoccupied with philosophy—which happened quite early in life—I dropped painting altogether and started writing philosophical novels instead.

I should like to say more about my experiences in the Cadet Corps. When I watch the young men of to-day, carried away as they often are by the ideals of war and grim-visaged militarism, a feeling of exasperation overwhelms me: I am too well acquainted with the effects of belonging to a military organization and with the harm done by military education and regimentation. My time in the Cadet Corps had a great influence on me, in the sense, above all, that it brought about in me a strong reaction against the military spirit and *milieu*. There are people who always tend to put themselves over against their environment, who dissent from and resist their surroundings, and I am one of them. This is, undoubtedly, a way of being dependent on as well as independent of one's environment: it is an inability to remain detached and aloof. I have always broken with every group to which I belonged; I could never conform to any collective. I was never able to go with the stream of the world around or bow submission to anyone or anything; my life has taught me that this could not have been otherwise. As a child, even before I joined the Cadet Corps, I used to enjoy putting on my father's cavalry uniform and my grandfather's ribbons and orders. I took an interest in working out strategic plans, and would figure myself in the shoes of Suvorov, who interested me very much. My bellicose inclinations, however, did not go beyond this, and appear to have passed, eventually, into the sphere of ideas, where I kept on waging real and imaginary battles. My dislike of soldiery issues from an innate instinct to resist and set at naught the power of the collective. I even made a special effort to avoid, as far as possible, looking like a cadet. I did not cut my hair short, as we were supposed to do, and I tried to keep out of the way of generals, so as not to salute and draw attention to my appearance. As I have already said, I never became friendly with a single one of my fellow-cadets. This was, to some extent, due to my diffidence and reserve; my hot, quick temper must also have made friendly relations with me exceedingly difficult. It was not a great pleasure to play cards with me, because I took it all very seriously: I was apt to fly into a rage with my partner. My love of playing cards and gambling, by the way, came to an end while I was still a boy, and I never indulged in these things in later years. It seems that philosophy, the 'love of wisdom', and the search for truth and meaning made a clean sweep of everything. I may still have something of the Guardsman in me—some instinct or residue perhaps—but it is hardly recognizable as such. I had to struggle in order to quell and master these inclinations, and this must have instilled a certain complexity into my nature. I will return to this at a later stage. Before the change came about in me I suffered from a number of painful habits and characteristics, which I did not get rid of until much later.

In the course of time I was transferred to the Corps of Pages, and was supposed to go to Petersburg to live with a cousin of my father's, who held some high office in the capital. But I had other dreams and other designs: I left the sixth form of the Cadet Corps and began to prepare for the University entrance examination. As I recall the past, I must avow that the only way of life for which I was cast was probably the life of the Russian country gentleman. In a certain sense I cherish this life and feel homesick for it to this day.

Illnesses have played a considerable part in my life. From childhood I was subject to a kind of *tic douloureux*. I believe I am fearless and courageous, both morally and physically, which may have something to do with my military background. But in one respect my courage fails me: I am a coward as far as illnesses are concerned. Malady and disease fill me with almost supernatural horror. This is in no way due to any innate fear of death, which I have never really known—at least I do not think this is typical of me. If death inspires fear in me, it is not my own so much as the death of people dear to me. But I am frightened and alarmed by disease, sickness, infection, and I am always picturing to myself some frightful outcome, some seizure, some visitation. I am nervous and apprehensive about health, alike my own and that of others; and I am always imagining the worst. I do not think I was ever alarmed at the thought of being hit by a bullet or a bomb, as indeed I had occasion to show during the October Revolution of 1917 in Moscow, when bombs flew around our house, and one exploded in the court-yard, while I went on writing all the time; neither was I frightened by the air-raids on Paris during the last war. But I am forever haunted by the fear of catching typhus, diphtheria, or even plain influenza. This may be partly the effect of an unending series of illnesses in our family. Although I am not particularly susceptible of suggestion from without, I was yet as a child profoundly impressed by the fact that life appeared to be a continuous illness.

Our house was periodically visited by every kind of medical specialist, who examined all the members of our family. My mother suffered for fourteen years from a serious liver complaint. She had frequent attacks at night, and I would hear her cries of agony; on every such occasion it was thought that she might die. Such experiences were deeply distressing to me. My father was perpetually undergoing cures of some kind, and I myself was constantly treated for one complaint or another. Some members of our family suffered from neuroses, and I have inherited a nervousness which expressed itself in spasmodic movements. My family was particularly prone to nervous disorders, and my mother used to say that, unlike the Kudashevs, the Berdyaevs were not quite normal. My brother was distinctly neurotic, and some considered him quite abnormal. I suspect that this background must have affected my subconscious.

It often fell to me to play the part of peace-maker in the tensions which accompanied our family life. My brother's family provided contacts for me with the world outside the restricted circles of the local landed gentry. He was extremely wasteful and extravagant; he squandered money right and left and was always in financial difficulties. He was very handsome, and had a face of almost Grecian beauty. From time to time, however, he would go for days without shaving or washing and dressed like a tramp, and then suddenly re-appeared elegant, polished and graceful. He had abilities which I did not possess; he had a wonderful memory and a gift for mathematics and languages. He wrote poetry in Russian and in German, but he had no taste whatsoever for philosophy. Through him and his family I became acquainted with occultism, which, however, always evoked opposition in me. My brother had distinct powers as a medium: sometimes he gave play to these and spoke in verse or in some unintelligible language. He claimed to be in communication with some Hindu Mahatmas. During one of his trances he uttered a prophecy, alleged to have come from a Mahatma, to the effect that 'your brother (i.e. myself) will be famous in your old Europe'! For my part I disliked all this mystifying mumbo-jumbo, though it created an atmosphere which was not uninteresting to me.

There were none of the traditional religious patterns of life in our family—patterns which tend to produce stifling and oppressive conditions. Our family seemed to be uprooted and exposed; it was not all of a piece; it had, as it were, affinities with the Tolstoyan world and yet had something of the intensity and complexity of Dostoevsky. It marked a transition from an age of stability and settled equilibrium to one of disquiet and instability.

I was never constrained or obliged to do anything in childhood.

I cannot even recall that I was ever punished. I may have behaved
—from motives of pride—in such a way as to give no cause for punishment. I was not a naughty or capricious child and was hardly ever mis-
chievous as children habitually are. My only conspicuous vice was
exhibitions of fits of temper. Above all other things I cherished my
independence, as, indeed, I do now. My whole feeling for life is born
of an intense love of freedom. Thus it is that in freedom was formed
within me a world over against the world without. I was fond of
stressing my state of being apart in various, possibly naïve ways. I
liked arranging my own room and kept it separate from the rest of
the house; I could not bear anyone to encroach on my domain and the
things pertaining to it. Already as a child I began to collect my own
library. No doubt I was egotistic, though this was primarily a defensive egotism; but I was never *egocentric*, that is to say, I was never concerned exclusively with myself and did not live by relating everything
only to myself.

I have always been almost pedantically regular in my habits: I liked
the day to be ordered and arranged according to plan, and I could not
bear the least disturbance of things on my writing-table. This is the
reverse side of my inborn anarchism and suspicion of all authority,
social or otherwise.

I shall never forget one memorable conversation I had with my father,
in the course of which he began to cry. This experience stirred me
deeply and was of immense significance for me: thereafter many things
changed in me, and I always carried it in my thoughts with gratitude.
My father was very fond of me—with a love that seemed to grow as
time went on. Relations with my mother were more difficult and less
consistent. There was a quality of 'Frenchness' about her, which was
not altogether congenial to me, and she was more mundane than my
father; but she was very kind and generous. I did not like the worldly
society of the upper class, and at one time this dislike turned into a
positive and deep repulsion: I longed for a complete break. The repugnance which I felt with particular intensity for upstarts, for *nouveaux
riches*, for people who push their way from the bottom to the top, betrayed perhaps a genuinely aristocratic quality in me. The same applies
to my abhorrence of snobbishness, of preferential social treatment and

class selectiveness. Aristocracy, after all, is a hereditary phenomenon: it is not a human quality, and it is not an achievement of the human spirit. As a child I certainly shared some of the aristocratic prejudices; but I overcame them very soon in the subsequent stormy reaction, or rather rebellion, against my environment. I was unable to recognize true aristocracy, that is to say, the aristocracy of the spirit, in the aristocratic society to which I belonged: what I saw was mostly arrogance, presumptuousness and contempt for those 'below', mixed with unnatural secretiveness and diffidence. There were no true aristocratic traditions in Russia.

I myself did not, of course, escape the psychology of the 'ruling class', for all my forbears had belonged to it. But it was found in me together with an intense revolutionary impulse which made me look for justice and compassion. I am in this one of the 'conscience-stricken, repentant noblemen', even though at one time I was opposed to and actively combated their influence in Russian culture. Later on my father used to laugh at my socialism, and he contended that it was I rather than he who was a gentleman rolling in luxury. In point of fact this was unfair. I never aimed either at so-called equality or at the domination of one class over another, but at the creation of a special world of my own.

As a child I lived in this world of mine and never merged with the world around, for the latter never seemed to belong to me. I was acutely aware of being peculiar, unlike everyone else—an expatriate with the feelings of an expatriate. André Gide in his Journal speaks, in another context, of a similar experience. Outwardly, so far from trying to accentuate my peculiarity, I did everything in my power to seem the same as other people. My sense of peculiarity or isolation should not be confused with conceit. A conceited person can feel himself at one with the world around him; he may, in fact, be wholly immersed in the preoccupations of society and confident concerning his place, position and importance in it. But I had no such preoccupation and no such confidence; I was ill-adapted to society and had an abhorrence of occupying a position in it. Later on it was a source of dismay to me that, despite my lack of adaptability, I seemed to have become famous in Europe and found myself occupying a 'position in the world'. I even turned 'respectable'—a strange comment on my lawless, rebellious nature.

My anti-social instincts should not be confused with what is known as 'inferiority complex', which is, in fact, entirely absent in me. I am not at all shy, and I have always spoken and acted openly and with confidence, as long as there were no questions of practical, everyday life involved—a sphere in which I have always felt singularly helpless. As regards everyday life I have been rather timid, clumsy and lacking in confidence: my courage and confidence were displayed solely in the struggle of ideas, and in situations of real danger.

A way of describing the attitude of which I want to give an account is to say that my feeling for life has always been accompanied by non-acceptance of the world as it was given to me, by inability to be merged in the world—a deep-rooted disinclination to the habitual state and course of things, and an almost morbid weariness of the commonplace. Some have called this, in my opinion quite inaccurately, 'individualism'. My wish to withdraw into myself does not conflict with a desire and an ability to enter a world of thought which is not my own or, indeed, to feel profoundly engaged in the problems and struggles of society. Man is a complex and perplexing being. I am aware of my self as a point of intersection of two worlds; while 'this' world, the world of my actual living, is known to me as unauthentic, untrue, devoid alike of primacy and ultimacy, there is 'another world', more authentic and more true, to which my deepest self belongs. Leo Tolstoy likewise continually contrasts the false, conventional world and true, divine nature: Prince Andrey in the Petersburg *salon* and Prince Andrey on the battlefield, gazing at the starry sky.

I think that all this has something to do with the predominance of imagination and vision over the brute matter-of-factness of life, though it has nothing to do with addiction to illusions and wishful thinking. I did, however, occasionally fall into fastidiousness, which seemed to me particularly wrong and worried me a great deal. I was over-delicate and sensitive, both physically and mentally. I have tried to overcome this, but have met with little success. I am not aware of despising anyone or anything: I am just fastidious. I have noticed this even with regard to food and to the physiological side of life in general. I have therefore gone through life, as it were, with half-closed eyes and holding my nose. I am particularly sensitive to smells: hence, perhaps, my predilection for scent. I should have liked the world to be turned into a symphony of odours: I am intensely and painfully sensitive to 'bad odour' in the world. And a bad moral odour pains me as much as a bad physical odour. I am fastidious when I come up against the schemings and intrigues of life, against the falsehoods, simulations and duplicities of politics. My fundamental attitude to life, however, is not that of an aesthete, and I have an antipathy to aestheticism: my approach is predominantly ethical, and my thought is concerned above all with the *ethos*, the moral quality and character of life.

Nevertheless I am profoundly appreciative of physical beauty, of aesthetic forms and loveliness. I have always been fond of beautiful human faces, and beautiful things, clothes, furniture, houses and gardens. It was not only seeing lovely things which gave me pleasure; I also desired personal beauty. I suffered from even the slightest disfigurement on a human face and from slovenliness in dress. I had exceptionally good eyesight and, on entering a room, I became immediately conscious of anything that might draw the attention of the eye, of any aesthetic blemish or defect. This is hardly a virtue, and I never considered it as such; indeed, I thought it a misfortune. In the world, among ordinary human beings, there is much more ugliness than beauty, and one has to come to terms with it. My sensitiveness in this respect is due, no doubt, to my not being a whole-hearted and unreserved participant in the to-and-fro movements, contentions and rivalries of this world. I am quite incapable of experiencing jealousy, I am not subject to envy, and I am as far removed as possible from any impulse of revengefulness. I am devoid of the slightest inclination to occupy a position in the hierarchical order of society, and the will to power and domination evokes in me an unspeakable nausea and revulsion. There are many passions which rule men's lives which are utterly foreign and incomprehensible to me. I do not pretend that this is the effect of any moral perfection on my part; as a matter of fact, it may even issue from certain defects in my nature, such as indifference and lack of ambition. I have fought battles with the world not as a man who desires or is able to conquer and subjugate it to himself, but as one who seeks to emancipate himself from this world, as one who resents its ascendency over the lives of men.

I have no descriptive literary gifts, and I realize that my power of expression is exceedingly poor. I can never find the right words and images to embody my thought. I was never able to write a novel, although my mind has certain attributes essential to a writer of fiction. Sometimes I feel I have in me the makings of a novelist, in respect of ideas rather than of any ability to render and describe the surface of life. A novelist requires above all an ability to grasp imaginatively the problems and events of life. I am conscious of being endowed with an imagination of this kind. Imagination has played a great, if sometimes an unhappy, part in my life. I have frequently suffered in imagination, and the sufferings were the more agonizing for not having been experienced in actual fact. I have been able to find spiritual strength to bear the death of those I love, after being completely unnerved by the expectation and anticipation of that death. When I first read Chateaubriand's *Mémoires d'Outre-Tombe* I was astonished to find myself at one with him, despite differences in many important respects. For Chateaubriand and myself alike there are, owing to an exaggerated imagination, no ways of making one's peace, of being satisfied with actuality. So far as I am concerned, however, the power of imagination is not due, as with Chateaubriand, to any visual, descriptive artistic talents. Chateaubriand's attitude to women was essentially imaginative or, perhaps, even delusive: he was all his life the prey of profound disappointment and melancholy, notwithstanding the exceptional success, fame and brilliance of his literary career. For me, too, imagination is a privilege of man, and I am prevented by it from assenting to or being satisfied with any given state of affairs. Like Chateaubriand I withdraw into myself from every arresting instant of life. Every moment seems to me abortive, time-worn and profoundly unsatisfying. Something which has been said of Nietzsche is equally applicable to me: he is said to have been in need of ecstasy to enable him to live; he was driven by a sense of dissatisfaction and disappointment in the actuality of existence. I too felt the need of, and longed for, ecstasy, and I have, indeed, known it. I have known the rapture of creative ecstasy; but my fastidiousness, as well as the demon of sobriety and a strange inability to surrender myself to the fancies of inspiration, as it were, cut the ground away under my ecstatic experience.

My attitude to life, so far from being romantic, has, in fact, always been very realistic; it is my attitude to what transcends life and is accessible solely to vision that was romantic. Maurice Barrès, with whom I have little else in common, said what might be applied to me: '*Mon évolution ne fut jamais une course vers quelque chose, mais une fuite vers ailleurs.*' I was always conscious of being at a distance from what is commonly called 'life'. As a matter of fact, I had a positive dislike of this so-called 'life'—in my youth even more than at present. I must, however, qualify this statement, for, while not liking 'life', I am in love with that quality of life which transcends life, with life, that is to say, which, in the act of ecstasy, surpasses its own limitations.

This brings me up against something profoundly and fundamentally contradictory in my nature. I have never suffered from lack of vitality; I have always lived keenly and intensely: my vitality has indeed been sometimes excessive and extravagant. Nevertheless, I dislike so-called 'life'; and my dislike is not physiological or even psychological, but spiritual in origin. I had a strong and well-formed body, yet I was always conscious of a feeling of revulsion against its physiological functions, and, as I have already noted, my fastidiousness extended to all things, material and spiritual alike. I am drawn to the individual form, the idea, the figure of the body rather than to the body as such. I always disliked stories about the sexual side of people's romantic adventures and could not avoid a feeling of distaste for them: they did not seem to concern me, even when they affected the lives of my intimate friends. I was even more revolted by anything bearing upon the sphere of squabbles for social position, rivalries, ambitions and the struggle for power. I would try not to listen whenever these things were brought to my attention and felt relieved when they were over, so that I could revert to the things that really concern me. Now it is true beyond question that sexual love and the struggle for power constitute what is known as 'life'. It has often seemed to me that, in reality, I have no part in 'life': it resounded in me from a distance, but scarcely touched me. Yet, at the same time, I have been deeply involved in many things pertaining to 'life', and others have relied on me in the struggle for it. In the last resort, however, I remained out of the world, on some different, wholly other plane. I was imbued with an irresistible eschatological impulse, which could not be satisfied by any given world. My love for life was a love for the meaning of life, and my love for the world was a love for a world that had denied its worldly fashion. I am not so presumptuous as to claim that I was above the temptations of 'life': I was, indeed, as much their victim as anybody else. But I was never tempted to provide them with moral sanctions or to justify them spiritually. The problem of 'the flesh' was never a particular concern of mine, as it was, for example, for Rozanov, Merezhkovsky, or D. H. Lawrence: the problem which preoccupied me above every other was that of freedom. I could never think of 'the flesh' in terms of either its 'sinfulness' or its 'holiness'. I could only ask whether or not the flesh denies or does violence to freedom. My early love for philosophy and metaphysics is, in some sense, related to my revulsion from 'life', as the ugly, the commonplace, which violates true life, that is freedom. Living, as distinct from creative living, has given me little satisfaction. I think I have derived more enjoyment from memories of the past and dreams of life to come than from the actual stuff of life.

My greatest sin has probably been my inability and refusal to bear the burden of the commonplace, that which constitutes the very stuff of 'life', or to see light through the unspeakable darkness of the commonplace. None the less, my philosophy is a philosophy of existence, and it has been described as such by others, that is to say, it gives expression to the problems and wrestlings of man: it is, in this sense, very close indeed to life, to life without inverted commas.

I should like to enlarge on the subject of my attitude to 'life' in yet one other respect, namely that of asceticism. The needs of the body have never seemed of much concern to me; I regarded these as primarily dependent on one's state of mind, on the motivations of the spirit. Those who knew me best have sometimes ascribed to me a tendency towards asceticism. In point of fact, I had no such inclinations and was never attracted by the ascetic way of life. From childhood I was pampered and surrounded by comfort; yet I have never been able to understand why it should be difficult to deny oneself comfort or live ascetically. The alleged merits and difficulties of ascetic life seem to me a form of self-delusion and self-glorification on the part of those who practise it. I was astonished to hear someone say to me that to abstain from meat is a heroic deed; anyhow I never liked meat and always had to force myself to eat it. There is, of course, no merit whatsoever attached to this. I never knew the meaning of fatigue: I could argue into the early hours of the morning without being the worse for it; and I was a very fast runner. Age and illness have taught me at last what fatigue means, but in the past even illnesses, which frequently beset me, did not prevent my having an almost athletic physique. I have always regarded the well-known and well-worn notion that the spirit should struggle against the flesh and the temptations of the flesh as a pernicious figment of the human brain. The spirit should struggle rather against the spirit, against the temptations of the spirit, which informs the body and not the other way round.

There was, however, an evil spirit in me, since everyone has, as it were, his positive and his negative 'Other One' within himself. My evil spirit was typified in Stavrogin.[1] When I was a young man people used to call me Stavrogin and I secretly relished this identification. I liked being 'the aristocrat of the Revolution', 'the dark-haired nobleman, gleaming with life and wearing the mask of cold aloofness'. It was perhaps naïve but no less tempting for that. There was, as a matter of fact, something of a Stavrogin in me, although I believe I have successfully got the better of it. Later I wrote an article about Stavrogin which reflected some of the intimate connection between him and myself and, incidentally, provoked an uproar of indignation.

It is a sign of ignorance and narrow-mindedness to be surprised at the conflicts and contradictions in man. Man is fundamentally a contradictory being: and this denotes something deeper and more important than any seeming absence of contradiction in him. I can identify a series of contradictions within me, which cannot be reduced to any one of them or explained by simplification. Such, for instance, are pride and humility, which are both present in me and somehow co-exist in a tension. I was always conscious of myself as living in many dimensions and on many levels. I have invariably been dismayed, and sometimes amused, when people praised me. It never occurred to me to be superior

[1] The hero of Dostoevsky's novel *The Possessed*. (Tr.)

or disdainful towards others; indeed, I made it even a point to consort with 'simple people' and frequently engaged in the most trivial conversations. I liked to escape observation and to be as inconspicuous as possible. It was particularly repugnant to me to display any intellectual superiority.

All these characteristics are perhaps in part the result of my extreme reserve, of a desire to preserve my inner peace, and of my insufficient capacity for human intercourse. But they also conceal a pride which I was unwilling to show to other people. When, in my old age, I was occasionally regarded as something of a celebrity, this gave me little satisfaction and did not in the least feed my self-esteem: as a matter of fact, it caused me considerable embarrassment and even shocked me. The idea of an incognito has a great attraction for me. I was proud and self-assertive indeed, but my pride was kept beneath the surface and in no way affected my relations with other people; and, at a still deeper level of my nature, I was genuinely humble, though I do not see anything particularly virtuous in this: it is just a natural trait rather than a spiritual attainment. Generally speaking, I know of very few moral attainments to my credit. The fact is that I am both rebellious and humble, unruly and unresisting. If I come to look into myself, I must, in all conscience, avow that I have not a high opinion of myself. I have hardly ever taken anything ill to heart, and even if I tried I never seemed to succeed. I could not understand the meaning of wounded self-esteem and felt no sympathy with its manifestations in others. I am not aware of any obscure, 'subterranean' tendencies in myself like Dostoevsky's 'man from the underworld', although to say this is far from implying that I am free from evil. I am altogether not given to introspection, except, presumably, in writing an autobiography, nor am I inclined to be perpetually at war with myself. I do not express in my writings, as some people manage to do, the reverse of what I am in reality. Probably I keep myself back and reveal myself at the same time, but the 'compensations', 'repressions' and 'sublimations', to which modern psycho-analysis attaches such importance, are not applicable to me, just as they are not applicable to so many other people.

The absence of conceit or ambition in me may have been a peculiar form of spiritual pride. At any rate, I have never sought after fame or reputation, which appears to have had such an attraction for Tolstoy and his hero Prince Andrey Volkonsky. Indifference, too, played no small part: I had but little interest for what people wrote about me and often left articles about myself unread. Sometimes it seemed to me that those who praised me were, in a way, putting pressure on me and depriving me of my freedom. I was apprehensive of those who claimed to be, or even were, like-minded; I was equally apprehensive of 'disciples', who appeared to me in the shape of obstacles to the exercise of my creative freedom and their own. I felt at my best when in conflict, for only then my thinking acquired its greatest intensity. The true spirit of freedom seemed to me to be closely linked with anonymity. When at some meeting or other people admired me as a notable figure or a famous man I was ready for the earth to swallow me up. No one would call this humility: it is, rather, evidence of a lack of desire for direct association with men and women—a little pride, a little indifference, a little reserve. In fact I am a horse for single harness, not cut out for 'society'.

There is yet one other contradiction in me, of which I have always been conscious. In spite of what I have said above, I was extraordinarily sensitive in my reactions to the things around me. All suffering, for example, even when it was least apparent to an outsider, whether in those who were near to me or in those who were not, caused me untold pain. I noticed the slightest shades and changes of moods in others. Yet, at the same time, this hypertrophied sensitiveness was accompanied by a strange emotional dryness or aridity. My very sensitiveness is arid: a thing which has not escaped the notice of many people who knew me. My inner world has the likeness of a desert, a waste land bare of all but stark and solitary rocks. The moments of greatest exultation in my life are devoid of all adornment, of all frills and furbelows, and their closest symbol is to be found in a bare flame. I feel most akin to the element of fire; and I am a stranger to the elements of earth and water. I have, therefore, seldom felt life to be well-grounded and secure, or relished it in the living. And yet I am far from being stern and rigid. Strange though it is in view of my sensitivity, I was never able to experience tender, soul-stirring emotions, and never liked such experiences. I am altogether unemotional, and I have never suspected any lyricism or 'high sentiments' in myself. On the other hand I am profoundly susceptible of the tragic in life, which issues from my intense awareness of suffering in the world and in human existence. The element most congenial to me is the dramatic.

I have never been able to achieve any harmony and balance between my spiritual and emotional life, and the spiritual always predominated over the emotional. This resulted in a weakening of my affective, emotive powers and reactions. My spirit was whole, but my soul was sick. I have never been conscious of any instability or uncertainty of thought or division of will in myself, but I have been frequently conscious of emotional confusions and indecisions. I have never failed to assert my spiritual independence; but there has never been anything which caused me greater torment than my relationships with other people and my failure in this respect. My quick temper was only one of the many symptoms of these short-comings. I was not only subject to outward fits of anger: sometimes, when alone in a room, I would conjure up my foe and become enflamed with anger.

I have already said that I have never liked soldiers; I was repelled by everything associated with war and had an abhorrence of force. Yet I am by nature militant, and I tend instinctively to react violently to my environment. At one time I even carried a revolver about with me. This suggests a similarity between myself and Tolstoy, who was imbued with the same aversion from force combined with the same militant attitude to life. I found it easy to express my emotions only towards animals: all my unexpressed tenderness was poured out on them. I seemed to find with animals a relief from my solitude. I am passionately fond of dogs, cats, birds, horses and other animals, but most of all of dogs and cats, for which I feel a particular affection. The company of animals, especially of those which have lived with me, gives me very great delight, and I would like this companionship to continue after death. I was greatly attached to two dogs: my wife's pug Tomka and, later, another dog called Shulka. Their loss (one died in very old age, the other was left behind at the time of my exile from Soviet Russia) gave me some of the most despondent hours in my life and left a large place vacant in my heart. I wept as I seldom wept before. But the animal I loved most dearly was my cat Mura. Its beautiful eyes seemed to reveal to me some unknown depths of experience, and I endured agonies when it fell ill and died.

I have already had occasion to note that there are in my attitude to life elements of the imaginative, the visionary and of the realistic alike. This does not necessarily involve conflict, because these things are concerned with different objects, and can therefore co-exist without inconsistency. It is not in my nature to idealize everyday reality: I am not prone to illusions, I do not tread on enchanted ground, nor am I easily disillusioned. I am a stranger to what is known as the romantic approach to reality. In one sense only can I be called a romantic, if indeed it is romanticism: I have striven relentlessly towards the transcendent in an intense endeavour to cross the boundary and surpass the limits of this world. This issued in a realization of the ultimate unreality or, rather, falsehood and 'fallenness' of this world of ours—a realization which is more fundamental to me than any theory or philosophical allegiance. I have no illusions whatsoever in regard to the world: but I believe that the world itself is to a large extent illusory, though in a different sense from that suggested by Indian thought or by philosophies derived from it. The pressure of history and the weight of the material universe do not impress me. The attempts to assign a sacred character to historical phenomena and to the hierarchical order of society carry no conviction with me. I have likewise, and above all, never been able to acquiesce in the ephemeral, perishable achievements of time, in all that lives but for an instant. The happy moments of life have continually escaped my grasp. I could never be reconciled to the fact that time is in a perpetual flux and that each moment is devoured by, and vanishes into, the succeeding one. This terrible aspect of time has caused me intense and unspeakable pain. To part with people, with things, with places, has been a source of agony to me as dreadful as death.

I must have always belonged to a type of men for whom dissatisfaction with the given and yearning for the eternal were the supreme and decisive imperatives in life. All my life I have re-echoed Zarathustra's immortal words: 'Eternity, I love thee.' It is impossible to love anything but the eternal, and all love is love eternal. If eternity is not, then nothing is. An instant in time possesses value to the extent to which it is united to eternity and provides an issue out of the issuelessness of time—only in virtue of being an atom of eternity, as Kierkegaard says, rather than of time. My sickness lay in that expectation and the anticipation of events before their actual occurrence has haunted me all my life. Such a state of mind is, admittedly and unfortunately, not consistent with the counsels of wisdom and the precepts of the Gospel. I have desired that time should cease to be, that eternity should contain and conquer time, past and future time alike. And yet, at the same time, I look forward and await the future. The problem of time may well be the fundamental problem of philosophy, especially of the philosophy of existence.

It has never occurred to me to think of the world as having no limits or finality. I have, on the contrary, always thought of it as limited, as in fact limitation itself, in contrast to the boundlessness and infinitude of that which was known to me within myself. The world within me is indeed much more real than the extraneous world without. Some have often reproached me with inability to acknowledge the movement from within outward—achievement, realization, success, victory. I should like to comment on this point in the present context, though I shall return to it later on. It is true that I have no liking for the victors and the successful: they seem to me to pursue the course of mere adaptation to a world which is situated in evil and is largely evil. I do not, admittedly, believe in the possibility of true realization on the level of an alienated, objectified universe: tragedy has struck too deep at the heart of the world. This attitude explains my dislike of Classicism, which creates the illusion of perfection in the finite, whereas, in reality, perfection can only be attained in the infinite. The illusion of finite perfection obstructs our view of, and aspiration towards, the infinite and eternal. Every form achieved or actualized is relative and can never lay claim to finality; every actualization in the here and now is but a symbol of something other beyond—a feeble attempt to embody our striving towards the infinite and eternal and, thereby, to arrest it. This provides the source of the revolutionary character of my thought: viz. revolution from beyond, from the transcendent into the immanent. In contrast to what is generally believed, I think that it is spirit which is revolutionary, whilst matter is conservative and reactionary. Indeed, matter is as a rule detrimental to true, i.e. spiritual, revolution and makes a travesty of its achievements. Matter concerns the temporal, but spirit seeks after the eternal. Attainment in itself signifies eternity.

As I recall my childhood and adolescence and even my last years I realize the tremendous significance which Dostoevsky and Tolstoy had for me. I always felt some peculiar bond with the heroes of Tolstoy's and Dostoevsky's novels; with Ivan Karamazov, Versilov, Stavrogin, Prince Andrey, and even with those whom Dostoevsky called 'the pilgrims of the Russian land', with Chatsky[1], Evgueny Onegin, Pechorin[2] and others. This feeling marked, perhaps, my deepest ties with Russia and her destiny. I have received an equally profound impression from such Russians as Chaadaev, some of the Slavophils, from Leo Tolstoy and Vladimir Solovyev, from Herzen, and even from Bakunin and the Nihilists.

Like many of these Russians, I was born into the gentry and broke with it. This rupture with the society to which I belonged, which was later on followed by another break with my associates in the Revolution, constitute two of the most fundamental events in my inward and outward biography. They were part of my struggle for the right to free thought and creativity.

I was never uncertain as to where my calling lay; I had sufficient strength and determination to pursue this calling, and I could be fierce in the struggle for its fulfilment. I have never excelled in restraint, but neither can I pretend to have surmounted the tensions, contradictions and inconsistencies within me. Steadiness and constancy were in fact never my virtues. My only enduring and my greatest love was philosophy, although I never surrendered myself exclusively to its pursuit. Few philosophers have been so deeply involved in life as I was, though, as I have tried to show, I have not liked 'life'. Likewise, few philosophers were so much involved in society as I was, although I had a positive dislike of 'society'. I had a taste for asceticism, even if my life was far from being ascetic; I was extraordinarily compassionate, but seem to have done very little to practise compassion. I have always been aware of the action of irrational forces in my life. My own actions have never been inspired by reason, and I tended to be swayed by impulse. I have

[1] Hero of Alexander Griboyedov's comedy *Woe from Wit*. (Tr.)
[2] Hero of Lermontov's novel *A Hero of Our Time*. (Tr.)

been conscious of a great virtue or energy of spirit in myself, of great inward liberty and release from dependence on the world around me; but in everyday life I have often been overwhelmed by the pressure of confused sensations and emotions. I was temperamentally a fighter, but I seldom fought to the end, and my moods and manifestations of belligerency gave way to a thirst for philosophical contemplation.

I often thought that, in the end, I failed to realize all the possibilities inherent in me and to be consistently true to myself, for, as someone once pointed out, there was something of an incorrigible aristocrat and dilettante about me. This quality left an almost metaphysical mark on me, and I was never able to overcome it. Had I been of another, more 'democratic' origin I should probably have been less inconsistent and, while lacking certain traits which I cannot but value, I should have achieved more or applied myself with greater consistency to what I have achieved.

I cannot acquit myself of egotism, but my egotism concerned the sphere of creative mind rather than the pleasures of life or happiness in life, upon which I have never set my heart. I was capable of cruelty in the defence of my own and other people's creative vocation: but I suspect that this is inevitable in a world in which the creative mind is confronted by inertia, sloth and dullness. A thinker, an intellectual, is, in some sense, an oddity and a monster. I was torn between a violent urge to pursue my intellectual battles and carry the fight into the enemy's camp, on the one hand, and moral and intellectual compassion, on the other. When speaking of egotism we must not confuse it with mere selfishness, for there is a legitimate form of egotism, which acknowledges the primacy of man's ego as his irreducible personal centre, as opposed to that of which Pascal said that it is 'hateful'. Thus man's very self is divided, and this accounts for my own discordant and complex nature and the equally divergent and complex pathways of my life.

CHAPTER II

SOLITUDE. ANGUISH. FREEDOM. REVOLT. PITY.
DOUBTS AND WRESTLINGS OF THE SPIRIT.
REFLECTIONS ON *EROS*

Solitude and communion, in their polarity and co-inherence, are fundamental to life. Withdrawal and communication are acts of human existence, round which revolves the whole religious life of man. How are the distance and the estrangement bred in withdrawal to be overcome? Religion provides an answer to this question, for it is concerned with creating a bridge between two worlds and thus with the realization of kinship and intimacy. I was never conscious of being a part of the objective world, or of occupying any given place and position in it. The experience I have of my self is one which sets me apart from the objective world, and I come into relation with this world only on its periphery. My sense of uprootedness and disestablishment in the world, which later I came to express philosophically as objectification, is at the heart of my whole world outlook. From childhood I dwelt in a world unlike the one which surrounded me and only feigned implication in the world of my environment. I was on the defensive against the world and kept watch over my freedom.

I began reading novels, plays, and a certain amount of poetry in early childhood, and this reading served to strengthen my impression of living in a different, peculiar world of my own. The heroes of literary fiction had a greater reality for me than the people amongst whom I lived. As a child I had a doll, dressed up in an officer's uniform, which I endowed with all the qualities I most admired: it was, as it were, significant of what happens to a myth. I read Tolstoy's *War and Peace* very early, and gradually the doll, whose name was Andrey, became an incarnation of Prince Andrey Volkonsky. I had conjured up a being endowed for me with a reality greater than that of my comrades of the Cadet Corps. Life in this world of mine did not, however, belong

33

merely to the sphere of phantasy and make-believe. I never lacked a
sense of reality and, in particular, of the reality of the afflicted world
around me. My experience has been, indeed, not so much of the
unreality as of the alien character of the objective world; but I have
never lived in some illusory sphere. My reaction to the world around
me was if anything too sober and realistic. But I had a sense of this
world's remoteness, and I could never merge with it. Later, when I
began to think in philosophical terms, I spoke of man's estrangement
vis-à-vis the world and of the world's exteriorization vis-à-vis man, and
I saw in this human condition a source of enslavement. I strove to preserve the wholeness of my own world and not to allow it to become
exteriorized. I had a vision of man as a being who had neither arisen
out of 'this world' nor become adapted and, thereby, enslaved to it;
and I began to identify myself as such a being. But I never thought that
I was in any sense 'better' than other men, better than those who were
rooted and firmly established in 'this world': indeed, sometimes I
thought I was worse, and worse off, than they.

The agonizing consciousness of estrangement extended to my attitude to all groups of people, to all movements, to all parties and classes.
I have never consented to be placed in a category, and I could not
imagine myself as part of a 'general', 'normal' human condition. The
sense of estrangement, which caused me sometimes real suffering, was
aroused by any gathering of people, any workaday occurrence in life.
There is even much within myself that is alien to me. I was an absentee
even when I was actively present in life. I cannot say, however, that
with me the sense of alienation was ever a sign of indifference: I was
if anything not sufficiently indifferent; I always found myself deeply
and actively committed in life. But this was combined, in a paradoxical
way, with a tendency to what may be called a non-social attitude; and
I frequently thought in this connection of the feudal lord sitting in his
castle with the drawbridge up and shooting at everyone who attacked
him.

Yet I am sociable. I have spent my life in intercourse with other
people and I have enjoyed such intercourse. I have also taken an active
part in social affairs and political movements. My thinking, moreover,
is not a solitary monologue: dialogue and the impact of the thought of

others have stimulated and intensified my own thinking. I have always inclined to be a controversialist. This is evidence of one of the contradictions in me, which has misled some of my critics. But I have seldom revealed myself outwardly in words as I really am. I have, as it were, worn a shield to defend my own world. I wonder if anyone was ever aware, when I seemed to be actively engaged in some conversation, how very remote and how much of a stranger I in fact remained. I felt most lonely in the company of other people; and loneliness amongst others is loneliness heightened and intensified.

Lonely people are said to have a predominantly inactive, contemplative frame of mind, whereas I was both lonely and active, albeit not 'activistic' or businesslike. I always felt, and I always do feel, passionately about social questions, and yet every social order and movement is completely alien to me. In my youth I belonged to, and was very active in, a number of Marxist groups: I addressed meetings, I argued, I engaged in propaganda. But the feeling of distance, the knowledge of having come from some other world, to which I would return, never left me. I have, therefore, never been quite able outwardly to embody that which was within me; and my attempts to shape my environment after my own heart were never crowned with great success. I have nothing in common with the 'pillars of society', with established persons and the guardians of the principles of life and civilization, whether these principles be conservative, liberal or socialist.

There are two fundamentally different types of people: those whose relationship with the world is accommodating and harmonious, and those who are continually at variance with it. I am of the second type. The disharmony between the 'self' and the 'non-self' and a deep-rooted inadaptability peculiar to me have always caused me pain and disquiet. Thanks to my reserve and my tendency to appear other than I am in reality, people, as a rule, formed a wrong opinion about me, whether it was favourable or not. In my youth certain sympathetic souls used to call me 'the darling of women and the gods'. This is perhaps very flattering, but I could scarcely recognize myself in this mirror, designed, as it appears to be, for a facile, happy and easy-going sort of person— a type, in fact, from which I am as far removed as possible. The experience of solitude and anguish is hardly conducive to high spirits and jocundity. To be solitary is not to be able to comply and to come to terms with the world as it stands over against one. This non-acceptance of the world may have been my first metaphysical cry on being born into it. When my consciousness awoke I became aware of a collision with the things and habits of commonplace, everyday existence. The life of the world and of men is, in fact, largely under the domination of the commonplace, of *das Man*, in Heidegger's words, attuned to the consciousness of that well-known abstraction 'the ordinary man'. Every established way of life among men was repellent to me, and I longed to break out of the world of workaday existence.

My realization of the alien character of the world resulted in an inability to acquire a firm footing in it and explains, perhaps, why I never entertained any ambitions in life. I have always been indifferent to the things which concern my person, in particular, to the appraisement of my work by others. Human appreciation struck me as touching only the superficial level, or the outer shell, of my thoughts, without ever reaching its real core. Some people were fond of me, or even enthusiastic about me, yet I was under the permanent impression of being disliked by 'public opinion' and 'society': I was disliked by the Marxists, by wide circles of the Russian intelligentsia, by politicians, by the representatives of 'official' and academic philosophy and science, in literary and ecclesiastical circles. I never showed much capacity for team-work and collaboration and always found myself in conflict and opposition. I rebelled against the society of the gentry and the revolutionary intelligentsia; against conservatives, liberals and communists; against the Russian *émigrés* and French society. Women have always shown greater regard for me than men; but their love cast a shadow on the years of my youth. I asserted my freedom too forcibly and habitually deceived their expectations. In the same way I disappointed all ideological movements which counted on my unreserved adherence. As a matter of fact, I adhered to no one except myself: I had my own 'idea', my own vocation, my own search for truth. I have never experienced the delight and rapture of full union, either religious, or national, or social, or erotic; but I have often experienced the rapture of liberation and revolt.

It would be quite erroneous to infer that I am a solipsist, that is to say, one who denies the reality of the other and of others for himself. On the contrary, the movement of self-transcendence is to me a matter of intense concern. Always and everywhere I am allured by and drawn towards the transcendent, the Other, which reaches out beyond all boundaries and limitations and holds within itself the mystery of life. I am not immersed exclusively in myself or preoccupied with self-analysis and self-reflection, even while aware of my solitude and painful estrangement from the world. Sometimes I have prevailed over my loneliness; at other times I would experience untold joy on returning to it, as if I had come home from a foreign country to my own native land. The native land was still not myself, yet it was within me. Paradoxical though it may be, I am aware of something in my self that is other than and alien to myself, and, conversely, of something that is closer to myself than my own self. But I cannot hope to express this in any sufficiently intelligible way, except by referring to St. Augustine and Pascal who speak of a similar experience.

From childhood I have had a strong sense of vocation. There was never any question for me what I should choose in life and which path I should take; for, while still a boy, I was sure that my calling lay in philosophy. This did not mean that I would specialize in a certain subject—viz. philosophy—produce theses, and become a professor. Generally speaking, I never looked forward to any career, and had no disposition whatever to an academic life. I disliked scholars as a class and could not stand the scholastic mentality in any shape whatsoever. In my opinion the very conception of conventional learning is a monstrosity. I could no more imagine myself in the rôle of a professor than in that of an officer, a civil servant, a *paterfamilias*, or, indeed, in any rôle in 'life'. As I became conscious of my vocation as a philosopher, I thereby became conscious of myself as dedicated to the search for truth and for the revelation of meaning in life.

As a child I developed very early, although I had little capacity for regular study and showed little regularity in my work. I read Schopenhauer, Kant and Hegel when I was fourteen, having discovered Schopenhauer's *World as Will and Idea*, Kant's *Critique of Pure Reason*, and Hegel's *Phenomenology of Mind* and the first part of the *Encyclopaedia* in my father's library. I watched the formation of a subjective world

which gradually evolved in me and which I opposed to the objective
world around me. But then, as indeed in later more mature years, I
was at a loss to express all the intensity of my awareness of this world.
The other, the objective world, always seemed to me somehow of less
interest. I was really able to recognize and comprehend the world
without and be one with it only in virtue of its inherence in me and
as an inner component of the world of 'self'. I could understand
Schopenhauer, or Kant, or Hegel when I discovered their universe of
discourse within myself. All the things which confronted me as an
object to be penetrated from without left me uncomprehending; I
understood only by returning to the subject, from within. Hence, perhaps, the misunderstandings which my thought caused in the minds of
other people. It is never possible to express adequately a knowledge
wrested from within. I may have succeeded to some extent in conveying my 'thoughts', but not my ultimate insights. I was equally incapable
of expressing my feelings. This is probably also a case of self-defence—
a desire to preserve and keep alive one's own world, rather than one
of frustration and inhibition.

I always found intimate conversation with another person difficult,
and, paradoxically enough, it was much easier for me to speak in society
or to an audience. When *tête-à-tête* I became acutely conscious of my
separateness, and reserve seemed to take the upper hand. Accordingly,
I always gave the impression of lacking sentiment and all 'lyrical'
qualities. But if the truth were known, an extreme sensitivity, compassion, and even a strain of the lyrical might have been discovered in
me. When I came into contact with people, however, I was utterly
unable to give these things expression. André Gide writes in his *Journal*
that he could never stand the slightest exhibition of sentimentality, and
its manifestation in others made his marrow freeze. My reactions are
similar to his: I cannot bear any emotional flutter, softness and unctu-
osity. Sometimes it has seemed to me that I had no need at all of people.
This is certainly an objectionable attitude, both morally and meta-
physically; but such was my temperament.

It is characteristic of my attitude to the world outside, to my social
environment and to the people I came across in the course of my life
that I never tried to attain anything, to seek success and prosperity in

any sense whatsoever. I followed my calling in the absence of the advantages and qualifications which the outer world can offer; and it always surprised me that occasionally I received such advantages. I never moved a finger in order to gain anything. I was fairly tolerant in personal relationships and I never felt any inclination to judge others. But I could be intolerant too: I became unsparing and uncompromising in confrontation with the things I was actively combating at the time. I was frequently conscious that 'inwardness', to which I attached so much importance, did not suffice after all: there was need of 'outwardness', of exteriorization, of action without. To use Jung's terminology, I acknowledged the legitimacy, for myself and for others, of extroversion as well as introversion; yet, at the same time, I could not help being aware of the tragic failure of every outward action. Nothing satisfied me, not one book I have written or one word I have uttered. I have felt an overwhelming urge to realize my vocation in the world, to create, to write, to leave the imprint of my thought on the world. Had I not been able to express myself in writing, I should probably have been utterly thwarted and downcast. I have never had any doubts as to the validity of the creative act. But I had no thought of the impression produced on others while engaged in the creative act. I will, however, say more about this at a later stage.

It would be quite wrong to read what I have written about solitude as implying that I had no close friends, or that I did not love anyone and owed no one enduring gratitude. Actually, my life did not pass in solitude, and the attainments that may be ascribed to me are largely due to others. But this did not relieve what I would call my metaphysical loneliness. I was powerless to express the painful implications of that loneliness, nor was I desirous of so doing. For this reason I was unable to experience happiness and sought an issue in eschatological expectation.

The other basic element in human existence of which I want to speak is anguish. All my life anguish never left me, although my awareness of it varied and was more or less intense at different stages of my inner development. It is necessary to distinguish between anguish, fear, and tedium. Anguish points to the world above and is associated with the experience of the insignificance, precariousness and transitoriness of this world. Anguish bears witness to the transcendent and, at the same time, to the distance, the yawning gulf that exists between man and the transcendent. Anguish is also a longing for another world, for that which is beyond the boundaries of this finite world of ours. It spells solitude in face of the transcendent; it is the point of greatest conflict between my existence in the world and the transcendent. Anguish can awake my awareness of God, but it can also signify my God-forsakenness. It intervenes, as it were, between the transcendent and the abyss of non-being, of void.

Fear and tedium, on the other hand, consign me to the nether world. Fear is evidence of danger, coming from the lower world; and tedium denotes this world's triviality and emptiness. There is nothing more frightful and hopeless than the tedious and wearisome void of life. Anguish admits of hope, but tedium is devoid of hope. There is no issue out of tedium, unless it be in the act of creation. Fear is always associated with external danger and must be distinguished from terror, which is an experience in the depths of spirit and concerns the transcendent realities of being and non-being. Kierkegaard draws a distinction between *Angst* and *Furcht*; and for him *Angst* is a primordial religious phenomenon. Anguish and terror are related experiences; but the experience of terror is the more poignant, the more intense and overpowering, while anguish is the gentler, the more tranquil and untroubled. Terror may deliver man from tedium, and, when it turns to anguish, man's diseased condition ceases to be acute and becomes chronic.

It is easier to endure anguish and terror than sadness of heart and sorrow, and I always sought to escape from these as quickly as possible. I felt helpless in face of anything that stirred my emotions: I was too deeply sensitive and impressionable. Sadness, which is of the heart, looks towards the past. Terror, which is of the spirit, looks towards the eternal. Turgenyev is the artist of sadness *par excellence*; Dostoevsky is the artist of terror. Sadness has a poetical quality; terror is inherently dramatic. I knew anguish and terror and bore them with fortitude; but it seemed to me that if I were to surrender to sadness, I would pass away.

Sadness is often associated with the sensation of pity, which I have always feared, knowing the power that it is apt to acquire over my soul. I was driven to raise barriers against sadness and pity, as indeed I did against anything that moved my emotions. But I was powerless to resist anguish, and it had no such destructive effects on me. To use an old-fashioned and rather inaccurate distinction, I combined in myself two types of temperament, commonly considered incompatible: I am at once sanguine and melancholic; and the sanguine element in me was perhaps even more pronounced than the melancholic. I was very easily roused, and my quick reaction issued, amongst other things, in the irascibility of which I have already spoken. But melancholy in me had deeper roots. Sometimes I suffered agonies of nostalgia and was driven by pessimistic moods, even when I appeared outwardly cheerful and content.

It is interesting, perhaps, that at the time of my spiritual awakening it was the philosophy of Schopenhauer rather than the Bible which impressed me—a fact which may have had far-reaching consequences for my later life. I found it difficult to recognize the alleged 'goodness' of creation. It is strange that I should have suffered most acutely from anguish during the so-called happy moments of life, if indeed it is at all possible to speak of such moments. I have always been afraid of happy, joyful experiences, for they have always brought me the most vivid memories of the agony of life. On great feast-days I almost invariably felt anguish, perhaps because I was awaiting some miraculous transformation of ordinary, workaday life: but it never came. The tragedy is that I was unable to idealize and romanticize, as some succeeded in doing, the painful condition of man—his anguish, his despair, his doubts, his sufferings and conflicts. I often thought of this condition as a frightful betrayal of life.

There is anguish which is characteristic of adolescence. In my youth I have known greater anguish than in later and more mature years: this anguish springs from an abundance of unrealized powers, from doubts and uncertainty as to the possibility of realizing them. Youth lives in the hope of a life rich, colourful, momentous and eventful; but there is disparity and contrast between life as it presents itself to hope and life as actually lived, life distorted and betrayed by untold disappointments, injustices, suffering and pain. It is a mistake to think that anguish is born of weakness: on the contrary, it is born of abundant strength. In life's very intensity there is contained an element of anguish. I believe that the young endure more of the anguish and longing of life than others are generally ready to admit. But different people experience this in different ways. I was myself particularly prone to anguish at moments which are commonly said to be joyful; for there is agony in the joy of the given moment when it is experienced against the background of life as a whole, pervaded as this is by tragedy and torment.

Anguish is always evidence of longing for eternity, of inability to come to terms with time. When we face the future we are moved not only by hope but also by anguish; for, in the end, the future carries death within itself and thus gives rise to anguish. Both future and past are hostile to eternity. I have often experienced a burning anguish under a wonderful starry or moonlit sky or on a glorious sunny day; in the quiet of a blossoming garden or in the silent immensity of the steppes; on looking into the face of a beautiful woman or at the moment of the awakening of love. Such moments called forth a vision of contrast between these and the darkness, decay and ugliness which fill the world to overflowing.

I was always struck by the unspeakable pain and destructiveness of time: I always foresaw the end in imagination and found no strength or desire to adapt myself to the process which led up to it. I was impatient. Love in particular seemed to me to carry within itself the seed of anguish, and I have frequently been amazed that people could experience the exultation of love as sheer joy and happiness. Eros is in anguish, for it is concerned with, and deeply rooted in, the mystery of time and eternity: it concerns time athirst for eternal fulfilment, and yet never attaining it. Likewise, there is anguish in sex, which does not merely denote a passion for satisfaction of desire, but also bears the signature of the fallen nature of man. It is impossible to quench the thirst of sex in the conditions of this fallen life, for this thirst gives rise to illusions which make man the tool of an inhuman, biological process. Dionysos, the god of dying and rising life, gives birth to tragedy, from which sex cannot ever extricate itself: Dionysos and Pluto are one. Sex shows man wounded, fallen apart and never able to attain true fulness through union. It bids man go out into another; but he returns once more into himself and the anguish of his longing for unity continues unrelieved. The desire for wholeness inherent in men cannot be satisfied, least of all in sexual passion, which indeed only serves to deepen the wounds of disunity. Sex is, in its very nature, unwholesome, unchaste: it is evidence of the divided nature of man: only true love prevails over the division and attains wholeness and chastity. This is a profoundly tragic problem, on which I shall dwell at a later stage.

I have known anguish at unusual times and in unusual circumstances. Summer twilight in the streets of a big city, especially in Petersburg and Paris, with their drifting, half-formed images, has frequently inspired anguish in me. I have always found it hard to bear the hour of twilight. It is the hour of transition between life and darkness—a time when the fount of daylight is already spent, and when the other light, which springs from the starry mystery of night, or when the man-made artificial light, by which we try to protect ourselves against the power of darkness, has not as yet illumined human existence. Twilight intensifies the longing for eternity, for eternal life. It is also at the hour of twilight, in the ghostly atmosphere of a large town, that the veil over the nightmares and the evil of human life is drawn aside. But the anguish of twilight is different from the anguish of night: the latter has a depth, a transcendence unknown to the former. I have known both: I have known the anguish of misty twilight and the anguish of night which turns into terror and which no human language can convey or express. But this experience vanished in time. There were periods when I could not wake or sleep in darkness, and I was haunted by terrifying dreams and nightmares. Dreams have altogether been a source of torment to me, although I have sometimes had remarkable dreams of great illumination for me. Night conveyed to me some alien presence which terrified and pursued me into daylight. Thus we would go, four of us, for a walk in the country, into forests or fields; and I would suddenly have a sense of the presence of a fifth, come I know not whence, and I would forget how many of us there were. I can see no other source of these experiences but this mysterious and unaccountable anguish.

Modern psychoanalysis describes these phenomena as having their origin in the sub-conscious, but this explains little and elucidates nothing. I am deeply convinced that the transcendent is present in human life: it allures man and acts in human existence. I have known the depth and power of the sub-conscious and the subterranean, but I have also known that other and greater deep which is transcendence. Anguish is present in the very fabric of so-called life (though it may be unknown to those who take this life for granted and ask no questions), and all living beings are imbued with its deadly poison.

It has been said that 'green is the tree of life and grey the theory of life'. Paradoxical though it may seem, I am inclined to think that the reverse is true: 'grey is the tree of life and green the theory thereof'. But I must explain, lest this should give rise to misunderstandings. Have I not always been a declared enemy of scholastic conceptualism and the desiccated theories of discursive reason? Have I not always been a Faust rather than a Wagner? What is known as 'life', however, is as often as not an embodiment of the commonplace and consists of nothing but the cares of workaday existence. 'Theory', on the other hand, may be understood as creative vision, as the Greek *theoria*, which raises us above the habits of daily life. Philosophy, the 'green theory of life', is free of anguish and boredom. I became a philosopher and a servant of 'theory' that I might renounce and be relieved of this unspeakable anguish. Philosophical thinking had always freed me from life's ugliness and corruption. To 'being' I have always opposed 'creativity', that is to say, not 'life', but the breaking through and flight from 'life' into 'existence', from the finite into the infinite and transcendent.

Anguish, then, takes its rise in 'life'—in the twilight and the mists of life—and drives man toward the transcendent; while creativity is that very movement towards transcendence and the evocation of the image of the wholly other in relation to this life. In the realm of creativity all things acquire depth, meaning, character and interest, in contrast to the shallowness, insignificance, fortuitousness and insipidity peculiar to the realm of tedious external fact. A world endowed with beauty, unknown to this objective world where ugliness reigns supreme, unfolded itself before me, and called upon my creative spirit.

Has tedium, which rises from the waste and vacant regions of being, ever filled my heart? I have hardly ever been bored, and time never seemed to suffice for the accomplishment of my life's work and the fulfilment of my vocation; nor have I ever wasted time. And yet many, all too many, things have bored me. I have been bored by the views and opinions of the majority of men; by politics; by ideologies; by the affairs of state and nation. The commonplace in life, the repetitions and imitations, the fetters and repressions of life have produced in me a sense of tedium and drawn me into a void of nothingness. Indeed, when man submits, through weakness or through ignorance, to the pressure of these things, the world becomes flat and empty, devoid of depth and meaning, and tedium comes into its own, in anticipation of that kingdom of utter emptiness which is hell. The final and infernal limit of tedium is reached when man says to himself that nothing is. Suffering is, no doubt, a relief and a salvation in such a human condition, for it is a way of regaining the depth of life. Anguish too may bring salvation. There are people who feel happy in the midst of their own and the world's emptiness, and this state may well be the supreme instance of triviality and the commonplace.

Many people are, or say they are, in love with life. But I have never been able to feel or, indeed, to understand this. I could only be 'in love' with creativity and with the rapture of the creative act. I could never escape the feeling of anguish when confronted with life in its inexorable finality, and always believed that man's stature and significance is in proportion to that in him which breaks through to infinity. This issued in my inability ever to master the art of living and to profit by life. 'The misfortune of man', says Carlyle in *Sartor Resartus*, 'has its source in his greatness; for there is something infinite in him, and he cannot succeed in burying himself completely in the finite.' The 'objective' world and 'objective' life are indeed buried in the finite; and burial is the most fitting thing that can happen in the finite world. 'Life', then, is, as it were, the dying of the infinite into the finite, of the eternal into the temporal. There is in me a strong anarchist instinct: I revolt against the power of the finite, the circumscribed and the limitatively determined. The commonplace, which is the epitome of finiteness in the life of man and of the world, has either struck me by its utter insignificance, or it has roused me to revolt; and any attempt to ascribe a sacred character to finite things was repulsive to me.

Anguish can denote a religious experience. Religious anguish involves longing for immortality and eternal life, for redemption of the finitude of existence. Similarly, art appeared to me as imbued with anguish and, therefore, as evidence of the longing for transcendence. The magic of art is its power to wrench out the roots of finitude and to turn man's gaze to the eternal, archetypal forms and images of existence.

Anguish has persistently weakened my activity in the world: I thought to withdraw, whilst life was there to be re-shaped and transformed. That is, perhaps, why happiness and the sense of satisfaction were denied to me. From time to time it seemed to me that I would have known joy and happiness, had the cause of some particular pain at a particular moment been removed. But when this did happen the sense of anguish would persist and intensify some new and hitherto unknown torment. Nothing gave me a feeling of complete satisfaction and sufficiency; indeed these very states betrayed to me their fundamentally sinful character.

Some have called me the philosopher of freedom, and a reactionary Russian bishop once said of me that I was 'the captive of freedom'. I do indeed love freedom above all else. Man came forth out of freedom and issues into freedom. Freedom is a primordial source and condition of existence, and, characteristically, I have put Freedom, rather than Being, at the basis of my philosophy. I do not think any other philosopher has done this in such a radical and thorough-going way. The mystery of the world abides in freedom: God desired freedom and freedom gave rise to tragedy in the world. Freedom is at the beginning and at the end. I might say that all my life I was engaged in hammering out a philosophy of freedom. I was moved by the basic conviction that God is truly present and operative only in freedom. Freedom alone should be recognized as possessing a sacred quality, whilst all the other things to which a sacred character has been assigned by men since history began ought to be made null and void.

I look at myself as pre-eminently an emancipator, and I am in sympathy with every emancipation. Thus it was that Christianity presented itself to me and called upon my allegiance as emancipation. From my early childhood I was wedded to freedom; already in the second form

of the Cadet Corps I was meditating on and dreaming of the miracle
of freedom. Dependence on other things and other people offended me,
and the spirit of independence moved me in all my thinking and
actions. Even the slightest, manifestation of servility aroused in me a
storm of protest and hostility. I could never agree to abdicate freedom
or even to curtail it, and never consented to anything at the price of
freedom. I found strength to renounce many things in life, but I have
never renounced anything in the name of duty or out of obedience to
precepts and prohibitions: I renounced for the sake of freedom, and,
maybe, also out of compassion. Nothing could ever tie me down, and
this, no doubt, has to some extent weakened my efficiency and dimin-
ished my possibilities of self-realization. I always knew, however, that
freedom gives birth to suffering, while the refusal to be free diminishes
suffering. Freedom is not easy, as its enemies and slanderers allege:
freedom is hard; it is a heavy burden. Men, as Dostoevsky has shown
with such amazing power, often renounce freedom to ease their lot.

When I was young people used to call me 'the free son of the ether'.
This was true only in as far as I am certainly not a 'son of the earth':
I have always been a stranger to the stubborn and crushing element of
earth; rather, I proceeded from and sought for freedom. If, however,
the label 'free son of the ether' denotes a kind of easy-goingness, a
lightness and lack of the sense of affliction and pain, then this cannot be
true of me at all. I won freedom with difficulty and with untold pain.
'Freedom led me to the crossing of the ways in the impenetrable darkness of night.' All the things to which I have borne witness throughout
my life spring from some initial experience of freedom and have been
inspired by freedom. Freedom is not, as Hegel maintained, the creature
of necessity; just the reverse: necessity is the creature of freedom, or, to
put it differently, a certain tendency or orientation of freedom. I cannot
agree to accept any truth otherwise than out of, and in, freedom. I am
not, however, using the word freedom here in the sense current among
professional philosophers, viz. not as denoting 'free-will', but in a much
deeper, metaphysical sense. Truth can make me free, and yet I can accept
truth only through, and in, freedom. Thus there are two kinds of freedom, and the problem of their relation has exercised my mind in most
of my writings. The primordial, undetermined and underived char-

acter of freedom has been expressed in the proposition that the 'self'
cannot receive the 'non-self' unless it makes it (the 'non-self') the content of itself, unless it takes it up into its own freedom.

The war for freedom which I have waged all my life was to me the
thing of the greatest value and importance. But it also had its reverse
and less fortunate side: it entailed opposition, estrangement, disunion,
and even hostility. Sometimes freedom drove me into conflict with
love. In contrast to the widespread opinion concerning these things I
have always held freedom to be aristocratic rather than democratic in
character. The majority of men do not in the least love freedom and
do not seek after it. The revolutions of the masses have never displayed
any great love of freedom. I may have gained many experiences in life,
but I could not say that I have 'gained' freedom or the experience of
freedom: freedom appeared to me as the initial, primary reality, as the
a priori of existence. The idea of freedom denotes for me something
more fundamental than even that of perfection, since freedom is the
key to perfection and in its absence perfection turns into compulsion
and enslavement, and thereby belies its very nature.

All things in human life should be born of freedom and pass through
freedom and be rejected whenever they betray freedom. The true
meaning and origin of the fallen condition of man is to be seen in the
primordial rejection of freedom. When I recall my whole life from the
very first step into it I realize that I never knew or admitted any
authority or extraneous power whatsoever. I could not recognize their
admissibility for, and compatibility with, the dignity and freedom of
man. I have not known authority either at home, or at school, or in
my philosophical enquiries, or, most particularly, in my religious life.
As a child I already decided that I would not comply with any orders
or consent to bow submission to any superior. I could not even visual-
ize becoming a university teacher, since this too would inevitably entail
conforming to the high priests of academic wisdom. The value I attach
to freedom accounts, in some measure, for the fact that my thought
could never crystallize itself into any fixed traditional pattern. I do not
mean to say, of course, that I refused to learn from others, from all the
great masters of thought, or that I was subject to no influences or not
indebted to anyone. I was constantly stimulated by the minds of all

those whom I had the privilege of meeting and reading, particularly of those whose universe of discourse was congenial to me. But all these influences and stimuli were received in freedom or, even more, were the outcome of the exercise of my own freedom. I cannot think of any intellectual influence which has not been assimilated by me in the very depths of freedom and self-determination. I have never complied with any philosophical tradition, and I am one of the most untraditional philosophers. I did not even need to break with authorities, since I never acknowledged any. There were, however, a number of thinkers and writers who nourished my love for the freedom of the spirit, who confirmed this love and attended to its fruition in me. The most important of these was Dostoevsky, particularly in his 'Legend of the Grand Inquisitor'. Among thinkers I have always regarded Kant as the philosopher of freedom *par excellence*, although his philosophy of freedom is, in my opinion, not sufficiently radical and consistent. At a later stage I discovered the great importance of Ibsen: I read him as one would read a prophet, the prophet who is moved by a longing for the liberation of man.

All my differences and dissensions from individual people as well as from religious, social and political movements had their origin in the matter of freedom. The struggle for freedom was for me not primarily a social struggle but one which concerned man standing over against society. Roger Secrétain says in one of the most remarkable books on Péguy (*Péguy, soldat de la vérité*) that Péguy's secret passion in life was his anarchism and his repudiation of all authority. He also speaks of Péguy's solitariness, which made it impossible for him to have any followers: those who did follow him were encouraged by Péguy himself to break away. And, significantly enough, it was his very anarchism which brought him face to face with God—on condition, however, as Secrétain puts it, that God himself be '*un liberal, un libertaire, presque un anarchiste*'.

It is perhaps characteristic of me that I never underwent what is known as conversion, neither did I know what it meant to be a complete unbeliever. I can only revolt against false and servile ideas about God in the name of another idea which is freer and nobler. But I shall try to explain this when I come to speak of my religious convictions.

I displayed great vehemence and passion in my fight for freedom, even when I was quite young. I have said before that our family did not uphold authoritarian principles, and I always succeeded in maintaining and defending my independence. Nevertheless, I broke with the social *milieu* into which I was born. Everything which did not originate directly in spirit and in freedom repelled me, and I came to realize that all things belonging to the genus, class, family, were opposed to freedom. My dislike·of the genus and of everything concerned with birth, as distinct from creation, should be seen in the light of an insensate love of freedom. Family has always appeared to me as the enemy and enslaver of personal freedom. Family is of the order of 'necessity' rather than of 'freedom', and the struggle for freedom is the struggle against the power of the genus. The antithesis of birth and creatorship is, in fact, at the centre of my thought. I set out by placing freedom, personality and creatorship at the basis of my whole outlook; but, in due course, my concern for freedom became more intense. When I broke with the life and traditions of the gentry and joined the revolutionary movement I began to struggle for freedom within that movement, among the revolutionary intelligentsia and in the midst of the Marxist world. I came to realize quite soon that the revolutionary intelligentsia did not really cherish freedom, and that its true inspiration was to be found elsewhere.

While still a Marxist I saw elements in Marxism which were bound to lead to despotism and the betrayal of freedom. Here as elsewhere I witnessed the clash of person and group, of person and society, of person and public opinion; and I invariably took the side of the person. I devoted many years of my life to fighting public opinion among the intelligentsia and, in doing so, failed to pursue the more creative and constructive work of philosophy. For a long time I was completely carried away by the task of solving the problem of the relation of socialism and personality and endured agonies of inner conflict and anxiety on this account. I considered the usual arguments provided by liberalism and individualism against socialism to be both unconvincing and hypocritical, and the defence of freedom put up by them altogether spurious. But it was clear to me that socialism may develop in different directions: it may lead to the emancipation of man, but it may also lead to the destruction of human freedom, to tyranny and to a system such as pre-figured by Dostoevsky in his 'Legend of the Grand Inquisitor'. In quite early days, while still active in Marxist circles, I had presentiments of the possibility of totalitarian communism and I endeavoured to combat and to prevent this. But I was combating similar things in every ideological movement and circle with which I came into contact. All ideological groups, all gatherings of people in pursuit of 'ideals' are known to encroach on, and to betray, the freedom, independence and creativity of man. On becoming associated with ecclesiastical orthodoxy I experienced the same anguish which I felt amongst the nobility and the revolutionaries: I watched the same apostasy from freedom, the same hostility to the independence of the human person and the same forfeiture of man's creativity. It was an identical phenomenon presenting itself on a deeper level, because religion touches the very depth of the human soul.

I persisted in my struggle for the freedom and dignity of man during the communist revolution, and this led to my exile from Russia. When I became an *émigré* and lived among the *émigrés*, I found myself, not unexpectedly, face to face with the same problem. I came to realize that the Russian 'emigration' denied and hated freedom as much and more than the Russian communists, with the difference, however, that the latter had more right to such hostility, seeing that the most monstrous crimes against freedom have been committed in the name of freedom. After the first World War a generation grew up which resolved to set itself against freedom and took to loving authority and force. This, however, in no way took me by surprise: I felt alone in my search for freedom and devotion to the human person as I had done all my life long. I could not discover any such searching or devotion either among the ruling classes of the old *régime*, or among the old revolutionary intelligentsia, or in historical Orthodoxy, or among the communists, or, and least of all, in the new generation of men, vowed as it is to the service of Fascist ideals and instincts. Every mass of people banded together is hostile to freedom. I might put this more emphatically by saying that every society which has so far been organized or is in process of organization is inimical to freedom and tends to deny human personality. This results from a fatal falsification of human consciousness misguided by a confusion in the hierarchy of values. Among the post-war (it should now be called the pre-war) generation there is no evidence of a single original thought: it lives entirely by the odds and ends and aberrations of nineteenth century mentality. The realization of the value and primacy of freedom and personality sets man, alone and apart, over against society and the mass processes of history. The democratic age is the age of the bourgeois: it reveals not so much the demoralization of man as the impoverishment of the type and of the human personality.

All my life I have devoted much thought to the problem of freedom, and I have formulated my conclusions in two works which express my approach to this problem at different stages in the development of my philosophy. Both are evidence of the avowed difficulties and com-plexities which I have encountered in attempting to present my con-clusion. Freedom is the source of many misunderstandings and it has been found to denote many different and even contradictory things. Freedom is not a static concept but a living reality to be known dynamically through the exercise and the experience of it. There exists a dialectic of freedom, which is duly revealed in the destiny of man and of the world. Freedom can even turn into its opposite and issue in abject tyranny.

Philosophical text-books generally speak of freedom as identical with 'free-will', that is to say, as the possibility of choice, of turning right or left. Such a choice, however, presupposes man's confrontation with a norm which determines a distinction between good and evil. Thus it is that the concept of free-will became particularly useful as a basis for criminal law, guaranteeing man's accountability and hence his punishment or acquittal as the case may be. For me freedom has always meant something quite different. Freedom is first and foremost my in-dependence, determination from within and creative initiative; its reality does not depend on any norm and its exercise is not a mere choice between a good and an evil standing over against me: rather, freedom is my own norm and my own creation of good and evil. The very condition of choice may result in a sense of repression, indecisive-ness or even in the complete disappearance of freedom on the part of man. Liberation comes when the choice is made and when I have begun to create. The problem of man and of human creativeness is indeed closely associated with that of freedom. I have always believed that life in God is freedom, untrammelled flight, anarchy in the true sense of the word. The real call of freedom is not to be thought of in moral or psychological but in metaphysical terms: God and freedom, evil and freedom, creative novelty and freedom—such are the problems which must be primarily taken into account in any discussion of freedom.

The antagonists of freedom like to contrast it with truth, which commands the allegiance of man and forces recognition by him. But truth as an object which intrudes itself and wields authority over me— an object in the name of which it is demanded that I should renounce freedom—is a figment: truth is no extraneous thing; it is the way and the life. Truth is spiritual conquest; it is known in and through freedom. Truth which forces itself on me and in the name of which I am required to relinquish freedom is no truth at all but a temptation of the evil one. The dictum 'knowledge of the truth will make you free' evidently and paradoxically entails two kinds of freedom—a final and an initial one. I come of my own freedom to know the truth which (in its turn) liberates me. There is no authority in the world which has the power to constrain me to truth. I cannot be liberated by force.

I have never admitted and I do not now admit any orthodoxy intruding itself on me and asserting its possession of truth apart from my own free quest, my own asking and demanding. I have always found myself resisting any orthodoxy, be it political or religious, which has attempted to limit or destroy my freedom. It could not have been and cannot be otherwise. I am even inclined to think that compelling orthodoxy has no relation at all to truth and, indeed, holds truth in abomination. The greatest falsifications of truth have been brought about by the orthodox. Orthodoxy has a social character and origin and denotes the authority of an organized collective wielding power over the free personality and the free spirit of man. I believe in the scandal and stumbling-block of freedom. Freedom itself is a constituent and basic element of truth as it gradually reveals itself in and to me. The freedom of my conscience is an absolute dogma, in the face of which no mid-course and no compromise are possible. The whole value of Khomyakov's thought lay in that he discovered *sobornost'*[1] as a reality belonging to the realm of freedom. Yet he did not carry his discovery to its logical conclusion. *Sobornost'* can in no way be regarded as implying an external authority, for here too absolute primacy belongs, at each and every moment, to freedom. Khomyakov did not take into account the possibility of a conflict between freedom and *sobornost'*, in which the ultimate decision must needs lie with freedom. I cannot accept as truth that which is thrust down my throat; I can accept as truth only that which is wrung out from within myself. I cannot acknowledge as falsehood that in which I see truth, and I cannot acknowledge as truth that in which I see falsehood, merely because I am obliged to acknowledge them as such. In point of fact no one has really ever consented to do this. If the Church wields authority by driving me into conformity with the collective consciousness of ecclesiastical society, I find myself up against the same kind of phenomenon as the ugly but very instructive Moscow trials of the veteran communists.

But *sobornost'* signifies a quality of life which affirms the reality of freedom by widening the scope of freedom and by revealing its transcendent, universal dimension. The recognition of the absolute priority of freedom does not, therefore, denote, as some would like to make out, individualistic self-assertion. Freedom of the spirit has in fact nothing in common with individualism: to be free is not to be insulated; it is not to shut oneself up, but, on the contrary, to break through in a creative act to the fulness and universality of existence.

When I come to consider my struggle for freedom, however, I must admit that my endeavours often served to increase my sense of solitude and intensify my conflict with the world around. The call of freedom also gave rise in me to inner tensions and, above all, to the tension between freedom and compassion, to which I shall return in this chapter.

All my life I have been a rebel: I was a rebel even while making great efforts to humble myself. Rebellion marked not a phase in my intellectual development but an innate quality of my thinking and living. I was easily roused to revolt, and injustice and violence done to the

[1] For a further explanation of this term see pp. 156-157. (Tr.)

dignity and freedom of man evoked angry protests in me. As a boy I was given a book with the inscription 'to the dear protester'. At different periods of my life I have remonstrated against different kinds of ideas and behaviour. But I have throughout sympathized with all the great rebels recorded in the annals of history: with the revolt of Luther against ecclesiastical tyranny, and of the Enlightenment against authority; with Rousseau's revolt of 'nature' against 'civilization', and the revolt of the French Revolution against oppression; with the revolt of Idealism against the power of the objective, and Marx's revolt against capitalism; with Belinsky's revolt against the Hegelian world-spirit and world-harmony, and the anarchistic revolt of Bakunin; with Leo Tolstoy's revolt against history and civilization, and Ibsen's revolt against society. Christianity itself is to me the embodiment of the revolt against the world and its laws and fashions.

I am conscious that this tendency to revolt, opposition and dissent exposes me to the temptation of self-sufficiency and arrogance. Still I am compelled, by the very nature of this book, to speak of all that self-knowledge requires. But in doing so I wish to avoid striking the note of pretentiousness. I am aware, moreover, that no one can live by revolt alone, for it is but a partial judgment and a partial valuation.

Have I ever revolted against God? Is not the very expression 'revolt against God' open to misunderstanding? It is impossible to revolt, except with reference to and in the name of some ultimate value by which I judge that which I resolve to oppose; that is to say, except in the name of God, the supreme judge and redeemer. In the last analysis even militant atheists revolt in the name of God, although they may be unaware of it. But I have often rebelled against the ideas and beliefs about God framed by men, that is to say, against false gods rather than God himself.

The other question which has exercised my mind is whether the Christian condition is compatible with the posture of revolt or rebellion. The Christian, or pseudo-Christian, teaching of humility understood as servility precludes, of course, any possibility of revolt and involves obedience and submission to whatsoever demands obedience and submission. Actually, it was this very thing which roused me to revolt and rebellion: to be a Christian cannot possibly mean to be an obedient slave.

I was a rebel; but my rebellion was never such as to approve revolutionary terror. I rebelled against the world and its slavish order; but revolutionary terror is precisely a relapse into the world and obeisance to the world's norms and exigencies. Mine is the revolt of the spirit and of personality against the collective which defies spirit and personality.

Spirit is freedom, and freedom is spirit, and the matter of revolt is closely allied to that of freedom. Revolt embodies a passion for freedom and invests its fierce element for the destruction of servitude and oppression. Sometimes this passion inundated me, set me astir and lashed me into fury. Admittedly, revolt cannot settle any issue, but it can play a great part in the liberation of man. It is a matter of regret that Christians have expressed their piety in bows, fawnings and prostrations—gestures that are symbolic of servility and humiliation. It cannot be denied that the gravest stumbling-block in the way of believing in God is not the object but the subject of this belief: i.e., the professions and manifestations of the believers; it is these which are often obnoxious and intolerable. The fact that man is sometimes unable or unwilling to acknowledge God may well mean that he cannot accept the profession of faith in God by men, or men's ideas about God, rather than God himself; that he defies the substitution of slavery and pious gesture for the worship of the living and ineffable image of God. The foundation of the knowledge of and faith in God is the awareness of the mystery of God, which puts to the test and purifies all our notions about him. Everyone ought to be a rebel, that is to say, should cease to tolerate slavery in any shape whatsoever. I am not generally prone to doubt, but from time to time a terrible thought crossed my mind: what if obsequious orthodoxy is right and I am wrong? In that case I am lost. But I have always been quick to cast this thought from me.

I shall have to refer more than once in the course of this autobiography to the presence of a strange duality in me, of a Janus-like quality, of two visages and conflicting elements which may produce the impression of inconsistency and discordance. But these conflicting elements can be traced to a single source. Man is not only a creature enduring solitude and anguish, an expatriate in the world whose heart is filled and torn by pity for afflicted and suffering creation; he is also fierce in revolt and capable of great daring in a desperate war of ideas. The world, strange and alien as it is, evokes a twofold reaction in me: one, as it were, from within outwards and one from without inwards. This is why I have never achieved wholeness in my life. After having delivered the challenge I would feel an intense need to withdraw into my inner world. The posture of revolt was but a moment in my inner life and in the spiritual conflict which went on within me. My creative endeavours, which I always regard as of primary importance in my life, were above all a matter of my own subjective condition: their declaration and embodiment in the objective world, on the other hand, always came short of perfection. Revolt marked my innate dissociation and inadaptability to the objective world and contained a strong eschatological element. All my life I have felt distaste for the fixed patterns, habits and conventional signs of human life. This was no mere feeling of uneasiness, but a symptom of my resistance to the objectification of human existence, a desire that the conventional pretexts for truth may at last give way to the revelation of truth itself. And this, in its turn, accounts for the supreme value I attach to sincerity and truthfulness.

Freedom can be pitiless. Dostoevsky's Grand Inquisitor charges Christ with laying the unbearable burden of freedom on men and thereby showing no pity towards them. Freedom brings forth suffering and tragedy, and real tragedy is not of fate, as the Greeks believed, but of freedom. During my life I have frequently had an intense experience of the conflict between freedom and pity. I am instinctively excited to pity and compassion; I cannot resign myself to the sufferings of men and of animals; I cannot suffer cruelty. I am sometimes overcome by compassion for the whole creation, which groaneth and travaileth, waiting for the redemption of the whole world. I feel utterly one with Ivan Karamazov, who was driven mad by the tears of a single little child. The problem of the justification of God in face of the measureless pain in the world has always been a source of infinite torment to me. I cannot admit the conception of an almighty, omniscient, punitive deity beholding this stricken world of ours; I can con-

sent to and understand only the image of a loving, suffering, crucified
God; I can, that is to say, only accept God through his Son. Indeed, it
is impossible to respond to God unless he takes upon himself and bears
the sufferings and afflictions of mankind, unless he is at once the High
Priest and the victim. I have, therefore, always had a liking for Marcion,
although this was an emotional rather than an intellectual sympathy.

I have never been able to acquiesce in the cold and cruel ruthlessness
of the state and in the penalties and retributions it inflicts on men. I
have persistently and passionately rejected capital punishment to the
extent even of dividing mankind into those who defend and those who
reject it. I have sometimes felt intense hostility towards its champions,
and regarded them as my personal enemies. Such a reaction against this
particular monstrosity perpetrated by the state is probably a characteristically Russian trait. I found it difficult to bear any condemnation of
man, still more his final condemnation. The Gospel words which have
most profoundly impressed me are 'judge not that ye be not judged'
and 'he that is without sin among you, let him first cast a stone at her'.
The end of the other parable, however, where the wicked are cast into
hell-fire, caused me pain and bewilderment. Revenge, in particular
the systematic, organized revenge of the state, revolted me more than
anything else. This revolt may well be the only Christian virtue to
which I can claim possession. It has occasionally crossed my mind that
if I go 'to heaven' I shall be admitted solely on account of my disinclination and inability to judge others: all the rest in me has seemed
utterly unworthy of 'heaven'.

There is evidently a connection between this reluctance to judge and
the impulse to pity and compassion. I have, as a matter of fact, always
been more aware of human unhappiness than of human sin. A religion
which sees human life in the law-courts is repugnant to me. I am a
wilful and obstinate creature, but it was very easy to impress me by
arousing my feeling of pity, and some people have no doubt taken
advantage of this. I struggled against this impulse, and at one time went
so far as to wage an ideological war on pity, and made Nietzsche's idea
on this matter my own. I was almost afraid of not being able to endure,
and of dissolving completely into, the sensation of pity. My weakness
and my misfortune, however, lay in that my compassion was passive

rather than active. I suffered from the sensation of pity most intensely because I suffered from it in a passive manner. I was active in freedom but not in pity: my pity did not radiate love and caused no warmth in others. I did little to put my compassion to use in life, and did not do much to help others or to alleviate the sufferings of other people. My feelings of compassion remained bottled up within me, and they would have been less agonizing to me had I been able to release them in some outward activity. The doctor who performs an operation on a sick man suffers less than he whose heart only goes out to man in pity, and who is unable to help him in any way. Sometimes I resisted my own passivity and inaction in this respect, but I could do little to overcome my shortcomings and to embody my impulse. I must have given to many the impression of being indifferent rather than compassionate, although I was, in a passive way, well disposed towards others.

As I have already had occasion to note, my sensitivity was combined with aridity: the mind predominated over the heart, and imagination over feeling. Yet my mental activity, my thought, themselves, were emotional and passionate. As to compassion and sympathy with others, these went hand in hand with an egotistic desire for self-preservation. Again and again I avoided or tried to escape that which was capable of evoking compassion in me: and for this I despised myself. In fact, I failed hopelessly to fulfil the precepts of the Gospel, and my compassion proved to be not a virtue but a weakness. This weakness, however, made me greatly admire active and radiating compassion in other people, and I valued it highly.

The experience of pity has always been associated in me with that of anxiety. I am by nature apprehensive. I was perpetually haunted by anxieties and apprehensions about those near to me, and was never able to brave the thought of their death. I tended to exaggerate the dangers threatening them, and was always concerned for their well-being, particularly that of my parents'. Sometimes my anxiety became quite unbearable, and I felt completely crushed by it, though I tried to conceal this from others, who scarcely knew of the extent to which I suffered under the pressure of these sensations. It seemed to me that it depended on me, that it was my business, whether a man perished or not.

Every disappointed and blighted human hope arouses acute pity, as does every parting. But it is kindled also by memories of the past, of all the things that have gone beyond recall, and by the realization of irreparable mistakes and of sufferings caused to others, especially those near to one. I have often felt a burning, piercing sense of pity when looking into the eyes of an animal. Their expression of suffering is unspeakably and almost unbearably moving: it seems to lay bare the affliction of the whole world, invading you and taking possession of you. Many a time I have visualized people threatened by death or dying, and I imagined the young and gay as ill and aged and despairing. It seemed to me that what evokes the greatest compassion of all is the disappointment of the hopes with which man and animals alike come into the world. I do not think this is evidence of sentimentality, for sentimentality is incompatible either with dryness of heart or with the predominance of the intellect over emotions, to which I have referred above. The sense of pity in me is not so much psychological as metaphysical in character. It is, perhaps, not unlike the impassioned, 'metaphysical' compassion in Buddhism, proceeding from a realization of the fallen and stricken state of the world at the deepest level of its being.

I am inclined to pessimism, although this does not hold full sway over me. I have never been able to believe in the possibility of lasting happiness, which, however, denotes a realism rather than a pessimism. I have sometimes thought that I did not desire happiness: I was apprehensive of it. Every joy in my life has been accompanied by a sense of guilt and wrong. I feared the happy moments of life; I could not surrender myself to them, and even turned away from them. I always wavered between an ascetic denial of the world—a religious, 'revolutionary', or 'Tolstoyan' denial—and a creative affirmation of the world of beauty, love, art, and the triumph of thought in life. I sought and awaited the transfiguration of the world, and at the same time resisted the world with all my heart and mind and desired complete withdrawal from it into some 'monastery' of unimaginable other-worldliness.

In my opinion the very notion of happiness is devoid of any content and meaning. Happiness cannot be objectified into a state apart from other states; it cannot be thought of, if indeed it can be thought of at all, in terms of quantities comparable with other quantities. No one knows what makes another person happy or unhappy. I have little sympathy with André Gide's insistence in his *Nourritures Terrestres*: I can see in it nothing but the struggle of a Puritan against the taboos and prohibitions imposed on him from without. I do not believe that man is born for happiness and bliss as a bird is born for flight. All hedonistic and eudaemonistic morality, even, or perhaps particularly, if it is presented in terms of the Christian or pseudo-Christian hope of eternal felicity for oneself, is false. There is no need to assert the right of every human being to happiness; what is needed is the assertion of the dignity and supreme value of every human being, who cannot or should not be treated as a means to any end whatsoever. Eudaemonism is wrong even when it assumes the subtler form of Christian perfectionism; whereas Kant is right, even though he may have betrayed his position by a tendency to ethical formalism. Eudaemonism must be rejected not on ascetic or altruistic, but on personalistic grounds. 'It is better', said John Stuart Mill, rather inconsistently in view of his general utilitarianism, 'to be a dissatisfied Socrates than a satisfied pig.'

It was always difficult for me to suffer anything that degrades the dignity of man, even of a single human individual, and I protested with all my strength against every sign of such degradation. The sufferings of man roused me to pity and compassion; yet I was aware that the struggle for the dignity of man' and for the condition of 'dissatisfied Socrates' involves a readiness to meet and accept suffering and affliction on the part of those who join the issue. It is a case of a painful moral antinomy, which cannot be surmounted within the dimensions of this world. Man is called upon to be compassionate towards all living things, and, at the same time, to assent to the suffering which is implied in the recognition of and the struggle for the dignity and freedom of man. Such is the paradox of pity and freedom, of descent into the afflicted world and ascent away from it, of *agape* and *eros*.

I suspect that the sense of pity and compassion has a bearing on my concern for social problems and my sympathy with socialism. I have always felt an instinctive dislike for men of rank, for rulers and masters, for somebodies and notabilities, for the rich and the privileged; and I have consistently avoided them. Even when I did not dislike them personally, something always stood between us. Yet I was as far removed

as possible from any resentment, and, having myself been one of the
privileged and a member of the ruling class, I could scarcely suffer from
any social inferiority complex. I always preferred the oppressed, the
persecuted, the poor, although the misfortune of my privileged position
prevented me from being completely one with them. But this privileged position did not consist in the possession of riches and power, for
I had neither: rather, it was a question of a certain way of life, in virtue
of which I remained a 'gentleman' even when there was nothing to
warrant it. People persisted in regarding me as such, and in some cases
had exaggerated notions about my material resources. In point of fact
the 'gentleman' was exceedingly modest and his means were more than
moderate.

I was surprised to discover in myself a capacity, which, as is well-
known, other members of the Russian intelligentsia seldom betrayed,
for contact and intercourse with 'the people'. During my Marxist period
in Kiev, for example, a number of workers who were hostile to the
intelligentsia made an exception in my case, welcomed me and treated
me with great friendliness. While in exile in Vologda, I was the only
one among the other exiles to mix with the deported *khitrovtsy*,[1] who
were regarded as the dregs of society, and of whom everyone was
afraid. One of them even became an intimate friend of mine. More
important still were my relations with the 'God-seekers from the
people', about which I shall have more to say later on. I do not claim,
however, to have succeeded in completely identifying myself with 'the
people', as many members of the intelligentsia tried and failed to do.
As a matter of fact, I never desired to be a 'populist': I was too much of
a Marxist for the populist doctrine to become my own. Altogether, I
must say emphatically that I am lacking in any ability to play a rôle
in social affairs, to lead others or to be led by others, to seek for power
and glory or to conceive ambitious worldly schemes.

I have already said that the conflict between pity and freedom is a
conflict between descent and ascent. Pity may lead to the rejection of
freedom, and freedom may result in pitilessness. Human life is characterized by these two movements—by ascent and descent. Man dares
to climb upwards, to transcend himself and his environment, to rise to

[1] Criminals from the Slums of Moscow. (Tr.)

God. On this path he gains spiritual strength, he recreates the natural configuration of life and creates new life and new values. Yet he cannot forget those left below, those weak of spirit and incapable of reaching out to the summits of creative knowledge and vision. He is compelled from within to begin the downward motion, to descend so that he may share his spiritual treasures and attend to the needs of his brothers, who are all destined for a high calling. As he soars upward man does not, or ought not to, disregard the world and humanity outside and disembarrass himself of responsibility for others. Eternal life breaks down the barriers between myself and other men, and involves salvation for all and responsibility for all. Freedom never spells irresponsibility, and it is pity and compassion that render freedom responsible. Later on I shall have more to say about this in connection with the problem of creativity and compassion.

At one time in my life I experienced an intense conflict between what may be called the Tolstoyan and the Nietzschean impulses in me. There was a period when the Nietzschean element had the upper hand, but in the end it was the Tolstoyan that prevailed. I have never consented to renounce freedom for pity's sake, and there was a fierceness about my fight for freedom: nevertheless I could not bear freedom turned cruel or falsified into the will to power. At bottom I have always believed that Christianity has been brought down to the level of human, all too human, instincts and turned into a rallying-point for the evasion of Christ's truth; that it has been thrown into the gutter so as to prevent its revolution taking effect. Christianity has not only remained unfulfilled in life, which can easily be explained in view of the sinfulness of human nature, but has been disfigured and compromised in the very teaching of it. Men have accommodated Christianity to this world and have greedily seized a thus accommodated Christianity in order to bolster up their rôle and position in the world. The shamelessness displayed by Christians in this respect is beyond measure. There are some, indeed, who have managed to extract from Christianity a number of principles which are not far removed from sadism; but for me it has always and pre-eminently meant mercy, compassion, forgiveness and humanity.

To return to the question of 'ascent' and 'descent', it must be noted that ascent shows a certain priority which man acquires *vis-à-vis* the world and other men. The Christian Gospel speaks, in its customary paradoxical language, of 'the first' who are to become 'the last'. This applies, presumably, not only to those who possess worldly rank and power, but also to those who have attained a certain spiritual stature. It is a warning to those who are 'ascending' and who may well find themselves 'the last', unless they identify themselves with and, indeed, become 'the last', of their own accord. Christianity is the tension and unity of ascent and descent, of freedom and pity, of loftiness and lowliness, of 'quality' and 'quantity', of love of divine altitudes and love for those who suffer below.

Men have so excelled themselves in the pursuit of their own interests, advantages and desires as to achieve for that purpose a Christian transmutation and sublimation of the primitive instincts of revenge. I felt driven more than once to denounce such falsifications. I have come to the conclusion that, e.g., the atrocious doctrine of eternal torments in hell is largely a projection of sadistic instincts into the sphere of religion. Many traditional Christians set store by this doctrine and are occasionally found to have a positive liking for it, although, as a rule, they show much less inclination to apply the possibility of these torments to themselves than to others: indeed, they have devised a whole system of terrorization by means of this doctrine. The idea of eternal damnation has had an enormous sociological significance, for entire societies and social groups were ruled and oppressed with the aid of this idea. It has undoubtedly contributed to the ordering of society and the control over the barbarous and sinful instincts of men. But it was put to a wrong use while Christendom still firmly believed in it; in fact, it was exploited for the gratification of men's sadistic instincts and for the ascendency of 'the first', the rulers and the powerful, over 'the last' and the lowly. It has often occurred to me that, had the ecclesiastical authorities, at the time when man generally believed in the doctrine of hell, threatened with damnation, excommunication and the deprivation of the sacraments those possessed by the will to power and domination, those vowed to the service of greed and engaged in the exploitation of their fellow-men, the course of history might have been very different. Instead, threats of eternal torment were directed against heresy, doctrinal deviations, disobedience to the hierarchy, venial sins which were regarded as mortal, and, occasionally, against things that were quite nugatory. I cannot help thinking that this has had a fatal effect on the destiny of Christendom.

In considering the idea of eternal damnation, one must not fail to acknowledge that, quite apart from its hideous and sadistic elements, it presents a serious philosophical problem. For my part I contend that its implications deprive man's spiritual and moral life of all value, turning, as it does, life into a trial in a court of law, whereby man exists under the threat of penal servitude for life. The fact that man could frame such an idea is evidence of some of the most sombre motives in his sub-conscious. I do not question the existence of hell: indeed, I think hell is a very common and a very profound human experience—a terrible and ghastly contingency on the pathways of human life. But I regard the erection of an ontology of hell as monstrous.

My reaction to traditional eschatology is due to the value I attach to pity and compassion; I am unable to conceive of any joy or bliss in face of the immeasurable suffering and agony of the world, and I am not in the least discouraged in this by St. Augustine's derisive statements about *Misericordes*. Salvation is inconceivable except in the company of the whole of mankind; and *sobornost'* should be seen as having eschatological as well as ecclesiological implications. I could never admit that there is less compassion and pity in God than in myself, imperfect and sinful as I am. In effect, I have always protested against any and every condemnation of men; I disliked intensely all the eloquent declamations about and pleadings for retributive justice, and, as I have said, all my life I had more sympathy for the judged than for the judges. This has more to do with my propensity to lawlessness and non-conformity than with any virtuousness on my part. I could not bear cruelty; and yet in the struggle for freedom I did not stop short of cruelty, and sometimes felt compelled to break with my friends. I was capable of desiring hell for those who advocate and prepare it for others. But I was cruel in yet another sense. I am haunted by the terrible thought that things which should never have been forgotten have died away from my memory: this is the cruelty of oblivion, no less cruel and destructive than the infliction of pain. Once I remembered again, I was overcome by a sense of guilt and remorse. I made the idea of *sobornost'* my own first and foremost on account of its implied recognition of men's mutual and common responsibility and guilt.

I am not a sceptic by nature. My thinking is not of the suspicious or doubting kind. I am prone to inward conflict and contradiction rather than to doubt. In fact, I do not doubt, but I revolt; and even in revolt I am affirming rather than denying or calling into question. My thinking does not proceed by way of some inner dialogue, in which I meet and resolve doubts and objections raised by my own mind. On the contrary, I always tended to project the objections to my thought outwards into the opponents of my ideas and convictions, with whom I then proceeded to wage war. My thinking has always been affirmative and assertive, even while I was remonstrating against or criticizing something. It would be wrong, however, to infer that it has a dogmatic character. I have believed in the truth which I sought, and I have believed in the God whom I sought. But I was a seeker first and foremost, engaged in a constant creative movement in which the seeking, as it were, evoked the very end which it pursued. I look upon myself as different alike from sceptics and dogmatists. In point of fact, a sceptic does not seek anything and does not move anywhere at all. Absolute scepticism, were it possible (which it is not) is the posture of complete motionlessness and, indeed, of death. Actually the sceptic belies his scepticism every time he asks a question or expresses his doubt and disbelief, and only by thus belying his scepticism is he capable of living and thinking. Unmitigated scepsis is, in the last analysis, one with the most rigid dogmatism; the one and the other alike spell immobility and the end of creative life.

It is a mistake to think that doubt can be an exclusively intellectual attitude. Man deceives himself when he claims that his doubting has no affective and volitional causes. Lasting, impassive and frigid scepticism, that is to say, a scepticism which, from a momentary experience, has turned into obduracy, is evidence of lack of character and of incapacity for free choice. When, on the other hand, people deny, for example, the existence of God on the grounds of its incompatibility with the existence of evil and suffering in the world, this kind of scepticism signifies no impartial and detached intellectual point of view, but a passionate state of mind, an affective experience which, by the way, deserves great sympathy.

There are, however, also very objectionable passions which prevent man from acknowledging the existence of God, the passions, namely, which make him adopt a worm's-eye view of life, and subject him to the power of this world. God is denied either because the world is 'too bad' or because it is 'too good'. But in both cases we are faced with a kind of denial or doubt that has an affective rather than an intellectual character. Likewise, certainty is eminently affective and intuitive. The intellect plays an entirely subservient part in these attitudes. There is no such thing as purely intellectual intuition: intuition combines intellectual and emotional elements alike. I would, however, attach to emotion itself a transcendent quality. Indeed, one may speak of transcendental emotions and postulate an emotional *a priori* of knowledge, and, most particularly, of religious knowledge.

All my life I have spent in wrestlings of the spirit; but I seldom expressed this in any direct way in my writings. Usually I have projected them into the external world, i.e., displayed them in the struggle with religious, social and political movements hostile to me. My manner of thinking and self-expression shows few signs of doubt, indecision and uncertainty: I always wrote and spoke boldly and resolutely, and I did so because I was always aware of performing an act of choice and decision. Have I ever doubted at all? I do not think I have at any time entertained any final, irretrievable doubts. I was aware of, understood, and entered into, the objections against my beliefs and convictions, but I always endeavoured to overcome them from within, creatively, while outwardly expressing merely the result of these endeavours. I have lived, and still live, through doubts of a religious character; but these were, and are, more a matter of passionate moral reactions, of repugnance, wrath or indignation. Had I repudiated God, it would probably have been in the name of God. But intellectually I reject the traditional proofs, ontological, teleological, or any other, for the existence of God. I am unable to think of God as a 'necessary being'; I disclaim altogether the categories of Being as applied to God and regard them

as figments of abstract human reasoning. God is, he is existent, and I
am able to think of him only as such, that is to say, existentially and
symbolically. My relation to, and thinking of, God are existential and
dramatic acts, and the wrestlings of the spirit which denote this relation
enter into my certainty concerning God. I suffer torments of religious
doubt only when I am compelled to admit the force of traditional,
static dogmatism, which exasperates me and rouses me to protest. It
suffices to reflect on the unreality and falsehood of such dogmatism,
for my faith to be strengthened and every doubt to disappear. This is,
perhaps, unlike the usual kind of doubt: it is simpler but no less agonizing for that. I could never reconcile myself with inner defeat, and my
mind was set towards inner victory, although I was quite indifferent
to and never sought external conquest.

Probably none of my writings has reflected all the extent and intensity of the spiritual wrestlings through which I passed. A declaration of
faith and conviction marks a state of mind and spirit when the inward
differences and conflicts have already been composed, and when a
relative integration of personality has been achieved. Lasting and persistent doubt and scepticism, on the other hand, are evidence of corruption and disintegration. Their effect is not unlike the impact of
dreams on human consciousness, in which loose and disjoined images
break out from the sub-conscious and throw man's personality out of
gear (although there are, admittedly, other dreams which come from
the supra-conscious, rather than the sub-conscious, and which do not
imperil the wholeness of personality). The final ascendency of doubt
turns life into a ghastly dream; and it is only faith, the creative, integrating act of faith, rather than assent to dogmatic propositions, which
prevents the whole world being turned into a nightmare. I have always
resisted the dissolution of the image of man, and have come to know
that in this very resistance man stands or falls according as he has, or
has not, faith. Scepticism is, indeed, the disablement and, in the end,
the destruction of man.

Before setting forth some of my reflections on *eros*, I want to say
that I do not propose to present the reader with descriptions of love

affairs: all such descriptions are distasteful to me. I do not intend to speak of my intimate relationships with women, least of all with those nearest to me and to whom I am particularly indebted. I noted at the outset that this autobiography is not concerned with 'inside stories'. What I am going to say on this matter, however, is based on experience, observation and intuition. I ought probably to be regarded as pre-eminently a philosopher of *eros*, but ethical passions (I speak deliberately of ethical passions and not of ethical norms) were stronger in me than erotic passions. I have perhaps been tempted most of all by the freedom and beauty of renunciation. I belong to the kind of people, and perhaps to that generation of Russians, who opposed love to the principles of family and domesticity, and who regarded love as alone valid and real. I have reflected a great deal on the relations between the various types of love, particularly between love-pity and love-*eros*, between love as charity and love as passion.

Sex is not merely one function of the human organism: it pervades man's being as a whole—a fact which is, by the way, recognized by modern psychology. Sex, moreover, is evidence of the fallen condition of man: his attitude to sex even reveals something shameful and demeaning to his dignity. In this matter he is constantly attempting to draw a veil, to withdraw and to conceal. I could not help asking myself why it is that it does not occur to man to keep his pity in the dark, but that he inclines to screen and to befog the love of sex. The sexual act in itself is unseemly and ugly. Leonardo da Vinci says (I do not remember his exact words) that the sexual organ is so hideous that the human race would have come to an end, if men did not become possessed and demented. In a very definite sense there is something degrading about sexual life. Our own age, as expressed in modern psychology and fiction, has fully revealed the degradation and dissolution of man brought about by sex. This is, however, evidence not only of the depravity of our age but also of our deeper awareness of human nature and our greater sincerity.

I have always insisted on the distinction between *eros* and sex, for, however much they may be interrelated, they remain radically different. The life of sex is impersonal, generic; it reduces man to a plaything of biological and physiological processes. The sexual act contains nothing that could be recognized as even remotely individual, unique, singular and personal; on the contrary, it is the mark of his identification with the animal world. Sexual attraction does not by itself reveal the personal image of the object of attraction, rather it blurs that image. Sex is 'faceless' and blind to the visage of man: indeed, there is in it something indiscriminating and pitiless towards man and subversive of his specifically human character. To individualize the sexual appetite is tantamount to limiting the power of sex. Love is personal and individual—that which inclines towards the unique, unrepeatable and irreplaceable person of man or woman. Sexual passion easily agrees to substitution, and substitution is in fact possible. So far from increasing, intense love-*eros* may even weaken sexual passion. The lover is less intent on sexual satisfaction; indeed, he may even prefer to refrain from it. True love is always concerned with the particular and not with the general, with something, or rather somebody, not with anything or anybody. Admittedly, erotic love is grounded in and is significant of sex; but, at the same time, it marks a victory over and redemption of sex. *Eros* is a wholly new experience and reveals a dimension which is transcendent in character.

The nature of love-*eros*, however, is very complex and contradictory, and it creates innumerable conflicts in life. I have myself observed some of these contradictions. Love-*eros* allured me, but, even more strongly, it appalled me. I have always stood for the freedom of love and I have defended this freedom passionately and ruthlessly against those who denied it; I have always abhorred moralism and legalism in this matter, and I could never stand the preaching of virtue. But sometimes this looked to me more like concern for freedom than for love, and I remained quite uninterested when told of other people's love-relations. Real love is a very rare flower. I felt the fascination of the sacrifice of love for the sake of freedom as much as, if not more than, the freedom of love itself. Love which has been sacrificed in the name of freedom or pity and made subject to these is love deepened and exalted. People completely at the mercy of love were comical and repulsive to me; and some manifestations of love made me positively angry. Nevertheless, my recognition of the intense conflict between love and freedom and love and pity did not preclude a realization of the immense value of erotic experience which, in its Dionysiac inspiration, is capable of transcending and liberating human life from crushing norms and laws. No one should renounce love, his right to and his freedom of love, in the name of duty or law, of public opinion or social conventions; but he may and should renounce it for the sake of pity or freedom.

There is no denying that love has come to be so debased, profaned and degraded in its meaning that it is almost intolerable to utter the word 'love': new words will have to be found for its truth to become apparent again. True love cannot be a matter of chance or circumstances: it arises in the encounter of two human beings whose destiny it is that they should meet. In point of fact, however, most of what is called love is the result of chance, which might as well have brought about any number of other and different combinations: yet it turns out irrevocably binding. This accounts for the vast number of absurdly unsuitable marriages.

I have always felt indignation at the interference of society in the erotic love of men and women. All the limits set by society and social conventions to the right of love aroused my protest. Love is the most intimately personal experience in life, and society should not dare to interfere in it. I have already spoken of my profound dislike of, and rebellion against, 'society'. Elsewhere (in *The Destiny of Man*) I have written that where there is love between two human beings, the presence—even a 'verbal' presence—of a third person is entirely superfluous; and, whenever I was told of some love-affair of an 'unlawful' nature, I always retorted that this concerned no one, neither me nor, least of all, those who talked about it. Love is by its very nature lawless and defies the law: lawful or legal love is love that has died. Legality is only valid on the level of the commonplace; but love rises above the commonplace. The world should remain ignorant of the love of every human being, since love is entirely beyond its pale. The so-called institution of marriage is, in fact, a piece of shamelessness, exposing as it does to society that which should remain hidden and scrupulously guarded against the eyes of strangers. The socialization of sex and love is one of the most disgusting phenomena in human history: it cripples life and causes untold suffering. Family is essentially a social business, subject to the same laws as political and economic phenomena. It is, indeed, closely associated with the economic order of society, and has but little relation to love, either erotic or sexual, although it can be a sphere for the exercise of *agape* or charity. Family has been, and still is in a large measure, a means of enslavement: it is a hierarchical institution based on domination and submission. The institution of marriage (though, of course, not love), on which the family is based, is a very doubtful sacrament. As a matter of fact, the Christian Church does not know any sacrament of marriage *of its own*: it merely confirms the old pagan and Jewish, that is to say, the 'natural' institution of marriage. But in marriage there does take place a socialization of something that by its very nature eludes society, including the Church as an external social institution. It is love which ought to be recognized as a true sacrament, a *mysterion*. This mystery lends itself to no social fixation and rationalization, which in fact are largely responsible for the tragedy of love in the context of social life, seeing that society is invariably hostile to, and often rejects, love. The lover in the true sense of the word is the enemy of society. The 'republic of letters' alone has defended the right and the dignity of love, but its plea was precisely for unsocialized love. The first to do so were the Provençal troubadours. Literature— not, of course, literary ribaldry or the sex-ridden stories which flood the book-market—has indeed rendered a service of profound religious significance to mankind. Legalistic theology, ethics and public opinion alike have never concealed their hostility to literature on this account, or at best have just tolerated it. I may note in this connection that, despite my great admiration for Tolstoy, I always repudiated the idea underlying *Anna Karenina*. I regarded the marital relations between Anna and Karenin as culpable and immoral, while believing in the excellence and nobility of the love between Anna and Vronsky.

As to the question of divorce, I always thought that the very way in which it is commonly stated opens the doors to insincerity and formalism. The real question is not of the right to divorce (a right which I believe to be beyond all question), but of the duty of divorce when love is no more. The perpetuation of marriage without love is immoral, for love alone, love of *eros* and of pity, can vindicate human relationships. The question of divorce is, it must be admitted, considerably complicated when there are children to be taken into account, but even then love should be regarded as the supreme standard, for lack of love between parents has disastrous repercussions on children.

I am not unaware that this point of view is likely to be stigmatized as highly dangerous and anti-social. But this does not deter me in the least or dissuade me from my conviction. There may be justice in the socialization of economic relations in society; but the attempt to socialize man himself—a process that has in fact marked the entire course of history—is a source of slavery and every reaction. Above all, I am unable to acknowledge the validity of the concept of danger: not, that is to say, as something iniquitous or reprehensible. Man should not shrink from danger and 'let "I dare not" wait upon "I would" '.

Chernishevsky's[1] novel *What is to be Done?* is worthless from the literary point of view, and its basic philosophical ideas are pitiful and decrepit: none the less, I am in complete agreement with him on moral and social issues, and feel nothing but admiration for him in this respect. Chernishevsky is profoundly right and shows true humanity in advocating the freedom of the bonds uniting man and woman and in repudiating conventions, hypocrisy and jealousy in human relationships. His novel, widely calumniated by the reactionary circles of the right, exhibits a remarkable degree of moral purity, disinterestedness and generosity. It is significant that Chernishevsky himself had a profound and touching affection for his wife: his letters to her from prison are the record of a love such as is seldom found in the annals of history. This nihilist and utilitarian was a true free lover, paying unreserved allegiance to 'eternal womanhood'. His love was completely devoid of intolerance, invidiousness and jealousy. I myself have always regarded intolerant love and jealousy as one of the most unattractive, slavish and enslaving impulses in man. Jealousy is indeed incompatible with freedom: it is all domination, insolence and possessiveness. The right of love, then, must be acknowledged unreservedly, but the right of jealousy must cease. Chernishevsky's importance lies in his undertaking to do this, even though he may have simplified things and lacked subtle psychological insight.

Jealousy is the tyranny of man over man. A woman's jealousy is

[1] A Leader of Russian Radicalism who laid the foundations of the utilitarian 'civic' criticism of literature in Russia. (Tr.)

doubly tyrannical and repulsive. Women are, therefore, particularly
prone to demonism. There are demonic women—a most unpleasant
and terrifying phenomenon. There is something distinctly unequal between the love of woman and that of man. A man's love is partial, that
is to say, it does not engulf his whole being. The love of woman, on the
other hand, is more whole-hearted: she is, therefore, liable to be lost
in and possessed by love. Her love can be envenomed, perilous and
deadly; it is full of magic power; it is relentless, obdurate, pitiless and
despotic. It becomes particularly unbearable in view of the tragic disparity between the concrete woman and her ideal image conjured up
by man's imagination. A woman's beauty is, more often than not, deceptive: she is inclined to lie more than man—in her appearance, in
her behaviour and in her words. Her lying, however, is largely a form
of self-defence, due, in a measure, to having been deprived of some of
the most elementary rights ever since the patriarchal system prevailed
over the matriarchal. Yet a woman's love may rise to remarkable
heights. Such is the love of Ibsen's Solveg or of Marcel Jouhandeau's
Veronique. This is love redeemed by and redeeming others in eternal
purity and fidelity.

It has always seemed to me that what is hardest and most agonizing
is not, as many believe, unrequited love, but love which it is impossible
to share; and, strange though it may seem, in the majority of cases it is
impossible to share love. Hence a peculiar feeling of guilt which fills
men in face of love. I have had, on the whole, more intimate and
friendly relations with women than with men: it even seemed to me
(or was this a mere illusion?) that women understood me better than
men. Women have indeed a remarkable capacity for giving rise to
illusions, for seeming other than they really are. I was by no means
unsusceptible of feminine charm. But I have never indulged in what
is known as the cult of eternal womanhood, so dear to many of my
contemporaries in early twentieth-century Russia, when 'fair ladies' in
Dantesque or Goethean guise were so highly popular. I even suspected
in myself positive dislike of 'the feminine', although I was never indifferent to it. I felt particularly inclined towards medieval romanticism
as expressed by the troubadours of Provence, who were the first to bear
witness to the greatness and nobility of love-*eros*. But the introduction

of eroticism into religion and into man's relation to God was quite foreign to me. Rather, I was attracted by Jacob Boehme's conception of the androgyn, who marks the ascendency of integral human nature over sexual differentiation. I had no liking at all for the eroticism of Vladimir Solovyev, even though I regard his essay on *The Meaning of Love* as one of the most important contributions to the discussion of the problem of love. I suspect a very fundamental contradiction between the views expressed in this remarkable essay and Solovyev's teaching on the Sophia, or Wisdom of God. Nevertheless, womanhood is symbolic of the cosmos and as such empowers man to participate in the cosmic life of nature; it fulfils his manhood, inasmuch as manhood is the unity of nature and personality.

Sex pertains to the genus and love to personality. I have already more than once referred to my reaction against the genus and the generic— a reaction which is quite ineradicable and fundamental in me. I am repelled by the very sight of pregnant women: but I do not take any pride in this; in fact, I am distressed by such reactions. I never disliked children. I was, for instance, very much attached to my nephews. But I could not help seeing in child-bearing something hostile to personality, something that is evidence of the dissolution of personality. I am at one with Kierkegaard, who bore witness to the evil and sinfulness of birth. There is intense opposition between generic and personal immortality —a fact which Solovyev has discussed with great insight in the essay just mentioned. But even before reading Solovyev I was conscious of the intensity of this opposition. The genus may evoke pity, but it cannot inspire love-*eros*. The latter is ultimately incompatible with family life, which is of the genus. Love betokens a victory of personality over genus and sex, which are devoid of uniqueness and individuality. Love-*eros* must and does prevail over sex. When love is strong it has a depth which reaches out to infinity: sex, on the contrary, carries within itself the sting of finitude; it fails tragically to attain fulness, and is doomed to remain an isolated, separate sphere of fallen nature. It is this disparate character of sex which is in a measure responsible for the horror of atomization characteristic of modern man. But man must fight against the autonomy of sex.

I have already noted that love is a way leading out of and above the commonplace; for many it is, indeed, the only way to such liberation. But the liberating power of love is easily spent, and love falls once more under the sway of the commonplace. It contains an urge towards the infinite, but, at the same time, it places limits to infinity. Love is a breach in the objectified, natural and social order. It penetrates beyond the appearances to the archetypal beauty which is in God, and spells victory over the ugliness which reigns supreme in this fallen world of ours. Love cannot grow within the confines of this world; indeed, its effects may be destructive and agonizing unless it is united with pity. Pitiless love is obnoxious and repulsive. But the relation between erotic and agapetic love is very complex and presents a series of difficult problems. Plato's *eros* is still confined within the sphere of the impersonal; it denotes man's desire for the divine principle of beauty which is reflected in the created universe, rather than for the concrete, personal manifestation. From the Christian point of view, on the other hand, *eros* signifies personal relations. Again, the naturalistic and pantheistic eroticism of a Rozanov[1] marks the return to a pagan exaltation of sex, which he advocated in avowed opposition to Solovyev's and my own views. Solovyev himself betrayed his personalism by taking over Plato's idea of *eros* and interpreting it in terms of eternal divine womanhood, which appears to reduce concrete women to shadowy and deceptive reflections of an abstract idea. *Eros* gives rise to all kinds of more or less alluring illusions, and makes it rather difficult to disentangle the real from the unreal. The dream of love, as Chateaubriand has admirably shown, is natural to man. Nevertheless, *eros* is by no means all fancy: its evocation of eternity is supremely real—it is 'eternal memory' which stirs the waters of Lethe and redeems the pain of oblivion. Oblivion spells betrayal, the burden of which may be removed by a dream or a vision. There are visions in which man re-lives the great but isolated and forgotten moments of erotic inspiration, but these visions are ineffable, and I was never able to communicate such experiences.

Love is deeply rooted in the tragedy of life, and it is no chance that love is closely linked with death. There is, likewise, tragedy in the conflict between love and creativity—a theme of which Ibsen treats in such

---

[1] A Russian writer and publicist, advocate of a naturalistic religion of sex and procreation. He was an older contemporary of Berdyaev. (Tr.)

a remarkable way in his dramas. To me it has always seemed strange that people could speak of the pleasures of love. Given a deeper attitude to life, it would be more natural to speak of the tragedy and anguish of love. When I see a happy, loving couple I experience mortal sorrow; for I know that, in actual fact, the hopes of love can never be fulfilled. One does, admittedly, on occasion meet comparatively happy family lives, but this is the happiness of the commonplace. Had I been a romantic, mine would be a romanticism devoid of all illusions, bright prospects and propensities to idealize actuality, a romanticism, in short, which knows life to be all too unromantic and 'realistic'.

CHAPTER III

FIRST CONVERSION. SEARCH FOR THE MEANING
OF LIFE

There is a rhythmic quality in the life of every human being, which I have experienced in my own life. The successiveness of temporal moments and periods as experienced by man derives from his inability to contain the fulness of life and to remain on the summits of inspiration. I have known periods of great inspiration which bordered on ecstasy; but I also knew times of dullness and heaviness of heart and mind when the creative flame faded and I felt deprived of spiritual strength.

As I look back on my spiritual path I do not discern any experience which could be properly described as a 'conversion'. I know of no point in my life at which I underwent a decisive crisis, partly perhaps because my whole life was a series of continuous crises. 'Conversion' plays altogether a far greater rôle amongst the Roman Catholics and Protestants than among the Orthodox; and Western Christians are apt to exaggerate its importance. Even if we do experience it, we are reluctant to drag it into the day or to proclaim it from the housetops. I shall speak of my religious experience at another stage of this autobiography: now I only want to dwell on one particular point which accounts for a rather important event in my inner life.

I have few childhood memories of traditional Orthodox beliefs and practices: I had no occasion to fall away from, or to return to, a traditional faith. The fact that no such memories remained with me, that, as a child, I was nurtured by no Orthodox religious environment, was of enormous significance for my entire spiritual make-up. I see two initial motives in man's inner life: the search for meaning and the search for the eternal. The search for meaning preceded in me the search for God, and the search for the eternal was prior to the search for redemption. Once, on the threshold of adolescence, I was shaken to

78

the depths by the thought that, even though there may be no such thing as a meaning in life, the very search for meaning would render life significant and meaningful. It is to this that I desired passionately to dedicate my life. This insight marked a true inner revolution which changed my whole outlook. There followed a time of great vision and inspiration: I even wrote an account of this inner change in me, but the manuscript was taken away from me when I was arrested for the first time in Russia, and I never saw it again. I should have liked now to read what I wrote then, so as to re-live and re-capture a first initiation into the mystery of life. This was undoubtedly a kind of conversion— the most powerful and perhaps the only one in my life. It was the conversion to the search for truth: a search which itself implied faith in the existence of truth; a search for truth and meaning which conflicted with commonplace and meaningless actuality. But the change was not evidence of a conversion to any religious confession, either to Orthodoxy or even to Christianity in general. It was above all a re-orientation towards spirit and spirituality.

Henceforth I was convinced that there is no religion above Truth (a statement, by the way, which has been much used and misused in theosophy); and the awareness of this supremacy of Truth has put a lasting stamp on my spiritual and intellectual development. This 'spiritualism' became the ground and framework of my whole philosophical attitude and probably of my very existence. As I understand it, however, the word spiritualism does not denote any philosophical or mystical or, indeed, any occult school of thought, but an existential awareness. I came to believe in the primary reality of the spirit at a level which is deeper than, and transcends, the sphere of discursive reasoning, for this latter has a secondary, derivative nature and belongs to the 'symbolic' and 'reflected' world of externality. I never abandoned this fundamental attitude, not even throughout my Marxist period. I do not think that people holding such a basically 'spiritualist' conviction can ever be thoroughgoing materialists, or are susceptible of any orthodoxy, religious or otherwise. I have always been struck by the fact that materialists, once they have become 'converts', adapt themselves very easily and readily to religious orthodoxy. From the 'spiritualist' point of view spirit is one with freedom, whereas to the materialist, unable as he is to acknowledge the primary reality of spirit, the spirit is an extraneous fact wielding authority and forcing recognition. Unlike the materialist, the spiritualist never undergoes any violent confessional conversion; he is in no way determined or influenced or shaken from without, and his movement is always one from within outwards. Now religious orthodoxy contains undoubtedly a strong tendency to materialism, and it is this which provides the authoritarian element in religious life. In contrast to the current view, one must, therefore, ascribe a revolutionary significance to spirit and a reactionary significance to matter.

I have always been tormented less by theological, dogmatic and ecclesiastical questions, or by questions of academic philosophical interest, than by problems concerning the meaning of life, freedom, the destiny of man, eternity, suffering, and evil. The heroes in Tolstoy's and Dostoevsky's novels were of greater importance for me than philosophical and theological schools of thought, and it was at their hands that I received Christianity.

As a result of my spiritual re-orientation I acquired a new inner strength. My whole life changed and I felt as if carried on the wings of some spiritual rapture. I had found a sense of spiritual stability, of the unshakable spiritual ground of life: not, however, because I had assented to some specific truth or truths, or some explicit belief, but by virtue of a decision to dedicate my life to the search for truth and meaning. To seek truth is, indeed, in a significant sense, to have already found it, and to arrive at a conviction concerning the meaning of life implies a state of being imbued with that meaning. St. Augustine and Pascal have, in their own way, borne witness to this paradoxical experience.

I was brought, then, to a belief in the higher meaning of life, yet there was nothing dogmatic about this belief. I committed an act of faith in the power of the spirit, and this faith never left me. Only the outward, 'symbolic' forms which the spirit assumed in its acts of self-determination were subject to change, to transformation or conversion, and were accompanied by a desire for moral amendment and purification, and even by a tendency to asceticism. I became conscious of the independence of the spirit of all the things in which it might find expression, and came to understand the meaning of sacrifice and self-surrender for the sake of the undefiled freedom of the spirit. Since then

I have frequently desired to re-capture this initial experience, for it is here, and only here, that man reaches the height of sincerity, penetration and insight into the ever new meaning of existence.

I have already had occasion to note that I have never known the gradualness and continuity of spiritual life and development. Truth appeared to me as a reality always intervening in and, as it were, puncturing the process of life, and every revelation of truth in my life was an innovation, a unique and unrepeatable event. Even an old and well-known book would sometimes strike me on re-reading as new, and I would react to it each time in a new way. It was the initial, the creative experience alone, which roused my interest. Creative passion may burn us to dross; but the words of truth are brought up from the creative well of life: they break in their immediacy all the laws and forms of so-called development and evolution and point to the order not of necessity but of freedom.

This may have left a mark on my manner of thinking, which is intuitive and aphoristic rather than discursive and systematic. I am unable to expound or demonstrate anything by way of ratiocination, and I do not believe in the need to do so. I have, for instance, a great admiration for Kant and I regard him as the greatest of all philosophers; but his thought always struck me as being overlaid with the trappings of academic and scholastic argument and with long-winded abstruse demonstrations which only serve to shackle and obscure his genius. It is almost comical to imagine that Spinoza claimed to attain knowledge *modo geometrico*: as a matter of fact the true origin of Spinoza's philosophy, as indeed of any other philosophy, is intuitive. The claims of 'pure', neutral and 'scientific' philosophy are a snare and a delusion. Intellectual discursiveness is not an original quality pertaining to philosophical cognition: it is ultimately irrelevant and is a piece of opportunism *vis-à-vis* those whom the philosopher hopes to convince of his insight. What carries conviction, however, is not discursive argument but the original insight. Discursiveness is, as it were, a sociological phenomenon, whereby man attempts to project his vision in the sphere of the social commonplace.

For my part I saw no way of communicating my thought except by inviting others to share my intuition, that is to say, not by discursively compelling them to the recognition of philosophical propositions. But, though my style and manner of writing may be fragmentary and disjointed, my thinking is not so: on the contrary it springs from a single, all-embracing vision, and aims at the discovery of integral and integrating meaning. I believe, indeed, that the aphoristic style is much more expressive of the philosophy of wholeness than discursive systems: an aphorism is, so to speak, a microcosmos reflecting the macrocosmos. I had no interest in the niceties of academic philosophy, which are regarded as problems, but are in fact mere quibbles. In a sense I know of no multiplicity of problems, but only of one single problem which contains them all. My great defect as a writer is that I am not sufficiently aphoristic, and that my manner is, therefore, not consistent and homogeneous.

I have already admitted that I am not very much concerned with the written products of my thought or with their literary perfection. My only desire is to express myself, however inadequately, to call out to the world in testimony of the truth as I see it. Between the time of my spiritual awakening and the present I can trace nothing that could be properly described as an ordered development marked by distinct stages of growth and resulting in an advancement: what I can discern is a series of illuminations and crises made intelligible to me in intuitions of which I am unable, and indeed not desirous, to frame any adequate concept at all. What has been revealed to me once in the past has remained with me all along and was present in the here and now with all the freshness of an original experience. The past as mere past is an unreality: it is real only in so far as it is a present.

After the inner change, of which I have spoken above, had taken place, I began to be intensely interested in philosophy and devoured philosophical books, each of which carried me off into untold exaltations. I had read a great deal before, but never with such intensity and concentration. Nevertheless, I was only stimulated by books: my thinking had another source and proceeded from some primal experience which cannot be acquired by means of study and reading. The reading of books provoked thought, but my reactions to what I read were often quite negative and unlike those apparently intended by the author. The key to the thought of others was my subjective insight.

Thus it was that what I found and appreciated in their thought became an experience on my own spiritual and intellectual path. Men delude themselves in believing that to know is to shed one's skin. Knowledge is an approximation to truth wrought out of personal experience: it is a process from within, from the 'self' outwards, into the 'non-self'. Man is capable of knowing and understanding only in virtue of his being a microcosmos, a point in which the whole world converges; and though he be a mere atom in space and time, his destiny has yet universal significance and value.

It is dangerous and tedious to apply labels to oneself, but I want to assert the predominance in myself of *homo mysticus* over *homo religiosus*: this, I think, has set a seal upon my whole philosophical outlook. An original mystical conviction was with me from the very moment of my 'conversion', while the specifically religious and credal element played a secondary part. Eckhart, Jacob Boehme and Angelus Silesius are more congenial to me than many doctors of the Church. Mysticism, understood as a mode of knowledge rather than a finished product, has always exercised my imagination. I believe in the existence of a universal mystical experience and a universal spirituality which cannot be described in terms of confessional differences, although, in another sense, I always looked for the meaning of confessional differences in the various types of mysticism which, while pursuing the same objective, developes along different lines. There is more depth and insight in the gnostic and 'esoteric' type of mysticism than in that which has received the official sanction of the Church and is not suspected of heterodoxy: orthodox mysticism has, in effect, frequently been identified with asceticism and thereby deprived of its genuinely mystical character.

I have already spoken of my great indebtedness to such writers as Tolstoy and Dostoevsky. Their impact served to clear my eyes with the re-discovery of the truth concerning man, and Tolstoy, despite all his later self-mutilations in this respect, instilled in me in my early youth a deep awareness of my mother country. Among philosophers I owe a great deal to Schopenhauer, who brought home to me and confirmed my sense of the unallayed pain of human existence. His conviction concerning the unreality of the world of appearances and of man's empirical environment was, in a measure, akin to my own. And, though I could not agree with his conception of the evolutionary process as the self-expression of a blind will, I agreed with him in his general voluntarism. Hermann Oldenberg's and Max Müller's classic works on Buddhism as well as Prince S. Trubetskoy's book on the metaphysics of Ancient Greece were among the first writings of the kind to impress me. I was also greatly stimulated by Carlyle—Carlyle the prophet rather than the preacher—and I remember being completely carried away while reading his *Heroes and Hero-worship*. 'Great men' were always the object of my admiration, although it was not in the ranks of conquerors and statesmen that I found my own heroes. My admiration for men of genius did not cease when I became ideologically hostile to them: such, for example, was the case with Marx. I bought and read with enthusiasm Pavlenkov's *Lives of Great Men*, which had come out at the end of the 'eighties as part of a rather uneven and spectacular series. I was interested not so much in the tricks and the vagaries of the behaviour of 'great men' as in human destiny, in men's struggle for release from the bonds of environment. I told myself that he who is conscious of his destiny, with all the tragedy that it involves, alone embodies true humanity. Even now I am fond of reading biographies, although I am less inclined than I used to be to treat history as a parade of unique and sparkling personalities. As a matter of fact, I feel a positive dislike for statesmen and politicians, who are known to history as 'great', but whose greatness is very questionable. If there is greatness among them, it is usually betrayed and destroyed by the functions they are expected to fulfil in society. It has always puzzled me that man could invest power, especially social power, and the exercise of power with a sacred or even divine significance. My passionate interest in social justice and social responsibility has always stood in curious contrast to a marked tendency to dualism (some have even called this sectarianism) and to metaphysical anarchism.

My favourite writers were the Old Testament prophets and the Book of Job; the Greek tragedians, Cervantes, Shakespeare, Goethe, Byron, Hoffmann, Dickens, Balzac; I liked Victor Hugo, and above all, Ibsen and Baudelaire. I do not, however, claim any consistency in this choice. I also enjoy, in a somewhat old-fashioned manner, the novels of Walter Scott and Alexandre Dumas. Among Russian writers—apart from

Dostoevsky and Tolstoy—Lermontov was nearer to me than any other; I shared his vision of 'a distant land', his scorn and indignation at the mob around him and his later 'realism'. Russian literature as a whole sustained me spiritually and intellectually throughout my whole life. Pushkin for some reason appealed to me least of all, and I came to appreciate him only considerably later. I thought very highly of Tyutchev, one of the few convincing metaphysical poets, who has, moreover, successfully embodied (and transcended) the classic and romantic elements. All literary rhetoric and grandiloquence, on the other hand, were distasteful to me: I was, for instance, never able to acquire a liking for Cicero. But all these literary interests and preoccupations were linked up with an initial disquietude about and search for truth and meaning as well as with a deep-rooted, even if powerless, desire to change the world in accordance with that truth and meaning. My early and passionate love for philosophy raised no ambitions in me for an academic career. To become anything of a public figure, a 'teacher' or 'master', was quite unpalatable to me; I desired only to lead what I thought was my chosen life in pursuit of truth and be no more and no less than just myself, keeping, as far as it is possible, at a distance from the battles of life. In actual fact philosophy brought me into the very midst of this life, into the turmoil of revolution, away from every possible ivory tower. Indeed, my participation in the revolutionary movement towards the end of the last century and at the beginning of this century, which was accompanied by spiritual renewal in Russia, proved to be a ferment for my own spiritual development.

CHAPTER IV

THE DOMAIN OF PHILOSOPHICAL KNOWLEDGE. PHILOSOPHICAL SOURCES. EXISTENTIALISM AND ROMANTICISM

When I finally took up philosophy as my life's work, I entered a domain of untold riches—not, admittedly, of 'consolations', as some believe, and yet one very unlike the dull and insipid world of the commonplace. It was, above all, a world in which the limits and limitations of time and space cease to have power. As I have already noted, once aware of my vocation as a philosopher, I never experienced any doubts as to its validity. My conception of this vocation was in some ways similar to that of Marx, who proclaimed in his famous Theses on Feuerbach that hitherto philosophy had been concerned with knowing life, but that the time has come for it to change life. It was, therefore, conceived by me as primarily a creative vocation, committing me to the fulfilment of a creative task. Accordingly, my main philosophical concern was of an ethical, anthropological and historiographical character, and the greater number of my books are devoted to the problems of ethics, history and to the metaphysics of freedom. I found much in common with the German philosopher Franz Baader, who placed freedom at the basis of all philosophical enquiry, and who conceived of the philosopher as living in his object, or rather making his object live in him and, indeed, of creating that object in freedom. As with many of my contemporaries in Russia, my initiation into philosophy proceeded by way of German Idealism, but especially through Kant's *Critique of Pure Reason* and Hegel's *Phenomenology of the Mind*—the only philosophical works I found in my father's predominantly historical library. In this library I also discovered the works of Voltaire in luxurious bindings, and in his ideas of a new kind of history, to be called the philosophy of history, I took an enormous interest. Without having ever been a Voltairian, I nevertheless shared his concern for the emancipation of man and even his revolt against religion. His polemical attitude towards life, however violent and one-sided, remained with me all my life.

I remember a somewhat trivial occasion in connection with my first acquaintance with Hegel's writings. I was at the time paying court to one of my cousins. She had an album in a blue velvet binding into which she copied verses: I could find nothing better to write in it than quotations from Hegel's *Phenomenology*. It was surprising that she did not take me for a freak, as no doubt I must have been at the time. I have already noted the extent to which my intellectual and philosophical pursuits set me apart from my comrades in the Corps and elsewhere.

Very soon I was able to find my way in the sphere of intellectual tendencies and philosophical schools of thought, to understand their relation with one another, and to see them in their proper perspective. My own thought moved increasingly towards the problems of ethics. The idea of what 'ought to be' came to predominate over the idea of what 'is', although, at the same time, I can claim to have safely avoided, and indeed exposed, moralism and the philosophy and religion of moral codes.

My thinking proceeded from, and my books were written out of, passion and a 'point of view': the will ruled the intellect and the philosophical imagination. In the sphere of knowledge decisive importance was to be attached to the affective element, however difficult it may be of articulation in intellectual propositions, to the emotional acceptance or rejection of this or that idea or fact or behaviour. I believe that the value of intellectual insight is in proportion to the awareness of conflict and unresolved opposites, and hence of evil and irrationality. Thus even an apparently most convincing and powerful system of monism seemed to me a piece of artlessness and *naïveté*. Hegel's monistic philosophy is redeemed by his vision of a dialectic and a struggle of opposites at the heart of existence. The most extreme intellectualism and rationalism usually spring from a passionate emotion, since, in the last analysis, they go back to some original intuition, which must be explained in emotional as well as intellectual terms. People, and particularly philosophers, who are engaged in intellectual pursuits, are apt to believe that the world consists exclusively of the figments of their intellect and is the embodiment of their rationalizations. In point of fact, the world is both torn and held together by passions, which alone make it worth the knowing, while the extinction of passion brings the commonplace, with its unmeaning and unreality, into being. This conviction has led me to disbelieve in the relevance of logic, although I have not, of course, escaped the study of logic and the reading of a host of books on this subject. I cannot help thinking that those who hope to attain knowledge would be better employed in trying to communicate with the mystery of being than in analysing and defending the truth of logical propositions.

It is customary in certain quarters to explain intellectual convictions by reducing them to certain processes in the subconscious, and thereby making it appear that their proper place would be in a psychiatrist's note-book. Far from attempting to disprove here this piece of psychoanalytical nonsense, I only want to state that, so far as I am aware, my thinking has been a constant dialogue, or intercourse, or battle—not with myself, but with an external friend or foe. Even my love for metaphysics is largely the result of a reaction against the external environment, against the 'necessities' of empirical reality and the commonplace. Hence also my insistence on freedom. Philosophical knowledge itself appeared to me as a way of liberation. Unlike my friend Leo Shestov, who engaged in the undoing of philosophy for the sake of liberating man (he did so, however, by means of philosophy!), I discovered in philosophy a source of freedom. I found in it a point of many dimensions from which man can undertake the struggle with finitude in the name of infinity. To use Nietzsche's words, I always felt myself to be a 'robber' rather than a 'shepherd'. The very process of thinking and philosophical knowledge are to me a revelation of meaning, a way of communicating with the mystery of life. But this attitude has little in common with the exercise of analytical and discursive reasoning, for which I have altogether little if any capacity. It is a mistake to believe that philosophy must deal with abstractions and generalities, with abstract laws and general ideas. I, for one, could never see the need of, or the justification for, discarding the concrete, the particular and individual in the choice of the object of philosophical knowledge: on the contrary I chose the concrete and the individual. Philosophy does not, admittedly, concern itself with disjointed things which stand to each other in the same kind of external relation as the facts of nature. Nevertheless, the universal, by existing at all, exists in the particular and concrete, and not the reverse. Its reality is revealed and known neither as a phenomenon presented from without nor as an abstract idea, but as lived and experienced in the subject and in proportion to the subject's awareness. Every particular philosophical insight, therefore, contains for me a whole universe of truth.

Sometimes I felt that the fate of the world might hang on the outcome of some single meeting, or conversation, or argument. Many people have been surprised that I could attach such importance to an informal talk: but this was due to my conviction that every single occurrence has literally universal implications. Sometimes an apparently insignificant conversation, a film or an unimportant novel provided an occasion for new insights. The entire plan for one of my books occurred to me while I was at the cinema. This is reminiscent of Plato's *anamnesis*, remembrance, which was for him an eminently transcendent instrument of knowledge, and also of Leibniz's idea of the microcosmic monad.

Despite the established and venerable tradition of confining philosophy to logic and epistemology, I was never able to conform my mind to such a limitation or to see any possibility of true philosophical knowledge along those lines. On the contrary, knowledge appeared to me as creative understanding, involving a movement of the spirit, a direction of will, a sensitivity, a search for meaning, a being shaken, elated, disillusioned and imbued with hope. Who will deny that suffering, joy, conflict, ecstasy are sources of knowledge? Reality is, in fact, closed to those who pretend to know in a state of indifference, disinterestedness and neutrality, for they suppress the evidence of the very reality which they attempt to know. In point of fact nobody, not even Spinoza, has ever been consistent in applying the principles of such allegedly 'pure' knowledge. Philosophy signifies the love of wisdom, and love implies emotion and passion. Philosophical knowledge, then, springs from the integral life of the spirit; it is preeminently spiritual experience. All the rest, the various philosophical disciplines propagated in philosophical text-books and taught at the universities are, at best, of secondary importance.

Is knowledge intent on eliminating mystery? I do not think so. Mystery abides even on the summits of knowledge: indeed it is made more real and more significant in knowledge. But knowledge destroys the false mysteries proceeding from, and maintained by, ignorance. There is a mystery before which we pause because our knowledge has acquired depth. God is Mystery, and the knowledge of God denotes a participation in a mystery, which, in consequence of such participation, becomes even more mysterious. That is why apophatic theology, the theology which bears witness to the *Deus absconditus*, is the only adequate theology. The knowledge of God attained by means of ratiocination, on the other hand, cannot be called a true knowledge of God, since it betrays and destroys Mystery.

Knowledge does not bring only joy and liberation: it brings bitterness too, for it exposes illusions and strips off their pretexts. Many things seemed to me more important and attractive before I came to know them. Too great a knowledge of life and men brings untold sadness in its wake: I should be glad now not to have seen or known many things so clearly and so intimately. But to do so had the effect of shattering, and freeing me from, the false illusions in which our life abounds: it has cleared the way to true mystery; indeed, it has enhanced the awareness of the mystery of life which is closed alike to ignorance and to the empty pretensions of omniscient positivism.

In discussing philosophical problems I have chosen the method of witness, of intuitive description and of characterization. I always desired to discern and to express the ethos, the character or quality of the object of my enquiry, rather than to present others with fragments of ideas and phenomena. This method is evidence of my 'existential' attitude, although in many other respects I do not identify myself with modern existentialism. Knowledge in the sense of objectification, of objective study—although it may have its valid place in scientific enquiry—is an unreality to me. In the last resort the 'something' which is known can never be set before the knowing subject as a ready-made object, independent of the subject and known in its objectivity. Nevertheless I did not look down on science and scientific methods, and I acknowledged their immense critical power and purifying function, particularly when applied to history and the history of religion. To establish the limits and limitations of science and to refuse its claim to solve all the problems of life is another matter, which I vigorously pursued, especially in Russia, in face of the positivistically-minded Russian intelligentsia.

The course of my philosophical wanderings was a complex and uneven one and is marked by many transformations. To some these appeared to be almost somersaults and were evidence of extraordinary inconsistency. Yet I can claim to have remained faithful to myself and never to have betrayed my original vision. Much that I discovered at the beginning of my philosophical path has now again, after the experience of a whole life, become a matter of intense concern. Thus I have throughout seen and endeavoured to know the world and man not as they are but as they are becoming—their destiny and their movement towards the incalculable and unpredictable end. My philosophy has never been 'scientific': rather, it was prophetic and eschatological in manner and orientation. I have studied and discovered and learnt much in the course of my life; but what was there in the beginning has, after all, remained with me all the time. Such indeed is the paradox of man, that he is invariably the same even as he changes. I regard it as a real achievement that I have now a much lower opinion of the extent and quality of my knowledge than I had thirty years ago, although, in the course of these years, my knowledge has presumably increased. I am beginning to know that I know nothing.

When, as a student, I came to take an active part in revolutionary university circles, I had great advantages over the other students in view of my knowledge of philosophy and my wider education. My associates were aware of this, and it explains, perhaps, why at one time I played a leading intellectual rôle amongst them. But, unlike most of them and, indeed, most of the Russian intelligentsia of my generation, I have never been a materialist or a positivist, although at one time I denied God. Even my atheistic convictions had other roots than those provided by materialism and shared by my fellow-students: it was, in fact, an inverted religious conviction, an anti-theism rather than an atheism, implying a denial not of God but of the man-made image of

God, of what I believed to be the traditional religious conceptions and travesties of him. I was not an atheist if atheism be taken to mean the denial of the supreme reality of spirit and of absolute values independent of the material world. Neither was I a pantheist believing in some homogeneous primary matter extending through infinite space and identical with God. My intellectual position at that time (that is, during and after my university years) may most adequately be described as ethical Idealism as represented by Fichte. The God in whom I believed was the God of German Idealism, a God who is involved in the process of becoming. But this Idealist phase was soon left behind: I lived through Idealism, I thought out its problems, I tasted its poison and was enriched by its partial insights; but I did not rest there, as some seemed to believe. The same must be said of my attitude to Marxism. I identified myself with Marxism only in so far as this did not involve me in the acceptance of social and economic determinism, and, whatever the truth and prophetic power of Marx's critique of bourgeois society and its assumptions, he could not shake my faith in the ultimate freedom of the spirit. I fought for this freedom in the very midst of the Marxist world, just as I fought for it amidst the Russian Orthodox. Even while denying God, the consciousness of mystery surrounding my own life and the life of the whole universe, and the consciousness of the inadequacy of all achievement within this two-dimensional world of ours, never left me.

Although I experienced the impact of German Idealist philosophy, I never became an 'adept': in fact, as I have already noted, I did not ever adhere to any school of thought. I have never succeeded in impressing academic philosophers, and, to tell the truth, I never desired to do so. I seem to have irritated them a great deal and, indeed, frequently accused them of cowardice and lack of imagination. I may have been influenced in this by Schopenhauer's and, to some extent, by Tolstoy's attitude towards the philosophy of the schools. But, still more, it was evidence of my 'individualism', of my inability for direct association with anybody or anything, of my constant desire to withdraw into myself, and also, perhaps, of my 'revolutionary' spirit. My own years at the university appeared to me as an ordeal which made me feel isolated in a sea of littleness and mediocrity. Afterwards, when I came to know that at the root of life, with all its wretched ramifications, there lies an unexplained and inexplicable mystery, and that it was my task to bear witness to that mystery, my hostility towards official, professorial philosophy increased: indeed, I failed to see how it could be called philosophy at all. The same was true of my attitude towards official Marxism when I became a Marxist. Later on, when circumstances forced me into closer association and even co-operation with academic circles, I could never feel at home and, on the other hand, must have caused considerable uneasiness to my colleagues.

I regard my type of philosophy as 'existentialist', even though one should qualify this by pointing out that true existentialist philosophy is represented by St. Augustine, Pascal, Kierkegaard and Nietzsche rather than by Heidegger, Jaspers or Sartre. I have, however, nothing in common with what is called the 'philosophy of life' or with pragmatism. I am an existentialist because I believe in the priority of the subject over the object, in the identity of the knowing subject and the existing subject; I am, furthermore, an existentialist because I see the life of man and of the world torn by contraries, which must be faced and maintained in their tension, and which no intellectual system of a closed and complete totality, no immanentism or optimism can resolve. I have always desired that philosophy should be not *about* something or somebody but should be that very something or somebody, in other words, that it should be the revelation of the original nature and character of the subject itself.

My true master in philosophy was Kant, and I have devoted most of my studies to his thought: to Kant himself rather than to Kantianism or neo-Kantianism. Nevertheless, I could hardly call myself a 'Kantian', just as I could not call myself a 'Tolstoyan', or a 'Marxist', or a 'Nietzschean', however great my indebtedness to the men behind these labels may be. Kant provided me with something that underlies my fundamental philosophical attitude, and I am conscious of this now more than ever before. My consciousness awoke with the realization of the distinction, or rather the radical difference, between the realm of phenomena and the realm of 'things in themselves', between the order of nature and the order of freedom; it also awoke with the realization of the truth that man is an end in himself.

My attitude to Kant has gone through different stages. At one time I fought against a wave of Kantianism, or rather neo-Kantianism, which threatened to flood the intellectual life of the Russian intelligentsia. I was particularly up in arms against Cohenism[1] which seemed to have produced a great impression on the younger Russian philosophers. At that time I was already living in Moscow, where I discovered a number of interesting, or at least interested, philosophical circles, and, despite my general aloofness in regard to the prevailing philosophical movements, I made an effort to take part in the intellectual life of Moscow, in the hope of finding something more important and, perhaps, more traditionally Russian than the prevailing fashionable neo-Kantianism. This latter school claimed to have improved on Kant, although, in point of fact, it made a travesty of him by reducing his philosophy to a rigid and intellectualized moralism which could not and did not really inspire anybody. Contrary to the opinion commonly found among academic philosophers, Kant must be regarded as primarily a metaphysician, rather than an epistemologist or even a moralist—a metaphysician who, even if he has no constructive metaphysics to offer, has yet cleared away all the obstacles which impede true metaphysical thinking. The metaphysical development of post-Kantian German Idealism, as represented by Fichte, Schelling and Hegel, was really a betrayal of Kant, whatever merits it may have had in other respects. This betrayal proved disastrous, since it ended in the elimination of the 'thing in itself', in the substitution of immanence for transcendence and of necessity for freedom, in the complete triumph of the world-Logos over everything, including God and man—in monism, pantheism and evolutionism. Nevertheless, even in Kant there were elements which I found thoroughly uncongenial: such were his ethical formalism, with its categorical imperative, his failure to show the relevance of the 'thing in itself' for every kind of knowledge, his rationalization of religious experience and his too great reliance on natural science (a science, moreover, which is now quite out of date). I dislike most particularly his formalistic and rather tedious and prosy moralism. As a very young man I wrote an essay entitled 'The Morality of Duty and

[1] H. Cohen, founder of the neo-Kantian school, who used Kant's ideas for the erection of a system of 'logical ethics' (*Logik des Sollens*). (Tr.)

the Morality of Desire', which was confiscated by the Tsarist police during a search. In it I attempted to define my position in regard to Kant's moralism. The essay expressed my original deep-rooted concern for moral philosophy and displayed, perhaps, something of a specifically Russian approach to moral problems. *The Destiny of Man*, written much later, in the early thirties, was merely a development of this essay.

If Kant's affirmation of the priority of ethics over all other philosophical problems has been responsible for moral formalism and a glorification of abstract moral codes, my own moralism has led me to the assertion of the radically individual, unique and unrepeatable character of moral acts and moral values and to a repudiation of every common, universally binding morality, which must needs result in enslavement and dehumanization. The concepts of duty, obligation, oath, contract, vow (marriage and monastic vows alike) must be regarded as hostile to moral life, for they lay down general rules to which the individual must submit under penalty of moral and social retribution, and thereby betray his freedom and absolute individuality. In this respect I was always a moral revolutionary, especially in view of the fact that it is society which became the bearer and the guardian of the moral law, of moral prohibitions, norms and standards. I considered it a moral duty to defy and to condemn the claims of moralistic and legalistic morality. In this, as in some other respects, I took up the position of Kierkegaard and Leo Shestov, even though my temperament and my manner of thinking are very different from theirs. I could never understand why and how a man who has transgressed a universally binding law of morality, which is in any case not in the least interested in the destiny of the concrete, living human being, should be regarded as a reprobate and an outcast. I am inclined to think that the reverse is true, that the guardians of the universally binding law, whoever or whatever they may be, are utterly immoral, and are the true candidates for hell, whereas the outcast and the reprobate is the moral man, because he has fulfilled his sacred duty of lawlessness.

I remember a moment in my life when I came face to face with the problem of man's personality and individuality; it arose in my consciousness with the power and impact of a sudden vision. Thereafter it was no more a matter of a philosophical or religious point of view,

but one of life and death for me. This experience had, as I shall explain
at a later stage, a considerable influence on the final outcome of my
association with Marxism, as well as on the way in which many other
conflicts in my life were to be resolved. I could not consent to the subjection of myself or of anybody else to the power of the general, the
universal, the total which spells the undoing of existence in its individuality, uniqueness and irrationality, and makes of man a means and
a tool of conceptual, or moral, or social abstractions. Man, the individual, unrepeatable image of man is always an exception, always
betraying and invalidating rules and norms. This attitude accounts,
perhaps, for my profound sympathy with Ibsen, whatever his artistic
merits or demerits may be, as also for my admiration for Belinsky and
his rebellion against Hegel's world-Spirit. Similarly, I responded to the
appeal of Kierkegaard and Shestov against the Hegelian or any other
delusion of having composed all differences and found a rounded-off
universe in which there is no more individuality, risk, or new creation.
In all monistic, optimistic and rationalistic types of thought man is, in
fact, suppressed, and becomes a mirror and a victim of 'objective'
unreality. My whole philosophy may be put in relief with references to
the fundamental antithesis in which it is conceived towards all monistic
tendencies, on the one hand, and to my radical personalism on the other.

I proceeded from Kant in my conception of the theory of knowledge.
But before long I arrived at a different view, which I endeavoured to
elaborate and bring to perfection in the course of my whole philosophical career, without ever being able to formulate it in a systematic
way. This view was set against every kind of rationalism which believes
in the possibility of pushing abstraction to the limiting case of Being
and of expressing Being in concept: in other words, which believes in
the rationality of Being. But Being is susceptible of rationalization and
conceptualization only if it is itself conceived as a concept, containing
something to differentiate it from something else; or, as I came to
formulate this later on, Being of which rationalistic epistemology and
ontology treat is itself a product of reasoning. We may speak, however,
of Being, of true and original Being, which precedes the process of

rationalization and is not to be known conceptually. This accords, in a measure, with the Kantian distinction of 'thing in itself' and its manifestation or phenomenon. I could never understand, however, why Kant refused to face the problem and explain how the world of phenomena, which is not the real, noumenal world, came into being. Moreover, Kant's assumption concerning the unknowability of the real, noumenal world ('thing in itself') puzzled me, and I could not understand why the derived, unreal, phenomenal world should be regarded as the only subject-matter of knowledge. This is evidence of a fundamental difference between Kant and Plato. There is, in my opinion, no denying that Plato is right whilst Kant is wrong, although there is something to be said for Kant's profound and ingenious teaching of the 'transcendental illusion'. My own interpretation of Kant in this context may be made clear with reference to the distinction, known in modern psychology, between the sub-conscious and consciousness, even if the facts as described by modern psychology are devoid of any philosophical connotation.

Among the neo-Kantians I had most in common with Windelband, Rickert and Lask. They were the only representatives of the revival of Kantianism who ventured to break out of the iron framework of rationalism. I even went to Heidelberg for a term to hear Windelband lecture. At that time—I was still a young man—I had, however, already moved away from Kantianism and was concerned with finding ways and means of going beyond Kant, without, at the same time, losing sight of his problems: I endeavoured to find a justification for the knowledge of original, noumenal reality prior to every kind of rationalization and before the emergence of the special problems and the special methods characteristic of scientific knowledge. I came to assume a 'primary' and a 'secondary' form of knowledge and, correspondingly, a 'primary' and a 'secondary' consciousness, from which knowledge springs. The 'secondary' consciousness originates in the process of objectification, whereby reality is seen as broken up into the realms of subject and object. The 'primary' consciousness, on the contrary, pertains to the subject, and proceeds from it as from a fountain of living water: it marks the fundamental identity of subject and object. In more recent years I called the process of objectification 'estrangement', which belies reality as it is, that is to say, as an experience and a subjectivity, as the act of him whose experience it is. The objective world is the product of estrangement: it is the fallen world, disintegrated and en- slaved, in which the subject is alienated from the object of his know- ledge. I have described true knowledge as, paradoxically, the objectivity of the subjective and the subjectivity of the objective. The subject is created by God, whereas the object is a product of the creature. The subject is noumenon, the object is phenomenon. For me reality is in no way identical with 'pure being', which I regard as a sheer abstraction, or indeed with what is called 'objectivity' (in accordance with the dictum that 'the real is the objective'). As a matter of fact true reality can be ascribed alone to subjectivity and personality.

I have already noted that, despite the vagaries of my philosophical development, I am conscious of having always remained true to my original insight. I remember an international conference of philosophers in Geneva which I attended in 1904. There I made the acquaintance of the famous materialist Georgi Plekhanov, who was a poor philosopher but, none the less, genuinely interested in philosophical problems. We used to discuss philosophy while strolling down the wide streets of Geneva. I tried to convince him of the *naïveté* of rationalism, particu- larly of materialistic rationalism, based as it is on the dogmatic pre- supposition concerning the rational nature of Being in general, and of material Being in particular. Then already I maintained that the rational world with its laws, its determinations and causal connections can have no primary reality: it is, I said, derivative—a product of rationalization, the validity of which is a figment of rationalistic human consciousness. Owing, perhaps, to his lack of philosophical culture, Plekhanov was at bottom unable to understand what I was trying to convey, while I myself did not pay sufficient attention to his one-sidedly epistemological preoccupation. This is, no doubt, a defect in my thinking: in my con- cern for the affirmation of freedom and subjectivity over against the objectifications of rationalism I am unable to concentrate on episte- mology.

I arrived at a position which compelled me to reject ontology, or the science of Being, altogether. Indeed, I believe it to be a disastrous philosophy of nothing at all, except certain figments of the human brain. I am thereby breaking with a long-standing and venerable tradition, which goes back to Parmenides, Plato, Aristotle, Thomas Aquinas, and continues in many trends of modern philosophy. I am, therefore, also compelled to reject Vladimir Solovyev's and his predecessors' teaching of all-in-oneness, or, as it has been described by some, of pan-en-theism. At one time I even felt akin to some Hindu philosophers but, in the end, I found more affinity with Jacob Boehme and Kant. Existentialist philosophy ought to be radically anti-ontological; but this is not the case with the majority of modern existentialists and, in particular, with Heidegger, who even claims to have built up a new science of Being (*Fundamentalontologie*) derived from his phenomenological ancestry.

My rejection of ontology, then, issues in the recognition of the primacy of Freedom over Being, for, with regard to Being, man is not free at all; and this signifies, at the same time, the primacy of spirit, for it is with regard to spirit that man is free. The freedom of the spirit consists in the fact that man is not determined by anything but himself, since spirit is to determine oneself from within and to be oneself. Being is, as it were, freedom arrested and congealed. The primacy of Being over freedom, on the other hand, must needs lead to determinism and the denial of freedom: if freedom is, it cannot be determined by anything except itself. The greater part of the philosophical doctrines concerning freedom fail to satisfy me. This, as I have pointed out in a previous chapter, applies especially to the traditional doctrine of freewill. The only conception of freedom which I found satisfactory was that of Jacob Boehme, whose writings I came to appreciate more and more, and about whom I later wrote a number of essays. I do not claim to be true to Boehme in every respect, but I regarded his teaching concerning *Ungrund*[1] as susceptible of my own interpretation, and I identified *Ungrund* with primordial freedom, which precedes all ontological determination. According to Boehme this freedom is in God; it is the inmost mysterious principle of divine life; whereas I conceived it to be outside God, preferring, as I do, not to speak of the unspeakable and ineffable apophatic mystery of God's life.

[1] The term means 'groundlessness' rather than 'primary ground' (*Ur-grund*) and suggests the idea of the indeterminate nature of freedom. (Tr.)

About thirty-five years ago I wrote my first book on freedom, entitled *The Philosophy of Freedom*. I must confess that this book does not satisfy me at all any more; but I am dissatisfied with all the books I have written. I cannot, for instance, bear reading or re-reading any of my previous writings, and I dislike seeing quotations from them. The only thing to which I attach value is the experience of creative inspiration from which these books sprang—the impulse rather than its outward result and embodiment. I should have liked to write every one of my books afresh.

I have devoted another work, entitled *Freedom and the Spirit*, to the problem of freedom. This was written much later, in exile, and it appears to express more adequately my views on this subject, although I am conscious that even here they could have been expressed much better. The problem of freedom, however, is at the centre of all my writings, to some of which I shall refer presently.

I have already spoken of the presence of a distinct rhythm of ebb and flow in my life, marked by moments of glowing, creative inspiration and times of weariness and lassitude. These changes were more frequent in early years than they are now. I have never attained a lasting equilibrium of mind, and all my thinking was accompanied by continual tensions and inward conflict. I have also noted that some of my philosophical insights came to me in the most incongruous and apparently absurd circumstances—at the cinema, on reading some novel or newspaper, in the course of a trivial conversation, or a journey into town. I was capable of working, reading, writing in all conditions: when smitten by fever, with bombs falling around the house (as in the autumn of 1917), at times of great adversity. Sometimes I was moved in my thinking by anger, by a spirit of opposition to or dissension from this or that, and by other passionate emotions, thereby often falling into extremes, without, however, ever allowing my consciousness to be wholly obscured or my inmost vision to be troubled.

My first work, *The Meaning of the Creative Act*, which is of particular importance to me, and about which I shall speak at greater length later on, was born of a great passion. It was written in a mood of *Sturm und Drang*, in a state of almost feverish intellectual excitement. All the themes to which I devoted my life and work were contained or prefigured in this book: I spoke there of man's personality, freedom and creativeness, of his greatness and dignity, and of his tragic and afflicted situation, of God's desire for man and of man's desire for God. I have written many and, no doubt, more mature things since, but none of them are inspired to the same extent or express the same intensity of thought.

It was not possible for me to devote my whole energy to philosophical matters. I was frequently distracted by the social and cultural exigencies of the shifting world around me and was induced to participate in its affairs. Nevertheless, I never became a 'politician', and my very association with politicians and political movements had a non-political, spiritual, philosophical or ethical character; and of late years I have altogether concentrated my attention more and more on philosophical problems in order to carry out and, as far as possible, to bring to perfection my philosophical work.

The books which are of first importance for the understanding of my outlook are, apart from the already mentioned *The Meaning of the Creative Act*, *The Destiny of Man*, the most systematic of my books; *Solitude and Society*; *Spirit and Reality*; and *Slavery and Freedom*, probably the most radical and revolutionary of them all. As regards philosophical influence and ancestry, I am, as I have already said, increasingly aware of my kinship with Kant, and differ in that respect from many other Russian religious thinkers, who were under the predominant influence of Plato, Schelling, and, to some extent, of Hegel. I should like to work out my views on the problems of metaphysics more explicitly and more thoroughly, although I have never desired to elaborate a metaphysical system.[1]

My thought has often been misunderstood and misinterpreted, and for this I am probably myself largely to blame: my thinking is antinomic; I incline too much to extremes and occasionally jump to conclusions without testing them by the accepted methods of cautious philosophical enquiry; and I express myself in an extravagantly aphoristic manner. The paradoxical and even contradictory character of my thought has produced the curious result of my having sometimes won

[1] Since I wrote this I have attempted to formulate a metaphysical theory in two recent books: *The Divine and Human* and *An Essay in Eschatological Metaphysics*.

the approval of my ideological opponents. One of the main misunderstandings arose *à propos* of my dualism: this is usually interpreted as an
ontological dualism involving the existence of two disparate and un-
related spheres of Being. A similar ontological dualism is attributed to
my opposition of subjectivity and objectification, as well as to my
eschatological attitude. My critics thereby put me on the Procrustean
bed of their own presuppositions and impute to me categories of
thought which cannot possibly be applied to me. I have been at times
much distressed by this hopeless misunderstanding: to me it was evidence of that very process of objectification which I have combated all
my life and which has such disastrous repercussions on men's relationships and on their attempts to speak to each other.

I should like now to devote a few pages to the appraisal of existentialism and of romanticism, and to explain their points of contact
with, and divergence from, my own thought. Since the appearance of
the works of Heidegger, Jaspers and, especially, those of Sartre in
France, existentialism has become something of a fashion. Its origins are
very distant, more distant than Soeren Kierkegaard. Kierkegaard's impulse was provided by a passionate reaction against Hegelian rationalism, but his solitary, tormented mind could only be properly appreciated by the inter-war generation, beset as it was by sheer terror and
despair. I was an existentialist even before I came to know Kierkegaard's writings, and I was attacked on this account before existentialism
came to the fore. I believe that Russian thought has always been marked
by an existentialist tendency. This applies, evidently, above all to
Dostoevsky, but is also true of Leo Shestov. Existentialism is, indeed,
not a new phenomenon: we may discern its vivifying theme throughout the whole history of thought. The emphasis on the subject as
against the object, of the will as against the intellect, of the concrete and
individual as against the general and universal; the antithesis between
intuitive and conceptual knowledge, between existence and essence,
were understood by some medieval thinkers and, in some measure,
even in Greek thought; they are characteristic, in various ways, of St.
Augustine, Pascal, Maine de Biran, Schopenhauer and the representa-

tives of the historicist school of thought. They can even be detected in Spinoza, Leibniz, Hegel and Schelling. Nevertheless, contemporary existentialists have brought a distinct element of originality: their existentialism is more radical, even if not always very consistent. Thus Heidegger, proceeding though he does from Kierkegaard, has, ironically enough, rationalized the Kierkegaardian theme into a rigid and almost scholastic system. He puts a genuinely existential experience into the strait-jacket of rational categories which are really quite unfit for it, and, in so doing, conjures up a whole inventory of almost unbearable and incomprehensible terminology, the only virtue of which is its undoubted originality. The terminology, however, is more original than the thought. Still, no one would deny that Heidegger is endowed with unusual philosophical gifts, and his thought reveals great intellectual intensity and concentration.

Jaspers seems to be more faithful, and gives a more dramatic relief, to the original Kierkegaardian inspiration. His thought contains, moreover, strong Nietzschean elements. But, if we are to take his distinction between prophetic and scientific philosophy seriously, his own philosophy must be regarded as belonging to the latter type. Jaspers is richer and more sensitive as a thinker than Heidegger; his thought abounds in psychological insight, and he has a deep feeling for history. I have much more in common with him than with the other contemporary existentialists. An existentialist philosopher should be aware of an identity between his thinking and his personal and the world's destiny. This involves victory, or at least partial victory, over objectification. Existence cannot be regarded as the 'object' of knowledge: it is, on the contrary, the subject of knowledge, or, at a still deeper level, it transcends the very differentiation into object and subject. I have spoken of this before, and I shall return to it more than once. 'Objects' and the knowledge of 'objects' have never interested me; what concerns, and absorbs, and haunts me is the destiny of the subject, the microcosmos, in which there stirs and throbs the whole universe, and which bears witness to the meaning of its own and the world's existence.

Neither Kierkegaard, whom I did not read until late in life and whose morbid exaltation of sin is profoundly uncongenial to me, nor Heidegger, nor even Jaspers, had any particular influence on my thought. I have been nourished in my philosophical thinking above all by the experience of life, and I regarded philosophy as a function of life, or rather as a kind of symbol of spiritual experience, of a lonely pilgrimage of the spirit. All the tensions and contradictions in life are, and ought to be, reflected in one's philosophy, and one should not attempt to compose them for the sake of neat philosophical constructions. Philosophy cannot ever be divorced from the totality of man's spiritual experience, from his struggles, his insights, his ecstasies, his religious faith and mystical vision. It is the concrete person, not the epistemological subject or the abstract universal mind, who takes cognisance of and meditates on the object of knowledge, philosophical or otherwise. Plato, Descartes, Spinoza, Kant and Hegel were all concrete, living people, and into their philosophy went all their 'existential' humanity, even if they did not admit this. When a philosopher is a believing Christian, it is quite inconceivable that his philosophy should remain unaffected by his religious conviction. A mystic will remain a mystic while dealing with the problems of philosophy. Similarly, a militant atheist cannot disengage himself in his philosophy from his anti-religious conviction. As a matter of fact, philosophy has always been positively or negatively religious.

Modern philosophy from Descartes onwards has been in a very definite sense more Christian than medieval scholastic philosophy, since Christianity had not as yet sufficiently pervaded and modified the mind of the scholastics, and their intellectual terms of reference and their mentality belonged to the pre-Christian, ancient Graeco-Roman universe of discourse. Modern philosophy, on the other hand, is already to a very large extent a product of the Christian era, the principal evidence for which is the fact that in it the central position is occupied not by the cosmos, as in ancient philosophy, but by man. The victory over naïve and dogmatic objectivism, realism and naturalism, which glory in the power of things and objects over human existence and want to make us believe that thought merely reflects a world of objects, as well as the recognition of the creative rôle of the subject in life must equally be attributed to the impact of Christianity on the mind of European man. Kant is a profoundly Christian thinker, more so than Thomas Aquinas, and he could have lived and thought only in a Christian era.

Christian philosophy is pre-eminently a philosophy of the subject, not of the object, a philosophy of man, not of the world with its unending determinations: it is a philosophy which bears witness to the redemption of subject-man from object-necessity.

I have often wondered if I might be called a romantic philosopher, especially in view of the current association of existentialism with romanticism. But what does romanticism really mean? If it is the opposite of classicism, I must undoubtedly style myself a romantic. In the reaction against romanticism, current in the inter-war period, everything which met with disapproval or condemnation was called romantic. In the end, everything that showed the slightest signs of human depth and insight, both in art and philosophy, came under the charge of romanticism. It is not by chance that the nineteenth century has been singled out for the most destructive condemnation. E. Seillière, in his numerous works on romanticism and imperialism,[1] exceeded himself in endless charges of romanticism against everyone and everything. The origin of the alleged plague of romanticism is said to be Rousseau and, accordingly, everybody bears the curse of Rousseauism. When I first encountered this onslaught on romanticism—an onslaught which I regard as profoundly reactionary—I came to feel myself a romantic; I realized that romanticism stands for everything that is human, and I was prepared to fight for it. On the other hand, I found myself in opposition to romanticism inasmuch as it fell a victim to illusions, falsehood, insincerity, to high-pitched and spectacular emotionalism, to aestheticism and to self-indulgence in the imaginary depths of life. It is on this account that I criticized certain manifestations of the Russian cultural renascence at the beginning of this century, with which I was closely associated, and which has displayed a peculiarly Russian romanticism.

The very problem of romanticism and classicism, as arising particularly in the minds of some contemporary Frenchmen, seems to me a wrongly-stated and, indeed, an imaginary problem. Not one great writer can be classified as either 'romantic' or 'classical'. Are Dante, Shakespeare and Goethe, Tolstoy and Dostoevsky 'romantic' or 'classical'? These labels are especially inapplicable to Russian literature.

[1] cf. his *Philosophie de l'impérialisme* and *Le mal romantique*. (Tr.)

I am, however, concerned here with the problem in so far as it affects philosophy. I am prepared to call myself a romantic for the following reasons: because of my belief in the primacy of the subject over the object; because of my hostility towards the determinism of the finite, and my disbelief in the possibility of achieving perfection in the finite: because of my opposition of intuition to discursive reasoning and of my general anti-intellectualism; because of the importance I attach to the creative element in the life of man; because of my hostility towards normative and legalistic morality; and, finally, because of my insistence on the supremacy of the personal and individual over the general and universal. But the current interpretations of romanticism fail to satisfy me. I do not in any way descend from Rousseau, nor do I believe in the essential goodness of human nature and human exper- ience; I do not regard nature as 'divine' or idealize the life-force. So far as emotional life is concerned, I view its exaltation with something not far removed from distaste, and I cannot admit the rule of aesthetics in life.

Some have described romanticism as a revolt of nature in general, and of human nature with its passions and emotions in particular, against reason, against norms and laws, against the binding principles of society and civilization. But for me the problem had a rather differ- ent connotation. I have never urged any revolt of 'nature' and 'instinct' against the laws of reason and society: rather, I have urged a revolt of the spirit and have demanded the recognition of the primacy of the spirit over nature, society and civilization alike. 'Nature', in its fallen state, is wholly subject to causal determination and, as such, is the figure of necessity. Spirit, on the contrary, signifies freedom; and all my life I have preached resistance to the power of necessity as embodied in nature and society.

I have never had a liking for German romanticism as represented by Friedrich Schlegel, Novalis, or even Schelling and Schleiermacher, and I have nothing in common with their idealization of the 'organic', or their reactionary idea of life as a process governed by natural laws which are blindly obeyed. Yet it cannot be denied that even this romantic naturalism could not but bring a lively ferment into philo- sophical thought and represented a healthy reaction against the rationalizations of the Enlightenment. At any rate its worship of nature is definitely superior to the worship of society and civilization which it was combating. While my romanticism is one of spirit and freedom, I am yet ready to join forces with traditional romanticism in the war for the liberation of the individual from the shackles of externality. But my conception of the ultimate aims of such a war and such a liberation differs from that of the romantics. To understand the true aims of man's liberation one must transcend romanticism and classicism, naturalism and rationalism alike: and I have endeavoured to do this.

If I were confined to the conventional terminology, I would say that my temperament is of the romantic rather than of the classical type. But this is admittedly misleading. I am a seeker after truth and meaning above everything else, and to that extent, perhaps, a romantic. But in my search I was more concerned with the 'what' than with the 'how', while, at the same time, never admitting that truth and meaning are expressive of objective laws and norms, rational, moral or religious. Romantics are, as a rule, preoccupied with the experiences and sensations which accompany that search rather than with the attainment of truth and meaning. They tend to exalt the emotional life with its thrills, pleasures and delights, or its gloom, bitterness and desolation, and easily take to melodrama and sensationalism. I have never surrendered to emotional self-indulgence and, as I have already said, even resisted emotions. The value I attached to inspiration, to creative ecstasy, to ardour and passion is evidence of a concern for truth as I saw it, that is to say, as something that affects, and is affected by, man's inmost being and liberates him from the dreariness and insipidity of the commonplace. I could never agree, as many romantics do, to man's surrender to, and final dissolution in, a blind and elemental search or longing for nothing at all. Such a search or longing only serves to imperil his sense of personality and freedom, which I believe to be the mark of supreme truthfulness. I could not regard 'nature', 'life', 'instinct', 'flow of heart', the 'organic', the 'collective', and all the rest as substitutes for truth. Truth is God who transcends all things, and yet reveals himself to man, in man and as man.

CHAPTER V

CONVERSION TO SOCIALISM. THE DOMAIN OF REVOLUTION. MARXISM AND IDEALISM

It is borne in on me that to carry out the plan of this book and adhere to a chronological order is a task which I find well nigh impossible to achieve.

After my break with the gentry I found myself banished into complete solitude. I had dissociated myself from my environment and could as yet see nothing to replace it. I did not even, to begin with, meet any people congenial to me, or capable of exercising influence on me. I associated for the most part with women, who gave me the illusion of being understood. Women have always been my chief 'admirers' (I do not use the word 'followers', because I have never had any). As to boon companionship, this never had any attraction for me, and I had no friends of this kind. But the time came when I abandoned my solitude and began to find my way into revolutionary society. It is not easy for me to give an account of the reasons for my association with this new world, or to answer the question as to what made me take this step. My adherence to revolutionary ideas appears to me a very complex matter, and I do not think I merely followed the trail of the majority of the Russian intelligentsia. What struck me above all was the prospect of a spiritual revolution: a rising of the spirit, of freedom and meaning against the deadly weight, the slavery and meaninglessness of the world. Actually, I was not much of a political revolutionary, and displayed little activity in this respect. I even went through the experience of a revolution of the spirit *against* political revolutionaries; for, at times, they seemed to me not revolutionary enough, and indeed positively reactionary. I exposed their dislike of freedom and their betrayal of man's personality. My temperament revealed, as it were, the operation of a constant duality, embodying a revolutionary and an aristocratic impulse—a duality which, however, affected my feeling for life more than my intellect. The revolutionary impulse sprang from an innate inability to acquiesce in the world-order and to submit to its exigencies. It had, therefore, primarily a personal, not a social significance. I was concerned with the revolution of the human person rather than of the people or the masses.

I have already spoken of my rebellious temperament; and this implied rebelliousness in regard to reactionary and revolutionary enslavement alike. At the outbreak of the communist Revolution a former Social-Revolutionary, who tended to adapt himself very readily to the new régime, said to me: 'I confess I am much less of a revolutionary than you are: you are a born revolutionary.' I do not, however, see any special merit in my non-conformism, and, although I was probably worse off than those who are more compliant, I was not even conscious of anything peculiar or outstanding about my attitude. I have, for instance, often been surprised when told that some article or speech of mine was imprudent, daring or reckless. In my attitude towards so-called public opinion, in all its manifestations, there was something not far removed from contempt. I never took it into consideration: it simply did not exist so far as I was concerned.

Such a frame of mind is evidently not conducive to professional political activities, not even to revolutionary professional politics, which after all, require no less adaptability than the politics of the *status quo*. Politics are altogether inseparable from the reign of 'public opinion', and that is perhaps why I always had such an intense dislike for them: politics are one of the most fruitful means for objectification to take effect in social life. They are remarkably successful in emptying human existence, even though, or perhaps because, they display such a feverish activity. But my dislike of politics did not lead me to a withdrawal from the world into some blissful ivory tower: I desired the overthrow of the old order, with all its fictitious political values, and the building up of a new one upon its ashes, which would eliminate, or at least reduce, the ruthless power of politics over the heart and mind of men. Purely political revolutions were repugnant to me not only in virtue of the means which they use for the attainment of their ends, but, above all, in virtue of their almost fatal tendency to betray the spirit and to belie the real, i.e., the spiritual revolution. Now it is only the revolution of the spirit which has any creative power, even though it may not be primarily concerned with the masses, the collective, the 'average man', with *raisons d'état*, conventions and objective morality, revolutionary and counter-revolutionary alike. What it does primarily take account of is man—the concrete, living human being, his personality and freedom.

And yet every liberation embodies a truth and contains a promise of true freedom. I believe revolutions to be inevitable: they tear down in perpetual recurrence the various shapes of organized exploitation in history; essentially they force change and are a threat to every social endeavour which fails to embody the power of creative spirit.

Even before I came to take a more active part in social life I was awakened to the realization of the boundless falsehood and evil which pervade and underlie the life of the world, society and civilization. My reading of history only served to confirm this impression. History unfolded itself before my eyes as a progression of crimes and falsifications, even if I recognized that it is no mere pointless game but a process endowed with some mysterious, if tragic, meaning. The very concept of 'sacred' history (unless it be understood in a very narrow and specific sense) struck me as a contradiction in terms. At one time I made a serious effort to acknowledge and accept the reality of so-called sacred traditions, but this effort only served to enhance my resistance. I was too deeply conscious of belonging to an era born of the Renaissance and the Enlightenment—an era of revolutions and revaluations. I reflected in my attitude the changes and the shifts of consciousness brought about by these historical experiences. Such experiences may be mastered —*aufgehoben*, as Hegel would say—but cannot be simply left behind, and, having gone through them, one cannot behave and think as if nothing had really happened. I could not accept the claims of some religious tendencies in early twentieth century Russia, or, for that matter, elsewhere, because they purported to live in a naïve, pre-critical age and indulged in an artificial primitivism. My very irrationalism, or supra-rationalism, of which I have already spoken, had passed through the experience of humanism, and the value I attached to the emancipation of man, as well as my distrust of authority and authoritarianism, were, to some extent, a result of this experience. Hence, also, my appreciation of and sympathy with Tolstoy in his revolt against history and civilization, although I was never a 'Tolstoyan', and indeed disliked the Tolstoyans. I was apprehensive and sceptical of every form of the glorification of history, past or present, and felt that true, authentic life is not to be found within the precincts of history and civilization, with its dictates, conventions, customs and conformities. But, unlike Tolstoy, I could never assume the posture of a spectator or judge *vis-à-vis* the world, and my sense of history made me identify myself with the historical destiny of man.

Aristotle says in his *Politics*: 'Man is naturally a political animal, destined for life in society, and he who is not naturally part of a state is either a God or a Beast' (i.e. lower or higher than man). In Aristotle's view such a being is incapable of submission to anybody or anything. I do not consider myself to be either lower or higher than man, and yet I suspect I must have something in common with that peculiar being of whom Aristotle speaks. I believe also that this points to a characteristic difference between man of the pre-Christian, ancient world and man belonging to the Christian or post-Christian age, a difference which is likewise reflected in the attitude of Western man and the Russians respectively. Russians are, indeed, much less inclined to accept and comply with the established and sanctified values of civilization than Western man. Their attitude is more questioning, 'revolutionary', and 'subversive'.

I have already spoken of the moment when I felt compelled to break with the society of the gentry. Apart from any ideological considerations, I simply felt uneasy, and my life seemed to become a series of constant protests and displays of anger and indignation. At the time of my entry into the University I went so far in this reaction to my environment as to seek only the company of those (particularly of Jews) of whom I knew for certain that they were neither of the gentry nor my relatives. When one of my Jewish friends came to see me my mother would put the traditional question: '*Est-ce un monsieur ou ce n'est pas un monsieur?*' But I bullied her to such an extent that she even stopped using the term 'Jew' in my presence and would say 'Israelite' instead.[1] My dislike of the gentry went hand in hand with a dislike of

[1] The Russian original distinguishes '*jid*' and '*evrey*': the former has acquired a derogatory meaning, while the latter is the proper equivalent of the English 'Jew'. (Tr.)

the military. It is on this account that I decided to leave the Cadet Corps and sit for the matriculation examination to the University—a rather difficult undertaking for me, in view of my inability to pass any examinations.

All these reactions, and my general resistance to authority, established institutions and social convention, were apparently deeper in me than even any intellectual convictions and beliefs. I remember that when I was a small boy the sight of a government building or state-institution filled me with abhorrence, and I desired its immediate destruction. Naturally the fact that my family was on friendly terms with Governors and Governor-Generals did not make it any easier for me. The state appeared to my youthful imagination as a Leviathan, embodying all that is monstrous, cruel, suppressive and inquisitorial, and its representatives as the torturers of men. Yet when we met at home or in society drawing-rooms I saw that these same people were often kind and delightful men. I could not help drawing some distinction between this society, which still preserved a tangible link with the patriarchal way of life, and the order of the state, which remained extraneous and terrible in its extraneousness. The latter seemed to produce some frightful change in men; they stopped being human and acquired the characteristics of beasts. Thus the Chief of Police N. used to visit my parents, and was always pleasant when I met him at home, but he looked quite different in his official capacity, on state occasions, when cross-examining prisoners. I do not remember a single occasion when I was positively impressed by an event or display in connection with the affairs of the state. It was surprising to me how unlike my own reaction was to that of others.

I have already observed that even active revolutionaries showed a greater sense of recognition *vis-à-vis* those in authority than I was ever capable of showing. Revolutionaries who have made their way in the revolution are indeed very quick to accept and to enjoy high office. Such is the irony of revolutions. I could not even (or, should one say, quite particularly?) be impressed by the 'high office' and 'rank' attained as a result of intellectu achievement, which, after all, is a much more convincing and impre sive matter. I was hopelessly lacking in a sense of hierarchical order,   d could never discriminate between people according to the position they occupy in society. All the symbols, labels, insignia, conventional devices, signs and emblems of social life evoked in me a sense of unreality, and I tended instinctively to oppose all this to life as it is and becomes before its falsifying reflection in workaday existence. I extended this even to Church life, where many things which struck me as worthy of being cast into outer darkness in fact received both endorsement and sanctification.

There is a widespread, though not always articulate, belief that the rank a man holds or the office he occupies is in itself a positive quality or even something that may redeem his worthlessness as a human being. I believe that, so far from redeeming, they usually increase the wretchedness of his condition. I am speaking here of all ranks and offices, not excluding those the legitimacy of which is acknowledged by the revolutionaries. Neither society, nor the state, nor the nation, but man alone should be regarded as sacred. My 'anarchistic' instincts and convictions, however, have nothing in common with the romantic and optimistic utopianism based on evolutionary theories: rather they are born of a realization of the conflict and tension between history and the end of history, of a belief in eternity, and of an inability to believe in or be the servant of time.

The revolutionary period through which I passed in my youth had a great influence on my moral development. Revolutionary convictions and the whole revolutionary 'atmosphere' gave rise to a peculiar mood and a peculiar attitude in regard to the future and the adversities, trials, and sufferings of the present. I did not persist in this frame of mind, but its effect on me was lasting and consisted in a kind of resilience and tenacity. It may be of interest that it is precisely the revolutionary rather than the Christian period in my life which produced these qualities in me. This may have something to do with the tendency to revolutionary asceticism characteristic of the Russian intelligentsia, which enabled them to endure persecution, although I cannot say that I have ever suffered persecution to the extent to which it is true of other Russian revolutionaries, and therefore possessed less of these ascetic qualities. The asceticism in question, however, was not of the usual kind, and had no specifically religious connotation. Whenever I thought or dreamt of the future, I imagined almost invariably that I should have to suffer and endure great sacrifices in the name of my convictions. I accustomed myself to the thought that prison, exile and, generally speaking, a life of endurance awaited me; and this prospect did not alarm me in the least. After all, I never looked forward to any successful career or established position in life, while my actual position, privileged as it was in many respects, often produced a sense of guilt in me. This, I felt, was in full accordance not only with my revolutionary but also with my 'aristocratic' attitude. My convictions, however, never induced me to become a professional revolutionary. For this I was, admittedly, too much of a theorist, a philosopher in the stricter sense of the word, and an ideologist: such was, no doubt, my vocation.

The estrangement *vis-à-vis* my environment was not confined to the gentry, but extended to the Liberals and even to the Radicals, who were the recognized 'opposition', but who, at the same time, were firmly rooted in lawful society, enjoying the good things of life and exposed to no dangers. I remember, too, that I was rather suspicious of 'legal' Marxists,[1] who struck me as being mainly preoccupied with professorial circumlocution. When I had just embarked on my literary activities, but was still a student, I was taken, on my first visit to Petersburg, by Prince Turgan-Baranovsky to a literary gathering of Marxists and Radicals. The group consisted mainly of people connected in one way or another with the magazine *Mir Bojii* (*God's World*), which was already then (that is to say, towards the end of the century) publishing Marxist articles, and to which I myself had begun to contribute. I was struck by the atmosphere of complacency and imperturbability prevailing in these circles, and returned from the meeting with a sense of profound disappointment. But I have already admitted that such feelings were to a greater or lesser extent evoked in me by practically all the social groups with which I came into contact.

What I have called the resilience and tenacity which accompanied my revolutionary outlook and activities had rather wider implications than a mere readiness to serve the revolution. They proved to be the moral and psychological leaven in all my reactions to social phenomena

[1] So called because they worked in the 'legal', that is to say, the home press. Their most outstanding spokesman was Peter Struve, who later abandoned Socialism and became the leader of the National Liberals. (Tr.)

—to the Liberal-Radical society, to the society of the men of letters, of lawyers, of professors and academicians, and, during my life abroad, to the world of parliamentary politics. It also proved decisive for my attitude to communism as it materialized after the Bolsheviks' rise to power. It necessitated my break with every society which is safely anchored in and enjoys the good things of this life, whether it be arrayed in the respectable philosophy of self-interest or, in general, relies on assured and unquestioned foundations. Nevertheless, I do not think I suffered from self-righteous purity, unsullied by any closeness to life, or from ascetic other-worldliness. But revolution and, in a different sense, religion led me to question all human values and urged me to face the terrifying abyss which imperils human existence. I was completely and sometimes even angrily convinced that the bourgeois spirit is no mere sociological phenomenon characteristic of capitalist society (although there it is particularly prominent), but, in fact, may attend socialism and communism, Christianity and Orthodoxy alike. I felt then, as I have felt many times since, an instinctive dislike for the strong and the triumphant of this world. I grew increasingly conscious of a painful clash between power and value: I realized that the greatness of value is in proportion to the decrease in power, and that the prominence of power is in proportion to the decrease in value.

My revolutionary and socialist sympathies and convictions had crystallized before I entered the University and began frequenting Marxist circles. The basis of socialism was provided for me by ethical considerations, and these considerations carried me into the Marxist fold. Among the socialists (or rather Populist socialists) I had a great admiration for Nikolai Mikhailovsky, the leader of Russian radicalism. His philosophy may be very poor, but his sociology and his socialism were built on ethical foundations and on a belief in human personality. I was attracted by his genuine moral passion and by his repudiation of class-morality and the superstitious faith in the laws of evolution. He belonged to the 'seventies, when the intellectual climate in Russia was under the pressure of the positivism of Auguste Comte, John Stuart Mill and Herbert Spencer. But his 'subjective method in sociology'—which meant that social science was to be studied not disinterestedly, like natural science, but in terms of human progress, in which man's individuality was the supreme and only value, not to be sacrificed to society—contained for me an indisputable truth. Few Russians have felt personal freedom as keenly as Mikhailovsky, although Alexander Herzen is, perhaps, even more important in this connection. The problem of the relation of personality and society was the focus of my own struggle for man, and it is this problem which brought me face to face with and made me adopt Marxism.

The encounter with Marxism took place in 1894. I soon became aware that something new and decisive had intervened in Russian life, and that I must meet the issues raised by the Marxist movement. I was not sufficiently familiar with Marx and began to read his and his followers' works. During my first year at the University I came to know a student attached to the Faculty of natural sciences, David Logvinsky: he was the only person with whom at this time I had a real friendship. He had a lively and brilliant mind, far above the level of the other students, and wide interests. Together we explored social questions, discussed a great deal, argued, concurred and disagreed, and as a result I felt myself greatly in his debt. Logvinsky was a man of unusual height, with a narrow chest and a generally emaciated appearance—a physique which disposed him to consumption. He was arrested subsequently to my first arrest for being mixed up with an illegal, Social-Democratic printing-house, and after a long imprisonment was exiled to Siberia, where he eventually died of consumption. His lot was one of the most tragic among the revolutionaries, and his extraordinary intellectual gifts, his moral integrity and passionate convictions, made it more, not less, tragic. He was a true companion throughout all the Marxist period of my life. We met again after his release from prison and before his exile to Siberia. But at that time I had already begun to move towards Idealism, and I was much distressed to find that he was quite unable to appreciate the change that had taken place in me, and the short time we were together was marred by a sense of mutual estrangement. My father was able to obtain an improvement of his position in Siberia; but this did not save him. Through Logvinsky I came into contact with a group of students who were active Marxists: one of them was Anatoli

Lunacharsky, who eventually became the first Commissar of Education and 'the literary man' *en titre* after the Bolshevik revolution. I began to participate in those unending discussions and conversations which go on until the early hours of the morning and are proverbially character-istic of the Russian intelligentsia. The first Marxist lecture I attended was in the rooms of a Pole who was later exiled with me to the province of Vologda. As so frequently happened on later and similar occasions, I felt very uneasy, and could not help feeling stifled by the lack of inner freedom, by the bigotry and prosiness which seemed to pervade the whole atmosphere. But the impression was not sufficiently powerful at the time to distract me from co-operation with these circles.

I have asked myself more than once what impelled me to become a Marxist, albeit an unorthodox, critical and free-thinking one; and why I should still have a 'soft spot' for Marxism. It is easier to answer this question in negative terms: I could not associate myself with the socialist Populists, or the Social-Revolutionaries as they later came to be known, because their outlook was infirm of purpose and their belief in social revolution by some internal process in the existing peasant commune was a piece of unimpressive idyllism. When they emerged in the shape of the 'People's Will' party, which adopted more active revolutionary methods (they were responsible for the assassination of Alexander II), they did not in the least change their basic mentality, with its implied submissiveness to the 'power of the soil', and its disguised Rousseauism. Marxism, on the other hand, denoted a complete re-orientation and marked a profound crisis of the Russian intelligentsia. The Marxist movement of the late 'nineties was born of a new vision: it brought with it not only emancipation from the routine of populism, but also a purpose and a new conception of man. It had, furthermore, a dis-tinctly higher intellectual and cultural standard than most of the pre-ceding movements. Marxism, at that juncture, was in fact a signal for the spiritual as well as social liberation of man. What attracted me most of all was its characteristic appreciation of the moving forces below the surface of history, its consciousness of the historic hour, its broad historical perspectives and its universalism. The old Russian socialism seemed provincial and narrow-minded in comparison. The fact that Marxism took root among the Russian intelligentsia was evi-

dence of a further Europeanization of Russia and of her readiness to
share to the end the destiny of Europe. I myself felt very anti-national-
istic and was never tempted to assert Russia against the West.

I remember distinctly the tremendous impression produced on me
by the sheer genius of Marx when I first read him. I accepted his critique
of capitalism without reservation. I realized that his insight into purposeful conflict as a part of the structure of things was pregnant with
enormous revolutionary possibilities, in comparison with which the old
socialistic theories appeared weak, ineffectual and rudderless. I also felt
that here was a focus for embodying a vision of life in a way which
might reflect something of the original creative impulse. The cumu-
lative weight of all these and other more elusive considerations thrust
me towards Marxism. I began to give lectures and read papers to the
members of the Kiev committee of the Social-Democrats, who soon
came to regard me as one of their ideological leaders. On returning
from one of my journeys abroad I even brought back with me a
large amount of Social-Democratic literature in a trunk with a false
bottom.

At this time the activities of the Committee did not always succeed
in winning the co-operation or the confidence of the ordinary workers,
who occasionally even displayed active hostility towards the intelligentsia. They demanded leaders from their own ranks and a right to
independent action. L., a tall, red-haired Jew, a worker at a printing-
house, was an ardent spokesman of this movement. He was particularly
hostile to the Social-Democratic intelligentsia. Yet for some reason he
was fond of me: he would come and see me and even hoped that I
would consent to become the leader of their movement. This was
strange, because, to judge from my outward appearance and manner,
I was even further than my Social-Democratic friends from the working-class *milieu*. L. went so far as to forgive me my philosophical deviations and even to take a positive interest in them. I have already had
occasion to remark on this comparative ease with which I consorted
with the members of the working-class. It may be that my innate dislike of leadership, and my disinclination to assume leadership, for which
other members of the intelligentsia sought, appealed to them. On the
other hand, I never suffered from that well-known guilt-complex

vis-à-vis the people, characteristic of the Russian intellectuals, which served to emphasise the gulf between them and the people, or at any rate made both parties feel uneasy in each other's company.

I did not actually anticipate becoming the object of any definite persecutions on account of my ideas or activities. But as it happened I was imprisoned, deported, tried and eventually exiled from my country —in fact, a rather eventful life for a philosopher, who, according to the current notion, uses his brains as an excuse for doing nothing. No doubt professional revolutionaries had to suffer far more than I; but then revolutionaries and philosophers may have the same fiery intensity of aim, yet their ways and means are different, and, for better or for worse, the philosopher's lot is to lead a rather quieter life.

I must say, from personal experience, that the prisons of the old *régime* were somewhat patriarchal and certainly less drastic institutions than the more perfected prisons of the post-revolutionary time. There were, of course, the ghastly fortress of Peter and Paul and the Alekseyevsky military prison; but these were not known to me from experience. The average prison conditions were a more timid affair. The prison-guards were generally good-natured Russian soldiers, to whom the prisoners were not 'enemies of the people', but enemies of the government, while the prison governor held patriarchal sway over his domain: if, that is to say, he was not by nature a brute, though this was occasionally the case. Under the revolutionary Soviet *régime* the prison-guards saw in the prisoners (I mean political prisoners) precisely 'enemies of the people' and of the Revolution, and the prison government was purposeful, fierce and ruthless rather than patriarchal. On the first occasion I was arrested in Kiev, for a few days in all, as party to a large student demonstration. All the participants were arrested, and we all sat together. We had gone to the demonstration anticipating that we should be shot at and that not all of us would return alive. We were surrounded by Cossacks, and several clashes followed; but it all came to very little in the end. I myself attended the demonstration from a sense of duty: I had taken practically no part in the student movement, which was too strictly organized for my liking. The Social-Democrats did not regard the student movement as their business, and their attitude towards it was somewhat patronizing. In their view, the real and most

effective revolutionary work consisted in agitation and the spreading
of propaganda among the workers.

In 1898 I was arrested in connection with the first big Social-Democratic affair and expelled from the University. About a hundred and
fifty people were arrested. For the first few days the men were together
in the large Lukianovsky prison on the outskirts of the town. Kiev was
one of the chief centres of the Social-Democratic movement at the time:
there was a secret printing-press, and revolutionary literature was produced in considerable quantities. The movement in Kiev was also in
touch with the *émigrés*, that is, with the group led by Plekhanov,
Akselrod and Vera Zasulich. When I went to Switzerland I always met
the founders and leaders of the whole movement. At the time Lenin
was in exile in Siberia and was unable to play the decisive part which
he assumed after 1900 when his term of exile expired, and that is why
I never came into direct contact with him.

My memories of this more serious occasion on which I was arrested
are of a time of great excitement: at no other time have I known such
a sense of a community of fate with my fellow-men. When I was
arrested and cross-examined I did not feel cast-down or dejected: on
the contrary, my mood was one of exhilaration, defiance and militancy.
My subsequent arrests were accompanied by similar experiences. I must
confess, however, that my own state of mind and that of many others
at the time was altogether rather peculiar, and, as I see it now, there
was something almost farcical about it. For we had no sense at all of
any failure: on the contrary we were conscious of being victors; it
seemed to us that a new era was beginning in the movement of liberation, that the news of our arrest would echo everywhere, even in
Western Europe.

My life in prison has had its bright and even pleasant sides. In the
course of the first few days, which we spent all together in a large hall,
I read a number of papers. On the second day the Governor-General
of Kiev, General Dragomirov, who was a friend of my parents, came
to see us. He entered in the company of the Chief of Police and the
Public Prosecutor. He addressed us, and I still remember some of his
words. 'Your mistake', he said, 'is not to see that the process of social
development is organic and has nothing to do with logic (!): a child

cannot be born before the ninth month.' The Chief of Police, who could not stand Dragomirov and had informed against him more than once, looked at him with undisguised suspicion. After this I was transferred to a separate cell, but with an unlocked door which opened on to the corridor. The prison *régime* was not very exacting, and I succeeded in penetrating into the upper corridor of the same prison building, where some ladies of my acquaintance had their cells. When we went out for walks we all collected in the prison courtyard and often had meetings, at which I usually took the chair. Eventually I was placed in real solitary confinement behind a locked door; then intercourse with the others ceased and I was able to read.

Thanks to my father's friendship with the Governor-General I was released at a comparatively early date. I had been in prison less than two months, but, on my release, was not allowed to leave Kiev, and remained under police-surveillance until a decision had been taken on my case. During the cross-examination the Chief of Police told me that it could be ascertained from my *dossier* that I aimed at the overthrow of the state, the Church, private property and the family. All these heinous crimes resulted in my exile for two years to the province of Vologda, where my friends and I continued to enjoy free intercourse with one another. But, as was usual in such cases, the whole affair, having begun in the law-courts, ended by being dealt with through administrative organs, and in fact dragged on for more than two years. I was seen off to my exile by a lady-friend of mine, a remarkable and very beautiful woman, who said to me: '*Dans la vie rien n'est beau que d'aimer, rien n'est vrai que de souffrir.*' I am not sure if and how these words of Musset were to be applied to me. I still remember my first sensation on leaving Yaroslavl and driving up to Vologda: looking at the spring-like and yet very dreary landscape, I was suddenly overcome by a wave of melancholy and a realization of doom hanging over my life. But this mood soon passed.

During this time I began to write: I wrote my first article and my first book (*Subjectivism and Individualism in Social Philosophy*). It is strange that my Marxist period was characterized by a much greater ease and adequacy where writing and self-expression were concerned than the later Christian period. I was less aware of the weight and inertia of the medium in which I endeavoured to embody my thought and vision. Marxism in those days was a less pedantic matter than the Marxism of the 'general line': it in no way prevented me from falling back upon my original intuition and justified my moral passion for the regeneration of man.

My first article, 'F. A. Lange and Critical Philosophy in its Relation to Socialism', was published in German in the Marxist journal *Neue Zeit*, edited by Kautsky. I became involved in correspondence with Kautsky on the subject of this article, and, in one of his letters, he wrote to me of his great hopes that the Russian Marxists would contribute to the future theoretical development of Marxism. He complained (ironically enough) that the German Marxists were too much absorbed in practical politics to be able to develop the theory of Marxism. Kautsky would however scarcely have sympathized with the way in which my thinking evolved. So far as the Russian Marxists were concerned, they sensed almost from the very beginning that I was not sufficiently orthodox and that I could not be regarded without reservation as one of them. An ideological conflict became thus inevitable and, indeed, was latent at the start.

My book contained a long preface by Peter Struve, who had also come to profess 'Idealist' or 'Spiritualist' Marxism. We occupied at the time similar ideological positions, though our temperaments, as also our motives, were different. I endeavoured to show the possibility of a synthesis of critical Marxism and the Idealist philosophy of Kant and partly of Fichte. Unlike most, if not all, Marxists I displayed no tendencies to, or even sympathies with, Hegelianism. The idea of the book sprang from a fundamental conviction concerning the ultimate independence of truth, goodness and beauty *vis-à-vis* the social environment or the revolutionary class-struggle, and from a belief in 'transcendental consciousness' as their source or origin. I held firmly to the Kantian *a priori*, which denotes a reality of the logical and ethical order. On the other hand, I maintained that, on the psychological level, consciousness is dependent on and determined by man's environment and the place he occupies as a member of a given class. There may be circumstances, I wrote, more or less favourable to the assimilation of truth and the approximation to justice, whilst truth and justice, in themselves, are rooted in transcendental consciousness. 'Class-truth', in my view, was a wholly contradictory and meaningless expression. There can, however, be 'class-untruth', such as the untruth which informs the bourgeois classes, implicated as they are in the evil of exploiting their fellow-men. This idea provided the basis for my theory of the messianic calling of the proletariat; for the proletariat is free from the sin of exploitation, and its social and psychological condition enables it to receive and bear witness to truth. I viewed the working-class as embodying, as it were, the proximity, or even the identity, of man's psychological condition with the transcendental consciousness. In my opinion this gave a much more adequate foundation for radical, revolutionary Marxism than the views of the other adherents of critical Marxism. I accepted the materialist interpretation of history over against the bourgeois illusion, according to which things in heaven are commodities relegated to another life because they are unobtainable by the workers, from whom they have been stolen by the representatives of a ruthless individualistic society; but I repudiated the metaphysical implications of materialism. I believed, above all, that truth cannot be imprisoned in any social net, socialist or capitalist, and that those who pursue the knowledge of truth step tiresomely and boldly out of neat prisons into worlds that have more to them than sociology or science could ever contain. My thought was thus left free to move in whatever direction it chose. Subsequently I defended the freedom of philosophical knowledge in the context of religious orthodoxy.

Plekhanov, whom I met in Zurich about this time, was fully aware of my position: he even prophesied that with a philosophy such as mine I would not remain a Marxist. During these years I continually found myself up in arms against Lunacharsky, whom I met frequently in our Kievian Marxist circles (like myself he was a native of Kiev); and it was just on the question of the autonomy of truth and of the knowledge of truth that we disagreed most. He accused me of a 'dangerous individualism', while I charged him with many other and more deadly things. Our conflict became at times very intense, especially as I happened to be a rather fierce controversialist and it was not easy to argue with me. I was left with the impression that Lunacharsky resented our altercations. But he himself was by no means a 'total' Marxist: he combined Marx with elements from the positivist Avenarius and Nietzsche. He was interested in new movements in the sphere of art. But, despite his many talents, a relatively superior culture and literary interests, there was something of a provincial schoolmaster with a dash of a journalist in him. He seemed already then to be destined to be People's Commissar of Education in a dictatorial government, although even his later authority could not make the official Soviet press admire his literary productions. There was, however, nothing particularly dictatorial about him personally, and he must have been shocked by the activities of the Cheka. His idea was to be a patron of the arts and sciences, but his patronage was not crowned with particular success.

Despite the immaturity of my book, *Subjectivism and Individualism in Social Philosophy*, I did, none the less, succeed in stating there a problem which had disturbed me all along and which later I endeavoured to express in a more adequate form. The problem is as follows. Knowledge depends in a sense on the extent and intensity of communion achieved by men. The character of knowledge is not only a matter of logic, but also of society, for the subject, in the act of knowing, is not the *Bewusstsein ueberhaupt* of German Idealism, or universal Mind, but concrete man endowed with certain mental and emotional qualities and placed within certain social relationships with other men. No *a priori* can be regarded as in itself a guarantee of authentic knowledge, because it is devoid of any special characteristics and belongs to the sphere of abstractions. The relevant question is that of the relation between *a priori* (assuming that there exists such a thing) and concrete man, and it is this relation which must be primarily defined. This line of thought eventually brought me to existentialist philosophy, which I later embodied in my book *Solitude and Society:* I might have entitled it 'The Sociology of Knowledge'.

The period immediately preceding the exile to Vologda was probably one of the most exhilarating, enthusiastic and creative in my life. Although it was associated with one dramatic episode which even cast a shadow on my whole youth, it is chiefly with joy that I recall this time. It was a time not so much of gaiety and high spirits, of which I knew very little, as of an experience of living in a world smouldering and almost bursting into flame—a time marked by insights into new worlds, by new experiences and new knowledge. I was never able to put these things into words, and, therefore, drove them as it were inwards. I became increasingly aware of the transcendent dimensions of life. I saw myself thrown into this world, and all around me were whirling the unknown, unseen forces of transcendence; I could not remain content within the closed circle of one-dimensional, flat, mundane existence. I read a great deal of Ibsen at this time, and found much in him that expressed my own shifting attitude and feeling for life; he even became one of my favourite writers. What others called my 'dangerous individualism', my intense consciousness of personal destiny, were echoed in Ibsen. I was also keenly interested in Russian symbolism which was at once an aesthetic and a mystical movement, and became part of the spiritual upheaval that changed the face of Russian culture on the threshold of the new century. All this served to alienate me more and more from revolutionary Marxist circles.

It would be a mistake to think that I moved at any time exclusively among the 'comrades': I was anxious to keep touch with other circles too. During my first year at the University I saw a great deal of Professor Georgi Chelpanov, who was a representative of academic philosophy: he was a popular teacher and produced at that time something of a sensation by his course of lectures, the burden of which was a pointed critique of materialism. He used to have regular 'at homes' on Saturdays, which I frequently attended, and at which I had long philosophical conversations with him. I enjoyed these and found them very useful, since they provided an opportunity of disengaging myself from the specific intellectual atmosphere of Marxist circles. Naturally, I could not agree with him on political issues, but this did not seem to have any great importance in our relationship. Chelpanov was, in his whole philosophical outlook and manner, pre-eminently a teacher, but he was also a man of wide and vivid interests—in fact, a new and exceptional type of University professor.

Somewhat later I met another man, who came to be a great and life-long friend of mine, and whose friendship I valued immensely. He was Leo Shestov. I regarded him then and regard him now as one of the most remarkable men I was ever privileged to meet. His books were just beginning to appear, and I was particularly interested in his work on Nietzsche and Dostoevsky. We disagreed on many issues, but we were preoccupied with and disturbed by similar problems. Every time we met I was conscious of a real companionship with him, of a kind of existential communion, of a common concern. A close and intimate relationship between us continued later in Paris, where he died shortly before the last war.

Despite the great change which had begun in me, despite my growing interests outside the pale of the Marxist world, the period before my exile was also the time of my greatest popularity. When I delivered my first public lecture I was given a real ovation. This may have been due in part to my approaching exile to the north, already a matter of common knowledge. But later on I suffered a long period of equally great unpopularity, and became the object of a flood of attacks and abusive articles. As I have already said, the time before my exile was marked by the experience of great elation, and this mood, which prefigured my later spiritual re-orientation, persisted into the early period of my exile in Vologda. I ventured then to publish an article entitled 'The Struggle for Idealism', published in *Mir Bojii*, in which I conveyed something of this mood. As was to be expected, the article evoked indignation among the left-wing intelligentsia, particularly among those who belonged to the old school. The epigraph for the article was taken from my favourite play by Ibsen, *The Master-builder*, which in itself must have struck them as a monstrosity. This article was the signal for a break with the traditional outlook of the intelligentsia, and its worm's eye view of the world. I proclaimed the primacy of spiritual and aesthetic values, smothered and suppressed by them. I had a strange sensation of the approaching spiritual upheaval in Russia which marked the first decade of the twentieth century. The article in question also embodied an experience of the conflict between personality and society —an experience possibly more characteristic of me than of the other representatives of this upheaval. I felt an urge, familiar to me before, to withdraw into myself: I seemed to lose for a moment the taste for social intercourse, for large numbers of people, for too close contacts with the political stage and political organization. Whether in society or solitude, in conflict or co-operation, however, I was equally and invariably concerned with man, called to freedom and fulfilling his personal destiny.

Spirit which does not work in a fixed and accepted scheme of things makes its own special order out of its special kind of chaos. I had my own chaos, which was the chaos of Dionysiac elements, and which frequently defied the spirit. This did not spring from any Nietzschean influences: it was, more likely, evidence of my Russian blood. But the spirit (or was it reason and sobriety?) prevailed, which, in its turn, may have something to do with the fact that there is some French blood in my veins. It is typical, perhaps, that wine never went to my head; I could drink a great deal and remain quite sober, while the rest of a party was drunk. Similarly, I never felt carried away or was infected by mass-psychoses, by communal emotional experiences, such as processions or military and patriotic demonstrations. I am completely impervious to hypnosis.

Yet I am susceptible of intoxication from thought, from spiritual and intellectual vision. My resistance to Nietzsche's feeling for life was due to his stubborn 'earthiness' and 'this-worldliness', to his confinement within the closed circle of this world, which made his very intensity stuffy and suffocating. My own feeling for life is fundamentally 'other-worldly', or to be more precise, transcendent. During the latter part of his life Nietzsche turned almost completely positivist, even though his positivism was of a deeper kind than the current meaning of this word suggests; whereas I am pre-eminently a metaphysician. This accounts, perhaps, for my tendency to dualism, which, contrary to Nietzsche's own claims, is in no way typical of him.

I was not much interested in happiness, and I lacked that particular *joie de vivre* which accompanies a deep conviction or a new spiritual discovery and vision. Nevertheless, paradoxical though it is, I seem to have been endowed with immense vitality, and my imagination, my occasional moody inconsequence and readiness to admit change was probably evidence of this. And it is this vitality which accounts for a period in my life of almost wholesale surrender to the Dionysiac element. I became for a time the prey of spiritual and cultural decadence, which covered, roughly speaking, the latter part of my exile and a year or so after it—a tendency which was characteristic in some measure of

the whole movement that began in the 'nineties and entailed a substitution of beauty for truth and of individualism for social responsibility.

It is significant that the time of greatest vitality was accompanied for
me by a decrease in creative intensity: I wrote comparatively little. My
strength was spent on other things, and, as it were, canalized into other
directions. I came to be almost exclusively preoccupied with the liberation of individuality and with the affirmation of individual man over
against society. A fellow-exile of mine, a typical representative of the
revolutionary intelligentsia, said to me then: 'No one can say what will
crown the tower you want to build above the habitations of men—it
may even be beauty.' For him this evidently seemed a most terrible
prospect. In short, I was regarded as a 'dangerous individualist', despite
the fact that politically I remained a Social-Democrat with strong
leanings to the extreme left. I underwent a strong reaction against the
asceticism and austerity of the Russian revolutionary intelligentsia, an
asceticism which appeared to aim at a complete extinction of the flame
of life and prevented man from breathing freely. Moreover, I came into
conflict with a phenomenon, long before it made its appearance in the
open, which might be called the totalitarianism of the Russian intelligentsia, and which demanded the unreserved subjugation of personal
conscience to the conscience (if any) of the group or the collective.
Once, to take a rather trivial example, when a large group of exiles
arrived in Vologda, there arose amongst them the somewhat childish
question whether we should shake hands with the police-inspector; the
majority wanted to decide the question 'as a body'. But I insisted on
deciding this, or, for that matter, all other questions of a moral character, for myself. The revolutionary intelligentsia seemed to live all the
time under the shadow of military discipline; and, in view of its
peculiar mentality, this was perhaps the only way to keep alive. But I
preferred to fight on my own, and would not agree to accept any military orders or organized group-morality.

My 'individualism' was by no means devoid of a peculiar revolutionary impulse. Much of what I did was a deliberate challenge to my
surroundings in exile. At that time Vologda was an important centre
of political deportees, and under my eyes a very great number of exiles,
mostly Social-Democrats, but also some Social-Revolutionaries, were

stationed in the town or passed through it. There were some *en route* for other places in the province of Vologda. Sometimes they were taken further north to Archangel; while others returned from exile through the town. I was able to observe them at close quarters. Many of them came to see me at the 'Golden Anchor', the inn where I was staying. I liked them; they were fine people, wholly devoted to their idea or ideals. Yet in their company the atmosphere became jejune and oppressive—an atmosphere which seemed to force one into a strait-jacket and made it impossible to breathe. There were some among them who were well-informed and well-read, but the cultural level of the average exile was pretty low. I just could not feign enthusiasm for this whole mental atmosphere, and I do not think my reaction was evidence of any intellectual snobbery. The exiles, in their turn, looked down on me as a romantic, an 'aristocrat' and a 'black swan'.

Still, there were other 'exceptions' among the exiles of my time: there were Alexey Remizov, Peter Shegelev, Boris Savinkov (one of the heads of the terrorist organization of the Social Revolutionary party), Kistiakovsky (who came to meet his exiled wife), and a Dane, Madelung (who later became a well-known writer and was at that time representative of an oil company), and, finally, the Marxist philosopher and empiro-criticist Bogdanov, and Lunacharsky. The two last-named arrived shortly after me. Remizov, Shegelev, Savinkov, Madelung and myself were known by the catch-word 'the aristocracy', while Bogdanov and Lunacharsky were called 'the democracy'. The 'aristocracy' assumed a more independent attitude *vis-à-vis* the decisions, judgments and behaviour of our collective and did not shun contacts with the local society.

My relations with Bogdanov were rather strange. He was a very fine person, extremely sincere and absolutely devoted to his idea, but rather narrow-minded and constantly engaged in hair-splitting and sterile sophistry. I was already known for my hidden and overt 'Idealist' and 'metaphysical' tendencies, and Bogdanov regarded these as symptoms of psychic abnormality! He began to visit me very frequently and, whenever he saw me, kept on asking all sorts of odd questions, such as, How did I feel in the morning? How did I sleep? What was my reaction to this or that? It eventually emerged that in his view my philosophical tendencies were evidence of an impending psychic disorder, and he, being by profession a psychiatrist, wanted to discover how far the process had gone. The irony of it all was that subsequently Bogdanov himself suffered from a serious nervous disease and spent a considerable time in a mental home, whereas I have safely avoided this institution despite my 'Idealism'. I was no psychiatrist, but I soon noticed that Bogdanov was the victim of a mania. It was a case of a tame and quiet madness, due to an *idée fixe*. Bogdanov behaved with great nobility during the Bolshevik revolution. He was a veteran Bolshevik and for a time a trusted collaborator of Lenin, particularly in the publication of a number of symposiums and journals. But when Bolshevism came into its own, he was strongly repelled by some of its uglier by-products and did not conceal his reactions; in consequence he was given a very modest position when the communist *régime* had been constituted. He was much more radical and uncompromising than Lenin, especially in connection with the latter's conciliatory attitude towards the *petit bourgeois* democrats, and advocated a revision of Marxism.

Among the many people with whom I came into contact while in exile was a man who, at the height of the Revolution, became Commissar for the whole of northern Russia, and was well-known for his cruelty and blood-thirstiness. The surprising thing was that, although I was not on very intimate terms with him, he always gave me the impression of a considerate, kind and even meek person. Such virtues (especially the latter one), alas, sometimes bear ghastly fruits. At the time of my exile the process of revolutionary selection had barely begun, but it was largely among such people that Lenin found the men for the actual making of the revolution. To these men pity for suffering became proof of weakness, and they were prepared to dirty their clothes (and their consciences) in the dust of the revolutionary arena.

Another fellow-exile of mine was A., who also eventually became an active Bolshevik, and until recently was Soviet consul in Paris. He was a rather different type, and I remember him chiefly as an organizer of bottle-parties and gay evenings. One woman exile with whom I had personal relations was V., a rather remarkable person endowed with great intellectual power and an outstanding gift for philosophy, things rare in a woman. Apart from the diverse and heterogeneous company of the exiles, I used to frequent the house of the president of the local *Zemstvo*,[1] where I would sometimes meet liberally-minded government officials, as well as actors and actresses from the local theatre.

I must say that I enjoyed a somewhat favourable position in exile, since the then governor of Vologda was a distant relative of mine and a great friend of my uncle. Six weeks after my arrival I received a paper saying that I had the right to live in a town of my own choice, provided it were not a University town. I was very much surprised, but decided to refuse the offer and remained in Vologda. It transpired that my uncle and godfather, Prince Lopoukhine-Demidov, had expressed his indignation to the Grand Duke Vladimir Alexandrovich at the deportation of his darling nephew and godson to the province of Vologda, and requested my transfer to the south. The Grand Duke at once gave the necessary instructions to the Minister of the Interior and the Chief of the Military Police. This intervention resulted in the offer in question, which, however, I was unable to accept. Moreover, life in Vologda caused me no serious hardship; I even grew fond of this ancient little town with a character all its own, which had the additional charm of novelty, for I was wholly unacquainted with the northern parts of Great Russia. In the summer I used to bicycle on the outskirts of Vologda in the direction of the ruins of the old monastery. As a matter of fact, I felt quite happy there, perhaps even happier than in Kiev. The police did not disturb me in the least, and I managed to win my independence even in regard to the dictatorship of the exiles themselves.

My first book, *Subjectivism and Individualism in Social Philosophy*, appeared while I was in exile. It provoked a great deal of argument even among the Vologda exiles. Reviews of the book kept on coming to my notice, and it seemed to have made me quite famous, although most of the reviewers attacked me for one reason or another. (I remember that one of the hostile reviews in a newspaper was based on a misprint

[1] *Zemstvo* (plural *Zemstva*)—self-governing, elective provincial and district councils which were established by Alexander II and preceded by some fifteen years the county councils in Britain. They were responsible for a great number of progressive social measures. (Tr.)

in the text.) It was widely discussed in Marxist circles, and this was more
to the point. Thus it was that I found myself, along with some others,
at the head of the movement subsequently christened by Sergey Bulgakov 'From-Marxism-to-Idealism'. When I received a copy of my book,
however, it no longer satisfied me: I had by now moved further along
the road of 'Idealism' and was engrossed in metaphysical problems.

Before my exile I obtained special permission (I was on bail at the
time) to go to Petersburg. The very different circles with which I came
into contact throughout my life seem to have been significant of
my rather discordant social and cultural background. On this occasion I dined with my cousin, Prince Trepov, and a director of the
Ministry of the Interior; in the evening I saw Peter Struve and Turgan-
Baranovsky. Struve, the *doyen* of the intelligentsia at the time, and a
central figure in its mental evolution, whom I met for the first time,
appeared rather friendly and interested; he said in a letter to a friend
that he had 'great hopes' of me. But, though we were part of the same
movement of so-called critical Marxism, I occupied a much more
leftist position than he. Struve gave one the impression of being attracted by the doctrine of Marx because it seemed to him to provide an
historical justification for industrial capitalism. There was irony in the
fact that when I came to see him on that first occasion he was with
Skvortsov-Stepanov, later a well-known Bolshevik and editor of
Izvestia. Yet at the time of this meeting the position of both Skvortsov-
Stepanov and Struve was further to the right than my own. I did not
meet the former again after he became editor of *Izvestia*.

As a result of my visit to Petersburg I formed a literary connection
with that movement within 'critical Marxism' which had most leanings
towards Idealism, and which comprised such men as Bulgakov, whom,
however, I came to know rather later in Kiev, where he was professor
of political economy at the Polytechnic Institute (I was permitted to
go to Kiev for a short visit during my exile). When I met Bulgakov
he had already definitely adopted a religious position, and was a
Christian and a practising Orthodox. Struve was always much more of
a politician than I; and he certainly was a most brilliant political writer.
But I am inclined to think that, though responsible for the composition
of the programme of the newly formed Social-Democratic party, he

was never a true socialist at heart. Significantly enough, from 'legal' Marxism he moved to revolutionary liberalism; thence, after 1905, to an acceptance of post-Petrine Russian imperialism, and finished up as a reactionary in the 'emigration'. So far as Marxism was concerned, his views were at the time close to those of Eduard Bernstein,[1] whose book was causing a great stir and revealed a crisis in German Marxism. I shared Struve's critique of Marxism; but I also shared Marx's prophecy concerning a new world, even if my world was not to be brought about by some inevitable social process passing dialectically through revolutionary stages, but was one which ends the domination of fate, whether historical, political or economic, and springs from the free creative act of man. My revolutionary conviction was, therefore, primarily ethical in character and was fast evolving in that direction.

Apart from my book there were other and shorter essays which contributed to my worsening reputation among Marxist circles and the traditional intelligentsia of the Left in general: 'The Struggle for Idealism' and 'The Ethical Problem in the Life of Philosophical Idealism' written in Vologda and published in the symposium *The Problems of Idealism*, were two of the more objectionable ones. The symposium contained contributions by other ex-Marxists and 'neo-Idealists', as well as by some representatives of 'liberal' academic philosophy, such as Novgorodsev and the brothers Trubetskoy. My own article, prefaced by a quotation from Pushkin ('Thou art a king, live alone and freely tread the open road whither thy lordly mind induces thee'), was a first attempt to formulate the idea of personalism which came to be my *idée maîtresse* and which I developed and amplified in later writings, but it contained, also, a great deal of Kant and Nietzsche.

Prince Sergey Trubetskoy said of my article that he would never have consented to contribute to the symposium had he known that it would contain such an outburst of 'Nietzscheanism'. All this obviously did not increase my popularity among my friends, Marxist or otherwise. I began to be considered a traitor to Marxism, despite the fact that I had scarcely changed in my views on political and economic matters. I

[1] Author of *Die Voraussetzungen des Sozialismus*, which appeared in 1889 and marked a movement, within the Marxist fold, away from thoroughgoing economic determinism. (Tr.)

found myself expending a great deal of energy on the struggle with and criticism of the traditional outlook and ways of thought of the Russian intelligentsia. This was to me a struggle for the emancipation of the spirit, long crushed and held in subjection; but, as I have already pointed out, it impeded my constructive philosophical work and, in addition, sometimes led me into overstatements, which I would have avoided in other circumstances, and to polemical unfairness.

During the time immediately following my exile I felt rather depressed and weary: all creative energy seemed to desert me. I wrote very little, although, on the whole, I am a prolific writer and write without much difficulty. I was in a critical mood, which was not conducive to positive productivity. I was seeking for the mystery and the beauty of life, but my mind was weary of its search amid the overpowering prose and ugliness around, and some demon seemed to trample underfoot the image of beauty which appeared to me in instants of love and ecstasy. I also felt the acute pain of the ever-growing break with the circle of friends with whom my life was so intimately associated, and I had as yet found no new ones.

The hostility of the Social-Democrats as a whole did not, however, prevent me keeping a few personal contacts with them, but I kept none with the Liberals, who, in any case, were at all times rather uncongenial to me. The Social-Democrats disliked me because of my 'Idealism' and my aberrations into 'metaphysics', and they fulminated against me in print; the Liberals, on the other hand, merely scoffed ironically. The hostility of the former sprang from their belief in dogma, and, as believers, they were prepared to 'burn the heretic'. The latter were hostile because they themselves did not know their own minds, because they were absorbed in a high-falutin claim for detachment, tolerance, objectivity and 'good manners' (the searchings of the spirit being, of course, regarded as 'bad manners'—in fact, as nonsense, even if harmless nonsense); they were sceptical, but not sceptical of their own scepticism.

My original connection with the Liberals came about when I decided to take part in the 'movement of liberation' and, for this reason, joined the League of Liberation. I knew the leader of the League personally, and vaguely sympathized with his ideas. I went to two conferences in 1903 and 1904, when the League came into being. The conferences were held respectively in Schwarzwald and Schaffhausen, beside the Rhine waterfalls. To be frank, the beauty of the surrounding country was more to my liking than the conferences. It was there that I first became acquainted with the Liberal circles grouped round the *Zemstva*. Later on many of them played an active part as members of the opposition in the Duma, and some of them joined the coalition of the Provisional Government of 1917. They included a number of outstanding people, but their readiness to compromise, their snobbish attachment to 'good form' and their kow-towing to the workers[1] made me feel uneasy in their midst. I shall not embark here on detailed reminiscences of the League of Liberation; I want to add, however, that even when some of its elements became the backbone of the party of the Cadets, for some time the most radical political body in the field, I never joined it, partly because I was, in any case, not much of a politician (though I was never indifferent to politics), but mainly because it was in its whole spirit too 'bourgeois' for my liking. I continued to regard myself as a socialist, even while a member—first in Kiev and later in Petersburg— of the Committee of the League of Liberation. I remained always conscious of a gulf dividing me from the Liberals—a gulf deeper than that which divided me from the Social-Revolutionaries and the Social-Democrats. Nonetheless, my attitude did not prevent me from carrying on negotiations on behalf of the League with the Social-Democrats, for example, with X., then a Menshevik, and subsequently a People's Commissar in the Soviet Government and an ambassador, as well as with Martov[2] and with the spokesman of the Jewish League.

As to my other public activities, these began when I first came to Petersburg. I made speeches at political gatherings and took the chair at meetings. Looking back on these days I cannot help remembering a feeling that my voice did not ring true whenever I appeared in that setting and that, in a sense, I deceived myself in assuming a part which did not suit me. The fact that I moved at a great speed away from the whole outlook of the intelligentsia (and eventually even from Idealism)

---

[1] Plekhanov, in his exuberant manner, said of them that they 'can do nothing but contemplate the posterior of the working-class'.

[2] Social-Democrat, an old comrade and later an enemy of Lenin. He became the leader of the 'Internationalist Mensheviks' in the first Soviet Assembly. (Tr.)

only served to enhance my sense of uneasiness and incongruity. The slightest move which revealed a spiritual re-orientation in the minds of a few members of the intelligentsia was regarded as politically reactionary. But the unfairness and the absurdity of this kind of valuation was demonstrated by the fact, for instance, that when the Idealist group, having broken with the positivism of the intelligentsia, started a journal called *Voprosy Zhizni* (*Questions of Life*), some of those very people who accused the group of reaction came to contribute to the journal. Thus it was that the Idealist movement won itself the right to citizenship in the eyes of Left public opinion. It was not easy to fume against and slander in print the same people with whom plans for the liberation of Russia were being worked out.

The generation which followed the revolution of 1905 did not experience all these conflicts and contentions. By then much ground had been won for the rights of spiritual and cultural values. The persistent conservatism of the intelligentsia, with its rigid materialistic and positivistic orthodoxy and agnosticism, had been shaken and already looked naïve and old-fashioned. Wider and wider circles of the intelligentsia became involved in the crisis, which eventually produced a wholesale shift in the mode of consciousness. This made itself felt most particularly in the growing awareness of aesthetic values, in the gradual substitution of aestheticism for public utility and in an intense search for new forms of art. As to the revolution of 1905 itself—an event which proved a turning-point in the cultural development in Russia—it became a source of real agony to me. The revolution, in my view, was quite inevitable; I welcomed it and disagreed with the Mensheviks who had given it half-hearted and lukewarm support, lamented its having been attempted, and accused its participants of embarking on 'adventures'. Nevertheless, these were not 'days of freedom'; indeed, to me they brought a sense of moral and spiritual suffocation. The atmosphere of bloody slaughter seemed to hover over one's mind, and the massacre of many thousands of revolutionaries and workers seemed to kill the last remnants of hope not only in the Tsarist *régime* but in the revolution itself and in the possibility of any change on this basis.

After the revolution the 'heroic' period in the history of the Russian intelligentsia came to an end. Their traditional attitude to life and to the world—their asceticism, their narrowness, their moral rigorism and their stuffy political religiosity—was shaken at its roots, and, in certain sections of the intelligentsia, an unmistakable moral disintegration set in as a result of disappointment in the revolution. To me this provided evidence for my own profound conviction that every political revolution is doomed and becomes stupefied by its own surfeit: the subject of true revolution must be man, rather than the masses or the body politic; and only a personalistic revolution can be properly called 'revolution'. Indeed, the radicalism of a revolution is in proportion to its personalistic, 'aristocratic' character. And the attempt to attain freedom by means of denying freedom to oneself or to others is doomed to failure. The failure of the 1905 revolution only served to intensify my longing for the revolution of the spirit.

In an article I wrote in 1907, re-published as part of my book, *The Spiritual Crisis of the Intelligentsia*, I foresaw with considerable accuracy that when the real hour for revolution in Russia struck the Bolsheviks would win the day. I did not imagine, like so many others, that a successful Russian revolution would be accompanied by the triumph of freedom and humanitarianism. Long before 1917 I wrote of my conviction that this revolution would, in fact, entail a supreme and terrible sacrifice of man's freedom. Such was to be the tragedy of the historical destiny of Russia . . . I withdrew entirely from politics and devoted myself entirely to the struggle for the spirit in face of the still prevalent inertia and blindness of the intelligentsia. But social problems did not cease to exercise my conscience and imagination, and, from time to time, I threw myself into the social battle. Much later, as an *émigré* abroad, I reverted to some of the most radical social and political ideas of my youth, but then they rested on a new and firmer spiritual foundation. Of this I shall have more to say at a later stage. At any rate I am conscious that I have always been and still am a revolutionary, and the very reasons which made me a revolutionary brought me up against the pseudo-revolution and the pseudo-revolutionaries of early twentieth century Russia. I understood that 'spirit' signifies freedom and revolution, while 'matter' spells necessity and reaction, and spreads reaction in the minds and hearts of the revolutionaries themselves. This is, in fact, the crucial problem underlying the demonic logic of the 'Grand

Inquisitor': men are all too ready to renounce spirit for the sake of bread (though it is not the business of those who have bread to denounce this logic in the face of those who have not). It is a problem which was intensely relevant on the stage of Russia's pre-revolutionary and revolutionary history, but it is no less, if not more relevant now on the stage of world-history.

I want to add here a few words on a question I was frequently led to ask in connection with some of the things described in this chapter, viz. the question of tolerance and intolerance. I think this question is largely one of temperament, and my temperament seems to have embodied and displayed both these qualities. I do not belong to the type of dogmatic orthodox (whatever form the orthodoxy may assume), which is commonly known as intolerant, fanatical, obdurate and inflexible. I am not a die-hard who takes no denial and flies in the face of life. Above all, I have always had an intense and spontaneous feeling for the sacred character of man's conscience and for the utter freedom of his religious and intellectual convictions.

Yet when I came up against violence done to the freedom and the spirit of man, or to other values which I considered precious and inviolable, I became extremely intolerant and even broke off relations with friends who perpetrated such crimes.

The combination of these two qualities gave rise to wrong and contradictory opinions about me. Man is, indeed, a being riddled with contradictions. I used to react violently and angrily against certain ideological tendencies; and there were certain questions which it was almost impossible to discuss with me. I have myself been the victim of my violent and contradictory temperament, and I made others its victims. My intransigence, however, was of a moral rather than a dogmatic character, although it could on occasion be aimed against moralists and legalists, whom I have never been able to stand. On the other hand, I never felt inclined to condemn people personally, that is to say, for reasons which concern their individual lives. As a matter of fact, I was very sympathetic and indulgent in this respect, and, for that reason, even became an easy target for attacks by other, more exacting, austere and virtuous people.

CHAPTER VI

THE RUSSIAN CULTURAL RENASCENCE OF THE EARLY TWENTIETH CENTURY.   ENCOUNTERS

In the autumn of 1904 I moved to St. Petersburg to take over the editorship of a new periodical. Before my departure an event took place which brought about a great change in my life: I met my life-long friend, Lydia. After a salutary experience of revolutionary enthusiasm she became a believing Christian: indeed, she seemed naturally predisposed to a religious conviction, and her faith proved on more than one occasion a tower of strength and support to me. She was endowed with remarkable spiritual gifts, and towards the end of her life approached sanctity. At the height of the communist revolution she became a convert to Roman Catholicism and passed through a phase of fanatical and intolerant religious dogmatism. Later her religious temper changed, and her attitude became more congenial to me: she was willing to admit her membership of the Church which transcends the limits of narrow confessionalism. Lydia was also endowed with a vivid poetical imagination and possessed unmistakable poetical gifts. She wrote a number of poems, a few of which were published, but she lacked any literary ambitions. Mikhail Gershenzon[1] and Vyacheslav Ivanov[2] thought highly of Lydia's poetry.

My other life-long friend was Lydia's sister, Genia, who came to live with us in 1914 and has been our companion ever since. She shouldered all my practical responsibilities, and I was sustained throughout my life by her infinite goodness, patience and understanding. She has a searching and sensitive mind and a discerning spirit. Constant illness failed to impede the intensity of her spiritual life and intellectual interest. Her friendship was of great significance for me. In accordance with the

[1] A writer and literary critic whose biographical and historical studies revived an interest in the Russian Idealists of the thirties and forties of the last century. (Tr.)

[2] See below. (Tr.)

character of this autobiography I shall confine myself to these brief remarks concerning my private life at the period in question and pass on to matters which are of more general interest.

It was at this time, that is to say, about the time of my arrival in Petersburg, that the meeting occurred between the ex-Marxist Idealists and the spokesmen of the new religious movement to which was attached the somewhat spectacular label *Novoye Religyóznoye Soznanye* (The New Religious Consciousness), and which centred round 'the Merezhkovskys' (a term including, beside Dimitri Merezhkovsky himself, his wife, the poetess Zinaida Gippius, and their friend Dimitri Filosofov), who were the principal editors of *Novy Put'* (The New Way). The plan for the new periodical, to which I have referred above, and which I was to edit, was worked out by Sergey Bulgakov and myself. We decided to make use of the already existing *New Way* by modifying and incorporating new elements into it. The group originally in charge of *The New Way* and the Idealists had many things in common, yet this journal was primarily concerned with literary matters, while we intended it to be also an organ of philosophical and political thought. A compromise solution was found by entrusting the literary section of the new journal to the group from the original *New Way*, whilst we were in charge of the philosophical and political side of it. The compromise, however, proved unstable: it concealed too diverse and conflicting elements. After a number of issues the combined journal had to be discontinued. It was succeeded by a new journal, *Voprosy Zhizni* (Questions of Life), which, however, in the difficult conditions obtaining in the early days of the revolution was only able to exist for a year. The editor of this journal was Dmitry Zhukovsky and its literary editor Georgi Chulkov.

Questions of Life was a wholly new attempt at representing current trends, but without falling a victim to their sectional interests. It was a new phenomenon in the history of Russian periodical publications. In view of the inherent tendency among Russians to quarrel on account of intellectual differences, such an undertaking was fraught with tremendous difficulties. The journal undertook the formidable task of giving expression to the crisis in the world outlook of the intelligentsia; to the spiritual searchings of the time; to the movement towards

Christianity, and to the change in the climate of religious opinion. It also provided a forum for the new trends in literature which had no access to the older journals, as well as to the political aspirations of the left-wing 'League of Liberation' and of the liberally-minded socialists.

On arrival in Petersburg I entered a literary world which I had formerly only known by hearsay. I always tended to expect—perhaps rather naïvely—something of a miracle as a result of meeting other people. I now found myself immersed in the highly charged and intense atmosphere of the early twentieth century Russian cultural renascence. Much of what I encountered in this new atmosphere recalled my former experience of 'Dionysian' *Sturm und Drang*. It is not easy now to re-capture the atmosphere of that time, and in trying to do so I am running the risk of striking too high a note. Much of that creative inspiration and enthusiasm has entered into, and become the permanent ingredient of, Russian culture, and, consequently, represents the heritage of all Russians, whatever their private reactions may be. But at the time we were simply carried away by a wave of almost ecstatic creative experiences, by new problems and new challenges which seemed to press in upon us from all sides. It was a time of the awakening of independent and original philosophical thought, of intense poetical imagination and aesthetic sensibility; it was a time marked by a profound spiritual disquiet and religious searching, and by wide-spread interest in mysticism and even occultism. We saw the glow of a new dawn, and the end of an old age seemed to coincide with a new era which would bring about a complete transfiguration of life.

But such moods were prevalent only in comparatively restricted circles, cut off from the wide and far-reaching social changes which were taking place at the time. There were unmistakable signs of incipient decadence in the whole movement: sometimes it seemed to breathe the atmosphere of a hothouse with no door or window open to the fresh air. We were in fact witnesses not of the beginning of a new era but of the end of an old one, and we were troubled by a sense of the approaching collapse of old Russia. And, significantly enough, while moved and inspired by great visions, we experienced no real joy. Moreover, signs of genuine creativeness were accompanied by mere fashions and imitations. For many it became simply a matter of *comme il faut* to be an aesthete or a mystic, or a 'seeker after God'. Moral values failed to impress anybody, and science was held in contempt. A belated rationalist or positivist could scarcely even hope for success in his love affairs: just as in the 'forties only an idealist or a romantic could be sure of success in such matters; in the 'sixties a materialist or a rationalist; in the 'seventies a 'populist' who had offered himself as a sacrifice for the liberation of 'the people'; or in the 'nineties a Marxist.

The principal cultural and spiritual tendencies were of a distinctly romantic nature, though it was the case of a peculiar Russian romanticism. Romantic aestheticism found its expression in Symbolist painting, poetry and art criticism. Russian literature of the early twentieth century broke with the ethical tradition of the preceding age. The Russian critics of the older generation were informed with lofty moral ideals, but they were lacking in true artistic culture and aesthetic feeling. The revival of aesthetic values and metaphysical interest brought about a new understanding of the Russian literary heritage and contributed to a deeper appreciation of such writers as Tolstoy and Dostoevsky. This can be clearly seen from Merezhkovsky's best work, *Tolstoy and Dostoevsky*, which I read with great interest before I came to Petersburg. Alexander Volynsky was one of the pioneers of the new trend in literary criticism: he attacked the prevalent 'social radicalism' in artistic appreciation, broke with literary 'enlightenment' in the name of philosophical idealism and aestheticism, and challenged the authority of Dobrolyubov, Chernishevsky and Pisarev, who still exercised a considerable influence among the intelligentsia. His work cannot, however, be regarded as of any great literary value; his philosophical position was vague and he lacked a sense of historical perspective. Nevertheless he had the courage to oppose standing literary orders, which cost him dearly: he was 'expelled from literature' at the instigation of Mikhailovsky.

Dimitri Merezhkovsky carried more weight: his book on Tolstoy and Dostoevsky produced a great impression, and it was the most important and readable thing he ever wrote. Like all his works, it was a brilliantly constructed, perhaps over-constructed, attempt to disclose a religious meaning in the creative work of these two great Russian geniuses. He stimulated a search for new or forgotten values in literature. The other figure usually associated with the new movement was Vassili Rozanov, who had begun to write already in the nineties. His true significance, however, was to emerge only later, as a result of his contributions to the 'religious-philosophical meetings' and to the journal *The New Way*. He was less active and prominent than Merezhkovsky, but as a figure in Russian literary history he is much more important.

The origins of the new movement are various, no less various than the currents which constitute it. The Russian sources are indicated by the two names of Tolstoy and Dostoevsky, and in part by that of Solovyev: the influence of the West came *via* Nietzsche and the French Symbolists. The new trends in philosophy were likewise under the influence of Tolstoy and Dostoevsky, particularly of the latter, and philosophical works often took the form of commentaries on Dostoevsky. The philosophical movement marked a search for and return to the original traditions of Russian thought as expressed in the work of these two novelists, as well as of the Slavophils and Vladimir Solovyev. This is true of my own philosophical thinking, despite its frankly revolutionary character and its Marxist antecedents. As I have already noted, I broke with the left-wing intelligentsia, but preserved its professed social and intellectual radicalism. The impact of Nietzsche, which in other Russian writers issued in vitalism, immoralism or the mythological theories of Vyacheslav Ivanov, prompted me to an increasing concern with moral problems. I read Nietzsche in the light of Ibsen and Ibsen in the light of Nietzsche. My mind was also greatly enriched by my association with Leo Shestov and Sergey Bulgakov. On my arrival in Petersburg I was, in fact, faced with intellectual vistas hitherto unknown to me. What impressed me most was the general intellectual and cultural expanse, rather than the weight of this or that philosophical or literary contribution.

Very soon, however, I became aware of something unwholesome in the prevailing atmosphere. No participant, and certainly no thinking observer, can imagine that so fundamental a cultural transformation could anywhere take place smoothly. But its most dangerous disease was some deep-rooted ambiguity—a divided mind and a divided consciousness. Men seemed to have lost their capacity for free choice; their eyes were blinded by their own powerful experiences. They were torn rather than illumined by the mysterious forces of which they were suddenly made aware and which surround and pervade human life and endeavour.

The principal contributors to *Questions of Life*, which became the organ of the new movement with all its varied ramifications, were, apart from the editors (Bulgakov and myself) the following writers: Merezhkovsky, Rozanov, Anton Kartashov, Ivanov, Fyodor Sologub, Alexander Blok, Andrey Bely, Valery Bryusov, Aleksey Remizov, Chulkov, Gershenzon, Simeon Frank, Struve, Prince Evgeni Trubetskoy, Pavel Novgorodsev, Fyodor Zelinsky, Volynsky and Vladimir Ern. Its political section was represented by radical liberals (*Osvobozhdentsy*) and the less doctrinaire social-democrats. It is distressing to me that, as I recall these colleagues of mine from *Questions of Life*, I realize that only a very few of them have remained my friends: most of the others I regard at present as my ideological opponents. Some of them, such as Merezhkovsky and Struve, are openly hostile to me and consider me a 'Bolshevik', whatever that may mean. No doubt, divergencies were already implicit in the original constitution of the group. There was, for example, a number of contributors writing on political and economic matters, who were isolated and had little in common with the central aims and aspirations of the journal.

However intense my subsequent estrangement from and even conflict with the Merezhkovskys, my meeting with them was of considerable importance for me, and I enjoyed a period of intense, even if short, intercourse with them (my relationship with Zinaida Gippius was indeed one of real friendship). I do not fully understand how it came about that we arrived at a stage when it was practically impossible to carry on a conversation or even to see one another. We were undoubtedly very different in temperament as well as in conviction; but much, I think, was also due to the aggressive attitude taken up by one side or the other. The Merezhkovskys always tended to form their own group, or even clique, of friends, on whom they relied implicitly to share and profess their ideas; and when someone on whom they had thus pinned their hopes left them or even ventured to criticize their ideas in print, they repudiated him. They were urged by a subtle love of power, and thought and lived in an atmosphere of unhealthy, self-assertive sectarian mysticism.

During the winter of 1905 I spent many long evenings in conversation with Zinaida Gippius, and later we carried on a stimulating correspondence. Even now I have a genuine affection and admiration for her, although we never meet. One of her peculiar characteristics was a profound understanding of others, blended with a capacity for inflicting pain on them. There was something snake-like about her. She was fragile, subtle, brilliant and entirely devoid of human warmth. She embodied an uncomfortable combination of the feminine and the masculine elements, and it was difficult to ascertain which was the stronger. Her femininity expressed itself mainly in her wilfulness and a somewhat capricious wit. She was by nature an unhappy person, capable of great suffering as well as of making others suffer. Apart from literary criticism, the most adequate instrument of her thought was her verse, but her outlook and attitude to life were definitely non-poetic; and this is true of the whole period—a period of poets *par excellence*, and yet strangely devoid of the poetic spirit. One 'poetic' quality which imposed itself then was extreme egocentricity and a kind of narcissism which, to be frank, were very distasteful to me. With Merezhkovsky himself I had no personal relationship, I even doubt whether such relationships were at all possible with him. He never listened to anyone and did not even take notice of other people. The Merezhkovskys' drawing-room was not a place where you would meet a real person, though it was frequented by a multitude of people; one felt absorbed by an impersonal whole. There was a kind of magic spell over-shadowing their lives—something similar to the atmosphere prevailing at the gatherings of mystical sects. Later I was to meet with the same phenomenon among the anthroposophists.

The Merezhkovskys always claimed to speak in the name of a hypothetical, mysterious 'we', into communion with whom they aspired to draw their friends. Filosofov was one of them; Andrey Bely nearly became another one. They called this 'we' the 'secret three', which in their imagination was destined to be the nucleus of the new Church of the Holy Spirit, in which 'the mystery of the flesh' awaited final manifestation. My personalist frame of mind, or, as it was sometimes mis-

takenly called, my individualism, was bound to come into conflict with
this strange mythology, and I was in every way unfit to take part in
the esoteric 'we'. Nevertheless, I did share some of their religious preoccupations, and inevitably found myself a spokesman of 'the new
religious consciousness', which indeed, in a measure, I remain even now.

My reaction against the Merezhkovsky atmosphere speeded me on
my way to the Orthodox Church, and other phenomena with which
I met and which I was bound to oppose in Petersburg at the time,
helped in the process. Even before I came to Petersburg, however, my
interest had already been aroused by the 'religious-philosophical meetings', in which representatives of the Russian Orthodox Church took
part. I had even written an article about these meetings in the journal
Osvobozhdenye (Liberation), although I did not sign it with my name.
These 'meetings' were very remarkable in that they marked the first
attempt at co-operation between the spokesmen of Russian thought
and literature, on the one hand, and the members of the hierarchy representing the traditional, even if progressive, elements in the Orthodox
Church, on the other. The Metropolitan Sergius, subsequently patriarchal *locum tenens* and late patriarch of the Russian Church, acted as
chairman at these meetings. The principal theme of discussion was the
relation between Christianity and culture, prompted by Ternavtsev's
book on the Apocalypse, which had just been published. This was followed by another theme associated with the names of Merezhkovsky
and Rozanov (whose concern in the matter, however, was more genuine than Merezhkovsky's), namely the problem of the body and sex.
I attached enormous importance not so much to the problems in themselves as to the need of openly confronting the new issues raised by
these problems from the Christian standpoint, and I felt that my own
approach to Christianity was in part dependent on such confrontation.
But as a philosopher I could not help detecting a confusion of ideas
from the way in which the problems in question were treated. Merezhkovsky was particularly guilty of such confusion by way of his in-
geniously designed but artificial antithesis of 'flesh' and 'spirit'. I challenged him many times on this point; but it was a futile effort on my
part, since Merezhkovsky was almost ecstatically enamoured of his
verbal constructions. In my view, the confusion arose from the fact

that, in reality and despite Merezhkovsky's protestations, the history of Christianity has been characterized not so much by a lack as by a superabundance of the flesh at the expense of the spirit. And for me, the 'new religious consciousness' opened up the possibility of re-affirming the primacy of spirit. Actually, the very antithesis of spirit and flesh is an erroneous one. The real problem lies elsewhere, namely in the opposition of freedom and necessity. Merezhkovsky's inflated insistence on the 'sanctity of the flesh' was, in the last resort, a reactionary posture hostile to freedom and personality. I came up against this problem in a different context in my encounter with Pavel Florensky in Moscow.

Despite my instinctive repudiation of the magical atmosphere around the Merezhkovskys, I was nevertheless profoundly impressed and attracted by their intense awareness of ideas, and by a complete absence in them of the commonplace. I remained quite impervious to their magical sophistication, and persisted, even in this dense atmosphere, in my original pursuit of the values of freedom and personality, which were if anything endangered by the hysterical naturalism of Merezhkovsky. In the end the Petersburg days only served to intensify my negative attitude *vis-à-vis* the forces which aspire to submerge or subdue personality, and make of man a victim of impersonal abstractions.

The manifold and colourful movement of the time touched me only superficially. I sought contacts with new people; I wanted to gain new insights, to extend my knowledge, to re-live the historical and cultural experience of my time; but at some deeper level I never lost a sense of loneliness in the very midst of these to-and-fro movements of an intense spiritual revival. It is not surprising, therefore, that I provoked criticism and even irritation among those who had completely identified themselves with these movements, and gave rise to mistaken judgments about my attitude. I desired to understand from within the spiritual and cultural currents of the age and to comprehend their significance, but I did not and could not surrender myself completely to them. The same was and is true of my position in regard to Marxism and to Orthodoxy. I was invariably driven into myself and thereby disappointed those who expected undivided compliance and non-resistance on my part. This may have been a sign of weakness as much as of strength on my part; but the weakness, if weakness it be, was not apathetic scepticism. Indeed, the creative literary movement at the beginning of the century stimulated me immensely: it provided me with fresh themes; it posed new problems and deepened my understanding; and I owe much to the people with whom I came into close contact in the course of these years. I succeeded, however, in remaining sober among the intoxicated, and thereby offered provocation to those whose temulent state deprived them of their critical faculties. Neither the pressure of occult influences in my early youth, nor the totalitarian enthusiasm of the social-democrat revolutionaries, nor 'the new religious consciousness' of the Merezhkovskys, nor the gnostic sectarianism of the anthroposophists, nor the mystagogical Orthodoxy of Pavel Florensky, nor the powerful spell of revolutionary Bolshevism, were capable of taking full possession of me and of forcing me to renounce conscience and freedom of the spirit. In the circumstances it was somewhat paradoxical that friends and foes alike suspected me of being the adept of some occult or esoteric society, a furtive Freemason or what-not.

My rebelliousness prompted me on occasion not only to defy demonstratively the demands made by the circles in which I moved and with which I was supposed to identify myself, but to sever all connections and move to another town so as to be able to remain free and unfettered. Few things were more repulsive to me than the stuffy, hothouse atmosphere of the literary circles, where one's allotted rôle was to feed the egocentric appetite of the poets who lived for men's praise of their verse; neither could I stand the intensification of occult enthusiasm in the closed and impassable horizons of a self-styled Church of the Holy Spirit. In one respect, however, I did yield to the temptation of the intellectual and spiritual movements of the time: I became less preoccupied with social problems. This may have been partly due to my mood subsequent to my conflict with Marxist circles, which did their best to impede my search for the things of the spirit. But it was in keeping with the absence of any real sense of social responsibility among the élite of the cultural renascence.

It cannot be denied that in one respect at least Merezhkovsky's work was of great importance: he introduced, and was himself expressive of, a whole unknown or forgotten world of cultural values, of Greek and

Roman antiquity, of the Italian Renaissance, of French literature, of Nietzsche and Ibsen, even if he lacked the spiritual earnestness of some other members of the new cultural élite. At the same time he embodied the intense polarity which is characteristic of the Russian mind, but which was blurred by generations of positivistically-minded Russians. This polarity found its expression in Merezhkovsky's love of antithesis: 'Christ and Antichrist', 'spirit and flesh', 'the abyss above and the abyss below', 'West and East', and so on. Unfortunately his polarities assumed the form of a kind of see-saw of scholastic contrapositions and were evidence of a fundamentally-divided, disintegrated consciousness, which has lost its capacity for choice and action. Merezhkovsky may have, in his usual high-pitched voice, called others to action; but his ideas provided no basis for any action whatsoever. None of the traditional concern of Russian literature for moral truth and justice had any place in Merezhkovsky's voluminous work. In his book on Tolstoy and Dostoevsky, for instance, there are some interesting pages on Tolstoy's artistic creativity; but it is, in the main, a shallow attack on Tolstoy: Merezhkovsky is quite insensitive to the justice of Tolstoy's cause against the lies and falsehood at the heart of human history and civilization. He is obsessed by his concern for justifying and sanctifying the 'flesh' of history, as others after him, particularly Florensky and the Orthodox of the new school, tried to do. He was devoid of the qualities of pity and compassion which are so characteristic of the Russians; he dismissed them as 'Buddhistic'.

Generally speaking Merezhkovsky professed a kind of Nietzschean Christianity, but without Nietzsche's aristocratism and intense awareness of the pain of human existence. His Nietzscheanism was a glorified religion of flesh and sex. But he himself suffered if anything from a lack of 'flesh': he was essentially a sexless creature, and his declamations and proclamations concerning the sanctity of sex were mental and aesthetic attempts at self-compensation. He often used the word 'freedom'; but no freedom could be detected in his flesh-worship. It was this which I found hardest of all to accept. For freedom is spirit and not flesh, which, more often than not, spells the enslavement of man. Freedom is attained neither through ascetic denial nor through naturalistic glorification of the flesh, but through inwardness, whereby no part of man's nature is external to him. Merezhkovsky was quite right in speaking of the truth and rightness of the love between Anna Karenina and Vronsky as against the falsehood of Karenin's legalism and pharisaism. But in my view this problem should be seen in terms of the struggle for the freedom and dignity of man against the order of law and authority, which falsifies human relationships and degrades man; whereas Merezhkovsky smothered it in the scholastic constructions of his mystical naturalism.

Vassili Rozanov (his name is usually associated with that of Merezhkovsky, but he is a much more significant figure in the history of Russian thought), also professed a naturalism, although he did not attempt to present his ideas as a new version of Christianity. His return to the pre-Christian, Jewish and pagan, religion of sex, however, was equally hostile to freedom and was a betrayal of the human person. Sex which is not integrated in and transfigured by spirit is always evidence of man's subjugation to the genus. Rozanov simply ignores human personality, although he possessed an inimitable gift for describing living human beings. For him life does not triumph through the resurrection of man into eternity, but through childbirth, in other words, through a process of disintegration whereby the human person is subsumed in the succession of new generations, in the continuation of the human race. Rozanov believed in a religion of eternal birth, and Christianity for him was identical with the religion of death, because, in his view, it implies a fundamental rejection, or at least a mere half-hearted acceptance, of sex and procreation. Merezhkovsky, on the other hand, was not concerned with procreation, or with nature for that matter. He was not a child of nature like Rozanov, but a feeble, sophisticated, *fin-de-siècle* intellectual, whose sexological theories became a repository of unconsummated erotic aspirations. But I should like at this point to say more about Rozanov.

Vassili Vassilyevich Rozanov was in every respect a most unusual figure, certainly the most unusual figure I have ever known. He embodied many typically Russian characteristics, and yet he was quite unlike anyone else. I often thought that he could have been conceived in the imagination of Dostoevsky; indeed, he was in some ways another version of Fyodor Karamazov turned writer and publicist. His external appearance was that of a red-haired peasant from Kostroma (actually, he was born in the province of Kostroma, and spent most of his early life in the capital of that province). He was exasperating, childish, vulgar, highly imaginative and extremely intelligent. As he talked he lisped, and from time to time he would eject a spray of saliva. He sometimes uttered the most surprising thoughts, whispering in your ear and spluttering all the while.

I greatly admired his books, for he was a writer of the first order and of exceptional originality. His most brilliant literary flights are usually contained in foot-notes and marginal comments to articles and essays of other writers. He is probably the greatest Russian prose-writer. His literary manner has the freedom and the richness of living speech, with its subtle shades of intonation, its undertones and overtones. He seemed to wield an almost magic power over words. But it is impossible either to translate or to expound him.

We had a genuine affection for each other. He used to call me 'Adonis' and sometimes 'the gentleman', and addressed me always as 'thou'. He wrote no less than fourteen articles on my book *The Meaning of the Creative Act*, most of which were attacks on what he called the Western spirit, with which I was supposed to be infected. Our views and our attitudes to life were at opposite poles. But I greatly valued Rozanov's critique of historical Christianity and his exposure of Christian hypocrisy in regard to sex. Inasmuch, however, as Rozanov's anti-Christianity was identical with his own naturalistic religion of sex, procreation, marriage and the family, I found myself decidedly on the Christian side, that is to say, in this case, on the side of personality as against the genus, and on the side of the freedom of the spirit as against the objectification of the flesh, which betrays and destroys the image of man. Rozanov did not fight the Church: indeed, he was profoundly moved by all the associations of the Russian Church, with its imagery, its patterns of piety, its warmth and ritual richness. He fought Christ himself, the crucified Lord who revealed the ultimate mystery of death. Rozanov used to say that he preferred a burning wax candle to God. A candle can be seen, touched, held in one's hand; while God is abstract and inaccessible to the human eye. He loved to invite priests to dinner to share his habitual plate of fish. His favourite company was the married clergy, who understood scarcely anything of his ideas but never seemed to bore him. Rozanov's attitude was another proof (if proofs are necessary) of the fact that 'the flesh' has not too small but too large a place in the life of the Church. This fact may have rejoiced Rozanov, but it repelled me.

When, on my initiative, a religious-philosophical society was founded in Petersburg, I read a paper at its first meeting entitled 'Christ and the World', which was directed against Rozanov's remarkable essay, *Concerning Sweetest Jesus and the Bitter Fruits of the World*; but this duel did not disturb our good relations. He was very fond of Lydia. About a month before his death, at the height of the communist revolution, Rozanov came to see us in Moscow and spent the night at our house. He made a painful impression: he talked incessantly without much sense, and yet, at times, he was absolutely brilliant. I remember him whispering in my ear: 'I am praying to God, but not to yours: to Osiris, Osiris'. Some of the Russian men of letters (among them Solovyev) despised him and charged him with moral perversity and opportunism. The latter charge was due to his practice of writing, under different names, political articles for conflicting factions. I think, however, that fundamentally he remained true to himself. He was hardly interested in politics as such: he was interested in the 'atmosphere', 'taste', and 'flavour' of politics or politicians rather than in political ideologies. But his principal contribution is to the discussion of the problem of sex, and he had remarkable intuitions about Judaism and Paganism in this connection.

I once wrote an article about Rozanov entitled 'On the Eternal Feminine in the Russian Soul'. Rozanov's genius is, indeed, completely devoid of the masculine virtues of discipline and form; his thinking was not logical but physiological; and his whole being was immersed in a kind of mystical sensuousness. He constantly provoked the charge of naked shamelessness, and many find him unspeakably shocking or even disgusting. Nevertheless, he is one of the most remarkable Russian figures and one of our greatest writers.

On the whole the advocates of Christian orthodoxy have failed to grapple with or even face the problems which tortured Rozanov. He himself was instinctively drawn to the conservatives, for the intellectual agnosticism and drab moralism of the radicals repelled him; but his conservative friends were equally afraid of him. I noticed, however, that right-wing Orthodox preferred Rozanov to Vladimir Solovyev, and forgave him much they would not forgive in prouder men. It was difficult to have any stable relations with Rozanov, because his own nature was so incredibly unbalanced; but I shall always remember him with warm affection.

The misfortune of the Russian renascence of the early twentieth century lay in the isolation of its cultural *élite* from the wider social movements of the time—a fact which proved fatal in the light of subsequent developments during the Russian Revolution. I also felt isolated, although my social instinct never became completely dormant, and I did not altogether sever my connections with the social-democrats. The Russians of that time lived, as it were, on different levels, or even, one might say, in different ages. The renascence shed hardly any light into the wider regions of social life. The attitude of the left intelligentsia, on the other hand, not only of the social-revolutionaries but also of the liberal-radicals, was one of drab, moral respectability and political stringency, and they failed to reflect the profound cultural changes. True, many adherents and spokesmen of the renascence sympathized with the Revolution (even Rozanov wrote a book during the events of 1905 full of praise of the revolutionary movement), but they lost a sense of proportion in their concern for the new problems of a philosophical, aesthetic and mystical character, neglected by those who for generations have been engaged in the social struggle. This division made itself felt even at public meetings, and on every such occasion I became painfully conscious of an ever-widening and fatal gulf. The sense of estrangement, so well-known to me from previous occasions, gradually took hold of me, and I began to react to the cultural élite as I had reacted to the social and political groups of my pre-Petersburg years.

The aim of our journal *Questions of Life* was, admittedly, to bring about a *rapprochement* between the cultural and social movements, but its resources for attaining such *rapprochement* were limited and imperfect. The result of these limitations made itself felt only much later, when the very existence of the journal was already a matter of a forgotten past. The Russian renascence suffered from a lack of moral decisiveness and readiness to choose and act. It was lost in a vague aestheticism and romanticism. It had more in common with the romantic movement in Germany than with the similar movement in France, where it was accompanied by an outspoken social and even revolutionary element. The creative expansion of ideas was confined to a small group of highly talented men and women and never reached either the broader masses of the people or even the wider circles of the intelligentsia.

The social revolution, on the other hand, developed under the banner of a world-view which rightly seemed to us primitive and obsolete— a view which came to dominate the cultural stage of Bolshevism. In the Russian Revolution the gulf between the higher cultural stratum and the lower strata, consisting of the main body of the intelligentsia and the people, was immeasurably wider than was the case in the French Revolution. The promoters of the French Revolution were inspired by the ideas of Rousseau and the scientific philosophy of the eighteenth century; they were carried on the stream of the most advanced thought of the time (whatever may be said of the value of that thought). The promoters of the Russian Revolution, on the other hand, were nurtured in and lived by the outworn ideas of Russian nihilism and positivism and were completely indifferent to the problems of the creative thought of their time. They were not interested in Dostoevsky, Tolstoy, Vladimir Solovyev, Nikolai Fyodorov and the thinkers of the turn of the century: they were satisfied with their Herwegh[1] and their Holbach[2] with their Chernishevsky[3] and their Pisarev;[4] their standard of culture rose no higher than that of Plekhanov. Lenin himself was a reactionary so far as philosophy and culture were concerned; he was not even fully abreast of Marxist dialectic: for, unlike Marx, he had not passed through

---

[1] German revolutionary poet with whom Alexander Herzen was associated. (Tr.)

[2] Eighteenth Century French materialist philosopher of German origin. (Tr.)

[3] See p. 73. (Tr.)

[4] Leader of the Nihilists and literary critic who admitted art only in so far as it was useful for the purposes of educating a 'scientific intelligentsia'. (Tr.)

the whole school of German Idealism, even though he had read Hegel.

This fact had a fatal effect on the character which the great revolution in Russia assumed: it began by perpetrating a real pogrom against what was best in Russian culture. In fact, the intelligentsia committed cultural suicide. It may be said that in pre-revolutionary Russia two human generations grew up side by side. The blame for this state of affairs rested with both sides, that is to say, alike with the leaders of the revolution and with the promoters of the cultural renascence, who were indifferent to social and moral problems. I belonged to the age and shared its weaknesses and contradictions. Yet, as I have already said on other occasions, I never fully merged with any one movement with which I was associated. And the precariousness of my relation to them, my loneliness and my misgivings, sharpened my perceptions.

The cultural renascence served greatly to enrich the mind and heart of its participants, but it also enervated them and deprived them of strength. Vyacheslav Ivanov said once that the movement offered hitherto unknown possibilities of experiencing the ecstasy of Dionysian inspiration, irrespective of the realities to which that experience was related (the 'how' rather than the 'what', as he said). The wings of Dionysos swept over the face of Russia, and set in motion a whole cultural movement. People sought ecstasy for ecstasy's sake, and, what is more, sometimes without being in the least capable of true ecstasy. Only a few were concerned with realities—whether the realities of the senses or of the mind. Eros held decisive sway over Logos: and this involved above all a disregard, especially painful to me, of the problem of personality and freedom. Andrey Bely, the most original and most influential of the Russian Symbolists, admitted to me frankly and proudly that he had no identity and no 'self'. It is not irrelevant, perhaps, to remember in this context the distinction between individuality and personality. For these people were vivid and highly pronounced individualities, but they lacked personality, or their personality was weak and shapeless. Personality involves moral self-determination: it is an axiological concept rather than an aesthetic or a psychological one. For those concerned with personality the origin and matter of ecstasy, the 'what' as distinct from the 'how', cannot possibly be indifferent.

The decadent elements in the Russian renascence were definitely destructive of personality.

It must be noted that some representatives of the renascence did make
an attempt to overcome individualism and revive the idea of *sobornost'*,
of 'symphonic' consciousness and 'symphonic' culture. But this *sobornost'*
differed greatly from the *sobornost'* of Khomyakov: it was more akin to
Wagner's idea of 'collective culture' and of a religious and cultural revival through art. The chief advocate of 'symphonic culture', designed
as an antidote to the individualism let loose in the European Renaissance, was Vyacheslav Ivanov. The Russian renascence, according to
Ivanov, involved a universal cosmic religion, a return to the ancient
sources and to the mysticism of the Earth. He went so far as to identify
Christianity with Dionysianism; and he opposed 'organic' culture to
the 'critical' culture of the Enlightenment. The artists of the time did
not want to preserve their personal freedom, but looked for dependence
on cosmic forces and on the life of the people as a whole. And, though
this time was marked by an extraordinary freedom for creative work,
artists and writers did not, ironically enough, follow so much the path
of freedom as the path of bondage. It was a means of seeking compensation for the state of isolation in which the cultural élite found itself,
just as populism was a compensation for the conscience-stricken
Russian nobleman who sacrificed his life to 'the people' in expiation
of the wrongs of serfdom. But, while the populists were impelled by
an intense awareness of direct social responsibility, the cultural élite of
the early twentieth century merely longed ineffectively for a world of
dream-like 'organic', '*soborny*' culture.

Yet not one of these writers and artists would have consented to
sacrifice his freedom of creativity in the name of any real community
whatsoever. And what an irony of fate awaited them! The Revolution
did, in fact, result in the overthrow of individualism and in the erection
of a collective 'people's culture', but the achievement was bought at
the price of cultural abasement and uniformity. Collective culture came
into being in post-revolutionary Russia only after the downfall of the
cultural élite and of their whole fragile cultural edifice. All the creative
artists of the Russian renascence proved entirely superfluous, and the
new leaders could easily and even contemptuously dispense with their

contribution. *Sobornost'* was realized: but how different it was from the *sobornost'* desired and sought by the men of the nineteenth and early twentieth centuries.

I believe that this irony of fate reveals something profoundly characteristic of Russia and of her tragic destiny. The Russian people are informed by a peculiar, instinctive tendency to collectivism—a collectivism, however, which should not be understood primarily in political or sociological terms. It would be more accurate to speak of a tendency to communism, which is a much more significant term, implying as it does not a mere collection of people, but their communion with one another. We never knew or experienced individualism in the Western sense of the word, as formulated in the humanist civilization of Europe; but this did not prevent us from deeply appreciating the problem of the relation between personality and universal social harmony. No one, in fact, has stated this problem with such power and understanding as, e.g., Dostoevsky or Belinsky. Russian populism, both of the left and of the right, the various religious and social movements of the nineteenth and early twentieth centuries: Herzen and Mikhailovsky, Khomyakov and the Slavophils, Vladimir Solovyev and Nikolai Fyodorov, Rozanov and Vyacheslav Ivanov, Bely and Florensky—all these, whatever the differences of their respective positions, were concerned with the relation of collective, organic and *soborny* culture to the individualistic culture of the West. But Russian practice was, more often than not, illustrative of distorted and falsified *sobornost'*. Thus Russian communism is a travesty of *sobornost'*, inasmuch as it subjects the creative freedom of man to the demands of a collectivized and mechanized society. And the Russians go on dreaming of *sobornost'* which would embody the integral unity of freedom and communion in religious, social, political and cultural relations.

One interesting movement which came into being in the course of this storm-driven age was so-called 'mystical anarchism', which was associated with the events leading to and following the revolution of 1905. This movement proved ephemeral: it was never very popular, even among the élite, and was in the main confined to a few literary circles in Petersburg. Some regarded me as responsible for 'mystical anarchism', and I admit that I was deeply interested in this movement, although, actually, I never identified myself with it and even opposed it in its later development. Its principal spokesmen were the young poet and revolutionary Georgi Chulkov and Vyacheslav Ivanov. My own interest in the movement was not unnatural in view of my rebellious past and the recent conflict with my ex-colleague Peter Struve, who about this time turned into a solid and respectable politician. The slogan adopted by the mystical anarchists was 'non-acceptance of the world',[1] and they claimed to be the champions of complete freedom of the spirit from all external conditions. I need hardly say that the cause of mystical anarchism was profoundly congenial to me, although I was apprehensive of the religious syncretism which it professed. Freedom, unconditional and uncompromising freedom, has been the fountain-head and prime mover of all my thinking. And to-day, as I near the end of my spiritual journey, I am more than ever before conscious of being a mystical anarchist, even if I am somewhat afraid of labels, especially as they serve to bring about the undoing of those who adopt them.

The trouble about mystical anarchism as represented by Chulkov and Ivanov was that, in my view, it was in the last resort regardless of truth and affirmed freedom irrespective of the truth either of man or of God. Their conception of freedom was abstract and formal, and their advocacy of freedom tended to be an aesthetic pose rather than a genuine concern. The movement had a purely literary character; and, while it served to promote the ascendency of Ivanov over the literary circles in Petersburg, its effect was on the whole a disintegrating one. My reaction to certain aspects of mystical anarchism proved another stimulus towards accepting Orthodox Christianity. I was, however, and I have remained, a mystical anarchist inasmuch as God for me is freedom: he is my liberator from the captivity in and enslavement to the world, and his kingdom is my kingdom of freedom and anarchy. I cannot regard the social catagories of power and domination as applicable to God or to God's relation to man and the world.

The Petersburg literary society became a source of growing irritation in me. I was particularly conscious of this when I came up against the

[1] The phrase refers to the words of Dostoevsky's Ivan Karamazov: 'I accept God, but I do not accept his world.' (Tr.)

easy-going way in which the literary circles adapted themselves to the revolutionary atmosphere of 1905-6; although my own negative reaction to it was as far removed as possible from that of the conservative politicians. Most of all, I resented their aestheticism which concealed a profound social irresponsibility, just as later on, in exile, I resented the attitude of the *literati* in France. It was not the word that became flesh here: but, on the contrary, flesh became word; and facile verbal constructions and literary prattle were taken as substitutes for real things and real human relations. I should like, however, to add a few words about Vyacheslav Ivanov, with whom and with whose wife, Lydia Zinovieva-Annibal, I was closely associated throughout my Petersburg period.

Ivanov was one of the most remarkable men of that age, rich as it was in talents. In view of his background there was something almost unexpected in his having become the most universally cultured and powerful intellectual figure of his generation. He was known among us by the nickname 'Vyacheslav the Magnificent'. Russia did not know his like. He was the son of a minor civil servant, and many of his ancestors belonged to the Russian clergy, deeply rooted as they are in the Russian soil. Yet he was pre-eminently a man of Western culture. For a long time he lived abroad and acquired there his immense erudition in Classics and ancient history, and his brilliant scholarship dominated the stage wherever he appeared in Petersburg. He was undisputedly the greatest Russian Classical scholar. He succeeded in combining an intense poetical imagination with an amazing knowledge of Classical philology and Greek religion. He was a philosopher and a theologian, a theosophist and a political publicist. There was no subject on which he could not throw some new and unexpected light. He possessed a rare personal charm, and was the greatest conversationalist I have ever met in my life. There was one trait in him, however, with which I found it difficult to sympathize and which made me quarrel with him on several occasions: his aesthetic sense seemed to drive him constantly to a kind of conformity or harmony with his environment and with the people amongst whom he lived. He always gave the impression of adapting himself and changing his views accordingly. After the great Revolution we parted company altogether and ceased to see one another. Probably at heart he remained true to himself, and merely tended to idealize and poeticize reality as he found it: it is difficult, therefore, to apply ethical criteria to him. He was everything: a conservative and an anarchist, a nationalist and a communist, and later a Fascist in Italy; he was an Orthodox and a Roman Catholic, an occultist and an advocate of religious orthodoxy, a mystic and a scientific positivist. And in all these situations and conditions he invariably exhibited his immense and brilliant gifts. His poetry, which belongs to the Symbolist school, is highly original, but difficult, scholarly, ornate and unspontaneous, and as a poet he is inferior to the greatest Russian Sym-. bolist Alexander Blok. He was, above all, a brilliant essayist. Despite (or perhaps because of) his adaptability, he was always tempted to dominate the minds and hearts of others.

Vyacheslav Ivanov's so-called 'Wednesdays' were the characteristic highlights of the Russian renascence. His flat, known as 'the Tower', on the seventh floor of a house overlooking the Duma in Taurida Park, was the meeting-place of all the most remarkable men of letters, poets, philosophers, scholars, artists, actors and even politicians of the time. They stayed until the early hours of the morning, engaged in brilliant conversation on every topic under the sun. For three years I was a kind of permanent chairman at these gatherings. Ivanov resented it every time I failed to appear and preside over the *symposium*. To be frank, I was a bad chairman, although others seemed to have a different view of the matter. I never succeeded in being objective, as behoves a chairman; I was too active and interfered frequently in the argument, passionately defending some ideas, and with equal passion attacking others. But I remained safely in the background on the not infrequent occasions when poets read their verse, and suffered agonies of embarrassment on such occasions, because poets seemed invariably to expect praise and admiration. Ivanov, on the other hand, was an understanding and very sympathetic critic of poetry, and knew how to discover and cultivate young poetic talents. In general he took a great deal of trouble with people, and devoted much of his attention to them. But his unmistakable gift for friendship was associated with a peculiar despotic desire to dominate the souls of others. We were at opposite poles in this respect. I have no gift for friendship, and I am incapable of devoting myself to others, or of teaching them; above all, I always had a real distaste for guiding or dominating souls. Indeed, even if I desired to exercise influence on the minds and hearts of other people or have a hold upon others, I would probably fail hopelessly. Ivanov, on the contrary, was a virtuoso in the art of mastering the souls of others, and his powerful personal magnetism soon made him a leader. His piercing, fascinating look was irresistible to many, especially to women. But in the end people abandoned him, for his relation to them, full though it was of attention and benevolence, had something of the vampire about it.

When recalling the 'Wednesdays', I cannot help realizing that 'the Tower' was in the fullest sense of the word an ivory tower, where mystical conversations and literary reading took place, while below in the streets of Petersburg the revolution was raging and the tragic destiny of Russia took its course. From time to time representatives of the revolutionary movement would appear in 'the Tower': for example Lunacharsky—a reminder of the harsh reality of the Hammer and Sickle. Once, when there was an unusually large attendance, we were searched by the police—an event which caused a great upheaval. Soldiers with rifles stood at every door, and we were questioned all through the night. This was of course no novelty for me, but the others were taken completely unawares. The only possible link between 'the Tower' and the revolutionary world below was Dionysos, whose destructive element swept the soul and mind of the élite as well as the soul of Russia herself in her revolutionary experience.

Ivanov was the chief spokesman of Dionysianism. Early on he was attracted by Greek mystery religions, and in 1903 he published a study on the religion of Dionysos—probably the most important work on the subject. His poems are full of Dionysian elements. He was fond of saying that, while for Nietzsche Dionysianism was a matter of aesthetics, for him it was a matter of religion, and, in fact, one of his characteristic ideas was the identification of Christ and Dionysos. Nevertheless, he was anything but 'Dionysian' by nature: to use the terminology current among the Romantics, he belonged not to 'nature' but to 'nurture'. In his magnificence and his scholarship was hidden the sting of a refined intellectualism rather than Dionysian forces.

I should like to mention one incident in this connection which subsequently proved a source of senseless rumours and gossip. The 'Dionysian' mood and a certain tendency to mystery-mongering prompted
a group of writers to attempt something like an imitation of the
Dionysian mystery-rites. They met one evening, on Ivanov's initiative
and with the active collaboration of Sologub,[1] in the house of Nikolai
Minsky, a poet and a member of the 'Nietzschean' group, and performed a mystic rite, as a result of which a state of ecstasy was to be
attained. Nobody engaged in any black masses or demonic ministra-
tions: the 'session' only showed the limits of humbug and exotic in-
genuity to which these people went. I remember this occasion as something very distasteful and repellent, even if perfectly innocent. Later
on somebody began to spread fantastic rumours, which were duly
exploited by the reactionary press, and a whole legend was built up
about 'the nest of satanic practices'.

The years in Petersburg, full of new impressions though they were,
proved a not very productive time for me. I had not yet fully discovered
or clearly defined the ruling motive of my life and thought. But my
mental horizon was considerably widened; I had a vision of new things
and I was enriched by new emotional experiences. I wrote a good deal,
but failed to produce anything of lasting value. I tried to express my
views on the subject of religious anarchism in what I regard now as a
very inadequate book (*The New Religious Consciousness and Society*).
There was, however, some hidden process going on within me as yet
not susceptible of expression, but pointing towards a deeper appreciation of the religious element. This, as I have already mentioned, coincided with a spiritual reaction against the contemporary literary tendencies, a reaction which finally issued in complete disillusion and break
with the literary world. Petersburg seemed to me poisoned. I still devoted much time to the Religious-Philosophical Society, of which I
was president, but I was uncertain whether I could remain in Petersburg.
Eventually I decided to go away. I left Petersburg in 1907, first for the
country and later for Paris, where I spent the winter.

In Paris I met the Merezhkovskys, but our meeting was an unhappy
one, and we seemed constantly to antagonize one another. I was in-

[1] Symbolist poet and novelist. (Tr.)

furiated by their utter unawareness of events in Russia. They persisted in living in the ivory tower of their stifling literary and religious constructions and did not even notice the momentous processes which were developing in Russia. The few months in Paris were altogether rather cheerless for me. Religious problems pressed in upon me, and I felt that I must face these issues in earnest in order to extricate myself from the half-truths and half-realities which dominated the scene of my life in Petersburg. The Merezhkovskys regarded my state of mind as an ominous sign of my imminent approach to the Orthodox Church, and in their company I felt indeed more Orthodox than, perhaps, I would admit to myself. Their quasi-literary and quasi-religious sectarianism provoked intense opposition in me. I resented all their attempts to create a bogus, sectarian church and refused to accept their version of the 'new religious consciousness' as an invitation to produce new sacraments. Thus the whole winter passed in violent argument and disagreement, and I never returned to Petersburg, but went to Moscow instead.

I should not like to give the impression that the Russian renascence was all corruption. There were many healthy symptoms in it, of which the specifically Christian ones were the most significant. The poets could not remain for long in the stuffy atmosphere of sheer aestheticism. They tried in various ways to transcend narrow individualism; and this was true in some measure even of Merezhkovsky. The leading Symbolists were the most outspoken in their advocacy of *sobornost'* as against individualism, and of mysticism as against aestheticism. Both Vyacheslav Ivanov and Andrey Bely (before his period of grim and cynical despair prior to the great Revolution) were mystics as well as poets, and their mysticism was after all not only a pose of irresponsible hieratic solemnity. There were signs of a possible *rapprochement* and understanding between the Symbolists and the movement which originated in Marxism and Idealism; and I found myself one of the chief mediating links in that *rapprochement*. The possibility of mutual understanding was reflected in the activities of the Religious-Philosophical Societies, with their centres in Moscow and Kiev as well as Petersburg. One of the most important figures in these Societies was Sergey Bulgakov, who also began his career as a Marxist, and, after a complex evolution, was the first to come to traditional Orthodoxy. The Moscow Religious-Philosophical Society was founded in memory of Vladimir Solovyev, and its most active and outstanding members were Bulgakov, Prince Evgeni Trubetskoy, Vladimir Ern, Georgi Rachinsky and later Vyache-slav Ivanov.

When I came to Moscow I joined this group. I was at once impressed by the earnestness of the atmosphere in which their deliberations were carried on; and this was highly refreshing after Petersburg. Though here too I did not feel entirely happy, the reasons for it were different from those which prompted me to leave Petersburg. The Moscow Religious-Philosophical Society was distinctly traditionalist and I found myself almost automatically in the position of a 'left-winger', a 'modern-ist' and an extreme representative of the 'new religious consciousness', notwithstanding my sincere desire to share in the life of the Orthodox Church.

The Moscow Religious-Philosophical Society seemed to have a wider appeal and gradually became a real spiritual and intellectual centre. Public lectures and discussions were well attended, and sometimes people flocked to the meetings in enormous numbers. The Society had worked out its own manner of stating and debating problems. No problem was discussed in isolation from the whole of which it formed a part. The guiding concern was to discover the ultimate spiritual mean-ing of the matter under discussion, whether it bore on philosophy, history, culture, economics or politics. But there was nothing premedi-tated or cut and dried about this procedure, and the discussions were spontaneous and on a very high intellectual level.

Much later, as an exile in France, I took an active part in debates with French intellectuals at Pontigny, and in connection with the '*Union pour la Vérité*', and I am bound to say that discussions in Russia were more searching, more impressive and more inspired. We never avoided considering a problem on its own merits and did not distract ourselves with comparative judgments. I remember, for instance, a paper read in Pontigny on the subject of solitude: we talked of influences and parallels, of solitude as defined by Petrarch, Rousseau and Nietzsche, but we never got down to the problem of solitude itself. This, I believe, is not without significance, for it shows that in Europe, and perhaps particularly in France, people are affected by a kind of spiritual weariness and have largely lost the capacity for asking ultimate questions and seeking ultimate solutions. For the Russians, on the contrary, these things are the only ones that matter. Belinsky would say, after an argument had gone on all night: 'We can't go home, we haven't yet decided the question of God.' So it was with us, when Bulgakov, Gershenzon, Shestov, Ivanov, Bely, and others foregathered.

Despite the response with which the Moscow Society met in many quarters, our group was a small one, and its outlook different from that of the typical representatives of the intelligentsia, particularly of the westernizing type. When they came to the meetings they usually sat through the paper and disappeared punctually before the real argument began, that is, before 'the question of God' was decided. No doubt, we talked a great deal and acted little or not at all: such was the fatal weakness of the whole renascence movement. Nevertheless, this weakness did not prevent us from exercising an influence on the minds of our contemporaries, or of serving as a cultural leaven.

I shall have more to say later about my relation to Orthodoxy, but I want to mention at this point that the Moscow period coincided with a serious attempt on my part to study, and to relate my thinking to, the theological tradition of the Orthodox Church. Among the Russian theologians I was able to find only one who, as it were, spoke to my condition: this was Nesmelov, a professor at the Theological Academy in Kazan, whose book *The Science of Man* produced a deep impression on me and played a considerable part in my religious development. His theology was avowedly anthropocentric, and this is the only theology which is palatable to me. I also embarked upon a systematic study of the Slavophils, for whose theological ideas I had had little sympathy in the past. Khomyakov aroused my greatest interest, and I began to prepare a book on him and his work. His idea of freedom as the ground of Christianity and the Church had a special significance for me. I also read a great deal of Patristic literature, but this, I must admit, did not on the whole excite my enthusiasm. Among the Doctors of the Church I took especially to Origen and even more to Gregory of Nyssa; and of ascetic and mystical writers I was greatly impressed and moved by Isaac the Syrian.

It was in Moscow that I made, through Bulgakov, the acquaintance of Pavel Florensky, a man of great gifts and originality, and one of the most curious figures among the recent converts to Orthodoxy from among the intelligentsia. From our first meeting I realized, however, that he stood for all the things which I held in abomination: he gloried in peace and tranquillity and in a rigid Byzantinism, exaggerated by the rigidity of his own mathematical intellect (he was a professional mathematician before he became a priest of the Orthodox Church); he fulminated against heresy and professed a kind of sublimated mystical sexuality; and he substituted Sophia for the living person of Christ and cosmic order for the freedom of man. But under this austere surface there was a soul full of strife, pride and boundless spiritual desire. This could be clearly seen even in his book *The Pillar and Foundation of Truth*, which made his reputation as a writer and a philosopher. The most significant and remarkable passages in this book are those in which he describes the agonizing torments of doubt identified by him with the torments of hell. He may in this respect even be regarded as one of the early existentialist thinkers, and there are elements in his manner of thinking reminiscent of Heidegger. But he also shared many things with Vyacheslav Ivanov. He seemed all the time to make the grave in his own soul invisible under a heap of flowers. There was even something lyrical about him: but his lyricism was suggestive of fallen autumn leaves. When his book came out I reviewed it in an article entitled 'Stylized Orthodoxy' and won his, and his admirers', lasting enmity. His very presence had a strangulating, suffocating effect on me. He spoke in a deliberately soft voice, with his eyes on the ground, and never looking straight into your face. He was always hiding something. Indeed, he confessed in an expansive moment that he was battling against the boundless Dionysian element within him.

Florensky, however, is inseparable from the history of ideas in Russia. He was the first Russian thinker who took Sophiology as a basis for theology. Bulgakov, the central figure in the movement of Russian thought towards Orthodoxy, owed much of his creative impulse to Florensky.

My own religious philosophy, which I came to express comprehensively for the first time in *The Meaning of the Creative Act*, was distinguished from the dominant trends of the day in that it was pre-eminently concerned with the problem of man and of his creative vocation. I regarded myself, therefore, as an anthropologist rather than a sophiologist or theologian. All or most of the other spokesmen of the Russian renascence, on the other hand, were preoccupied with cosmology and asked for signs of divine glory and wisdom in this world. Even their theology had a cosmological character. They lived and thought under the spell of the cosmos, oblivious of man and his tortuous historic destiny. To me the world was a source of constant torment. I saw man warped out of recognition, degraded and defiled in and by the world; I saw him tragically stricken and yet called upon to create and capable of creativity. But my experience of the evil and sin which attend human existence was quite different from that of Calvin, or Luther, or the Jansenists, or even that of Orthodox monastic asceticism. It was more akin to Marcion and the gnostics, to Dostoevsky and Kierkegaard. Whenever I came up against the ideas of a Merezhkovsky or an Ivanov, a Rozanov or a Florensky (whatever the differences of their respective positions), I saw man relegated to the cosmic cycle, in which he is paralysed and crushed by inexorable necessity and reduced to the semblance of a 'thing' or 'object'.

I did not share the newly-converted intelligentsia's sudden enthusiasm for the priesthood and other ecclesiastical functions. Pavel Florensky and Sergey Bulgakov, Sergey Solovyev (the Symbolist poet, nephew of Vladimir Solovyev, who later became a Roman Catholic), Durylin and Sventitsky (who produced a great sensation at the time by being expelled from the Religious-Philosophical Societies)—all took orders. My strong and inborn aversion against clericalism seemed ineradicable, and I was never able to overcome my misgivings *vis-à-vis* the clergy. Some accused me of old-fashioned Voltairianism on this account and saw in my reaction a survival of the old anti-clericalism of the Russian gentry. I must confess, however, that the atmosphere which prevailed among the Russians, especially those in exile after the Revolution, was not calculated to cure even the mildest form of anti-clericalism. I was much more favourably impressed by the *startsy* than by our newly-ordained priests from the intelligentsia. But I shall say more about *starchestvo* at a later stage.

From what I have described in this chapter there emerges a picture of two main tendencies which characterize the religious preoccupations of the time. One was represented by Orthodox religious thought, which however, was by no means representative of official ecclesiasticism: its chief spokesmen were Bulgakov, Florensky and the group of which they were the centre. The other represented a religious mysticism and occultism, the chief adherents of which were Bely, Ivanov at his most characteristic, the anthroposophists, and in a measure, Alexander Blok (who was, on the whole, rather indifferent to all ideologies), together with the group of young people who worked in association with the publishing-house 'Musaget'. Both sections were responsible for the spread of sophiological themes and doctrines; but whereas the former lived and thought within the framework of Orthodox dogmatics, the latter was vaguely irrational in its manner of thinking. The last-named group was responsible for the complete nullification of language, whereby words ceased to be signs and became vague phonetic symbols. In both cases 'cosmos' held sway over 'ethos', and 'eros' over 'agape'. They all used, or tended to use, the thought-forms and images of traditional Christianity and the Bible, but the moment they gave free rein to their ideas, it became apparent that the core of their thought was pagan rather than Christian. (The only and outstanding exception in this respect was Bulgakov.) True, never before were Russians so intensely aware of the illimitable unknown surrounding human life, of the mystery and the terrifying abyss with which man is faced; but even this tended in some cases to become a pose, and words like 'mystery' and 'abyss' became catchwords hiding a growing inward emptiness.

As I have already said, the cultural renascence at the beginning of the twentieth century was a time of tremendous religious, philosophical and poetic renewal, a time of intense spirituality. Only those who have themselves lived through that time know what a creative inspiration was experienced among us, and how a new breath of the spirit took possession of the Russian soul. And yet nobody, even the apparently most self-satisfied aesthetes, was given to that passive aberration to which a 'golden age' of cultural renewal may give rise, whereby man begins to dream that he has won a title to live in happiness and spiritual prosperity. On the contrary, there was if anything a profound and all-pervading restlessness. The Russian soul was filled and dominated by forebodings of approaching catastrophe. Whether in the form of Ivanov-Razumnik's later mystical revolutionary apocalypticism, or in Blok's self-intoxication by the passionate whirlwinds of revolution, or in Bely's obsession with a mystique of destruction, the atmosphere was one of expectation on the eve of some terrible and imminent event affecting Russia and Europe alike. The religious philosophers were likewise informed with apocalyptic moods.

It may be, however, that prophecies concerning the approaching end should in fact have been referred to the collapse of old imperial Russia. The whole historical setting of the cultural renascence was typical of a pre-revolutionary epoch overshadowed by the vast catastrophe of impending war and social conflict. There was nothing stable, no solid ground left anywhere. Nevertheless, the apocalyptic mood was not evidence of mere desolation which blinds all vision and destroys hope. Like the Jews, the Russians cannot exist without a messianic hope, a hope beyond men's daily hopes, without a longing for fulfilment beyond all partial fulfilments and partial failures. The final vision is the Kingdom of God, which involves the end (in a revolution or a Last Judgment) of this stricken world, begetting its own doom; and yet it illumines and gives meaning to its tragic pathways.

CHAPTER VII

THE MOVEMENT TOWARDS CHRISTIANITY. THE DRAMA OF RELIGION. NEW ENCOUNTERS

I began this chapter at a terrible and agonizing moment for Europe: in June 1940. Whole worlds are crashing in ruins, and other worlds, unknown and unpredictable, are coming into being. Men are cast into outer darkness in which they are reduced to the semblance of broken puppets. Again and again I am made aware of the question whether this fallen and stricken world, which paralyses and crushes man by its inexorable necessities, can be possessed of true, original reality; whether man is not driven by the very nature of things to look for a reality which transcends this world. This constitutes the religious question which has been a source of continuous disquiet for me even in my most irreligious moments.

As I have already had occasion to note, I do not regard myself as belonging to the type, *homo religiosus*, and yet the matter of religion has never failed to exercise my mind and heart. Since childhood I have been tormented by those 'accursed questions' which Dostoevsky believed to be characteristic of the 'Russian Boys'. And I have remained a 'Russian Boy' even now when my life is approaching its appointed end. I am naturally endowed with a consciousness, however dim and inarticulate, that reality is not and cannot be exhausted by this external world which forces itself on us; that we can exist only in the progress towards another world; that we are not fixed in a permanent position within a crude and self-sufficient universe; that we dwell in the midst of mystery. This confrontation of the human mind with a something or someone which is from the first felt as a transcendent presence—the wholly 'other', even where it is also felt as within man—is, to use Rudolf Otto's terminology, the experience of a *mysterium tremendum*. Our world appears to me as derivative: it is, as it were, at a remove from ultimate reality. God is at the centre of all things; and they become flat, petty, narrow and parochial in proportion to their remoteness from him. In such a world, deprived of the dimension of depth, there is no place for tragedy, and this is, in all probability, what attracts so many. The nobility and sublimity of Greek Tragedy lies in this, that it has raised men to a realization of destiny, to a conception of the mystery of life in which divine agencies are at work. I could never feel at ease in a purely immanentist attitude to life. I was always striving to pass beyond, to transcend life as a mere external datum. To know the transcendent, however, is in itself an immanent spiritual experience: it does not stand over against me forcing recognition of itself. Immanence and transcendence are in any case correlatives, since to be immanent in something one must in a sense transcend it, and to transcend something one must in a sense be immanent in it. I can have no experience of things which are not part of my spiritual path: they do not exist apart from myself; although I may come to experience that which is not included within myself and thereby make it my own. Religious life is always personal; and the deeper it is, the more personal it becomes.

Even as a child I had a dim apprehension of religious life as a realm of inward spiritual revelation, which by being exteriorized loses its authentic character. Historical revelation never does more than symbolize the mystery of the spirit and reflect the imperfect state of man's consciousness and his social environment. It has the function of a sign, and urges man away from external significations to the thing signified. Our natural world, with its infinite social and historical necessities, which serves as a medium for revelation, does not possess meaning and value in itself; on the contrary it tends to weigh down the spirit and to alienate the spirit from itself. Revelation, which comes to us through the channels of history and tradition, has therefore always appeared to me devoid of original reality, and I could accept history and tradition only in so far as their symbolic character was not mistaken for reality, only in so far as I was aware of their liberating influence. I never succeeded in identifying myself entirely with any one point in time and space. The centre of life both within and without is to be found on another plane, which frees us from the power of the world. At the same time I never held to the view which reduces the world to a self-con-

tained entity incapable of permeation by the spirit. Neither did I ever
lose touch with the so-called reality of our stubborn world. Indeed, I
could behave and talk as if all the happenings of workaday existence,
politics and economics, war and social depression, were the very stuff
of life. Yet no war-time attacks or bombardments were ever able to
convince me of the primacy or the ultimate reality of such happenings.
I am no realist in the current sense of the word and no positivist who
relies on the omnipotence of the world of sense. (Incidentally I have
often noticed a strong tendency to such reliance in the traditional faith
of believers.)

The present chapter is more difficult to write than any other in this
book: it requires of me a particular sense of responsibility. I want to be
truthful and candid in what I say. Yet it is not easy to be truthful, not
because I would not, but because, in the very nature of things, I cannot.
There are, no doubt, many who, for different reasons, will not like
what I have to say. There are many among my co-religionists who will
charge me with substituting my own philosophy for religion; others
will accuse me of muddle-headedness and inability to get away from
religion in my philosophy. But I am no Hegelian who identifies religion
with philosophy and makes the best of two worlds. I have never served
two masters: indeed, I have never served any master at all, except
Freedom, to which I was called by my Creator. But I have no wish to
break away from the Church or to assert myself in some sectarian
independence.

I was not brought up in the traditional atmosphere of 'naïve' Orthodoxy. Naïve Orthodoxy can be valid only for those who have inherited it from childhood as part of their natural make-up; for the rest
Orthodoxy can only be 'sentimental' (I am, of course, using the words
'naïve' and 'sentimental' in Schiller's sense). There was, as I have already said, no traditional Orthodox atmosphere in our home. My
father was a free-thinker and a Voltairian. Towards the end of his life
he had sympathies with the religious teaching of Leo Tolstoy. But
throughout he professed a kind of vague deism. He had a reverence
for Jesus Christ, but Christianity with him subsided into the injunction
to be nice to our fellow-men. He was fond of reading the Bible and
used to make his own critical comments on the margins, most of which

were strongly reminiscent of Voltairian rationalism. His attitude to the dogmas of the Church was negative, and he regarded them as a perversion of the teaching of Christ. He would often attack the Bible and the Church at dinner, pouring scorn on traditional beliefs. This always evoked indignation in my mother: '*Alexandre, si vous continuez, je m'en vais*', she would say.

I have already mentioned that my paternal grandmother was a nun. As a child my father was forced into a sort of semi-monastic existence, with fasts lasting throughout a large part of the year, the effect of which was, not unnaturally, rather different from the one intended by my monkish grandmamma. As he grew up, he slipped into the Voltairian enlightenment prevalent among certain sections of the Russian gentry. My mother, who was half French by birth and French by education, had adopted Roman Catholic ways, although she remained a member of the Orthodox Church. She disliked any references to differences between Orthodoxy and Roman Catholicism, and got very cross when reminded of these.

My childhood impressions of Orthodox church services had nothing captivating about them. As a child I used to be taken to the Governor-General's church. The atmosphere there was that of the established Imperial state Orthodoxy. I have unpleasant memories of generals in ribbons and stars, who went to church because it was their social duty to do so. In the monasteries of Pechersk there was a more genuine Orthodox atmosphere, but after my grandmother's death our family scarcely ever went to Pechersk. In any case I did not like monks. Every time I went to Pechersk I was overcome by its melancholy and sepulchral surroundings. I also had a somewhat irrational dislike of Old Slavonic;[1] I preferred the Latin of the Roman Catholic services. Throughout my life, whenever I entered a Gothic church, I was overcome by a strange sensation of re-living an experience in some previous existence. I was never able to explain this.

Generally speaking, I have never known any particular feeling for the sacramental and liturgical element in the religious life, and no intense experiences are associated in my memory with this side of the Church. My knowledge of liturgics was *nil*, and I have not changed

[1] The liturgical language of the Russian Orthodox Church. (Tr.)

in this respect since that memorable occasion in the Cadet Corps when I was given one mark out of twelve at my final examination in divinity. The priest who examined me would have been very much surprised had he known that I was to write a number of books on subjects pertaining remotely to his domain. I was quite hopeless at memorizing anything, including church services, and unable to relate these to my early searchings and quests for the meaning of life and eternity. As far back as I can remember there has been something uneasy, pained, divided in my relations with the Orthodox Church. I remained throughout a free seeker after truth and meaning.

My original religious impulse was bound up with a bitter feeling of discontent with and dissent from the world with its evil and corruption. And this was a first indication of my subsequent conviction that the existence of evil is not so much an obstacle to faith in God as a proof of God's existence, a challenge to turn towards that in which love triumphs over hatred, union over division and eternal life over death. But I had no stable religious beliefs to which I could turn; and I could never, as the expression goes, return to the faith of my fathers. Conventional religiosity if anything repelled me. It was only when I went to live in Moscow that I came to realize for the first time the beauty of Orthodox liturgical life and experience some of the things which were known from childhood to many of my contemporaries. I remember particularly the differences in this respect between myself and my close associate Sergey Bulgakov. Bulgakov's ancestors were priests, and his whole background was pervaded by the atmosphere of Orthodox tradition. His was a case in point of a return to the faith of his fathers, and it could not but affect his mind both before and after his re-orientation towards a religious conviction.

On the other hand, I cannot say that I possess a natural, 'pagan' religious disposition. I had too strong a sense of evil and of the fallen nature of the world to be thus predisposed. Few things are more alien to me than the feeling and conception of cosmic harmony and purposefulness. But this had little to do with the sense of sin or of the viciousness of human nature. The fallen, dejected state of man and the world denotes both something more and something less than their sinfulness. I believe I am much more sensitive to evil than to sin, which has acquired such a dominant and precious place in the systems of Christian theology. The depths of human misery, human pain and suffering strike me more than the sinfulness of man. The conception of sin as a crime provoking divine wrath and punishment, indeed, appeared to me a mockery of divine-human relations.

If I were to outline briefly my confession of faith which delivered me from atheism, I would say something like this: God reveals himself to the world in the prophets, in the Son, in the Spirit, in his chosen solitaries, men and women, who have attained the summits of spiritual vision and who, while sharing the destiny of the world, do not feel at ease in the world. But God does not dominate this fallen and dejected world. God's revelation to the world and to man is eschatological in character; in other words, it is a revelation of a Kingdom which is not of this world and which signifies that there is no making out anything in this world. I cannot, therefore, apply to God in himself or in his relation to the world the categories of force, power, government, or of anger, jealousy, vengeance and even justice. While repudiating the application of these anthropomorphic categories to God, I cannot think of divine life except in terms of sacrificial love, of an eternal movement towards the loved one. And this relative anthropomorphism is in turn bound up with a recognition of the central place of man in the world, about which I shall have more to say later on.

I always opposed the anthropocentric to the cosmocentric—a distinction the importance of which became particularly poignant to me in the context of the events described in the last chapter. I have frequently been reproached in this connection for a Manichean aversion to matter and for shunning the corporeal side of life. This reproach is evidently based on a confusion of matter and body. The body is not to be equated with matter. To adopt for the moment Aristotelian terminology, one might say that the human body is form which is not determined by its chemical composition. One might even say that, paradoxically, body is spirit. The splendour and the beauty of the body for me is contained in its form rather than in its material substance, which is a source of necessity. The form of the body pertains to man's personality and will inherit eternal life. But matter ('flesh and blood') do not inherit eternal life. (Karl Carus, the German physiologist, maintained that the 'soul' of man is contained not in his brain but in his 'form'.)

I was always apprehensive of fixed religious ideals and beliefs, precisely because they are largely determined by material necessities, by external pressures, and by the predominance in history of 'flesh and blood'. So far from being impressed by these pressures and necessities, I conceived in them an evidence of the fallen state of this world. I would often look for and find a sociological explanation for the attempt to ascribe a sacred character to this or that object in history. And sometimes, in my endeavours to understand the processes of history, I became conscious of the Marxist in me. I longed to strip off the moral and religious pretexts which Christendom has designed to cover up its basic materialism. Sometimes, again, I was driven to the conviction that Christianity as taught by Christians throughout the ages has turned into the ideology of a dominant religious collective, in ascendency or in decline, and has become a sociological phenomenon. The critique of such a Christianity is an urgent task; and this task can be fulfilled only from the point of view of eschatological Christianity, which puts itself consciously beyond the realm of natural and social determinations.

Earlier on I have stated that I can remember no event in my life which could be described as a 'conversion', to which Western Christians attach such great importance. But there must have been a moment when I became conscious of myself as a Christian, even if I am not able to relate it to any particular day in my life. I remember one experience when some strange knowledge and light were communicated to me: it happened one summer in the country; at a moment of great anxiety and depression, I went into the garden at twilight. Heavy clouds hung overhead, and the shadows were falling, when suddenly a burning light flared up in my soul. But I do not call this experience a sudden conversion, although it happened at a time of intense spiritual conflict, because before it I was neither a sceptic, nor a materialist, nor an agnostic; and because thereafter the conflicts within me did not vanish. I knew no time of enduring inner peace and went on labouring under the pressure of tormenting problems.

In describing my spiritual path I am again and again compelled to return to the *leitmotif* of my life, namely freedom. My experience of freedom, however, was not merely one of deliverance and release, it was also an experience of travail. For freedom is a burden rather than a right, a source of tragedy and untold pain. It is the repudiation of freedom which brings ease and respite and the happiness of obedient children. I experience freedom as divine: God is freedom; he is not Lord, but Liberator; he is the Saviour and Liberator from the slavery of the world. God never operates through necessity, but always through freedom; and he never forces recognition of himself. Herein lies the mystery of religious experience, and I see no evidence for it except the possibility and the reality of freedom. Every denial of freedom was for me a calling in question of my deepest and most fundamental Christian conviction. Whenever I felt like shouting in defence of freedom, I shouted. Freedom is highly unsettling and explosive: this was the burden of the Grand Inquisitor's argument against it. And Christ's silence in face of the Inquisitor is more unsettling than the Inquisitor's relentless logic. It is a grave fatal error to ask for and rely on safety devices, guarantees and infallible criteria in our religious life, since this life involves all the boundless possibilities, risks and insecurities of freedom.

I am not a theologian, and my approach to and formulation of these problems are not theological. Rather, I speak with the voice of free religious thought. But I am not oblivious of theology. I have read a great many theological works and tried to discover and determine for myself the nature and essence of Orthodoxy, as well as of Roman Catholicism and Protestantism. Numerous and varied contacts with the spiritual world of Orthodoxy and with the representatives of Orthodox thought have served to deepen and widen my understanding of Orthodox teaching. As a result, I was led to the conclusion that Orthodoxy is less susceptible of definition and rationalization than either Catholicism or Protestantism. For me this was significant of greater freedom, and hence evidence of the pre-eminence of Orthodoxy. I cannot, in all conscience, call myself a typical 'orthodox' of any kind; but Orthodoxy was nearer to me (and I hope I am nearer to Orthodoxy) than either Catholicism or Protestantism. I never severed my link with the Orthodox Church, although confessional self-satisfaction and exclusiveness are alien to me.

I have had occasion to observe a theologian who thought of himself as ultra-Orthodox, or even as the only true Orthodox. 'Orthodoxy', says this zealot and heresy-hunter, 'is I myself'. If he had asked my opinion about his attitude, I would have told him: 'the criterion you have chosen for determining the nature of Orthodoxy is formally correct; the mistake, however, lies in your contention that Orthodoxy is *you*: as a matter of fact, Orthodoxy is not *you* but *I*.'... For some time I have noticed that, actually, the spokesmen of orthodoxy and doctrinal authority acknowledge no authority whatsoever over themselves: in their view it is they who are the authorities, and they freely bring accusations against metropolitans and bishops whose authority should be guaranteed by their doctrinal orthodoxy; they allow great liberty to themselves and deny it only to others.

I have also noticed that, while the newly-converted advocates of Orthodoxy were studying and propagating the Church Fathers with great enthusiasm, they often ascribed to them views and beliefs which it is not possible to find in them, or tended to read between the lines where no 'between' could possibly be detected. For my part, I always valued the Greek Fathers more highly than the Western Fathers, especially the Scholastics. But Orthodoxy does not dispense with truthfulness and sincerity, and we must not indulge in make-believe in this as in all other respects.

Throughout my religious development I have been much exercised by the problem of theodicy. This was evidence of the heritage of Dostoevsky. I have said on many occasions that the only serious argument in favour of atheism is the difficulty of reconciling an almighty and benevolent Deity with the evil and suffering in the world and in human existence. All theological doctrines which deal with this problem appeared to me as intolerable rationalizations. Theodicy reaches down to the mystery of freedom, which is not susceptible of any rationalization, and which cannot be expressed in terms of easy-going deductive logic. The issues involved in this problem have led me to the recognition of uncreated or uncaused freedom, which is tantamount to the recognition of an irreducible mystery, admitting of intuitive description but not of definition. My first attempt at such description is contained in my book *The Philosophy of Freedom*, written a few years before the Revolution, which I regard as an unfinished outline of the matter in question. Already then I felt attracted to Jacob Boehme and his idea of *Ungrund*. Acquaintance with this greatest of all mystics has coloured my approach to the problem of freedom ever since, although there are important differences in our respective interpretations of *Ungrund*. To avoid misunderstandings I was always anxious to emphasize that the idea of 'groundless freedom' does not imply a kind of ontological dualism, which affirms the existence of two spheres of being, viz. God and freedom. Such affirmations are precisely evidence of rationalization, no less conspicuous than the affirmations of monism, which reduces everything to a single sphere of being, be it divine or human.

The fiercest opposition in me was provoked by the traditional doctrine of providence, which is a pantheism in disguise, less tolerable than overt pantheism. I have already touched on this. If God, alleged pantocrator, is present in all evil and suffering, in destruction and misery, in plague and cholera, then faith in God is impossible and rebellion against God is justified. This conclusion is valid even in its simplest and most primitive form. But God is spirit, and he acts within the order of freedom and not of objectified necessity. His activity cannot be understood in naturalistic terms. He is present not in external things and happenings, to which we attach divine names and in which we perceive a divine purpose, not in the power or powers of this world, but in truth, beauty, love, freedom, and creativity. This precludes all conceptions of God which make of him the subject of power and almighty influences. God has no power: he has less power than a policeman. Power is a social and not a religious phenomenon. And I considered it to be one of my most important tasks as a Christian philosopher to contribute to the purification and liberation of the Christian conscience from the power of sociomorphism. God can reconcile man to the sufferings of creation because he himself suffers, not because he reigns. Pure monotheism is inconsistent with the Christian conception of God: in fact, it is the supreme form of idolatry.

In opposition to Schleiermacher and many others it must be stated that religion is not a 'sense of dependence' (*Abhaengigkeitsgefuehl*) but, on the contrary, a sense of independence. If God does not exist, man is a being wholly dependent on nature or society, on the world or the state. If God exists, man is a spiritually independent being; and his relation to God is to be defined as freedom. It is unfortunate that Christians have come to speak or drone in the language of meek obsequiousness, called humility, and to conduct themselves accordingly, for this belies the Christian conception of man as a God-like spiritual being. This attitude, with its attendant sermonizing on sin, is undoubtedly also an offspring of sociomorphism: it is based on the concepts of subordination to a sovereign power, of liability and submission to a higher authority. This is the heritage of primitive beliefs. But even sin may be understood as a loss of freedom or the trial of freedom rather than disobedience. This is how I have always experienced man's sin and alienation from God.

When I became conscious of myself as a Christian, I came to confess a religion of God-manhood: that is to say, in becoming a believer in God I did not cease to believe in man and in man's dignity and creative freedom. I became a Christian because I was seeking for a deeper and truer foundation for belief in man. In this I have always been conscious of a difference from the majority of people who became converted to Christianity, whether Orthodox, Catholic or Protestant. And it is not possible for my faith to be shaken by man, however low he may sink; for this faith is grounded not on what man thinks about man, but on what God thinks about him. I have been a strong critic of humanism in the form it has taken in our modern age. Its belief in the self-sufficiency of man has brought about its own crisis, which may turn out to be the final undoing of man. Dostoevsky and Nietzsche alike have shown that this crisis marks an inversion whereby humanism issues in anti-humanism. But this has happened not on account of any undue emphasis on man: rather, the reverse is true. There has not been enough emphasis on man: there has not been emphasis on man to the point of affirming him in God. My critique of humanism, therefore, was based on a more extreme and consistent kind of humanism which implies a belief in the humanity of God. In the absence of this belief man must needs become inhuman. This primordial truth is overshadowed by, or escapes recognition altogether on account of, the fallen condition of man in which he is found estranged not only from God but also from himself. But the very ambiguity of this truth made me aware of the twofold, divine-human mystery of Christ—the mystery of the birth of God in man and of the birth of man in God. God has need of man, of his creative response to the divine summons. I did not hesitate, therefore, to take the motto for my book, *The Meaning of the Creative Act*, from Angelus Silesius's *Der Cherubinische Wandersmann: Ich weiss dass ohne mich Gott nicht ein Nu kann leben: werd ich zu nicht, er muss von Noth den Geist aufgeben.*[1]

To speak of the relation of God and man in such terms is to be avowedly mythological. This is the way the Bible speaks. The most arid rational theology and metaphysics, in the last analysis, derive their sustenance from the myths of religion. Knowledge which seeks to be living knowledge must needs be mythological and imaginative in character. I wish to deny the current identification of myth with invention and make-believe; with anything, in fact, which is contrary to reality. I see the greatest realities, the original phenomena of spiritual life, concealed in the myths of mankind—realities that are more real and more concrete than the concepts and ideas of discursive reason. No knowledge is free from mythology. Materialism mythologises about matter, and positivism about science. It is essential, however, to free oneself from a naïvely realist influence which myths exercise as a result of a superstitious attitude towards them. At any rate Christianity is mythological through and through, as indeed all religion is, and this is the only way leading to the realities underlying the Christian revelation. Christ the God-man is not susceptible of rational explanation, but we can give an account of the nature of his person in mythological terms.

If mythology represents an attempt to express and articulate the truths of religion, religious experience itself issues from living and direct contact with the ultimate mystery, and this is the domain of mysticism. When my religious interests were awakened I was instinctively drawn to mysticism. One of the first things that struck me in my study of religion and mysticism was the somewhat strained relations which seemed to exist between them. Religion has often been apprehensive

[1] 'I know that without me God cannot exist for a single second. If I cease to be, He too must necessarily cease to be.'

of mysticism, and mysticism appeared as a factor impeding the organizing function of religion and threatening to upset its established standards. I was also struck by the underlying unity of mystical experience irrespective of confessional differences—a unity which goes deeper or transcends the sphere of dogmatic precision and doctrinal differentiation.

But I also realized that mysticism may lead, and in many cases has led, to fallacies. There are types of mysticism which are hostile towards man and human personality. Such is the monistic type of mysticism: in Buddhism, with its repudiation of 'the heresy of individuality' or 'the doctrine of soul and self', in Plotinus, Eckhart, and in some forms of Christian monastic mysticism. Their impersonalism is in no way weakened by the fact that some monistic mystics pursue the ideal of self-improvement, impelled by the selfish motive of obtaining a better future for themselves. I would, however, emphatically exempt Jacob Boehme from any charge of monism, despite the fact that the textbooks on mysticism tend to represent him as a pantheist. The dissolution of the person and the annihilation of individuality in a nameless Godhead, or, for that matter, in the whirlpool of cosmic forces, remained abhorrent to me as a betrayal of my Christian conviction concerning the God-manhood of Christ and the indestructibility of the human person. God-manhood embodies the unity and interaction of two natures, divine and human, which are one but unconfused. Man is not subsumed in God, but is made divine, and his humanity endures in eternal life. Surely this represents the essence of Orthodox Christology, although its implications are largely forgotten by Christians and non-Christians alike, and need to be recalled again and again in face of the persistent tendency to monophysitism in Christian thought.

I have never, or very seldom, experienced what are known as the joys and comforts of religious life. Not only did an irreducible element of the tragic remain with me, but tragedy itself had for me an eminently religious significance. I have never had any sympathy for a religion which guarantees a calm and satisfying existence and supplies spiritual comfort to the bourgeois. I felt some oppressive and insinuating presence every time I came across manifestations of religious emotionalism. I am probably entirely lacking in religious warmth; and I have even envied those who possess this quality in a natural and spontaneous manner, while recoiling from the sentimentality which so often accompanies it. Emotional aridity, however, did not prevent me from being sometimes beset by visions, dreams and visitations of a religious and mystical nature. And these appeared to me not less but more real than the actuality into which I was thrown by circumstances beyond my control. The moments of greatest inspiration were associated in my life with experiences evoked by dreams. It is very unlikely that in my case this was evidence of possessing any special gifts of grace. I am entirely devoid of that sense of religious certainty and confidence which is characteristic of *homo religiosus*. I have known moments of intense creative exaltation, but often they were accompanied by an experience of godforsakenness and absence of all tangible presence of divine grace.

I remember one dream, the most remarkable I have ever had, which seemed to prefigure something of my spiritual pilgrimage. I saw an enormous, almost boundless square, in the midst of which were standing wooden tables covered with rich food, and benches drawn up to the tables. Here an œcumenical council was to be held. I approached the tables and wanted to sit down on one of the benches, in order to take part in the business of the council and enter into communion with others who were about to confer and among whom I recognized many of my Orthodox friends. But wherever I tried to sit down I was informed that it was the wrong place, or that no place had been provided for me. I then turned round and saw at the very limit of the square a bare and rugged rock. I went towards the rock and began to climb it; but my very first efforts to do so showed the awful difficulties which were to attend my ascent. I kept on succumbing to weariness and exhaustion, and I saw my hands and feet covered in blood. Having reached a certain height, I looked round and, to the side and below me, I recognized a winding, tortuous road, up which a great number of people were making their way. With agonizing efforts I continued to struggle up the rock. At last I reached the summit. And then I suddenly saw in front of me the figure of Christ crucified, his side pierced and blood flowing from the wound. I fell at his feet utterly exhausted and hardly conscious. Then I awoke, stirred and shaken by this extraordinary vision. When, later on, I recounted this dream to some of my Orthodox friends, their explanation was unanimous: they perceived in it an edifying proof of my spiritual pride and presumption. For my part, I was merely filled with a sense of unworthiness of the heights so strikingly prefigured in the dream: they marked my secret longing rather than attainment or even a capacity for attainment. I have, in fact, always been conscious of my unworthiness in the face of my own searchings and imaginings.

I have often been described as a 'modernist' from the point of view of traditional Orthodoxy. This is, of course, a very unfortunate term, suggesting as it does dependence on time and an ability to adapt oneself to it. As a matter of fact, I have no tendency whatsoever to exaggerate the importance of temporal conditions, present, past or future. But I am a modernist in the sense that I recognize the possibility of a creative process, of the emergence of ever new realities within Christianity. This conviction was helped by a recognition of the truth, so often concealed from the religiously wise, that there is no such thing as a fixed, immovable human consciousness, or other mental and spiritual faculties, natural or supernatural, pertaining to men. On the contrary, human consciousness is susceptible of change, of purification, of being strengthened and deepened; it is, therefore, capable of receiving new truths, or of understanding old truths in a new way. Truth is eternal, and only that which is of the truth is eternal. It is a piece of opportunism to assert that truth is relative. But there are degrees and varieties in the disclosure of truth and in the way in which it is received. This involves a possibility of distortion and even of betrayal with regard to truth. Truth does not fall on us from on high, and it does not hit the eye like some visible and tangible object. It is the way and the life rather than an objective reality standing over against me; and it is acquired as a result of a spiritual contest, of a movement from without inwards.

I was one with many representatives of Russian religious thought of the early twentieth century in the hope of a continued revelation in Christianity, of a new outpouring of the Holy Spirit. This hope I shared with Pavel Florensky, who was so uncongenial and hostile to me in other respects. Questions concerning Christianity and human creativeness, Christianity and culture, Christianity and the life of society and so on, demanded restatement and new solutions. There exists an eternal Christian truth transcending time and space, but that very truth, as revealed in history and related to a particular period and a given set of circumstances, was drawing near its end. And this end marked both a judgment on the preceding historical realization of the Christian truth and a token of other realizations to come.

I have frequently been accused of heresy, but every time I came up against this charge I could not help thinking that people who made it completely misapprehended my position and took the shadow for the substance. As a matter of fact, a heretic is a peculiar and highly pronounced representative of ecclesiasticism, who is possessed by a desire to cut an exclusive ecclesiastical figure and to be alone in the right with regard to the religious truth he professes. But this cannot possibly apply to me. I have never claimed that my religious thought was the teaching of the Church. I did nothing more or less than seek for the truth and bear witness to truth as I saw it. Historical Orthodoxy and all exclusive claims to Orthodoxy struck me as smelling strongly of heresy, i.e., of sectarianism, and as devoid of the spirit of universality. I am no heretic and no sectarian, but a believing, free thinker. As a free thinker I cannot submit to or admit any tutelage or censorship of my thought; but my thought is deeply rooted in an initial act of faith. Nothing and nobody could shake this faith; it is beyond all purely intellectual relations and I am unable to give an adequate account of it. (I see myself immersed in the depth of human existence and standing in face of the ineffable mystery of the world and of all that is. And in that situation I am made poignantly and burningly aware that the world cannot be self-sufficient, that there is hidden in some still greater depth a mysterious, transcendent meaning. This meaning is God. Men have not been able to find a loftier name, although they have abused it to the extent of making it almost unutterable. God can be denied only on the surface: but he cannot be denied where human experience reaches down beneath the surface of flat, vapid, commonplace existence.)

Throughout my whole religious development I have constantly sought communion with others, conscious of the immense importance

which relationships with other men and women have—in this sphere
no less, if not more, than in other spheres. Communion with others is
indeed a very special source of religious knowledge; and it belongs to
religious life that man, partaking of it, shall overcome his isolation and
enter into communion with his fellow-men. Nevertheless I have experienced particularly great difficulties in this respect, even though I
never wished to remain self-enclosed in an attitude of unrelieved
loneliness.

When I came to live in Moscow I made the acquaintance, through
Sergey Bulgakov, of a number of people from whom in former times
I was divided by what seemed to be an impassable gulf. They were
typical of a section of the Russian intelligentsia which had turned to
Orthodoxy and had assimilated itself in the Orthodox Church. This
meeting offered a unique opportunity of acquiring a knowledge of
Orthodoxy not from books but from direct contact with the life of the
Church as lived by its newly-converted, devout and loyal sons.

The heart and soul of this group was Mikhail Novoselov (I do not
know whether he is still alive or not); and the group included Vladimir
Kojevnikov (a great scholar and personal friend of Nikolai Fyodorov),
Fyodor Samarin and Boris Mansurov (survivors of the old Slavophil
movement) and Bishop Fyodor, rector of the Moscow Theological
Academy. Bulgakov was a comparative newcomer to the group, and
his eventual identification with it must have meant for him a decisive
move to the 'right', both from the religious and the political points of
view. Florensky was also a member of the circle.

We used to meet at Novoselov's 'monastic' flat, where the usual
papers were read and discussions and debates carried on. The group was
more orthodox and 'right-wing' than that of the Religious-Philosophical Society, which was associated with the name of Vladimir Solovyev.
Solovyev was highly unpopular among the 'Novoselovtsy'. They
were ardent church-goers and liturgical enthusiasts and had close
contacts with monastic hermitages and with the *startsy*[1]. Many had
submitted themselves to the spiritual guidance of the *startsy* and used
to visit the Zossimova Hermitage, which had come to replace the
Optina Hermitage as a centre of monastic and spiritual life. The *starets*

[1] Monastic elders who were great experts in the art of spiritual direction. (Tr.)

Guerman, of whom I shall have more to say presently, was especially renowned.

Novoselov himself was a former disciple of Tolstoy, but had become converted to Orthodoxy. He was engaged in editing and publishing a library of Orthodox writers. In his own way he was a rather remarkable person, deeply believing, boundlessly devoted to his idea, extremely active, even to the point of fussiness, full of solicitude for other people, and always ready to give help, especially of a spiritual kind. He had set himself to convert everyone. He gave the impression of a man who had secretly taken monastic vows. His cultural and intellectual interests were rather narrow. He was devoted to Khomyakov and regarded himself as his disciple. His *bête noire* was Vladimir Solovyev, whom he could not forgive for his gnostic tendencies, his eroticism and his Roman Catholic sympathies. Novoselov's was a conservative Orthodoxy with a strongly monastic and ascetic bias, but he was free of that clericalism and devotion to hierarchical authority which characterized the right wing of the post-revolutionary Russian ecclesiastical *émigrés*. He acknowledged only the authority of the *startsy*, whose spiritual gifts and experience were independent of their place in the hierarchy of the Church. He did not care at all for bishops and regarded them as ecclesiastical *fonctionnaires* who bowed and scraped before the state. Although he was a convinced monarchist and believed in the religious significance of absolute monarchy, he was implacably opposed to erastianism and the Church's subservience to the state.

I used to attend Novoselov's gatherings for a time, and took part in the debates. I was genuinely interested in this world so new to me, and, as I have already mentioned, I was attracted by a greater earnestness which distinguished it from the literary circles of Petersburg. But I need hardly say that in the end I proved something of an interloper in this society, and I had continually to restrain my natural self. Nevertheless, I had a profound respect for the individual members of the group, especially for Novoselov.

I remember one discussion we had about the proposed inclusion of the study of the comparative history of religions into the syllabus of the Theological Academies. Bulgakov and Kojevnikov defended the proposal. But Bishop Fyodor, rector of the Moscow Theological

Academy, which was regarded as the highest educational institution, objected on the ground that, as he put it, 'such a subject may undermine the faith of the young', and that, in any case, 'there is no point in engaging in scientific enquiries in view of the impending salvation or damnation of the soul'. This was the voice of traditional, monastic and ascetic Orthodoxy, which has frequently displayed its hostility to knowledge, science and culture. I shuddered at these exhibitions of obscurantism and just could not see my way to identify myself with Novoselov's cause.

Members of the intelligentsia returning to the Orthodox Church made a cult of *starchestvo* and sought spiritual guidance from the *startsy*. At the time this was even more typical of the intelligentsia, in its attempts at self-identification with Orthodoxy, than of the traditional Orthodox who had never left the fold. Some of those outside the Church, such as theosophists and anthroposophists, likewise developed a veneration for the *startsy*, whom they regarded as 'initiates'. *Starchestvo* became a kind of myth. People believed that, besides the famous *startsy* who lived in the well-known monasteries and hermitages, there were hidden ones, whose whereabouts were unknown, or known only to a very few. Men and women were in search of spiritual teaching and guidance. They contributed to the growing cult of St. Seraphim of Sarov,[1] whose way of life was represented as a new, 'white' form of monasticism, less other-worldly than the established monastic institution and informed with special gifts of the Holy Spirit. A new revelation of Orthodoxy was found in a recorded conversation between St. Seraphim and his friend and disciple Motovilov. Contemporary *starchestvo* was viewed as a continuation of the same esoteric tradition in Orthodoxy.

I read all the literature available in order to acquaint myself with the Optina Hermitage[2] and its greatest *starets*, Amvrosy. In the accounts of the latter I could, however, find nothing resembling the figure in the imagination of his early twentieth century admirers. He belonged to a very traditional type of Orthodox monasticism, of which he was a most worthy representative, but there was nothing 'pentecostal' about him.

[1] A Russian saint who lived at the beginning of the last century. (Tr.)
[2] The place where the movement of *starchestvo* in Russia began. (Tr.)

Unlike St. Seraphim, in whom the light of the Spirit truly shone, *starets* Amvrosy had something almost dreary about him.

At the suggestion of and accompanied by Novoselov I went to the Zossimova Hermitage to see the *startsy* for myself. We were joined by Bulgakov. The experience, however, proved highly disappointing and even painful for me. There were two *startsy* at the Zossimova Hermitage: *starets* Guerman, whose spirituality was rated especially high, and *starets* Aleksey, a hermit. The latter was to make the final choice by lot in the election of the Patriarch Tikhon in 1917. The Zossimova Hermitage is situated in the province of Vladimir, which is not distinguished by any special natural beauties. The day we arrived the Grand Duchess Elizaveta Fyodorovna was also there, and the conditions surrounding her presence only served to emphasise the unpleasantness of the bond between the Orthodox Church and the Imperial *régime*. The service occupied the greater part of the night. Pavel Florensky, who at the time was not yet ordained, stood behind me in church; on turning round I saw that he was weeping and tears were pouring down his face. I understand that he was going through a period of great spiritual difficulties and distress. I was meant to make my confession to *starets* Guerman. Starets Aleksey, who was in seclusion at the time, also agreed to receive us. The conversation with the latter was very unsatisfactory and even depressing, and with the best intentions I could not discover anything 'spiritual' in him at all. He kept on abusing Leo Tolstoy, employing the most violent and vulgar language and calling him 'Levka'. The meeting was in fact distasteful rather than edifying. When I met him a second time later on, however, he produced a much more favourable impression. *Starets* Guerman, on the other hand, was quite different. While Aleksey was 'educated' (which in his case proved a very doubtful virtue), Guerman was a simple peasant of no education at all. He struck me as being a man of great goodness and illumination, as well as of immense sympathy for his fellow-men. Still, I did not find the things which other people ascribed to him or sought in him. At any rate, I discovered nothing that could make me join those who surrendered their entire will to the guidance of a *starets*. As, early in the morning, I stood at the window of the hostelry of the Zossimova Hermitage and watched the wet snow falling,

I realized that mine was another, and perhaps a more difficult, path, and that, in pursuing that path, I must not count the cost, nor succumb to fear and hesitation. I was quite ready to repent of my numerous sins; but I could not repent of my search for a new spirit and for new ways of knowledge, of my love of freedom.

At one time I read a good many spiritual and ascetic writings of the *Dobrotolyubye* type.[1] These writings contain many incontestable truths. Yet, on the whole, my reading left me with a crushing feeling of the humiliation of man, and of the denial of man's exalted creative vocation. On the other hand, I liked *The Imitation of Christ*, in which I felt a great nobility and a sense of sorrow pervading man's way to God. I believe that mysticism of the ascetic type, as exhibited especially in Syrian asceticism, is a travesty of the teaching of Christ; it is intrinsically Monophysite and belies the Christian revelation of God-manhood. Still, even Syrian asceticism is preferable to the moral teachings of Bishop Theophan the Recluse, the most popular of our spiritual writers. It is impossible to describe the sense of repulsion I experienced on reading him. His doctrines of ascetic life and prayer do not differ from those of his more illustrious predecessors, but all his utterances about practical morality struck me as the quintessence of platitude, servility and obscurantism. Twenty years of cloistered life spent in prayer and solitude do not seem to have produced the slightest sign of mental or moral illumination in this man.

These and suchlike unseemly manifestations of Orthodoxy roused me to revolt. When brought up against them I could not possibly attach any significance whatsoever to the claim of certain ecclesiastical writers that the Church is heaven on earth, except one of astounding self-delusion. I would sooner say that the Church is earth in heaven, and leave it to the reader to decide whether this is a good or a bad thing.

I have already mentioned in the previous chapter that the time about which I am writing was marked by a number of occult movements which had a considerable appeal to certain sections of the intelligentsia. The most interesting of these was anthroposophy. Vyacheslav Ivanov and Andrey Bely were both ardent anthroposophists at one time. The

---

Dobrotolyubye or *Philocalia*, a collection of extracts from the Fathers, dealing with spiritual and ascetic life, prayer and mystical communion with God. (Tr.)

spokesman of anthroposophy was Alexandra Mintslova, Rudolph Steiner's emissary to Russia, and Ivanov was under her influence. The group of young men and women round 'Musaget' were all under the sway of anthroposophy or of other forms of occultism. People were looking for and discovering secret societies; they suspected one another of being involved in occult organizations; their conversations were full of allusions to occult phenomena; and they claimed occult knowledge which they by no means always possessed. Even the ultra-Orthodox Pavel Florensky took an active interest in occult matters; and he was one of the few who really possessed occult faculties, which were duly revealed in his magical conception of the world.

I am far from denying all reality to occult phenomena, and from regarding them as frauds or self-deception, or even from explaining them as a matter of psycho-pathology. I recognize the existence of occult powers in man and of occult phenomena in nature, as yet unexplored by science. Occult tendencies and attempts to control and organize occult agencies are to be found throughout the whole of human history, and this in itself is not without significance. Furthermore, I see no reason why the whole sphere of the occult should be ascribed, as it is by many Christians, to the influence of demonic forces. The latter is evident only where occultism claims to be a substitute for religion. My own critical attitude to occultism, theosophy and anthroposophy was based on a repudiation of the cosmic spell which seems to hover over these movements.

I am most of all familiar with Steiner's anthroposophy. Unfortunately, despite the promising label, man is, in fact, not to be found in Steiner's system; he is completely dissolved somewhere between or within the 'cosmic dimensions'. Similarly, in theosophy, I sought in vain for God: God is, in fact, dissolved into or identified with the cosmos. I explained the popularity of these ideas as a temptation of the age, lured as it was by the power of the cosmos, and by the prospect of merging with the 'soul of the world'. This promised an abrogation of freedom and personality. Part of the responsibility for the effectiveness of this temptation lies undoubtedly with official Christian theology, which was quite powerless to meet the problems that exercised the mind and the soul of the intelligentsia in search of truth.

Anthroposophy had a distinctly corrupting and disintegrating effect on those who professed it: it seemed to create a strange void in their souls. A typical example is provided by Andrey Bely, whose spiritual disintegration was hastened by his anthroposophical beliefs. Some of the anthroposophists struck me as being maniacs possessed by some power beyond their control. Whenever they uttered the magic words 'the Doctor (i.e. Steiner) said', they seemed to be seized by some demon, their eyes and facial expression changed, and it became impossible to continue the conversation. Believing anthroposophists are in fact far more dogmatic and authoritarian than the most rigid representatives of ecclesiastical orthodoxy.

Nonetheless, I wanted to acquire a closer knowledge of anthroposophy, especially as some of my friends became ardent adepts. Thanks to my friends among the anthroposophists, I had the opportunity of attending a course of lectures on the *Bhagavadgita* given by Rudolph Steiner in the anthroposophic lodge in Helsingfors. This experience confirmed my worst anticipations. Steiner himself made an extremely painful impression, although he did not strike me at all as an impostor. He was a man who convinced and hypnotized not only others but himself. He seemed to possess a number of characters which he changed like masks as the need arose: now he was a benevolent pastor (sometimes even dressed as a Protestant pastor), now a magician holding sway over human souls. Seldom have I met anyone so completely devoid of grace as Steiner. Not one ray of light seemed to fall on him from above. His sole purpose and aspiration was to obtain possession of all things from below, by his own titanic devices, and to break through by a passionate effort to the realm of the spirit.

I have always been bored by Steiner's books, which in my view show little talent. It is often said that this is only true of his popular works, and that to appreciate him one should hear his lectures. But I did not see much difference between the course of lectures which I attended at Helsingfors and his written utterances. He may have possessed oratorical gifts, but he lacked the true gift and feeling for words. His speech was a kind of magical act, aimed at obtaining control over his hearers by means of gestures, by raising and lowering his voice, and by changes in the expression of his face. He hypnotized his disciples, some of whom even fell asleep (presumably not from boredom). Andrey Bely, who hardly knew any German at that time, also came under his hypnotic influence. Apart from the course on the *Bhagavadgita*, Steiner gave a public lecture on free-will, extremely mediocre and of little philosophical interest. His philosophical work (as distinct from other theosophical and anthroposophical treatises) *The Philosophy of Freedom*, is similarly of little or no value. I summarized my impressions of Helsingfors in an article in *Russkaya Mysl* ('Russian Thought'), which aroused the indignation of the anthroposophists.

I should like here to add a few words about Mintslova, who at one time played a great rôle in literary circles under the influence of occultism. I first met Mintslova in Petersburg at the Ivanovs, but paid little attention to her then. After the death of Ivanov's wife, Mintslova acquired a great influence over him and acted as a kind of comforter; but her activity in this respect was of a distinctly occult nature. Later, when Mintslova came to Moscow to draw Bely and the young people with whom he was associated into the anthroposophical net, I became more interested in her. She was, as I have already said, Steiner's ambassador to Russia. She was an ugly, fat woman with protruding eyes; there was a certain likeness between her and Madame Blavatsky. Her appearance was rather repulsive; only her hands were fine and beautiful. She was intelligent and she had talent: above all, she was skilled in her approach to human souls, and knew how to speak to each different person. To me Mintslova's influence seemed absolutely negative and demonic. I remember a strange vision I had of her. It happened after her arrival in Moscow. I was lying in bed in my room half asleep; I could clearly see the room and the corner opposite me where an ikon was hanging with a little burning oil-lamp before it. I was looking into this corner, when suddenly, beneath the ikon, I beheld the outline of Mintslova's face: its expression was quite horrifying—a face seemingly possessed of all the powers of darkness. I gazed at her intently for a few seconds, and then, by an intense spiritual effort, forced the horrible vision to disappear.

Mintslova must have sensed my hostility towards her, and she did her best to dispel it. She announced herself one summer at our country-place near Kharkov on her way to the Crimea. She proved an inter-

esting companion in conversation, but she did not succeed in winning
me over to her side. One of the strangest things about her was her
disappearance. A few days after her return to Moscow from the Crimea
she went to Kuznetsky Bridge with a woman friend of hers with whom
she was staying. Her friend turned away for a moment and then suddenly found that Mintslova had disappeared. No one knew where
she had gone, and she was never seen again. This contributed still more
to her mysterious reputation. Some believed that she had gone into
hiding in a Roman Catholic convent somewhere in Western Europe,
a place which was associated with the Rosicrucians; others thought that
she had committed suicide because Steiner had condemned her for
failing to fulfil her mission in Russia.

People like Mintslova could only exercise influence in the atmosphere which prevailed among the cultural élite of that time, impelled
as it was by occult moods, and seeking as it did intimate acquaintance
and union with the secrets of the cosmos. There was a great deal of
perversion, falsehood, and self-deception in the air, and little love of
the truth. Men and women desired to be deceived and seduced, and
none could stand criticism. But this was no new phenomenon in Russia:
similar moods and tendencies characterized the previous *fin de siècle*,
when mystical Freemasonry held sway over the minds and hearts of
Russians in the late eighteenth and early nineteenth centuries. But there
was more spontaneity and simplicity then.

One of the most characteristic figures of the time of which I am
speaking was Andrey Bely (this is a *nom de plume*—his real name was
Boris Bugaev), who is the most influential of the Russian Symbolists
and occupies an important place in the history of Russian literature.
Bely was a very complex and outspoken personality; and yet he himself lived by a kind of passionate desire to lose his identity altogether.
Bely's literary world, for all its life-like detail, seemed indeed to be an
impersonal and immaterial realm into which reality is projected like a
whirlwind of phantasms. His impersonalism showed itself especially in
his monstrous disloyalty and his tendency to treachery. My relationship
with him was strange, almost abnormal. I had a personal affection for
him and, as a novelist, I valued him highly. When he published the first
of his novels, *The Silver Dove*, which was soon to have such an enor-

mous influence, but at first passed almost unnoticed, and later his second novel, *Petersburg*, I wrote two review articles: I regarded both novels as very powerful from the literary point of view, and highly interesting philosophically, since they deal in a most original manner with problems of the philosophy of Russian history. I may even have exaggerated their importance. Henceforth Andrey Bely was a constant visitor at our home. To all appearances he was a friend of the family. He always agreed with me in conversation, as, in general, he was incapable of disagreeing with anyone to their face. Then, for a time, he would disappear, suddenly and completely, from my horizon: during which time he kept himself busy with writing some lampoon or article fiercely attacking and ridiculing me. He did the same thing to his other friends, the Merezhkovskys, Emil Medtner, Rachinsky, Ivanov, and even his greatest friend Alexander Blok. I was left with the impression that he was squaring accounts for having acquiesced in my ideas when we met face to face; he was just paying back 'with interest' for his real disagreement with me. It was not possible to rely on Bely in any way whatsoever. When he became a Steinerite he lived for four years in the 'Goetheanum', Steiner's magical establishment at Dornach in Switzerland; but then he suddenly turned Steiner's mortal enemy and wrote the most ghastly things about him. Later he returned to the bosom of the anthroposophical faith. In the summer of 1917 he was a passionate admirer of Kerensky: he was literally enamoured of him and expressed his love and admiration in choreographical figures in our drawing-room. But later on he developed a feverish activity in favour of Bolshevism, in which he saw the dawn of a great mystical renascence of Russia.

Bely was tremendously gifted. He is perhaps our greatest satirist after Gogol. There was something really new and wildly original in his creative work, and, unlike the other Symbolists and Romantics, he was all turned towards the future. His novels are like musical symphonies (one of his first prose works is in fact called *The Dramatic Symphony*, which, as he says in his preface, has three senses: a musical, a satirical and a philosophical one). And yet he was unable to create a perfect work of art, and his 'symphonies' are unfinished and lack inward unity. In my opinion, however, Bely is more important as an artist than Ivanov, although Ivanov was a much greater scholar, while Bely knew very little, and what he knew was confused and incoherent. His mentality and feeling for life had something Germanic about them, and his first books are full of Teutonic allusions. But he did not know the German language well, and had not read anything in German properly. One could not help thinking that Bely was something of a maniac. He was constantly obsessed by apprehensions, fears, horrors and premonitions: he was, for instance, for some reason, mortally afraid of meeting a Japanese or a Chinese. But he had an irresistible charm, and it was difficult to be angry with him. He was surrounded by friendship and even adoration, and yet, as he confessed to me on several occasions, he felt utterly lonely and dissatisfied.

Bely belongs to the brilliant Pleiade of Russian men and women whom I have described in the last chapter—pioneers of a cultural renascence, which, though onesided and beset by many evils, infinitely widened and enriched the Russian mind, and was evidence of a profound consciousness of Russia's historic hour. The present post-war and post-revolutionary age strikes me as much poorer in talent and of a narrower vision, even though it is marked by more potent and momentous historical events.

My life in Moscow was a period which I regard as one of the happiest: this began when I first came into contact with 'wandering Russia', with the pilgrims, tramps and vagabonds of 'Holy Russia'. In a Moscow inn called *Yama* (the Pit), near the church of SS Florent and Laura, in the Myasnitsky district, there was a hall where members of the numerous Russian religious sects assembled. I heard about the meetings and became keenly interested in them. I began, therefore, to frequent these assemblies and from the very start they made a most powerful impression on me. It was, as it were, the epitome of Russia in search of God, truth and justice—courageous, untrammelled, spontaneous and boundless. Somewhat to my own surprise I began to take an active part in their religious deliberations. I even discovered in myself unsuspected gifts for intercourse with 'the people', who were as far removed as possible from all the customary paraphernalia of 'culture'. We seemed to have a mutual sympathy and understanding.

There was a vast variety of religious movements represented at the gatherings: *Bessmertniki* (Immortals), Baptists and various shades of Evangelicals, left wing Dissenters, *Dukhobors*, secret *Khlysty*, Tolstoyans and others. The *Bessmertniki*, a new mystical sect, which aroused my greatest interest, fell into three groups: the Old Testament *Bessmertniki*, the New Testament *Bessmertniki* and the Third Testament *Bessmertniki*. They were particularly remarkable for their language. The language of the intelligentsia seemed pale and abstract in comparison with their rich, vivid and powerful speech. The language of these sectarians combined the tender and the sarcastic, the humorous and the indignant; and their imagery was vigorous and daringly original. Nikita Pustosvyat was especially eloquent. The whole atmosphere was expressive of a passionate concern and search for truth and a great spiritual and intellectual intensity. These gatherings were undoubtedly of inestimable value for the study of the Russian people, as it is and not as others think it to be. Some of the sectarians were true gnostics from the people and had elaborated whole systems of spiritual gnosis in which salvation was regarded as dependent on the knowledge of truth. Some of them were of a distinctly Manichean and Bogomilian[1] character. I responded instinctively to the dualistic motive in their attitude, but I hotly contested the sectarian spirit and tried to break down their enclosed systems. Neither could I sympathize with their tendency to claim in each individual case an absolute possession of truth over against all others who were supposed to be plunged in darkness. The mystical sects were more interesting than the rationalistic ones. Least of all I liked the Baptists; I could not stand their harping on salvation and their stubborn self-sufficiency. Most of the Tolstoyans succeeded in exhibiting their great master in the light of their own dullness. The most pathetic spectacle, however, was provided by the Orthodox missionary, who was sent there to expose and refute the sectarians. His attitude was a kind of watered-down Orthodoxy, and even when he said something true, it was irritating, obnoxious and certainly quite ineffective.

I had many conversations with the *Bessmertniki*, who, as I have said, were of special interest to me. They also used to come and see me at

[1] An early medieval Manichean sect which is said to have originated in Bulgaria. (Tr.)

home. The principal tenet of their faith was that they would never die, that people die only because they believe in and rationalize death, or, to be more precise, that death has become a superstition. Like all sectarians, they took their stand on the texts of Scripture. They understood Christ's victory over death to mean not the resurrection of the dead, but a state of immortality actually attained. In fact, they denied the reality of death for those who believe in Christ. If men died, this was evidence of their lack of faith in Christ's victory over death. And if a *Bessmertnik* dies, this is due only to his loss of faith. It was evidently quite impossible to argue with the *Bessmertniki*, since to them the fact of death proved nothing but an absence or weakness of faith. One of them said to me that if it came to his burial and people would mourn and weep for him, he would stand beside his grave and laugh at these people of little faith. For him death was just such an illusion as illness is for Christian Scientists—a figment of evil imagination and bad faith to be fought and overcome by right imagination and good faith. I have heard that there was a more sinister sect of the *Bessmertniki* who were known by the name of Satanists and who believed only in their own immortality, while regarding all others as doomed to death. The significant thing about the *Bessmertniki*, however, was that they expressed the profound and inborn concern among the Russian people with the problem of death. The trouble was that they, like all sectarians, dwelt on one truth to the exclusion of all others, and consequently fell victim to misjudgment and even bigotry.

Nikita Pustosvyat, one of the left-wing Dissenters, once came up to me at a meeting and said: 'If you want to know the truth, invite me to come and see you.' Needless to say, I did want to know the truth, and asked him to come and see me. He duly arrived, sat down in the middle of the room, and began to expound to me in his vigorous and vivid language a very complicated gnostic system, which was centred round the problem of time. He saw in time the source of evil. But he considered it to be invincible, except through being what he called 'rolled up in the moment', whereby all things would pass into eternal life. But he was not in the least concerned with his hearers, and when I attempted to call some of his statements in question he simply would not listen. He was absolutely convinced that he was the bearer of the one redeeming truth. But his intelligence and imagination were quite stupendous. Many of these sectarians reminded me of Jacob Boehme and other Christian mystics and theosophists. Incidentally, Boehme was not unknown in Russia; he was introduced into Russia during the reign of Alexander I, who himself had strong mystical leanings. But Boehme's memory was kept alive only among 'the people', where he was even regarded as a saint and prophet.

The religious gatherings in 'the Pit' were soon prohibited by the police: this was typical of the old *régime*. When official state Orthodoxy became conscious of its powerlessness and spiritual incompetence *vis-à-vis* these religious movements among the people, it turned to the state, which proceeded to prohibit and even to persecute them.

During the period of my attendance at 'the Pit' Andrey Bely was writing his novel *The Silver Dove*, in which the hero, an intellectual who had drunk deep of the truth of European culture, but remained unsatisfied, seeks a new truth and finds it among a set of peasants belonging to the mystical and orgiastic sect of the 'White Doves'. I suggested that he should come to 'the Pit' and listen to the sectarians. To my great surprise he refused and preferred to rely on his artistic intuition. The result was very remarkable indeed: he succeeded in drawing the characters of the sectarians with almost Gogolian vividness and in conveying something of the spirit which informs their search for truth.

I should like to mention a few other encounters with the 'seekers after God' from among the people, which left an even deeper and more enduring impression on me. For a number of years we spent the summer in the country, in the province of Kharkov, near Lyubotin, with Lydia's mother. We discovered that nearby Vladimir Sheerman, a brother of the well-known theosophist and a Tolstoyan, had founded a colony or a spiritual community of the Tolstoyan type. The Tolstoyans were, however, by no means the most prominent or the most numerous there: it was a kind of nation-wide centre for all who 'hunger and thirst after truth and justice', both from the intelligentsia and from 'the people'. One could meet there members of all kinds of sects, wandering Orthodox monks and others who had discovered their own individual way of salvation. The latter were even in the majority. In this peculiar spiritual centre I first made the acquaintance of the *Dobrolyubtsy*, the followers of Alexander Dobrolyubov,[1] the 'decadent' poet who 'went into the people', became a pilgrim wandering homeless over Russia and the founder of a mystical and anarchist movement. He wrote a book (*From the Book Invisible*) which was published by the Symbolist poet Bryusov, consisting of fragments in prose which described his mystical visions, interspersed with poems of remarkable freshness and originality. It was difficult to communicate with the *Dobrolyubtsy* because they were tied to a vow of silence and could only answer your question a year later, which was not very considerate of them. Sheerman himself was a wonderful person, of great purity and devotion to the search for the good life. Unlike most of the other Tolstoyans, there was nothing moralistic, narrow-minded, bigoted or sectarian about him. As a rule, Tolstoy's followers were quite intolerant in this respect.

I often visited the 'colony', and its members, in turn, came to see me. The population was very fluid: many people only passed through it on their wanderings through Russia. I derived great insights from these contacts and a knowledge of the Russian people which is not available anywhere else, for this was the true fountain-head of Russian spirituality. I do not know what happened to this Russia after the Revolution, during the years of the wholesale socialization of the country. But I cannot imagine Russia without these seekers after truth, who may appear madmen to some but are saints and prophets to others. They were the true revolutionaries of Russia, more genuine and ultimately effective than the social and political revolutionaries.

My greatest friend was Akimushka. He was a simple peasant, an unskilled labourer, illiterate and almost blind. He seemed lost in the world of external things and objects; he was like a helpless child, not able to find his way about it; and one constantly felt that he was about to stumble against something and fall. In behaviour he sometimes reminded me of Andrey Bely. Conversation with him always involved one in incredible profundities. He appeared to be at home on the heights of the most sublime and difficult mystical topics. At the same time he seemed to breathe sympathy, pity and kindness—a childlike, natural

[1] Not to be confused with Nikolai Dobrolyubov, the most influential 'radical' literary critic after Belinsky. (Tr.)

and spontaneous kindness. He used to come and see me very often, and we spent hours together. Every time we met I felt that he was more congenial to me and conversation with him was easier than with the representatives of the cultural renascence. My friendship with Akimushka convinced me of the fallacies of the populist assumption that there exists a gulf between the 'cultured classes' and 'the people'. Akimushka told me that he felt cut off from a peasant who was immersed in the affairs of his material existence, and close to me, in whom he found spiritual kinship and community of interest. There exists a unity and a universe of the spirit transcending all the distinctions and differentiations which pertain to the life of civilization.

Akimushka once told me about a remarkable event in his life. He was a shepherd-boy, and one day, when he was tending the flocks, he was seized by a sudden thought that there is no God. Thereupon the sun grew dim and he was plunged in darkness. He felt that, if there was no God, nothing at all can be: there was only utter emptiness and darkness. Then, when he realized that existence itself was shrinking away into the void, and that he was thrown into the depth of nothingness, he had a sudden glimpse of light, which grew more and more, invading his heart and mind, and he became once more aware of God. Darkness turned into all-consuming light, and all things were restored to their original reality.

Later on Akimushka left for the Caucasus, and I did not see him again. But the memory of him is very precious to me.

From among the 'educated' I remember particularly the artist B. and his wife (who may both still be alive in Russia). They were nearest to the *Dobrolyubtsy*. B. had a strikingly beautiful face, and gave the impression of great spiritual power; but he was silent and inarticulate, and his spiritual power had nothing odd or conspicuous about it. His very presence had a luminous and transfiguring influence on those who were with him. His wife was of a more Orthodox type; she was fond of the *Dobrotolyubie* and used to read Eastern mystical and ascetic literature and discuss it at great length. I remember many stimulating evenings spent in the company of B. and his wife. They too left subsequently for the Caucasus, which became another centre for 'wandering Russia'.

Spoilt as I was by my upbringing and a selfish preoccupation with my own philosophical and literary work, I did little if anything in comparison with those men and women to attain the ideal of the good life. And yet I saw and felt as they did, and I was deeply conscious of a solidarity with their longing and their search for truth.

In the stormy and dangerous conditions which were gathering momentum in pre-revolutionary Russia, the days spent in our Ukrainian country-house seemed almost like a fairy-tale. I shall never forget those winter evenings when Sheerman would drive up on his sledge, each time accompanied by a new guest. In his wide fur-coat, with his white beard covered with snow, with his kind and gentle eyes, he was a figure reminiscent of Santa Claus. We would rush out of the drawing-room to meet the welcome guests, accompanied by the growls of our Tomka, who was lying by the fireside. Tea was brought in and we would start on the usual conversation, listening to our new guest's ways of bringing salvation to the world, discussing, pleading for this or that. The atmosphere gave a feeling of peace and tranquillity, but it was adumbrated against the background of the seething cauldron of world-events which was soon to boil over in a terrible war and revolution.

My resistance to official Orthodoxy and the appearances of Church-life was growing. It is a bitter thing for me to admit, but I was increasingly made aware of the terrible stumbling-block provided by historical Christianity. When the Russian hierarchy joined the Ministry of Foreign Affairs in its interference with and eventual suppression of the *Imyaslavtsy*,[1] I wrote an indignant article entitled 'Quenchers of the Spirit' and openly attacked the Holy Synod. I had myself no particular sympathy with the ideas of the *Imyaslavtsy*, but I was roused to protest by the use of force in purely spiritual matters and by the sanctimonious worldliness of the Russian Synod. The issue of the paper in which the article appeared was confiscated and I was given notice of my impending trial on a charge of blasphemy—an offence punishable by exile to Siberia for life. My lawyer told me that my case was hopeless. The

---

[1] *Imya-slavtsy* (lit., glorifiers of the name)—adherents of a mystical movement which originated among the Russian monks on Mount Athos. They ascribed a sacred or even a sacramental significance to the name of God. (Tr.)

hearing, however, was postponed on account of the war: some important witnesses were not available. The case was about to be heard when the revolution broke out, and put an end to it altogether. Had there been no revolution I should have been exiled for life to Siberia instead of to Paris.

In the summer of 1917, at the height of the Revolution, ecclesiastical gatherings were arranged in preparation for an all-Russian Council and the election of a Patriarch after two hundred years of Synodal Church government and subservience to the state. I have never liked ecclesiastical gatherings; but on this occasion I did attend several conferences, without taking any very active part in the deliberations. Some of these conferences gave the impression of assemblies of a 'tea-drinking Union of the Russian people'. Others were more significant. But all were held under the shadow of the deep bond between the Orthodox Church and the forces of reaction and supra-reaction, between the Church and the absolute monarchy with its policy of religious discrimination, its Black Hundred,[1] and the rest—a bond from which the Orthodox Church in the Russia of to-day is quite free. The level of the deliberations at the Council was rather low, and they were quite out of touch with the momentous and decisive happenings of the time. Not a single problem which exercised the mind of so many Russian thinkers throughout the nineteenth and twentieth centuries was raised. The Council was to a large extent a successor of complacent, commonplace Orthodoxy, concerned exclusively with secondary questions about external Church order and organization. Even men of the calibre of Sergey Bulgakov and Prince Evgeni Trubetskoy, who took an active part and drew up most of the memoranda for the Council, could do little in face of the extraordinary inertia of ecclesiastical officialdom. I remember how difficult it was for me to persuade our parish priest to omit the references to 'our autocratic Tsar' in the liturgical services. This priest was a fine man (there were, in fact, many very good and deeply believing priests, though hardly any good bishops, in pre-revolutionary Russia), but he was held in the leash of state-ridden ecclesiasticism. The downfall of the autocratic monarchy spelled for him the downfall

---

[1] A monarchist, anti-Semitic movement sponsored by the Tsarist *régime* and responsible for the Jewish pogroms. (Tr.)

of the Orthodox Church, and he clung to 'our autocratic Tsar' as a
shipwrecked survivor might cling to a straw. Yet when the persecution
of the Church and of the clergy was let loose many priests were found
devoted to their faith and prepared to face suffering and torture for its
sake: indeed, the persecution proved a purification for the Church.
Nevertheless, there were hardly any signs of a new and creative consciousness to be discerned within ecclesiastical Orthodoxy. The Church
as a traditional social institution governed by liturgical and canonical
practices turned out to be more stubborn and influential than the
Church as a mystical organism.

There were notable exceptions to this state of affairs. I remember
particularly my meeting with Aleksey Mechevoy shortly before my
exile from Soviet Russia. He belonged to the married clergy and was
regarded by many as a 'white' *starets*. There was indeed something
about him reminiscent of Dostoevsky's Starets Zossima. He seemed to
belong to a wholly different spiritual world from that of the majority
of the Russian clergy. Incidentally, he believed that no military intervention or counter-revolution would ever overcome the evils of Bolshevism, and that those Christians who rely on such intervention and
counter-revolution are not concerned with the Christian truth which
they claim to represent. Only a spiritual renewal within the Russian
people itself, he said, would purify Russia. Throughout my years of
exile abroad I have borne witness to just this truth. Father Aleksey told
me how soldiers of the Red Army came to him by night to make their
confessions. Through him I came to feel a new bond with the historical
Orthodox Church, which had in fact never been completely broken,
despite all my non-conformity and protestations against it. In this respect, there was something in common between my own religious
position and that of Solovyev, although his objectives were different.

My experience in connection with Church-life abroad will be dealt
with later on, but I want to mention here that, generally speaking, the
spiritual and psychological conditions of Church-life among the *émigrés*
had the same strangulating effect on me as those of pre-revolutionary
Church-life. As before, the majority of the Orthodox (including, I am
sorry to say, the young people), were beset by the heresies of the Sad-
ducees and the Pharisees. Russian religious thought seemed to have

almost entirely vanished, or been abrogated. It was upheld only by a small group of the representatives of theological and philosophical thought, whose Orthodoxy, however, was suspect in ecclesiastical circles.

Of my contacts with the Western Christian world, both Catholic and Protestant, I shall, likewise, have more to say later. In regard to the Church I always desired a reformation—not in any specifically Protestant sense of the word, but in the sense of a thoroughgoing spiritual reform, of which the Protestant Church stands in no less need than the Orthodox or the Catholic Churches.

The drama of my religious life appears to me as pre-eminently the drama of man and his creative vocation. I shall speak of this at greater length in the following chapter. The more I think about the predicament of historical Christianity, the more convinced I am that the only way out of it is the way of re-orientation towards creativity, which is the same as an eschatological re-orientation—the way of true messianism. God reveals himself to the world, but he does not rule the world: it is ruled by the Prince of this World. 'Thy Kingdom come' signifies that the Kingdom of God is not yet in the world, that we only await it, and move towards or away from it. Many historians of Christianity —Weiss, Loisy, Schweitzer, and others—believed that the Kingdom of God is to be understood eschatologically. But the Kingdom of God is not only to be awaited: it is also to be created. The eschatological attitude involves a profound and radical change in human consciousness —a change which differs from the one envisaged by Kierkegaard, for whom the central question was to know if one has or has not faith, or from those who are concerned exclusively with sin and salvation, or even from those who pass through the agonies of doubt and uncertainty. The change for me comprises above all a modification in man's experience and understanding of the relation between God and man. I do not doubt the existence of God; but I have known moments when my heart and mind were overwhelmed by the terrible thought that the current notion of this relationship may be right—the notion, namely, of God as master and man as serf, of ruler and subject. If this be so, then all is lost, and I am lost too. If this be so, then nothing remains for me but the gaping abyss of nothingness. The most monstrous religious nightmare is that of an evil God whom men, blinded by their slavishness, regard as good. But there is another religious experience, which knows of the inscrutable divine-human mystery of God expecting from man a daring, creative response to his calling. And this lays on man an incomparably greater burden and responsibility than any concept of law and of the fulfilment of the law could ever envisage. The summit of daring is reached in the awareness that on man depends not human life alone but divine life as well.

CHAPTER VIII

THE DOMAIN OF CREATIVITY. *THE MEANING OF THE CREATIVE ACT.* THE CREATIVE ACT AS ECSTASY

The matter of creativity and of the creative vocation of man is not only a facet or one of the facets of my outlook, reached as a result of philosophical reasoning, but a source of my whole thinking and living—an initial inner experience and illumination. But it has also proved a cause of the greatest misunderstandings. Creativity, as a rule, is understood as an aesthetic or cultural concept denoting the sphere of science and the arts: knowledge and the production of works of art. In the religious or Christian context it is often discussed in terms of the somewhat trivial question of the relation of Christianity to cultural activities, in other words, of the question whether Christianity is or is not obscurantist. But the problem of creativity can be approached on a different and deeper level. Creativity stands in no need of justification from the religious or any other point of view: it is its own justification in virtue of the very existence of man; it is that which constitutes man's relation and response to God. The question of culture, of cultural values and of the products of culture, on the other hand, is a secondary and derivative one.

I have been deeply disturbed by the problem of the relation between creativity, sin and redemption. I have experienced moments of acute awareness of the sinfulness of man; and such moments probably marked the points of my closest approximation to Orthodoxy. But I also came to realize that to remain fixed in that position, to surrender oneself entirely to the sense of sin, spells frustration and a disablement of life. The consciousness of sin may be a stage on the way towards spiritual renewal and illumination; but it may also prove an omen of unrelieved darkness. There can be no creativity and no illumination if life is reduced to the consciousness of man's misery, wretchedness and possible salvation. If regeneration is to come, the sense of sin must be transformed into another and loftier experience. How are we to overcome the *vis inertiae*, the lameness and impotence of the sense of sin, and to reach out to a more ardent and more creative attitude? The counsels of current religious spirituality invite us to deepen the awareness of our sinful and unworthy condition, thereby making us susceptible of divine grace and illumination. But the source of grace is in God: grace proceeds from on high, whilst the realization of our sinful condition proceeds from below. My question then is this: can we ascribe to grace, which redeems the frustrations and the insignificance of human existence, a quality which is not only divine but also human, which is from 'below' as well as from 'above'. Is man justified solely by obedience to a higher divine power, or is he also justified by his human endeavour and creative ecstasy?

It is imperative to bear in mind that human creativity is not a claim or a right on the part of man, but God's claim on and call to man. God awaits man's creative act, which is the response to the creative act of God. What is true of man's freedom is true also of his creativity: for freedom too is God's summons to man and man's duty towards God. God does not reveal to man that which it is for man to reveal to God. In Holy Scripture we find no revelation concerning man's creativity— not on account of its implied denial of human creativity, but because creativity is a matter for man to reveal. God is silent on this matter and expects man to speak. I have frequently been asked to justify my idea of the religious significance of human creativity by quotations from Scripture. I may or I may not be able to provide such justification —but in any case such a demand is evidence of a fundamental misunderstanding of the problem under discussion. It is, in fact, the concealed, rather than the revealed, will of God that man should dare and create, and such daring and creativity are a token of man's fulfilment of the will of God.

It is absurd to charge me with an attempt to defy God. Creativity for me is implied in the fundamental Christian truth of God-manhood, and its justification is the theandric theme of Christianity. God's idea of man is infinitely loftier than the traditional orthodox conceptions of man, which are as often as not an expression of a frustrated and stunted mind. The idea of God is the greatest human idea, and the idea of man is the greatest divine idea. Man awaits the birth of God in himself, and God awaits the birth of man in himself. It is at this level that the question of creativity arises, and it is from this point of view that it should be approached. The notion that God has need of man and of man's response to him is, admittedly, an extraordinarily daring notion; yet in its absence the Christian revelation of God-manhood loses all meaning. The drama of God and his Other One, Man, is present and operative in the very depths of divine life. This is revealed not in theological doctrines but in spiritual experience, where the divine drama passes into a human drama and that which is above is converted into that which is below. But this is in no way inconsistent with redemption: rather it is another moment on the same spiritual path and another act in the mystical drama of God and man.

I want to emphasize in this connection that my whole philosophical approach is radically incompatible with a belief in the possibility of a rational ontology, that is to say, of a science of being in which the process of abstraction is pushed to the point where Being is regarded as devoid of all peculiarities and all concrete characteristics. I can only admit a phenomenology which describes metaphysical reality in symbolic terms. Any rationalization of the divine-human relationship, any attempt at expressing it in terms of a rational philosophy of being, makes nonsense both of that relationship and of that philosophy. It can only be spoken of in symbolic and mythological terms which leave the door open to Mystery.

Creativity, in my view, is not an 'insertion' in the finite, not a mastery over the medium, or the creative product itself: rather it is a flight into the infinite; not an activity which objectifies in the finite but one which transcends the finite towards the infinite. The creative act signifies an *ek-stasis*, a breaking through to eternity. This conception laid open to me the tragic character of creativity as it is displayed in the products of culture and society, viz., the continuous but unavailing effort and the ensuing painful disparity between the creative idea and its embodiment in the world.

As I have noted, I passed through a phase of the crushing experience of sin, and in the wake of this experience darkness gathered around me.

Had I followed this path to the end, unable to dispel its evil charm, I should have grown accustomed to a perpetual contemplation of sin, to a brooding over darkness, rather than to a vision of light. It is, in fact, the aim of religious life to put an end to this oppressive attitude. The sense of dejection and lowness of spirit gave way in me to a sense of exultation. I can remember how one summer day just before dawn I was suddenly seized by a tumultous force which seemed to wrench me away from the oppressive spell of my despondent condition, and a light invaded my whole being. I knew then that this was the exalting call to creativity: henceforth I would create out of the freedom of my soul like the great artificer whose image I bear.

What lay for me, as a Christian, in this experience was a realization of two processes, seemingly incompatible but, by the paradox of life, really complementary, one redemptive, the other creative. I realized the fallacy of an exclusively soteriological religion. It is only in the creative act that man prevails over the oppression and enslavement of extraneous influences. The creative act reveals the absolute priority of the 'self', the subject, over the 'non-self', the object; but, at the same time, it strikes at the root of the egocentric, for it is eminently a movement of self-transcendence, reaching out to that which is higher than oneself. Creative experience is not characterized by absorption in one's own perfection or imperfection: it makes for the transfiguration of man and of the world; it foreshadows a new Heaven and a new Earth which are to be prepared at once by God and man. It is individual and indeed rebellious in nature, involving conflict between man and his environment, yet it is, in its liberating power, at the opposite pole of self-sufficiency, raising man to a vision of boundless and infinite reality.

This experience underlies my book *The Meaning of the Creative Act*, An Essay in the Justification of Man, which was written at a time of well-nigh intoxicating ecstasy, a book in which my thoughts and the normal course of philosophical argument seemed to dissolve into vision. It is an impulsive, unpremeditated and unfinished work (I am least of all satisfied with the section on Art), but it contains in that raw form all my dominant and formative ideas and insights. My misfortune is that, owing partly to the distraction provided by other themes and problems and partly to my unsystematic manner of thinking, I was never able to work out the principal thesis of this work.

The Meaning of the Creative Act was written when an irresistible reaction against the Orthodox circles of Moscow began to grow within me. I left not only the Novoselov group but also the Religious-Philosophical Society and no longer attended their meetings; I also ceased to work in the publishing-house 'Put', with which I had been associated since my arrival in Moscow. I withdrew into complete solitude. This period coincided with my first visit to Italy. We went to Florence and Rome and, on our return journey to Russia, speeded by my mother's illness, we paid a visit to Assisi.

Italy made a powerful impression on me. The pages in *The Meaning of the Creative Act* devoted to the Renaissance were entirely written in Italy. Italy revealed to me the Renaissance as the dawn of a new age in which the Christian soul became conscious for the first time of a will to creation; and, though I knew that the Renaissance was a failure, I realized that this was the most sublime, significant and tragic failure ever experienced by European man. I felt completely carried away, to the point of re-living the creative urge of the Renaissance man and the affirmation of his power to make freely and out of freedom. I was particularly stirred by the Renaissance of the *Trecento* and the *Quatrocento* of the Florentine period. Botticelli appeared to me as particularly significant of the drama and the paradox of creativity as I myself knew them. But the Italy of the sixteenth century was quite uncongenial to me, and I disliked the lifeless academicism of its architecture. St. Peter's was positively distasteful to me; neither could I develop any liking for Raphael. On the other hand, I was deeply moved by Leonardo. I liked the Baroque fountains, though not the Baroque churches. In the Campagna the monuments of human creativity seemed to me to have become a part of nature itself. As to Rome, whatever the past and present practical or ideological considerations in her favour or against her as the centre of Christendom, it was evident to me that she bore the signature of cultural universality.

I had always had a special devotion for St. Francis of Assisi, in whose unique personality I perceived the image of transfigured human nature. But the monastery of St. Francis did not in the least evoke that image, and nothing in it seemed to have caught St. Francis's fire. One Franciscan, a Dane by extraction, complained to me bitterly that St. Francis had fallen into complete oblivion and had become a lifeless symbol. Apart from the resident monks there was no one in the church. Before our departure from Assisi a special Mass was celebrated for us at St. Francis's grave.

I left Italy with a feeling of sorrow, as if I were abandoning a spiritual homeland. When I came back it was to a very different Italy, an Italy under the shadow of Fascism.

My return to Moscow marked a new phase in my life. Orthodox circles both of the 'right' and of the 'left' now no longer concealed their thoroughgoing suspicion and even hostility to my position, particularly in regard to the philosophy of creativity as expressed in *The Meaning of the Creative Act*. So far as I can remember the only critics in whom my book met with any response were Rozanov and Vyacheslav Ivanov. Sergey Bulgakov, on the other hand, in his book *The Light That Never Fades*, which was published shortly after, spoke of my defence of creativity as 'demonic', 'titanic', 'humanistic', and nearly akin to anti-Christ.

The problem of creativity was for me always one with the problem of freedom. The creative act of man and the emergence of new things and new values in the world are inconceivable within the closed cycle of Being, subject as it is to all kinds of determination, causal and otherwise. Creativity is possible only on account of Freedom, which is not determined by anything, not even by Being. The source of Freedom is in the void of non-being. Freedom, as I have repeatedly tried to show, is indeterminate, uncaused, gratuitous. But my original formulation of this idea, as found, for instance, in *The Philosophy of Freedom* and, to some extent, even in *The Meaning of the Creative Act*, was unsatisfactory because I was still beset by the associations of Idealist ontology and used the terminology characteristic of this philosophy.

My critics charged me with a refusal to admit the need of any given 'material' for the creative act of man. This charge was, of course, completely unfounded. I have never denied that man cannot create without a medium, that he cannot dispense with the world of external reality, and that he cannot perform anything in a vacuum. And yet the basic characteristic of a creative act consists in not being wholly determined by its medium, and that it comprises something new, something which cannot be derived from the external world in which it is embodied, or indeed from some fixed repository of ideal forms which press upon the creator's imagination. This, then, is the point where Freedom comes in—an untraceable, undetermined and unpredictable movement from within outwards. Creation is, in this sense, out of nothing. Without such freedom creativity would merely present a re-distribution of the given elements constituting the world, and the appearance of anything new and original would be pure illusion. I was much exercised by the problem as to how being arises out of non-being, and how the non-existent becomes existent. The movement from non-being into being, which is the very stuff of freedom, cannot be explained from within being, which is bound by its own laws of determination. To admit that freedom is rooted in non-being or nothingness, is to admit the irrational mystery of freedom. No rational concepts can possibly express this mystery, for concepts deal with and are dependent on the already existing. It is only accessible to spiritual experience and, as such, it can only be spoken of in symbols and mythological images.

I acknowledged that the gift of creativity proceeds from God; but man intervenes by virtue of his freedom, and, in his capacity of creator, he is no mere passive object in the hands of God. It is fruitless and absurd to ask whether creativity is justifiable from the point of view of the religion of redemption, because, though man be degraded and defiled by sin, there can be no redemption and no salvation without man's response to God. Redemption and salvation are, therefore, also acts of divine-human creativity. Similarly, the ultimate fulfilment of redemption and the coming of God's Kingdom comprises a creative act on the part of man. I have never failed to emphasise the religious, rather than the merely aesthetic or cultural, significance of creativity. My object has been not to justify creativity but to show that, in its divine-human character, it is itself justification, inseparable from all the other acts which characterize God's relation to man and to the world.

But there is another element in creativity which was very much in my mind when I wrote *The Meaning of the Creative Act*, namely the element of tragedy. Man's creative act is doomed to fail within the conditions of this world. It is a tremendous effort which is destined never to succeed. Its initial impulse is to bring forth new life, to transfigure the world and usher in a new heaven and a new earth; but in the conditions of the fallen world the effort turns out to be unavailing: it comes up against the inertia, the laws and compulsions of the external world, pervaded as it is by inexorable necessities. The attempt gives place to the production of aesthetic and cultural objects of a greater or lesser perfection. These objects, however, are symbols of reality rather than reality itself: a book, a symphony, a picture, a poem or a social institution; but all these are evidence of the painful disparity between the creative impulse and its partial and fragmentary embodiment in the objective world.

I will not repeat here what I have already said many times on this subject. But I should like to avert any possible misunderstanding, to which I seem frequently to have given occasion. I am far from denying the validity of culture and the value of its creative function in this world. Man is committed by virtue of his mundane destiny to the making of culture and civilization. And yet such making must not blind us to the fact that it is but a token of real transfiguration, which is the true, though unattainable, goal of creativity. 'Realistic' creativity, as distinct from 'symbolic' creativity, would, in fact, bring about the transfiguration and the end of this world, and the emergence of a new heaven and a new earth. The creative act, alike in its power and impotence, is eschatological—a prefiguration of the end of the world.

This paradox of creativity underlies my sympathy for romanticism and my hostility towards classicism (although the accepted distinction between these two notions needs considerable qualification). I have spoken of this in a previous chapter. I do not, of course, object to classicism, in so far as it aims at the achievement of perfection in the creative act. But the fallacy of classicism and of the intellectual type it has helped to produce lies in the fact that it admits of the possibility of perfection in the finite, within this contingent and fallen world of ours. I object to classicism because of its characteristically anti-eschatological attitude. The truth of romanticism (which in other respects is an easy target for criticism) lies in its pervading sense of the insufficiency of all achievement within the finite, in its longing for and aspiration to the infinite, or, to be more precise, to the trans-finite. The true aim of creativity, then, is the victory of 'reality' over 'symbol' and the desire for such a victory. To take symbols for reality is one of the chief temptations in human life, and it has proved, on more than one occasion, the undoing of man and the betrayal of creativity.

But is it possible at all to pass from symbolic to realistic or trans-figuring creativity? Or is this merely a dream which is destined to cause pain and torment to man but is never to come true? The Russian genius is characterized by a particularly intense concern with this problem, and the Russian writers, such as Gogol, Leo Tolstoy, Dostoevsky, and many others, have striven to transcend art and to break down the walls dividing art and life. Nietzsche, Ibsen and the Symbolists have followed a similar path. No doubt, even to raise this problem is tantamount to demanding a miracle from man. But a miracle is already involved in the very act of creation which conforms to no order the laws of which are known, and demands for its explanation an agency transcending the possibilities of a given and a determinate world.

We must not understand creation to mean a kind of process of moral perfection, whereby man hopes to be justified in the sight of God. The current Christian attitude to the problem of creativity wavers between asceticism, which is hostile to the world and yet perfectionist in regard to the individual human soul, on the one hand, and, on the other, an attempt to give a religious dressing to, or to justify and even to sanctify, the social and cultural habits of this world. I for my part was looking for another way of creativity which, while impelled by a sense of the utter insufficiency of every creative realization, aims at a real, not only a nominal and symbolic, transformation of this world.

My faith and hope, at first confident, elated and enthusiastic, but subsequently more temperate, difficult and painful, concerning the coming of a new creative epoch in human history, was never 'humanist' in the sense in which this is true of Renaissance humanism. I am a humanist, of course, since I believe in God-manhood and hence in the humanity of God. As a matter of fact, I believe that God is more human than man, or even that God is human, whereas man is inhuman. Belief

in man involves and indeed is, belief in God, and it cannot afford to
indulge in illusions concerning man. But it cannot be said of me
that I am at one with the humanism of the European Renaissance.
I have written a great deal about the crisis of humanism, and predicted
the coming of an anti-humanistic age—a prediction which has been
abundantly vindicated. I spoke already at the beginning of the century
of an inner dialectic whereby humanism is on the point of turning into
anti-humanism, the 'super-man' into 'sub-man', and the affirmation of
man's self-sufficiency into his self-annihilation. But these insights into
the existential dialectic of humanism did not distract me in the least
from my belief in creativity; on the contrary, they served to confirm
me in that belief, and, after the intense experience of ecstasy which I
have described above, I never went back on my faith in the creative
vocation of man.

The hope in the advent of an age of creativity, however, was shattered by the course of historical events: by the catastrophe of the first
world-war, by the Russian Revolution, by the cataclysm in Germany,
by the general and ominous decline in creativity in the inter-war years,
by a second world-war and the threat of a third one to come. Nevertheless, this did not invalidate my hope: it only went to confirm my disbelief in the stability and unchangeableness of the universal and social
order. That which many regard as immobile, solid and enduring is in
fact liable to be blown to pieces with the greatest of ease by the volcanic forces which always lurk beneath the surface of apparent harmony. Historical catastrophes, impelled though they are by a great
dynamism which may be mistaken for a creative power and on which
some rely for the creation of a new world, are by no means favourable
to creativity as I understand it. Indeed, as a rule, they usher in a period
of reaction so far as true creative activity is concerned: for they make
nothing of man and prove destructive of the freedom of the spirit.
Thus it is that the world was hurled into an anti-humanistic age.

But the historical experience of the dialectic of humanism is itself of
immense significance: its very irony is a symptom of a new phase in
the destiny of mankind. The path of man throughout the ages is not a
continuous, unbroken development. On the contrary, it is characterized
by the eruption of irrational forces: it is a trial of man's freedom, un-

determined, ambiguous and unpredictable. I was surprised, therefore, when some of my critics attached to me a belief in 'creative evolution' *à la* Bergson. In point of fact, 'creative evolution' is altogether a misconception, because creativity and evolution are mutually exclusive notions. Evolution is a process in accordance with certain laws immanent in or transcending the world, whereas creativity issues from freedom and is not subject to any laws whatsoever.

The happenings on the surface of history have always appeared to me as of secondary importance; I looked at them as signs of life in a deeper dimension. Consequently, I was never taken in by the formidable appearances of events and activities pertaining to the 'objective' world of history and society. This is true even of those activities in which I took part or of which I was the initiator. I treated with a kind of bitter detachment even those things in which I was most passionately implicated. This may have been due in part to the influence on me of Tolstoy and also of Russian Nihilism. It seemed as if life lay after all beyond or beneath all external affairs. Ordinary workaday existence, with all its endeavours and exigencies, was, however, interspersed with moments of true freedom and inspiration, and these alone infused significance, authenticity and nobility into a world of unmeaning, make-believe and degradation.

I devoted much of my time and many of my writings to the transient happenings of the day: I did so because, despite my detachment, history for me was not a spectacle to be observed from a box, but a human drama in which I was involved. But my constant inner withdrawal even in face of those things which I endured with passionate anguish made all my utterances and judgments like Nietzsche's 'uncontemporaneous meditations', marking as they did a deep conflict with the age and pointing to a distant future of which the present was but a negative revelation. I have never been a politician or a political journalist, although I have on my conscience dozens of newspaper articles about social and political matters. When I joined issue in social and political affairs I did so as a moralist in defence of man—in an age the dominant characteristic of which was hostility towards man. I tried to preach humanity in the most inhuman of ages. When I came to use existentialist terminology and described myself as an existentialist philosopher (with all the qualifications made in the previous chapter) many thought that I had betrayed my philosophical path. No one observed that, in point of fact, the change was a natural outcome of my original and fundamental concern for man.

The link between creativity and a 'pessimistic' attitude towards life as it is given, with all its necessities, compulsions and conventions, made me attach a great importance to imagination, since without imagination there can be no creative activity. A creative act always rises above reality; it means imagining something other and better than the reality around us. But just as there may be evil imagination, calling up before us evil images and phantasms, so there may be false or illusory creative acts. Man is capable of responding not only to the call of God but also to the call of Satan.

And yet can we really speak of evil creativity? An artist may be driven by demonic powers or may have a demonic imagination (Leonardo da Vinci is a case in point), but, inasmuch as it is given to him to perform a truly creative act, his demonism is consumed in the fire of that creativity. These things are not susceptible of moralization. I have frequently come into conflict with traditional religious beliefs on this account. The universe of discourse characteristic of religious orthodoxy is forced to deny creativity altogether, or at best only to tolerate it in a superficial way, because it is to a large extent the expression of an organized social collective, with its norms, taboos, prohibitions and conventions. The creative impulse, on the other hand, is absolutely unique, unbidden and lawless. The stuff of art is inner conflict, conflict between man and the society in which he lives, man and his moral conscience. It is impossible to write a play, a novel or a lyrical poem without coming into conflict with the accepted norms and standards of moral and social behaviour, unless one is satisfied with quasi-artistic pieces glorifying social, moral or religious puppets. Similarly, creative philosophical thought cannot exist if conflict and tragedy are ruled out, if all things are certain and well-defined, if no new questions can arise and the human mind is put at rest. Orthodox systems, whether social or religious, however, do not want to hear of these problems; their attitude to creative unrest, to the searchings and wrestlings of the spirit, is, quite consistently, one of suspicion and hostility.

Most Orthodox theologians either regarded my views on creativity as heretical or thought that I was just beating about the bush, although some conceded that I had raised an important problem. I met with exactly the same attitude among the representatives of Western, Catholic and Protestant, theological thought. (Incidentally it was curious to observe that people in the West wavered in their reactions to my thought between labelling me a 'gnostic' and representing me as an 'Orthodox theologian'!) Indeed, the more closely I became acquainted with the modern Catholic and Protestant world, the more I realized how uncongenial the problem of creativity (or, for that matter, many other problems raised in Russian thought) was to the majority of its spokesmen.

I have already spoken of the unsystematic nature of my thinking. I have been much criticized for my carelessness and apparent incapacity for thoroughgoing philosophical analysis. I accept this criticism, since I am aware that the discursive and deductive processes of reasoning give place in my mind to sudden and disturbing visions. The thoughts to which I attach greatest importance came to me like flashes of lightning, like instantaneous illuminations. When I begin to write I am sometimes carried away to the point of dizziness. My thought flows so fast that I hardly have time to write it down. Often I am forced to leave words unfinished so as to keep up with the rapid course of my thinking. I never think much about the form it takes: it seems to pour forth of its own accord, having, as it were, a word beyond or prior to the ordinary written or spoken words.

When I write I do not ordinarily read other books dealing with the subject with which I am concerned at the moment, nor do I even glance at them if they are lying on my table. To do so would, so it seems to me, constrain the freedom of my thought and weaken my creative powers. I have already mentioned that some of my books were conceived in the most unusual and inappropriate circumstances. Thus *The Destiny of Man* was framed in my mind suddenly while watching a

Diaghilev ballet. Sometimes I had a strange sensation of living and
thinking simultaneously on several levels: I could, for instance, suffer
agonies on account of my own or other people's pain or illness and yet,
at the same time, experience the joy and exultation of creative thought.

An artist must needs be concerned with the adequacy and effectiveness of his finished work. For my part, I have, so far as I can remember,
never been concerned with these things, and I have no claim whatsoever to artistic perfection in my writings. Nevertheless, the inner words
in which my thought is clothed bear their unique freight of sound and
appearance, however inadequate and ineffective their outward expression and their 'objectification' may be. I write in response to an inner
voice which commands me to transmit my mental experience. Writing
is no luxury for me but a means of survival, an almost physiological
necessity. I never looked back on my performance and have no regard
for myself while engaged in the process of performing. There may be
a creative or, rather, an artistic quality about my thought at the moment of its inception; but in other respects my manner is expository. I
write in order to testify to and free my mind from an overwhelming
impression. But when I see my work done within the objective world
and standing over against me as a fixed and irrevocable object, I suffer
agonies of discontent and embarrassment—perhaps something of the
kind one experiences when looking at one's own photograph. Only in
the white heat of creative ecstasy, when none of the divisions and differentiations into subject and object had yet arisen, did I experience
moments of fulfilment and joy. Creative *works* are within time, with
its objectifications, discords and divisions, but the creative *act* is beyond
time: it is wholly within, subjective, prior to all objectification.

There is an intimate link between creativity and contemplation,
although the current tendency is to oppose them. Contemplation must
not be understood as a state of sheer passivity or receptiveness: it comprises a distinctly active and creative element. Thus the aesthetic contemplation of natural beauty is more than a state: it is an act, a breaking
through to another world. Beauty is indeed that other world revealing
itself in our own. And in contemplating beauty man goes out to meet
its call. A poet who is possessed by his vision of beauty is not engaged
in passive observation but in an activity whereby he creates for himself

and re-creates in his imagination the image of beauty. Contemplation does, admittedly, preclude the experience of struggle, conflict and opposition. But it supplies that background against which struggle, conflict and opposition acquire significance. Man ought to be able from time to time to fall back on contemplation in order to obtain relief from the activism of existence which, as we know too well to-day, can tear him to pieces.

CHAPTER IX

THE RUSSIAN REVOLUTION AND THE DOMAIN
OF COMMUNISM

The experience of the Russian Revolution was a stage in my own personal destiny, not something imposed from without. The Revolution happened to me, although my attitude towards it was critical and I resisted its evil manifestations. There is a widespread tendency among the Russian *émigrés* to regard the Bolshevik Revolution as something brought about by the powers of evil and perpetrated by a band of criminal maniacs, while they, the *émigrés*, dwelt in untarnished truth and light. I find this tendency quite abhorrent. In point of fact, everyone is responsible for and implicated in the Revolution and, in the first instance, those reactionary forces of the old *régime* which now plead innocence. I believe that the revolution in Russia was inevitable and richly deserved, but I never saw it in rosy hues. On the contrary, I foresaw that in the Revolution the cause of freedom would be jeopardized, and elements hostile to culture would prevail. I wrote a great deal to that effect, but hardly anyone saw fit to agree with me. The expectations of the revolutionary humanists about the coming idyll of a bloodless revolution, in which the goodness of human nature in general and of the popular masses in particular would at last be revealed, seemed to me a piece of gross credulity and *naïveté*. A revolution is, in fact, a serious disease and a source of agony to those who undergo it; it is a symptom of creative disablement, of a neglected responsibility, or of the responsibility men incur by doing nothing. The Russian Revolution, like many other revolutions, was not the outcome of a creative act on the part of man: it was in a large measure dominated by fate.

I welcomed 'the Fall of the Holy Russian Tsardom' (the title of an article of mine published at the beginning of the Revolution): I regarded it as a just and ineluctable process of 'dis-incarnation', of the undoing of a series of historical symbols, which have been invested with a sacred meaning but, in the course of history, belied reality as it was, and not as the champions of the monarchy imagined it to be. This inevitable process of casting off false appearances and pretences, however, was not in itself a guarantee of the goodness of things to come.

The misfortune of the Russian Revolution did not lie in that it came too early, but in that it came too late. Its character was largely dependent on the circumstances caused by the war; and there was something sad and disappointing in the very fact that it arose out of the war. Undoubtedly the revolution had gathered momentum during the preceding hundred years; it had behind it a great tradition of heroic and implacable struggle against oppression, and many revolutionary movements gave impetus to its eventual outbreak. But when it came it did so suddenly and almost unawares: the autocratic monarchy was not really overthrown, rather it broke up and collapsed of its own accord. I remember how, about a month before the February Revolution, I was discussing with two old friends of ours, a Menshevik and a Bolshevik, the chances for revolution and the overthrow of the monarchy in Russia. The Menshevik's view was that we would have to wait for another twenty-five years, whilst the Bolshevik maintained that fifty years must pass before it could happen. The Bolsheviks did not so much prepare the Revolution as make use of a moment when everything got out of hand. This is evidence of that fateful character of the Revolution, to which I have referred. And, even while acknowledging the truth of the Revolution, we must not forget that a large element in it was a fateful, negative outburst of elemental and, indeed, demonic forces.

During the year preceding the Revolution there were a series of private meetings which seemed to mark a certain check in the longstanding and gradual process of disintegration among the intelligentsia, and in which the left was represented by the Social Democrats and Social Revolutionaries, as well as by some Bolsheviks, and the right by the Kadets. Elena Kuskova and Sergey Prokopovich were the central figures at these meetings. The revolutionary Social Democrat Potresov, at one time an associate of Lenin, used to come arm in arm with Vera Zassulich (a very old woman by then). The Bolshevik Skvortsov-Stepanov, subsequently editor of *Izvestia*, also appeared from time to time. As a constant participant in these meetings, I had ample opportunity of observing the psychology of the political elements which were about to play such an important rôle in the revolutionary destiny of Russia. These people gave the impression of being in the grip of some superior, irrational power, of a fate entirely beyond their control; and this is what seemed to unite them.

As was usually the case, however, I remained aloof even while actively sharing in the activities of the group. When the February Revolution flared up I found myself a complete stranger.[1] I was, above all, revolted by the way in which some members of the revolutionary intelligentsia were intent on making a career in the Provisional Government and by the ease with which they turned into respectable government officials. To see the fighters for freedom become almost overnight upstarts and timeservers has been one of the most painful experiences of my life, which I am now witnessing once more in France after her defeat.

The first and comparatively freedom-loving Revolution was not long-lived. Kerensky and his associates made nonsense of it by their complete misapprehension of the situation and their inability to grapple with the inescapable problems.[2] The summer of 1917 was like a night-

[1] During the days of the February Revolution N(ikolai) A(lexandrovich's) attitude was displayed in the following heroic act, of which I have a vivid recollection. News had reached us from Petersburg of the outbreak of the Revolution. Crowds filled the streets of Moscow, and the most incredible rumours were circulating. The atmosphere was highly charged and an explosion might have occurred at any moment. N. A., my sister and I went out to join the revolutionary crowd which was moving towards the Riding School. As we approached it we saw that a huge crowd had already gathered round the Square. The Square itself was occupied by a detachment of soldiers standing ready to shoot. The threatening crowd came nearer and nearer—a closed ring pressing in on the Square. There was a terrible moment in which we expected a volley from the guns and rifles. Just then I turned to say something to N. A.: but he was not there; he had disappeared. Afterwards we realized that he had pushed his way through the crowd and then through the wire entanglement: we saw him going up to the soldiers and calling on them not to fire on the crowd and not to shed blood. The soldiers did not fire. To this day it is a miracle to me that he was not shot on the spot by the officer in command of the detachment. (Note by E. R.)

[2] One day I was at home alone. The bell rang and in rushed Andrey Bely. Without any greeting he shouted in an agitated voice: 'Do you know where I have been?' But

mare. The heated revolutionary atmosphere seemed to be on the point of bursting into an unheard-of and all-consuming conflagration. During the spring and early summer I already had a distinct presentiment that the Revolution would not stop at the February stage and that eventually it would prove anything but bloodless. Strange though it may seem, however, I felt inwardly happier after the October Revolution, in the Soviet period, than during the preceding months: partly because the Bolsheviks showed greater awareness of the situation and a greater courage in facing the revolutionary storm, but also because by that time I had already lived through the initial shock and, having found an inner meaning in what had happened, I did not feel frustrated by the pressure of events. The events seemed indeed to provide an additional impetus for activity. I embarked upon an extensive educational plan: I gave lectures, read papers, wrote, discussed and took an active part in the All-Russian Union of Writers. I also founded the Free Academy of Moral Science.[1] The possibility of engaging in such activities is an illustration of the degree of liberty which the ideological opponents of Bolshevism enjoyed in the first years after the October Revolution. Contrary to the general impression, the Soviet Government did not use methods of wholesale oppression until it was faced with the task of wrestling with half the world without and counter-revolutionary terror within.

I watched with pain and bewilderment the flight of the Russian army from the front, which, by now, had turned into a kind of mass movement. My reactions issued from a mixture of patriotism and military honour, which must have been infused into me by my family back-

he did not wait for an answer and went on: 'I have seen him, him, Kerensky . . . he said . . . a crowd of thousands . . . ecstasy . . . prophecy . . . !' Thereupon Bely threw up his hands in rapture. 'I saw,' he continued, '. . . I saw how a ray of light fell on him. I saw the birth of New, Eternal Man . . .' While Bely was speaking, or rather proclaiming, Nikolai Alexandrovich had come unnoticed into the room, and at these last words he burst out laughing. Andrey Bely threw a lightning glance at him and without a word rushed out of the room. He did not come to see us for a long time after this. (Note by E. R.)

[1] The original Russian name is *Svobodnaya Akademya Dukhovnoy Kultury* (Free Academy of Spiritual Culture). The nearest German equivalent of *dukhovnaya kultura* is *Geisteswissenschaft*, which is sometimes rendered into English as Moral Science. (Tr.)

ground and upbringing. There were moments when I was almost prepared to identify myself with the attitude of the generals and professional soldiers of the time. On second thoughts, however, I would not
have surrendered to these instincts, in view of the unique circumstances
of a tremendous historical upheaval. Later on my attitude changed, and
I began to see events in a deeper and wider perspective. In any case I
did not doubt the utter inevitability of Russia's experience of Bolshevism. 'Historical inevitability' is, admittedly, often a grand name by
which people seek to fortify themselves and sometimes even to para-
lyse their antagonists: but this was a different inevitability, showing a
decisive experience in the inner destiny of the Russian people and
ushering Russia into a new world in which she was enabled to speak
the full truth about herself. There is no return to what was before the
Bolshevik Revolution, and all attempts at restoration, even of the
principles of the February Revolution, appeared to me as both powerless and harmful. After the experience of a catastrophe of the dimensions
of the communist Revolution there can only be a forward movement,
an *Aufhebung* (in Hegel's sense), and the facts of the past have no importance whatever except for the facts of the future. This realization
of the deeper significance of revolutionary events, however, did not
make me applaud the rule of the Bolsheviks.

As a result of a number of circumstances I found myself for a short
time a member of the Council (*Soviet*) of the newly proclaimed Republic (pre-Parliament)[1]—a position which, so far as I was concerned,
seemed almost grotesque. But it was another opportunity for seeing at
close quarters the currents and undercurrents in revolutionary Russia.
There I found many acquaintances from my political past, who now
thronged the political stage after years of persecution and 'illegal'
existence and presented a pitiful sight as political skipjacks and busy-
bodies. Kerensky indulged mainly in hysterical ravings. The whole
atmosphere was exceedingly unpleasant and nauseating, and my mind
was preoccupied with one thought, how was I to get away from this
nightmare? By the beginning of 1918 I succeeded in dispelling my
mood of irritation. Unpleasant facts have a way of getting more and

[1] Appointed before October by Kerensky but comprising at the beginning a
number of Bolsheviks. (Tr.)

more unpleasant if one does not face them. New and difficult problems and unpleasantnesses arose with the establishment of the Soviet *régime*. In the spring of 1918 I wrote *The Philosophy of Inequality*, the book which I dislike most among all those I have written. There is much in it which I regard now as unjust and untrue to my deeper convictions. Some people have reproached me with having written it at all; others with having disclaimed it. The only thing about the book which I am not prepared to recant is the fact that it was written out of an intense concern for freedom over against the spiritual—rather than social—egalitarianism let loose by the Revolution and the reign of the 'common man' and the 'collective mind'. I defended the evident truth that the only source of true social equality is to be found in a recognition of the dignity and worth of the human person. Inasmuch as Bolshevism repudiated this truth, I regarded it as an ugly phenomenon, even though I was not unaware that revolutions in their very inevitability are ugly and that in them moral purity is sullied by applicability. To say this was after all an expression of fidelity to myself. The five years of my life under the Soviet *régime* were in fact a continuous moral struggle, which, however, did not begin then, but was known to me whenever and wherever I came up against the pressures of this world. To have remained independent, and to that extent true to oneself, in the conditions of revolutionary and post-revolutionary Russia was no easy thing, and I confess to a certain pride in having withstood the pressure of these conditions.

One of the most tangible and painful changes which came about as a result of the revolutionary upheaval was the astounding transformation in the appearance of many men and women. A new type of man seemed to have emerged. There was none of the tolerance and kindness in him so characteristic of the pre-revolutionary type of Russian; none of the pining for what is not; none of the anarchism which respects no rules; no doubts, no subjective reactions, no melancholy, no introspection. All this gave place to a buoyant and somewhat aggressive optimism and a readiness to conform to anybody and to do anything. The faces showed eyes firmly fixed on the external realities; sympathy and mercy for others, especially for those holding heretical views, became an unknown quality. 'Pushing', self-confidence and thirst for recognition by others dominated human relationships among these people. With the disappearance of the Russian lie-abed many other and more positive qualities disappeared; but there was greater readiness than hitherto to face trouble and the attendant risk.

Despite this 'typological' change life itself in Soviet Russia was intensely interesting and even thrilling. The Revolution had released many forces—not only 'careers open to talent' but hitherto unknown spiritual energies. There was something almost supernaturally significant in the events which succeeded each other daily and opened up ever new vistas and new problems—a quality which is singularly absent in the catastrophe which France is experiencing as I write. As I have already noted, I also found myself plunged into feverish activities; but these were of a non-political character. The dangers and uncertainties of existence made personal relations for me easier, even though 'officially' the personal element came to be regarded as a matter of contempt. It is noteworthy that many people who later on, in the emigration, were dominated by mutual enmity and resentment showed a genuine capacity for friendship and understanding.

I did not conceal my attitude to communism. Indeed, I waged an open war against its spirit, or rather against its hostility to the spirit. Least of all did I desire restoration. I was entirely convinced that the old world had come to an end and that a return to it was alike impossible and undesirable. Sometimes I even believed that the attitude and psychology of the émigrés was almost a greater evil than the excesses of the Revolution. I was utterly opposed to every kind of intervention from without, and to the interference of foreigners in the destiny of Russia. Many émigrés were playing into the hands of Russia's external enemy, moved by the outrages of the Bolshevik régime of which they were the victims. But I could not adopt this attitude, for reasons which I have already stated, and also because the Russian people had their back to the wall, besieged on all sides and desperately struggling for survival. It was more than a question of 'which rule is to be preferred'. I was convinced that the guilt and responsibility for the horrors of the Revolution lay above all on the men of the old régime, and that it was not for them to sit in judgment on these horrors. Later I came to realize that the leaders of the Russian renascence, of whom I was one, also had their share in the guilt of the hostile attitude of the Russian Revolution towards spiritual values: we were guilty of social irresponsibility, of softness, self-sufficiency and pseudo-aristocratism. The supreme responsibility, however, lies with historical Christianity and with Christians, who have failed to fulfil their duty. Communism was for me from the very start a challenge and a reminder of an unfulfilled Christian duty. Christians ought to have embodied the truth of communism: had they done so, its falsehood would never have won the day. Throughout my exile in the West this conviction was the dominant idea behind my social activities. Communism marked a crisis of Christianity as well as of humanism. In addition, it proved of enormous consequence for much that was to happen in Western Europe—not because of any alleged *Drang nach Westen* on the part of revolutionary Russia, but, first and foremost, because of the spiritual implications of her revolutionary experience. But the impact was a complex one and the response of Western Europe to that impact was in some instances one of blind reaction. Fascism is a case in point.

The communist Revolution marked the end of the Russian intelligentsia. Revolutions have always been unrewarding to those who nurtured them, and the attitude of the Russian Revolution to the intelligentsia which paved the way to it was one of black ingratitude: it persecuted and threw overboard (in its initial stages) the whole of pre-revolutionary Russian culture and repudiated its historic value. This went to show that I was right in believing that freedom is not democratic but aristocratic: freedom is uninteresting and unnecessary to the masses in revolt, and the burden of freedom is too heavy for them to bear. Human existence is dominated and torn by the symbols of bread and freedom, and revolutions more often than not reject freedom in the name of bread. In Russian communism the will to power proved stronger than the will to freedom, and the element of power politics more decisive than that of genuine revolutionary socialism.

I have just said that there was something exhilarating in the atmosphere of post-revolutionary Russia. It was not possible to remain inactive, and, despite the overwhelming pressure of events, nobody felt crushed or downhearted save those who were frightened out of their wits and dared not say their soul was their own. Even when labour conscription was introduced and I had to clear away snow or to march in the early mornings through the cold, dark streets to dig outside the town, I did not feel at all depressed and unhappy, despite the unaccustomed strain of the pick and shovel on my sedentary muscles and the feeling of dizziness when engaged in hard physical labour. I could not help realizing the justice of my predicament. In Petersburg and elsewhere the hunger became real starvation. The shortages in Moscow were less severe, though we were pretty hungry on the little bread and potatoes we were able to get. But all food tasted better than in the years of plenty. I still lived in our flat (now permanently unheated) with its familiar furniture, with the portraits of my ancestors—generals wearing ribbons, stars and crosses. By some miracle the flat was not requisitioned. My library remained intact owing to the peculiar attitude of the authorities to paper! Every bit of paper, blank or not, in book form and in newspaper sheets, acquired a kind of sacred significance: Russia turned into a bureaucratic kingdom of paper.

At that time many writers went to the Crimea to avail themselves of the services of Lunacharsky, who, alongside Maxim Gorky, had become a patron of the arts and provided means of subsistence for the badly shaken republic of letters. I was opposed to any such move and felt no inclination to become a court philosopher to the comrade of my youth, Lunacharsky. I even quarrelled with some of my old friends on this account, for instance, with Vyacheslav Ivanov and Gershenzon. I do not think now that my attitude was justified, especially in regard to Gershenzon, who accepted the communist revolution not because he was an opportunist but because he sincerely believed that the devastating revolutionary storm would free the modern soul from the oppressive scales of excessive culture and knowledge.

The Soviet order had by then not yet been fully worked out or put into practice; it certainly could not as yet be called a totalitarian *régime*, and it was full of contradictions and inconsistencies. Before general 'academic rations' came into existence, a special, even if very meagre, food allowance was made to the better-known writers, irrespective of their ideological position; and they were jokingly called 'the immortals'. I found myself one of these. But this favour coincided with my first arrest and imprisonment by the Cheka. Fortunately, the Cheka was not entirely in control of the destiny of Russia. The Kremlin, which, as Herzen had prophesied sixty years ago, has now become the heart of the nation, and for the possession of which there was a fierce struggle ending in the establishment of Bolshevik control, was also inhabited by the representatives of the old Russian intelligentsia—Kamenev, Lunacharsky, Bukharin, Ryazanov and others. Their attitude to those members of the intelligentsia who did not join forces with communism was unlike that of the Cheka. They were disposed to act as the generous enemy and were probably genuinely concerned by the persecution let loose on their former political associates.

In 1918 I took part in a church procession headed by the Patriarch, which became something of a demonstration on a large scale. People joined it in the face of possible victimization, although actually the government did not interfere.

As usual I continued to write a great deal, but no opportunity for publishing presented itself. I wrote four books, among them *The Meaning of History* and a philosophico-literary essay on Dostoevsky, both of which were based on lectures and studies in seminars. The problems of the philosophy of history exercised my mind a great deal at the time, and the historical crisis and catastrophe which I was witnessing were propitious for such enquiries. My book on Dostoevsky was prompted by the social and religious implications of the 'Legend of the Grand Inquisitor'.

Apart from writing I actively participated in the administration of the All-Russian Union of Writers, which had to be registered under the category of printers (since there was, significantly enough, no professional branch dealing with the work of writers!); and, for a year, was its acting president. Whenever there arose a need of interceding for the members of the Union, of obtaining their release from prison or of averting eviction from their homes, I was, as a rule, asked to go and see Kamenev, the President of the Moscow City Soviet of Workers' Deputies, who later on shared the political vacillation and eventually the tragic fate of Zinoviev and was alleged to have been implicated in the murder of Kirov. Kamenev had a pleasant way with him; he in-

variably defended the interests of the scholars and writers and did a
great deal on behalf of the persecuted intellectuals. Yet each visit to
him meant a tremendous effort for me, and his somewhat genial manner
did not make it any easier. On one occasion I even had a meeting with
Kalinin, President of the Central Executive Committee, together with
another member of the Union of Writers, in order to intercede for the
release from prison of Mikhail Ossorgin, who had been arrested in connection with the Red Cross for the relief of political prisoners (this
relief society was organized by the intelligentsia, but, paradoxically
enough, was sponsored by the Soviet Government itself). In the course
of our conversation we referred to Lunacharsky, but Kalinin, the
nominal head of the Soviet State, made the following astounding
statement: 'Lunacharsky's recommendation has no significance whatsoever: it is as unimportant as any recommendation I might have given
you. It would be a different matter had you been authorized to refer
to Comrade Stalin.'

In 1920 the Faculty elected me Professor of Philosophy at the University of Moscow, and, for a year, I gave lectures in which I openly
and without any hindrance criticized Marxism. I was able to subsist,
however, and to make ends meet, only thanks to my share in the
Writers' Shop. The chief organizer of this Shop was Ossorgin: it became something of a literary club, which, apart from the opportunities
it gave of meeting other people, provided food, warmth and light.

Since the very first days of the Revolution and throughout all my
life in Soviet Russia until my exile there were gatherings every Tuesday
in our house in the Maly Vassylevski Lane, with the usual papers,
lectures and discussions. I also spoke a great deal in public; and I do not
think that at any time before or since have I had such enormous audi-
encies as during these troubled years. There were a number of anarchist
groups and movements, some of which proved decisive factors in the
development of the Revolution, and, until 1921 (the year of the
Kronstadt rebellion in which anarchist influences played a part) they
were tolerated by the Soviet Government and had their own book
stores, printing offices and organs of propaganda. One of the anarchist
clubs announced a debate on Christ (it must have been late in 1918 or
early in 1919), and I was invited, along with some bishops and priests

(who, however, failed to come), to address the meeting.[1] A number of Tolstoyans, followers of Nikolai Fyodorov, professing a mixture of Fyodorov's ideas and anarchist communism, some straightforward anarchists and communists also took part in the debate. As I entered the crowded hall, I had an almost physical sensation of terrific tension in the air. The crowd contained a great many Red Army men, sailors and workers. The whole atmosphere was significant of the elemental forces behind the Revolution, exulting in the downfall of intolerable restraints, wanton, unbridled, ruthless, and frank to the point of naked shamelessness. One worker read a paper on the Gospel, in which he affirmed as scientifically proved that the Mother of God was a prostitute and Jesus Christ the illegitimate son of a Roman soldier—a statement which was greeted with wild applause from the audience. He also dwelt incessantly on the 'contradictions' and 'inconsistencies' in the Gospels. He was followed by a Tolstoyan who made a sharp attack on the Church. A follower of Fyodorov, who described himself as a 'biocosmist', produced, in what sounded like unprintable slang, some incredible hotch-potch of science, gnosticism and the Gospels. He finished by proclaiming that, since the maximum social programme had already been put into practice, 'the cosmic resurrection of the dead' will occur any moment. This statement provoked an uproar of laughter in the audience. The next speaker, and the best of them all, was an anarchist. Having listened to all the speakers I felt completely paralysed, not knowing what to say or how to extricate myself from the frightful predicament. But I made an intense spiritual effort, concentrated all my powers, and got up to speak when asked to do so. With the very first words I felt as if I was seized by some power inspiring me and giving me strength and all the words appropriate for the occasion. Indeed, I do not think I have ever spoken better in my life than at this meeting. I said approximately what I expounded later in my pamphlet *On the Worth of Christianity and the Unworthiness of Christians*. At first the audience was extremely hostile and drowned my words in hisses, cries

[1] The anarchists were the only revolutionary group with which I was in contact in the years following the Revolution. They frequently asked me to speak at their meetings, and I gave a course of lectures on the 'Ethics of Language' in the State Institute of Language.

and derisive ejaculations. But gradually I gained control over it, and
ended my speech in a roar of applause. When I had finished people
came up to me, shook me by the hand and thanked me.

I also remember a public lecture on 'Science and Religion' in the hall
of the Polytechnic Museum. There were probably about two thousand
people present, mostly workers and Red Army men, as well as many
communists. After the lecture the public asked for the debate to be
opened. But I had to explain that the lecture had been authorized only
on condition that there should be no debate. On this a man standing
behind me suddenly came forward and said: 'In the name of the
Extraordinary Commission (Cheka) I declare the debate open.' The
atmosphere was similar to that of the previous occasion. And there was
the same keenness and interest in the questions under discussion. The
most interesting experience, however, awaited me when, on returning
home, I observed a large group of people, consisting mostly of workers,
following me across the Arbat Square. One of them approached me
and began with great vehemence to attack God and religion. I asked
him why he had stayed on and listened to my lecture, whereupon he
said: 'I want my convictions and arguments against God and faith to
be disproved. I want to see if I can stand up to God.' Nothing of this
kind could ever have been said by the young Russian émigrés, who seem
to have lost completely the searching mind and the intense spiritual
disquietude characteristic of the Russian.

The iconoclasm of the Revolution did not succeed in destroying all
vestiges of cultural life, and some links with the Russian spiritual
tradition remained intact. It occurred to me, therefore, that an opportunity should be provided for carrying on the cultural work and for
gathering together the available cultural forces. I did not envisage, however, a mere revival of the Religious-Philosophical Societies: I intended
the circle to be as wide as possible and to include representatives of the
most varied trends of thought united in a common recognition of the
independence and primacy of spiritual values. Thus it was that the
Free Academy of Moral Science, which existed up to the time of my
exile in 1922, came into existence. It was the counterpart of the Petersburg Volfila (Free Philosophical Academy). The Moscow and the
Petersburg Academies comprised those who 'accepted Bolshevism' and

those who, while rejecting it, accepted the new age as an age of material destruction and spiritual creation, as well as those who held a completely independent position. There were also a few Orthodox churchmen who condemned atheistic communism and looked towards a new era in which the persecuted and purified Church would be a freer and more genuine witness to the Christian truth. We arranged courses of lectures, seminars, public meetings and debates. Our Moscow Academy could not, of course, have its own premises, as it was independent of any of the existing state institutions; but the authorities made it possible for us to hire public halls. The courses took place in the lecture-rooms of the Women's University, and lectures and seminars were held in various other places.

I remember a course of lectures I gave in the premises of the Central Distillery. Subsequently a statement appeared in *Pravda* to the effect that a Soviet institution was being used by Berdyaev for religious propaganda, and that such occurrences should be stopped immediately. The author of the article, which was based on a denunciation, displayed his wit by ending his contribution with the remark that there had always been a bond between religion and spirit. As a consequence of this incident I was taken to the Cheka along with the chairman of the Central Distillery. I produced a paper, signed by Kamenev, which said that F. A. M. S. was registered in the Moscow Soviet of Workers' Delegates, whereupon I was asked to explain what moral science is, and why and how it differs from physical science. The task was not an easy one! But the Cheka man listened attentively. The incident came to nothing at the time, but it must have contributed to my subsequent expulsion from the Soviet Union.

The lectures on the philosophy of history and the seminar on Dostoevsky were both well attended, with a considerable number of communists among the audience, and in the presence of what looked like a young Cheka agent, invariably sitting in the front row and looking at me with a blank gaze. I always spoke freely without concealing my convictions in any way; and the debates which followed the public lectures were equally outspoken. The last year of F. A. M. S. was particularly successful. On one occasion (the subject of the lecture was Spengler's *Decline of the West*, or possibly theosophy) there was such a vast crowd that people stood in the streets; the staircase was blocked, and it was only with difficulty that I was able to penetrate into the lecture-room. On another occasion I received a note during the lecture from the management of the Women's University, to the effect that there was danger of the floor giving way under the weight of such a number of people. I may note that we never advertised the meetings in the papers (which, in any case, would never have agreed to print our advertisements), and, as a rule, it was only possible to find out about them through the Writers' Shop or through friends.

The success of the Academy's activities was evidence of great intellectual and spiritual interest among the Russians. Although the possibilities of finding this interest in the Russia of to-day are almost non-existent, I cannot imagine that the interest itself has vanished altogether, and I am, in fact, convinced that free thought continues to exist in Russia in one way or another. My conviction is confirmed by a very remarkable letter from a young man which I received in 1934 in Paris, and which was subsequently published in the journal *Put'*. While I was still in Russia the communist organization had not yet made much headway. The revolutionary element was still abroad, and the totalitarian tendencies of the Soviet state had left many aspects of life untouched, having spread chiefly to the sphere of politics and economics. Some non-communist and even anti-communist writers indeed succeeded in publishing a few books, despite the great shortage of paper and the rather ineffective censorship, exercised not directly but through the monopolization of practically all the printing industry by the state.

I never wanted to leave Russia and become an *émigré*, for I had faith in the possibility of the spiritual regeneration and liberation of communist Russia from within. I felt that there was some genuinely human element released by the revolution which might have given a new impetus to creative activity in Russia. But other factors intervened and forced me to leave my country.

I cannot say that the Soviet authorities subjected me to any persecution. But I was arrested and imprisoned on two occasions by the Cheka and later by the G.P.U.; the imprisonment, however, did not last long. The first arrest occurred in 1920 at the time of the affair of the so-called Tactical Centre (an anarchist organ), with which I had no connection, except indirectly through personal acquaintances, many of whom were arrested on the charge of counter-revolution. The arrests were followed by a trial, but my own case was dealt with separately.

One day (actually, it was in the middle of the night), when I was sitting in the inner prison of the Cheka, a warder opened the door of the cell and took me to be cross-examined. I was led through endless dark corridors and up and down winding-staircases. Eventually we came to a clearer and lighter passage with a carpet and entered a large, brightly-lit room with a white bear-skin on the floor. To the left of a writing-desk stood a man in military uniform wearing a red star. He had fair hair, a thin, pointed beard and dull, grey and somewhat melancholic eyes. His appearance and manner suggested good breeding and gentleness. He asked me to sit down and said: 'My name is Dzerzhinsky.' This, then, was the notorious head of the political police, believed to have much blood on his hands, at whose name all Russia trembled with horror. I was the only one among the many arrested who had the honour of being examined by this formidable gentleman. It was a rather solemn affair, with Kamenev and Menzhinsky, the vice-president of the Cheka, present. (I knew the latter in former times when he pursued an unsuccessful literary career in Petersburg.) I do not remember ever having felt frightened, panic-stricken or down-hearted in such or similar situations, which, on the contrary, inspired a fighting mood in me: and on this occasion also I decided to take the offensive rather than defend myself or behave apologetically. I said to Dzerzhinsky: 'Please bear in mind that my dignity as a thinker and writer demands that I should speak frankly and plainly.' To this Dzerzhinsky replied: 'That is what we expect of you.' I then proceeded with my attack and spoke for more than half an hour, giving reasons for my religious, philosophical and moral opposition to communism, while stressing that I was not concerned with party politics. Dzerzhinsky listened very attentively, from time to time interposing a short remark. Once, for example, he said: 'It is possible to be a materialist in theory and an idealist in life, or, on the contrary, an idealist in theory and a materialist in life.' After my speech he put several questions to me, mainly *á propos* of other people. Having already had experience of cross-examinations under the old *régime*, I knew this would come and naturally declined to give any information. Dzerzhinsky himself came to my rescue when he asked a particularly embarrassing question by answering it himself. I learned later on that most of those who were subjected to cross-examination on this occasion gave themselves away, so that the charges against them were based chiefly on their own evidence. When the proceedings were finished Dzerzhinsky said:'I will set you free, but you will not be able to leave Moscow without permission.' Then he turned to Menzhinsky and added: 'It is late and there are plenty of bandits about; would it not be possible to take Mr Berdyaev home by car?' There was no car available, but a Red Guard took me home, with my luggage, on a motor-bicycle. When I left the prison the governor asked if I had 'enjoyed' my stay with them. The *régime* of the Cheka was, in fact, much harder and the discipline far sterner than the prison *régime* in pre-revolutionary days. For one thing, we were kept in complete and strict isolation, and nobody was allowed to see visitors. But the Cheka was at first active largely against political and military rather than ideological enemies, and the murders of the first years after the Revolution were outbursts of popular passion and mob-law. The Cheka became more indiscriminate when dangers from without and from within thickened and fear took the upper hand.

Dzerzhinsky gave me the impression of a man of genuine conviction and sincerity. I do not think that he was an evil or even a naturally cruel man (later on I learnt that he did good work in the reclamation of waif children, though he never publicized his activity). But he was a fanatic, and there was, undoubtedly, something uncanny about him. He came of a noble Polish-Lithuanian family, and showed signs of great refinement. I understand that in the past he had almost become a Roman Catholic monk, but had subsequently transferred his fanatical faith to communism, and turned into a persecuting saint of his new creed.

A few weeks after my release the trial of the Tactical Centre took place. The public was admitted, and I was present at all the sessions. Among the accused there were some who were personal friends of mine. The trial made a grim impression on me: it was a stage-piece in which everything had been decided beforehand. Some of the accused conducted themselves with dignity; but others bowed and scraped. The sentences, however, were not especially heavy, and were conditional.

For some months after this I lived comparatively undisturbed. The situation began to change only in the spring of 1922, with the formation of an anti-religious front and the beginning of anti-religious persecutions. We spent the summer of 1922 in Borvik, an entrancing spot on the bank of the river Moskva, not far from Arkhangelsk, the former estate of the Yussupovs, where Trotsky was living at the time. The woods and the whole landscape round Borvik are some of the most beautiful in central Russia; and for a few weeks we were able to live remote from the post-revolutionary nightmares of city life. It was a relief to be able to spend hours gathering mushrooms. One day I had to go for a very short visit to Moscow. On the night of my arrival— the only one spent in Moscow during the whole summer—I slept in our flat. It was searched, and I was arrested for the second time. I was removed once more to the prison of the Cheka, now re-named G.P.U., where I was kept for about a week. In the course of the first examination I was told that I was to be exiled from the Soviet Union. The examiner produced a document stating that if I crossed the frontier of the U.S.S.R. again, after my exile, I would be shot. I had to sign the paper, and, having done so, I was set free. About two months passed, however, before I succeeded in leaving the country. A whole group of writers, scholars and people engaged in various branches of social work, which had no application to the changing social conditions of the country, were sent into exile. It was an unusual measure, never to be repeated again, except in certain individual cases. My own banishment was based not on any political but on ideological grounds. When I heard of the decision, I was overcome with grief and bitterness: as I have said, I did not want to emigrate, and the prospect of merging with the *émigré* world filled me with something like horror. Yet, at the same time, I could not help feeling that in exile, which I hoped would not last as long as in fact it did, I would be able to breathe more freely.

The German Embassy was of great assistance in arranging our departure: amongst other things, they declined the Soviet Government's request for a collective visa, and, instead, gave all the prospective exiles individual authorizations to go to Germany. During these last days I had to visit the G.P.U. on several occasions in connection with our departure. Once, on entering the offices of the G.P.U., I was surprised to see that the corridor and waiting-rooms were packed with clergy, all of whom turned out to be members of the Living Church.[1] It was a rather unseemly and painful sight. My negative impression of the Living Church was confirmed when I learned that its leaders were chiefly engaged in libellous denunciations of the legitimate representatives of the Russian Orthodox Church, and particularly in informing against the Patriarch, who was to be imprisoned in this same year in consequence of these machinations. This was, to put it mildly, a dubious way of bringing about the reformation which I myself desired. In the G.P.U. waiting-rooms I ran into Bishop Anthony, whom I had met some years ago in Petersburg. He was one of the most talented and progressive Russian bishops, and he played an active part in the Petersburg Religious-Philosophical Society. His part in the reformation of the Church, however, was a very ugly one: he kept on blackmailing other Church leaders and then informing against them. Bishop Anthony came up to me, embraced me and, bubbling over with affection, embarked on enthusiastic reminiscences of the past. His enthusiasm and general behaviour against the background of a G.P.U. waiting-room was positively nauseating, and I was very short with him. This was my last unpleasant memory of Soviet Russia.

It is not easy for me to speak of the experiences and emotions which stirred me when the moment came to take leave of my country, of all the things and all the people that had become the inmost part of my life. The experience was, indeed, more agonizing than I would myself ever have thought possible. But, though at the moment life in exile appeared to me as a mysterious and unwelcome Unknown, it proved in fact intensely significant for me and full of creative possibilities. And, maybe, I would not have fulfilled my calling without this providential displacement.

In the course of my life abroad I have returned more than once to the problems of communism and the Russian Revolution and have de-

[1] A dissenting body of the Russian Orthodox Church, which consisted mainly of opportunists and, besides advocating a number of church-reforms, declared its unconditional support of communism. The government granted this schismatic body certain concessions, but subsequently repudiated it as an unwanted ally. (Tr.)

voted a number of books and essays to them. I was intent on discovering the meaning of the revolutionary events which came to have such a far-reaching influence on the destiny of Russia as well as of the whole world. In my effort to evaluate these events I did my best to rise above the political *pros* and *cons*, to make a clean sweep of all *ressentiment* and vested interest, and to see not only the falsehood but also the truth of communism. I recoiled instinctively from the moods prevalent among the Russian *émigrés*, who were blinded by rancour and a desire to pay off old scores and recover their lost positions. If I opposed communism, I did so solely on account of the freedom of the spirit, not because I desired to preserve this or that social or political order. I opposed communism precisely because I believed in the freedom and ultimate independence of the human person *vis-à-vis* all social and political orders. Freedom may, as a matter of fact, still be tied by a thousand bonds to the reign of necessity. But communism, inasmuch as it lays down the law of that reign and acts accordingly, imperils the living principle of freedom and personality. I did not, however, oppose communism in so far as it deals with the delimited sphere of social and economic organization and is based on a scientific analysis of certain aspects of social life. I believe that the organization of material resources for the benefit of all and the curtailment of economic individualism will make men not less but more aware of those final realities and values of human existence which are imperilled by communism and anti-communism alike. I am prepared to describe myself as a socialist, but my socialism is personalistic, not authoritarian: it precludes the primacy of society over the person, for it springs from a recognition of the supreme value of each individual human being made in the image God and endowed with a free spirit. If Marxism is in earnest about its avowed aim to liberate humanity from servitude to economics, then I am a Marxist. I cannot assent to any exteriorization of the personal conscience—to its transference to the collective. For conscience is within man, in the depth of his freedom where he enters into relation with God. 'Collective conscience' is itself a mythological expression of a condition in which man has undergone a process of self-estrangement and lost the true centre of his existence. That is perhaps why communism has much in it that is religious in character—not only because, in fact, it has been the inheritor of many religious and Christian ideas and traditions, but because it possesses certain psychological qualities which serve as a substitute for religion. The worship of the collective is an unmistakably religious phenomenon—a form of idolatry, similar to that of nationalism, racialism, capitalism, and the rest. As a critique and judgment upon proleterianized capitalist society, with its privileges and vested interests, however, communism seemed to me irrefutable, and I regarded all attempts at refuting communism which proceed from the assumptions on which that society is built as unconvincing, futile and stultifying.

Shortly before my exile K., a communist of culture and learning (qualities which were unusual among the communists at the time) and president of the Academy of Arts, of which I was a member, told me in conversation that 'they hope in the Kremlin that when you find yourself in Western Europe you will understand on which side justice lies': in other words, that I would come to understand the injustice of the capitalist world. But I did not need to be exiled to Western Europe in order to understand the falsehood and injustices of the capitalist order. I had never failed to understand this and never had any liking for the bourgeois world. My views on this matter are expressed in many writings and, perhaps, most forcibly in *The Meaning of the Creative Act*. But I have probably become more socialist in Western Europe than I would have been had I remained in Soviet Russia, although my socialism had primarily a spiritual rather than a political or economic source. If my socialist leanings were particularly pronounced during my life in exile, this was due to a twofold reaction: a reaction, in the first instance, against the surrounding bourgeois-capitalist world and, in the second, against the tendencies prevalent among the Russian *émigrés*. I admit that such a reaction was itself evidence of a relative dependence on my environment. Still, I doubt whether I have fully justified the hopes of the Kremlin, for I have remained an enemy of totalitarianism, in whatever form it paraded, in Russia and in the West alike. As to the *émigrés*, I seem to have become a kind of permanent thorn in their flesh, and they did their best to disqualify me on account of my alleged 'communist' or 'bolshevizing' tendencies.

If I were to summarize the lesson I have learnt throughout this time of trials and ordeals in revolutionary and post-revolutionary Russia, I would say that it has imbued me with a bitter feeling for the verdicts of history. At times the historical stage is dominated by those who call out

> *Away from the shouts and the sniggers, the hands that are slimy with blood,*
> *Away, to the camp of the outlawed who struggle and perish for love.*[1]

And they go down into history as men and women who have made supreme sacrifices and surrendered their lives for a great cause. But then the hour strikes for them and their cause to triumph and be victorious: and lo, they too are quick to turn into those who shout and sneer and whose hands are slimy with blood. New generations follow and are impelled by a desire to join the camp of the outlawed. Thus the tragi-comedy of history goes on for ever in unremitting, perpetual recurrence. The Kingdom of God alone transcends and overcomes this spell-bound course.

[1] Translated by P. J. Thompson from a poem by Nicolai Nekrasov. (Tr.)

CHAPTER X

RUSSIA AND THE WEST

The group of exiles left Russia in 1922. We went through Petersburg, thence, by sea, to Stettin and reached Berlin in October. There were twenty-five of us, and, together with our families, about seventy-five. The boat (*Oberbuergermeister Haken*) for the voyage from Petersburg to Stettin was entirely occupied by our party. When we left Soviet waters behind us many had a feeling of being out of danger: until then no one was certain that we would not be sent back at the last minute. A new life was opening before us. We felt free; yet in me the sense of freedom was transfused by a sense of intense pain at parting, perhaps irrevocably, with my native land. The voyage across the Baltic was wonderful; the sea was calm and smooth; the sun beat down from an unclouded sky, and the nights were mild and starry. On arrival in Berlin we were met with courtesy and kindness by representatives of various German organizations, which also assisted us in the difficult practical matter of starting our lives in a foreign country. No Russian *émigrés* came to meet us.

Like so many Russians before, I had always been something of a 'European', and since my childhood our frequent visits abroad had been great events for me. Walking now in the streets of Berlin, however, I was conscious of the contrast between two worlds—a contrast which I was destined to bear within me for many years to come. I did not feel pity for myself as an exile, but I yearned for Russia. Germany at that time was a very unhappy country. Berlin was crowded with disabled soldiers; the mark was falling at an incredible speed; and '*Deutschland ist verloren*' never left the lips of the Germans. I saw what I had witnessed so many times before: the first prove to be the last, and the last are the first.

The first unpleasant experience in Germany was my clash with the *émigrés*. The majority of them met the exiles with extreme suspicion and even hostility. Some even began spreading rumours that we were hired Bolshevik agents sent by the Soviet Government with the secret aim of undermining and demoralizing the Russian *émigrés* (a task which the *émigrés* were already themselves successfully performing). Soon after our arrival there was a meeting of a number of exiles and some leading *émigrés* belonging to the so-called White Movement. At the head of this group stood Peter Struve, with whom I had been associated in the past (we had parted company some time ago and, except for this occasion and just before his death, we never met even in exile). The meeting took place in my flat and began in a spirit of apparent goodwill, but ended in a storm. For a time I tried to contain myself, but the provocation was too strong: I duly flew into a rage and began to shout (even the landlady came out and said she would call the police). Plans to overthrow Bolshevism by means of military intervention, which became a kind of day-dream among the *émigrés*, were for me a monstrosity or, rather, a monstrous farce, and I realized that it was hopeless to expect from them the slightest understanding of the real situation. I had no faith in or sympathy with the White Movement: it belonged to an irretrievable past; it was irrelevant—just 'sound and fury signifying nothing', but, at times, something very pernicious. For my part, I envisaged a wholly different way of saving Russia from the perils of Bolshevism: I believed in her regeneration from within, through a painful process of inner purification. This is not a very spectacular remedy, but it is no less effective for that. I was conscious that Russia in her revolutionary experience, and through her the whole world, was on the threshold of a new historical epoch, and that, as a result of that experience, she would come to learn her true vocation. I confess to an angry antipathy for the typical 'White' *émigrés*: their impenitence, their obduracy and self-infatuation were quite astounding. They did not so much as consider the possibility of themselves being or ever having been in the wrong. Their most significant and distressing characteristic, however, consisted in their open hostility to freedom, although they desired as much elbow-room as possible for themselves. They were, in fact, quite indifferent to the only relevant critique of Bolshevism, namely that which issues from the recognition of the supreme value of freedom. Freedom of thought was recognized no more among

the *émigrés* than in Soviet Russia. I came to the conclusion that they
were suffering from a phobia: they never stopped talking about Bolshevism and appeared quite unable to think of anything else, suspecting
Bolshevik agents wherever they looked. It was the case of an acute and
chronic psychological complex, by which many *émigrés* are beset up to
the present day.

In 1922 I made a suggestion that the Western powers should formally
recognize the Soviet Government and establish diplomatic relations
with it. This, in my view, would make it easier for Russia to come out
of her state of isolation and see herself in a wider perspective, which in
turn might serve to extenuate the less attractive aspects of Bolshevism
and ease the world situation. My suggestion horrified even the most
enlightened left-wing *émigrés*. In face of this opposition I resolved to
avoid contacts with *émigré* circles and met only those few exiles with
whom I had come to Germany. It was only on moving to Paris that I
began to mix with the wider circles of Russians abroad.

Soon after our arrival in Berlin some exiles embarked on a series of
cultural enterprises, and I found myself again immersed in social activities. But I devoted more time to study and writing. Since there were
a number of university professors and scholars among us, it was suggested that an independent educational institution should be founded,
and this resulted in the establishment of the Institute of Science in Berlin.
I became Dean of one of its departments. There was an immediate
response among the rank and file of the *émigrés*. The German Government, which was then led by the Social Democrats and the Catholic
Centre, took a considerable interest in our enterprise, and helped in
various ways in the running of the Institute. In general, the Germans
showed us great consideration, and we were constantly invited to attend
official meetings and dinners in our honour. In this connection I met
a number of German Social Democrat ministers, who struck me as
rather dull though extremely well-meaning. The interest and attention
shown to the Russian intellectuals by the Germans cannot even be
compared to the attitude of the French. Whereas the Germans displayed
an interest in the world outside and hoped to learn something from it,
the French remained shut in their own cultural universe and had very
little interest in anything else—despite the fact that the Germans are

far more nationalistically-minded and more aggressive than the French.

The Institute of Science did strictly academic work, and, though I did my best to contribute to this, it provided little attraction for me. I felt more inspired by the Russian Religious-Philosophical Academy founded in Berlin on my initiative and subsequently transferred to Paris. The name was somewhat spectacular and pretentious, but it was chosen *faute de mieux* and with a view to carrying on the tradition of the Moscow Academy of Moral Science and the Religious-Philosophical Societies.

We were greatly assisted in the foundation of the Academy by the Young Men's Christian Association (Y.M.C.A.), and it was in the flat of the secretary of the Y.M.C.A. in Berlin, Paul Anderson, a very fine man with a deep interest in and sympathy for Russians, that the Academy came into being. Cultural work among the Russians abroad was indeed made possible only thanks to the disinterested help of the Y.M.C.A. and its representatives Anderson and Donald Lowrie. The Y.M.C.A. also published many works of Russian writers and thinkers. Its help has proved of immense value to Russian culture and will undoubtedly be appreciated inside Russia when conditions return to normal. One of my closest collaborators in the Religious-Philosophical Academy was the Russian philosopher Simeon Frank.

Paul Anderson introduced me to Gustav Kullmann, a Swiss, who was also at that time a secretary of the Y.M.C.A. but subsequently joined the Secretariat of the League of Nations. We were surprised to meet in Kullmann a man entirely representative of the Western spirit and yet sharing our own spiritual and intellectual experience, and capable of a genuine understanding of our concern and our problems. He was a man of profound culture and great open-mindedness, which made it possible for him to do important work in the religious, social and political spheres alike.

The American Y.M.C.A. helped to create the Russian Student Christian Movement (the name is open to misunderstanding, since the Movement did not consist of students). The Religious-Philosophical Academy also had links with the Student Movement, and we took an active part in the Movement's first conference in Psherov in Czechoslovakia.

With a few exceptions, however, the work of the Academy had little response among the *émigrés*. Its emphasis on understanding the events and ideas in the post-war and post-revolutionary world and its spirit of free enquiry proved a source of constant provocation to their frightened and reactionary minds. The standard of intellectual interest and culture among the young people was on the whole rather low. The majority were mainly preoccupied either with ways and means of overthrowing Bolshevism and with the White Movement or with stuffy, ritualistic piety. As a result, I felt a growing desire to break away altogether from the closed circle in which the *émigrés* lived and thought, and to draw nearer to the people of the West.

In Berlin I made the acquaintance of a number of German thinkers, among them Max Scheler, whom I used to meet also later on in Paris. I read Scheler's works with great interest and found many of his ideas akin to mine. In many instances we seemed to arrive at the same conclusions, although we proceeded from different premises and thought in a different idiom. But my first meeting with Scheler was disappointing. I soon discovered that he had moved away not only from Catholicism but also from Christianity. He was brilliant in conversation and his thinking revealed a rich intellectual imagination. His spontaneous, gentle and almost child-like manner went hand in hand with an astonishing and rather shameless egocentricity. It was impossible to touch on any subject without his reverting to his own person, to his books and his rôle in life. In my opinion he was the most talented and original German philosopher of the day. I felt, nevertheless, the lack of any dominant and integrating idea in his outlook.

About the same time I also made the acquaintance of Count Keyserling, and we continued to meet and to correspond intermittently for many years. He was instrumental in the first German translation of a book of mine (*The Meaning of History*), to which he wrote a flattering preface. I seldom met such a many-sided and many-gifted man. He was a European first and foremost, or even a citizen of the world, rather than a German; he spoke many languages (including Russian) and was thoroughly at home in the culture of many countries. Many people found him difficult and were almost afraid of meeting him. It is true that he was incredibly self-centred; and his self-centredness had nothing of Scheler's simplicity. He was narcissistic and entirely absorbed in his own achievements. I do not know why Keyserling should have taken an interest in my thought in view of his self-absorption and the fundamental differences in our respective views and attitudes to life. I could never agree with his professed dualism of what he called the 'spiritual' and the 'telluric' principles, in which priority belongs to the latter and which has a strongly anti-ethical bias. His a-moralism, however, was Hindu rather than Nietzschean in character.

I also met Spengler in Berlin; I expected a great deal from this meeting but in fact it proved disappointing. Spengler struck me, both in appearance and mentality, as something of a bourgeois, which certainly could not have been said either of Scheler or of Keyserling.

In Berlin I began to work on a book on the philosophy of religion. I also wrote a smaller essay, *The New Middle Ages,* in which I attempted to interpret certain dominant tendencies and events in our age. The work, to my surprise, had a great success: it was translated into fourteen languages and was the subject of a great deal of discussion in many quarters. The essay was my introduction to European intellectual circles. For my part, I never attached a very great importance to it, and it certainly does not occupy the central place in my thought which foreigners have ascribed to it. Its success may have been due to its topical and relatively popular character.

The winter of 1923-4, the last I spent in Germany, was a difficult one: conditions grew worse and the general atmosphere had something ominous about it. We continued the traditional 'at homes' in our flat, which were attended by many young people, some of whom were not at all to my liking. It is interesting to note that at that time there was no absolute break between the Russian *émigrés* and Soviet Russians living or staying abroad (this was particularly true of Berlin). I attached a great importance to the possibility of intercourse between the two sections, and always welcomed at our gatherings Soviet intellectuals as well as *émigrés* who cared to come.

The two years of my life in Berlin were a prelude to my Western wayfaring, Germany being in every sense the boundary of the Russian

East and the European West. I came to share the life of the West fully
only in Paris. I came to Western Europe as a Russian, and it was by
virtue of being a Russian that I was able to love Europe and make her
my own. I feel what Dostoevsky says of all Russians: that they are
capable of being especially European *because* they are especially Russian.
Universalism is a specifically Russian quality. Keyserling complimented
me in one of his essays on being the first Russian thinker who could
be called fully European and for whom the fate of Europe was also his
own fate. It is true, perhaps, that I am less of a foreigner in Western
Europe than other Russians to-day, and share more passionately in her
life: and I am not prepared to admit that this is due merely to the fact
that I met with greater appreciation in the West than among my
countrymen. Nevertheless, I am more of a Russian than my Western
friends believe, and that is probably why I have caused so many mis-
apprehensions and misunderstandings in their minds. Inasmuch as I have
been able to contribute to the philosophical and religious discussion
in the West, I regard this contribution as an eminently Russian one:
I came to the West with a characteristically Russian 'idea', although
it is not easy for me to define in what lies its specifically Russian character. One of the things which made me vividly conscious of the fundamental divergence between the Western and the Russian approach to
the problems of life was the Westerners' excessive emphasis on what
the Germans call *Kultur* and the French *civilisation*. I have referred to
this *à propos* of the meetings at Pontigny, to which I shall return presently. It seemed to me that whenever Western people are confronted
with a problem they tend to be distracted by its historical context, by
its impact on this or that situation, by its 'when' and 'how' rather than
by its 'what'. They are, therefore, apt to think and speak *about* a thing
rather than bear witness to the thing itself. Their thinking is enslaved
and disabled by the excessive weight of history and cultural tradition.
On the other hand, inasmuch as the Western mind is capable of dis-
embarrassing itself from this weight, it reverts, as a rule, to abstract
systems of thought, which are dogmatic and objectivist and eliminate
personal interest and subjective impression. Thomism is a case in point.

I have frequently heard the French say that they are placed high in
the hierarchy of cultural development, whereas the Russians have not

yet left the stage of 'nature', i.e., barbarism. For my part, I believe in the priority (not only chronological but also logical) of barbarism. At the same time, it is the Russian's rather than the Frenchman's business to point out that in Russia the spirits and passions of 'nature' have not yet finally been checked or mastered by the civilizing power of man. Hence the well-known and characteristic 'elemental', unbounded tendencies in the Russian, which are reflected even in the Russian landscape, and which are largely lost in balanced, formalized, and 'civilized' Western Europe. This may also explain the comparative ease with which Russians engage in social intercourse (while possessing no gifts for social organization) and communion with other people: they are less beset by custom and the rules of the social game. Their way of life is less dependent on family conventions, domesticity and moral norms.

A well-known French writer once said to me that of all people the French are the most unforthcoming in human relations (this, however, may also be said of the English), and that this was a result of French individualism. There is, he said, something distant and unapproachable about the French, and their external vivacity only serves to emphasize their sense of fundamental estrangement. I was surprised at the extent of self-isolation pervading French culture and at their lack of interest in other cultures. Anything beyond the Rhine appears to them to be part of the domain of 'barbarism', outside the heritage of Graeco-Roman civilization. That is why Russians, despite the veneer of French cultural habits which they have adopted since the eighteenth century, were never able to penetrate to the sources of French culture. The French believe in the universal character of their own civilization and sometimes do not even suspect the existence of a plurality of cultural types. This attitude seemed to me an intolerable limitation, although I am myself a great admirer and lover of French culture.

I have given a great deal of thought to the problem of Russia and the West, and I discovered that my ideas on this matter proceed on lines similar to those suggested by the German philosopher of history Frobenius. But while his distinctions are applied to the relation between Germany, on the one hand, and the Latin countries and England, on the other, I am inclined to apply them to the relation between Russia and the West, including central Europe. Frobenius held the view that

Germany is endangered by the rationalism coming from the West, and that, in having assimilated this rationalism which issues in a civilization dominated by technology, she will exhaust her cultural energies. But this view applies more properly to the relation between Russia and the whole West. For us Russians Germany is no less Western than France, and we see in both the triumph of rationalism, just as, presumably, for India and China Russia represents the West. These distinctions are significant provided there is nothing fixed and naturalistic about them, and a people's character is seen as made what it is by that people's experience rather than, as in Spengler, by unalterable natural laws.

What, then, is the characteristically Russian 'idea' with which I came to meet the West? I think that, in the first place, I brought with me a pronounced eschatological sense of history, which people in the West, Christians and non-Christians alike, have almost entirely lost and which is only now beginning to re-awaken among them. I brought thoughts born of the catastrophic fire of the Russian Revolution and the experience of Russian communism, which had raised issues from which Christendom had been hiding for centuries. I bore in me a consciousness of the crisis of historical Christianity. My mind was torn by the conflict between personality and universal harmony, between the individual and the general, the subjective and the objective—a conflict for which I was unable to find any solution within the confines of history. I have also never concealed my 'anarchism', my hostility to every glorification or sanctification of power and the state—not merely of the modern state, communist or anti-communist, but the state as it has been understood by man from the beginning of civilization. I saw the ultimate guarantee that mankind will not forget the image of man and the God-created dignity of man in Christ's God-manhood. These themes are expressive of an existential attitude, but I received them as a heritage of Russian thought. Along with a bitter, perhaps even a pessimistic sense of history, however, I still hoped for and awaited a new creative epoch in Christianity.

In the early stages of my philosophical development I learned a great deal from Western thought, particularly from German philosophy, and I continued to learn much in the years of exile in Western Europe. The themes with which I was concerned evolved and took shape under the impact of my encounter with Western thought, however intensely I may have, at times, experienced a reaction against it.

In 1924 I went from defeated Berlin to victorious Paris; sixteen years later I was to know Paris in defeat too. There were many reasons for moving to France. To begin with, Berlin gradually gave place to Paris as the centre of Russian life abroad. But ever since my departure from Russia I intended to go to France, which was associated for me with many memories. On arrival in Paris I was struck by the city's splendour, richness, and colour in comparison with Berlin, which, on looking back, seemed completely devoid of character and style. But, at the same time, I had an inexplicable presentiment about Paris—as if her splendour were suggestive of a 'feast amidst the plague'[1] and a doom were hanging over her. The Religious-Philosophical Academy was likewise transferred to Paris, where its activities increased in scope.

The year 1926 marked the beginning of the monthly journal *Put'*, organ of Russian religious philosophical thought, which I edited until the beginning of the second world-war. It was published under the auspices of the Academy, but the initiative belonged to Gustav Kullmann, who did a great deal for Russians and in every way encouraged cultural and intellectual activities among them. *Put'* was also supported by Dr. Mott, a powerful personality and a great Christian. Dr Mott was a sincere friend of Orthodoxy and of Russians, and, as head of the Y.M.C.A. and the Student Christian Federation, his aid and sympathy were of enormous consequence. *Put'* united all the available intellectual forces, with the exception of those which were openly obscurantist and reactionary. It was not a journal representative of any particular school of thought, for there was no such school, but rather of a number of Russians who were qualified in one way or another to carry on the tradition of Russian religious and philosophical thought. As editor I did my best to be tolerant of various views and trends of thought and admitted contributions with which I did not agree at all. Sometimes *Put'* was a little dull for my taste, and I wished it were more pugnacious

[1] Title of Pushkin's tragedy in verse, adapted from John Wilson's *City of the Plague*. (Tr.)

and controversial. The most combative contributions came from me, and occasionally these provided considerable provocation and even scandal among the *émigrés*. Such, for example, was my campaign against the Karlovtsy episcopate;[1] my attack on those elements among the *émigrés* which severed relations with the Church in Moscow; on Metropolitan Sergey's condemnation of Father Bulgakov's teaching on Sophia; and on the Theological Institute in connection with the affair of Georgii Fedotov.[2] I must also mention an article of mine in defence of the Church in Soviet Russia which appeared in *Poslednye Novosti*.[3]

In all these and many other pronouncements I waged a war for freedom, for the freedom of the spirit, for the freedom of conscience, for the freedom of thought. I did not miss a single opportunity of coming out against those who quenched the spirit and violated thought and conscience. It is significant that these oppressive measures were perpetrated by reactionary religious and political elements, and I combated them in *Put'*, in the Religious-Philosophical Academy, and in the Christian Student Movement. I did finally succeed in forming a small group of the more enlightened elements around and within these enterprises. Where I was not successful, or where reactionary elements took the upper hand, I broke off relations and went my own way. On the whole, my success was rather meagre, and life among the *émigrés* came to be dominated by every kind of reaction, by obscurantism, clericalism, authoritarianism, servility and the rest.

As time went on, I became more and more of a bugbear to the *émigrés*. At first they described me as a spokesman of 'tolerance' and 'broad-mindedness', which were taken for some of the deadly sins, and, in view of the political manias obsessing the *émigrés*, invariably meant tolerance and broad-mindedness *vis-à-vis* Bolshevism (this point of view was true in a measure, because I was not obsessed by violent hatred of the Russian Revolution) as well as some of the 'left-wing' move-

---

[1] A branch of the Russian Orthodox Hierarchy representing, both politically and theologically, the extreme conservative sections of the *émigrés*. (Tr.)

[2] A professor of the Institute who published a number of articles in defence of Republican Spain. (Tr.)

[3] A Russian daily paper published in Paris before the last war. (Tr.)

ments with which I had frequent contacts. Subsequently people seemed to have changed their opinion, and began to describe me as very intolerant indeed: and I admit that, in the conditions prevailing in *émigré* life, it was difficult not to acquire angry convictions and not to lose one's temper. The *émigrés* reflected all the shades on the political scale known in Western Europe. I never had anything to do with the extreme right; but the more enlightened moderates (the 'left centre', to use the current and inaccurate phraseology), and particularly the younger generation among them, regarded me as fundamentally one of them, which, in actual fact, was never the case. Both intellectually and emotionally I was decidedly a 'left-winger' and a revolutionary, although such designations have for me a spiritual rather than a political connotation. In point of fact, it is our private interests and prejudices which substitute the misleading distinction between left and right for the true distinction between truth and falsehood.

I should now like to say a few words about the Russian Student Christian Movement, with which I was associated for some years. This association proved a source of painful disagreements, which contributed to the growing estrangement between myself and the *émigrés*. The Russian S.C.M., which is affiliated to the international organization of that name, existed in embryo in Russia before the Revolution; but I had no contact with it then. On arriving in Germany, however, I soon became an active participant in its various activities. Since then, and for some years to come, I was a member of the Movement's Council, a constant contributor to its publications and an active participant in its conferences and meetings. In all these activities I tried to impart some of the spirit of the traditions of Russian religious thought, to deepen the intellectual interest of the young Russian Christians, to foster their concern for freedom and to draw their attention away from sectional interests to the wider implications of Christianity. But my efforts bore practically no fruit. In fact, I became thoroughly unpopular and a source of constant misgivings. My association with the Movement was preserved chiefly through its Secretary, Fydor Pianov, for whom I had a great regard: I felt confident in him as one of the few among the S.C.M.

leaders who was true to his convictions. He always supported me in my struggle against the reactionary trends among the *émigrés*.

The time came when, so far as I could see, the sole reason why the members of the Russian S.C.M. tolerated my presence among them or even stood on ceremony with me, was the fact of my general 'reputation', especially among those Christians of the West who supported the Russian Student Movement. But I was regarded as an alien and uncongenial outsider: above all, I was to be considered not a true Orthodox, but a 'modernist', a 'free-thinker', a 'heretic'. This antipathy was reciprocal. After having been attracted by the Movement in its initial stages, I soon realized, as on so many other occasions, that, in the end, it would be difficult for me to adapt myself to an atmosphere of increasing hostility to untrammelled thinking, to freedom, creative imagination, justice—in short, to all the things which I valued most. Whenever I gave vent to my real convictions I was crying in the wilderness. I could hardly complain, considering that many leading members of the Movement received their religious initiation at the hands of such ecclesiastics as Metropolitan Antonii and Archbishop Theophan, who were the bulwark of every kind of reaction among the Russian *émigrés* in Serbia, where numbers of Russian citizens found themselves as a result of the defeat of the White Army. For my part, I regarded these two ecclesiastics as mischief-makers *par excellence*. At one conference I made a sharp attack on the whole Karlovtsy episcopate to which they belonged, and thereby provoked violent disapprobation. Henceforth I forfeited the little good opinion these people had of me. The religious life, even of the original members of the Russian S.C.M., some of whom were moved by a genuine religious interest, was of an exclusively liturgical type, which seemed to me an intolerable limitation. Those who joined the Movement later on displayed no genuine religious interest whatsoever; and eventually the Russian S.C.M. came under the ways of quasi-Fascist and nationalistic elements. I ceased to attend the conferences or take part in the work of the various groups and circles, and in the end broke entirely with the Movement. My name became a symbol of disgrace, and a new term was coined: *Berdyaevshchina*,[1] denoting all the most hateful things a Russian *émigré* could think of,

[1] A derogatory form of 'Berdyaevism'. (Tr.)

such as love of freedom, heresy, modernism, Bolshevism, and what-not. Meanwhile some groups of the Russian S.C.M. began to build up and elaborate an ideology of the 'Orthodox State'—an activity which I in turn regarded as the quintessence of abomination.

Russian thought among the *émigrés* of the younger generation was not entirely fruitless, as the examples of the Russian S.C.M. may suggest. The most interesting manifestation came from a group of young politically-minded men who adopted the name 'Eurasians', and who were representative of a 'post-revolutionary' mentality. Similar groups were known under the name of *Utverzhdentsy*[1] and *Mladorossy*.[2] I was much interested in these groups and had a number of personal friends among them, particularly among the Eurasians, while they sought my support against the hostile activity directed against them from the ranks of the older *émigrés*. What seemed to me to make these groups especially significant was that they were, in their outlook and interest, in tune with the events and tendencies inside Russia, and that for them Russia was to be re-created in relation to the far-reaching spiritual, social and political changes brought about by the Revolution. This had a considerable appeal to me, and, though I disclaim having exercised such a rôle of leadership in these movements as some Eurasians ascribed to me, I was ready to support them up to a point. There were, in fact, a number of factors which made it impossible for me to give them my whole-hearted allegiance, for they too showed little appreciation of freedom. Neither could I identify myself with their extreme 'Asiatic' nationalism and with their interpretation of Russia as a cultural world wholly apart from and standing over against the West. I was also not happy about their rather deliberate and pious churchmanship, which they were fond of opposing to 'seeking after God', on the somewhat inconclusive ground that they wanted to draw strength from religion rather than to give away to it all of theirs. I was equally apprehensive

[1] Those who affirmed (*utverzhdat'*) or accepted the Revolution as an inevitable stage in the historical development of Russia. (Tr.)

[2] 'Young Russians', who attempted to combine the post-revolutionary Soviet social system with the monarchy. (Tr.)

258 DREAM AND REALITY

of the importance they attached to the state. A number of Eurasians eventually became professed communists. The *Utverzhdentsy* were freer in their outlook and had no formulated dogmatic beliefs. They did not, however, command such a wide allegiance as e.g. the *Mladorossy*. The latter group was least of all acceptable to me on account of their great insistence on monarchistic legitimism. I was made aware, again and again, that despite my readiness and partial ability to share in the to-and-fro movements of history and assimilate the problems of my age, I must have always cut an untimely or, to use once more Nietzsche's expression, an uncontemporaneous figure.

My impressions among the Western Christians, both Catholic and Protestant, were in some measure similar to those I had among the Russian Christians. They too appeared to me to a great extent in the grip of religious reaction, although their intellectual and cultural standard was higher than that of the emigrated Russian Orthodox. This reaction took the form of a 'return', a going back to all kinds of things, in search of stable authority and tradition amidst the uncertainties of human existence. This was particularly evident among the neo-Thomists and neo-Calvinists. The preoccupations of Russian religious thought were equally alien and incomprehensible to my Russian contemporaries and to the Western Christians; and, so far as the latter were concerned, I was particularly conscious of a divergence in the understanding of man and in the appraisal of the historical experience of humanism and of the new age in general. I did, nevertheless, meet a number of kindred spirits, especially among the young, both Russian and Western, in whom I found that spiritual and intellectual disquietude which is the hall-mark of a proper attitude to life. These meetings were a source of great strength and joy to me.

Soon after my arrival in Paris I took the initiative in arranging a number of interconfessional gatherings between Orthodox, Catholics and Protestants, which took place at the Russian House in the Boulevard Montparnasse. It was significant, perhaps, that, so far as I knew, these gatherings provided the first opportunity for French Catholics and Protestants to come together for the purpose of discussing religious matters. It also proved an occasion for Catholic Modernists and Thomists to meet across the barrier of ecclesiastical sanctions. Orthodoxy provided a meeting-point between the various sections of a divided Christendom, uninhibited as it is by the weight of historical memories which impede mutual understanding between the various Western Churches. During the first year the meetings were extremely alive and interesting: there was even a danger of their becoming something of a fashion. There was a feeling that the members of the respective confessions were brought face to face with completely new worlds, unknown and yet unexpectedly akin to each other. We were all conscious of forming a Christian oasis in a desert of irreligion and hostility towards Christianity; and yet there was a complete absence of presumption and sectarian self-assertiveness. We discovered our fundamental unity in Christ and, at the same time, differences which we knew how to respect and understand. The most active participants among the Catholics were Père Gillet, subsequently General of the Dominican Order, Abbé Laberthonnière, a leading Modernist, and especially Jacques Maritain, of whom I shall have more to say in this chapter. The leading Protestants were Pasteur Boegner, head of the Protestant churches in France, Professor Lesserer, an orthodox Calvinist (both in appearance and conviction he seemed to have jumped into our age straight from the sixteenth century) and Wilfred Monod, representative of the liberal Protestant tradition in France.

My own part in the meetings was somewhat embarrassing to me. Everyone spoke as a representative of his own confession, and in the strength of his allegiance to an ecclesiastical body. The Roman Catholics and Protestants wanted to discover the nature of Orthodoxy and the character of the religious thought which has grown on Orthodox soil. In the first place, I was conscious that, unlike Roman Catholicism and Protestantism, there is no unified Orthodox intellectual tradition to which an Orthodox can appeal. There was only one participant from our side, Father Bulgakov, who could speak in the name of the Orthodox Church; but his was the voice of a theologian, not of a philosopher, and his theology was held in suspicion by the Orthodox ecclesiastical authorities. My embarrassment was due to my own ambiguous position: I was unable to speak in the name of any official body.

I could express only my own individual convictions, without claiming to represent anything or anybody except myself. But when these inter-confessional meetings began our non-Orthodox friends regarded my position as distinctly Orthodox, or even as the voice of Orthodoxy itself. This misunderstanding, which kept on recurring on other occasions, was rather disturbing, and I did my best to dispel it.

The misunderstanding was enhanced and spread to other quarters owing to the fact that I happened to be the first Russian Christian philosopher who became known in the West, and people began to form their opinion about the character of Russian Orthodoxy in accordance with my ideas. To my surprise, for instance, I became a kind of Orthodox thinker *en titre* to the Anglo-Saxon Christians and to High Anglicans in particular. The ambiguity was magnified by the attitude of the Russian Orthodox Institute in Paris, which did not conceal its hostility towards me in the context of our domestic ecclesiastical and political affairs, but, being intent on maintaining good relations with the Anglicans and American Protestants, placarded me as one of themselves. This policy of prevarication and insincerity, as well as other considerations, prompted my eventual break with the Institute, and I ceased to have anything to do with its staff. My Roman Catholic friends understood at last that I was to be regarded not as the mouthpiece of an ecclesiastical organization, but as an individual Christian philosopher. In the end my heterodoxy was duly acknowledged, and my so-called 'gnostic' deviations were tolerated in view of what has been described as my useful provocations in the social sphere and my success in reading the signs of the times. I confess I am not altogether happy with this truncated form of my thought, although I am glad that the ambiguity in regard to my ecclesiastical position has been finally dispelled.

After three years our interconfessional gatherings began to wear thin, and eventually gave place to a new and perhaps more fruitful form of inter-communication. The new meetings took place in our house in Clamart and were made possible by the help and co-operation of Jacques Maritain.

I met Maritain shortly after my arrival in Paris, in 1925, through the widow of Léon Bloy. I took a great interest in Léon Bloy while still in Russia, and introduced him to the Russian public a few years before his death in 1917. Lydia had also a great regard for him, and it was by way of her correspondence with Madame Bloy (a remarkable woman in her way, passionately devoted to the Roman Catholic Church and to the memory of her husband) that we came to meet Maritain. Maritain is a Roman Catholic convert from Protestantism, and Léon Bloy was his godfather. I had read some of Maritain's works, and understood him to be the chief representative of Thomism in France. I had also heard that he exercised a powerful influence on the young French Catholics. It is noteworthy that Maritain was an anarchist and a materialist in the past. On becoming Roman Catholic he ardently defended his Catholic faith and was well-known as a powerful critic of Modernism. I was prejudiced against Thomism, Catholic orthodoxy and those who harassed the Modernists. None the less, Maritain instantly won my heart. There was something irresistibly attractive for me even in his appearance. When he wrote about the opponents of Roman Catholicism or of Thomism he was harsh and caustic (his characterization of Descartes, Luther and Rousseau in *The Three Reformers*, for example, was very unjust), but in reality he was extremely gentle, urbane and generous, and possessed a remarkable poise of mind and character. Soon the most friendly relations grew up between us. I developed a deep affection for him—a feeling I do not experience often in my relation with other people. He seemed to forgive me my heterodox convictions, which were quite unacceptable to him and which he did not tolerate in others. This may be due partly to the fact that I came from an altogether different world, which for him had no associations with the problems and divergencies arising in a specifically French and Catholic context. We could practically never agree on philosophical issues. He was an Aristotelian both in the manner and matter of his thinking, and, despite all his qualifications and reservations, I could not help regarding his 'Christian philosophy' as a superstructure on a basis of Aristotelian rationalism. He was not in the least affected by the problems and preoccupations of German philosophy, which to him was an inimical and extraneous factor. I have no claims of any kind to be an academic philosopher, but I do not think it is possible at all to philosophize without having experienced the impact of, and lived through, the problems of Kant and Hegel. Maritain is a scholastic philosopher, not only because he happens to be a Thomist, but because the problems of German Idealism are for him in the last resort unreal and irrelevant. And yet our relationship was extremely fruitful. Maritain is a mystic, apart from being a philosopher, and to talk with him on subjects of mysticism and spirituality was extraordinarily stimulating. Moreover, he possesses a great sensitivity and responsiveness in regard to the social and cultural movements of the day, although it is a strange fact that these appear to leave his philosophy largely unaffected.

Despite the many changes which he underwent in the course of our enduring friendship, Maritain always remained a Thomist, intent on adapting Thomism to the ever-changing circumstances of his time. Such attempts are undoubtedly reminiscent of Modernism. Politically and socially he was 'right' when I first met him; in the course of a long evolution he shifted more and more to the 'left' and even became a leader of some of the left-wing movements in French Catholicism. As such he was a constant source of irritation and bewilderment to his conservative co-religionists. Maritain is that rare phenomenon, a Frenchman in whom there is not the slightest sign of national exclusiveness. He endeavoured to break out of the enclosed circle of Latin cultural habits and open the doors to the world outside: and he was singularly successful in this. He was very fond of Russians, and in his manner of living there was something of a Russian *intellectuel*. The Maritains used to invite anyone who could be induced to visit them in their home. Sometimes they held private meetings and discussions; but these were mainly frequented by Thomists, and it needed a strong digestion and even stronger breathing capacities to take the large and suffocating doses of scholasticism dished up on these occasions. Maritain himself, however, was entirely and invariably charming. He is not an orator or a controversialist, and has the best of the argument in writing rather than in speech. With me it is the opposite: I flourish in argument and am inhibited and incoherent in writing.

As the years passed Maritain's Thomism became less rigid and exclusive. I remember how intolerant and even disagreeable he used to be at our early interconfessional gatherings to Abbé Laberthonnière, who had suffered a great deal from Thomistic orthodoxy and its inquisitorial representatives, and could not stand Thomism. Laberthonnière was in fact a martyr to his convictions and, in the course of our deliberations, I found myself more often than not on his side rather than on that of Maritain. His anti-Thomism, however, was also rather rigid and fanatical: he even refused to regard Thomas Aquinas as a Christian. Least of all did I like the Dominican Père Gillet: his Torque-mada-like behaviour towards Abbé Laberthonnière was positively revolting.

As I have already mentioned, the interconfessional group at Mont-parnasse was succeeded by another one in our home. It was less formal and less concerned with questions of a specifically theological and ecclesiastical character: instead we concentrated on subjects of mysticism and spirituality. Maritain welcomed the idea of such discussions and took on himself the arrangements for the French membership. For various reasons he was, however, against Protestant participation. From the beginning the meetings proved very successful. A number of inter-esting people, who had not yet been at the previous interconfessional gatherings, joined the group. Among them were the writer Charles du Bos (who had concealed his conversion to Catholicism and disclosed it only shortly before our group began to meet), Gabriel Marcel, Massignon (the well-known expert on Mahommedan mysticism) and Etienne Gilson, who was an occasional visitor. Despite differences the conversations were always carried on in a very friendly atmosphere. But when, in a paper on mysticism, I referred to Jacob Boehme and Angelus Silesius, there was something of an uproar. A Roman Catholic priest, a professor of the *Institut Catholique*, said to his neighbour: 'that is how heresies are born'. It seemed to me that at times I distressed Maritain: some of my utterances were a test of his feeling for me.

The contribution of du Bos, who often took the chair, was particu-larly valuable in that he approached the problems of mysticism and spirituality in the context of literature. I shall have more to say about this remarkable man later on. Gabriel Marcel was another recent Roman Catholic convert: he was a philosopher and a playwright, but his philosophy was of a very different type from that of Maritain. He was at that time the only outstanding representative of existentialism in France. His philosophical utterances were brilliant, but he was rather at sea when it came to questions of theology and Christian doctrine.

Other people who came to the meetings were the melancholy Comte de Parges, Fumet, d'Ermenheim, Mounier (subsequently editor of *Esprit*) and some members of the clergy. It was in fact the flower of contemporary French Catholicism.

I have very pleasant memories of these gatherings, and I was distressed when, after three years, they came to an end. They touched something very intimate in me. And yet even here I could not overcome a sense of remoteness, an ultimate inability to communicate my inmost 'idea', even when I felt called upon and desired to do so. It almost seemed as if the consciousness of estrangement is in proportion to the intensity of association with others, however like-minded they may be. May it not be that the essence of human relationship involves an irreducible conflict and, consequently, pain and bitterness?

Apart from the meetings which I have just described, and which were an informal affair, I used to attend and speak at many official or semi-official international conferences, especially those organized by the Student Christian Federation. This enabled me to get to know, and be in touch with, the ways of thought of many different peoples. In the course of these activities I visited England, Germany, Austria, Switzerland, Holland, Belgium, Hungary, Czechoslovakia, Poland, and countries of which some are now no longer to be seen on the map of Europe. I always found travelling a difficult and upsetting business: consulates, trains, customs and passport examinations made me almost ill, although I do not remember ever having had any unpleasant incidents of a tangible nature in this connection. Still, every journey was to me a stimulating and nourishing, even if rather exhausting, experience. To go abroad may in itself be a significant activity, and this is duly expressed in the Russian language where 'to go abroad' means 'to pass the boundary' or 'to transcend', in other words, to extricate oneself from workaday existence.

In my numerous visits abroad it was brought home to me that Europe was increasingly becoming the victim of excessive nationalism: every European nation seemed to be obsessed by the idea of its own magnitude and by the crucial and world-wide importance which it has in human affairs. Even Hungarians and Esthonians kept on harping on the foremost and exclusive mission of Hungary and Esthonia. As usual, this tendency of national boasting and self-aggrandisement went hand in hand with a hatred of other, especially neighbouring, nations. Europe was in a state of unhealthy ferment. The Peace of Versailles and the policies which succeeded to it had evidently paved the way for a new catastrophe. But the causes of the orgy of nationalism lay deeper: nationalism has assumed the form of idolatry which darkens the counsels of the nations. Nationalism, like its twin, egocentricity, is not only immoral but frankly ludicrous and grotesque. My reactions to these manifestations were similar to those of Vladimir Solovyev, as expressed in his remarkable essay *The National Question in Russia*. In this, as in so many other respects, I found myself at loggerheads with the majority of the *émigrés*, who caroused on national self-adulation and concocted plans for a glorious Russia.

My own passionate love of Russia and the Russian people grew as time went on; but it was associated in my mind and heart with a sense of universality, and I could not conceive of patriotism as a kind of glorification of the piecemeal confusion of national developments. Internationalism, however, and, indeed, every conception opening with the prefix 'inter' ('interconfessionalism' is another such conception) had no meaning for me, and referred to no known sphere of existence. Internationalism is an abstraction as devoid of real existence as interconfessionalism, rejecting as they do the various degrees and stages of individualization which are inseparable from life. But in protest against the growing nationalism which threatened Europe with ruin I was prepared to defend even 'internationalism', which reflected, even if in a very distorted way, the truth of universalism. I believe that the innumerable nationalistic societies and associations of to-day present a strange and paradoxical picture of a betrayal of the idea of true nationhood—a kind of International of the right. To be frank, I dislike the very term 'foreigner' or 'alien' with all its evil undertones and overtones, and I cannot put myself in the position of distinguishing human beings according to their nationality. Every 'foreigner' is my compatriot. I may have a greater or lesser sympathy for this or that national type, but this cannot in any way determine my attitude to individual human beings. Few things are more repulsive than national conceit, arrogance and exclusiveness, and I find these instincts particu-

larly repulsive in Russians. This applies above all to anti-Semitism and
every other form of racial discrimination.[1]

But I want to repeat that, in repudiating nationalism, I am yet deeply
conscious of my 'Russianness'. More than this: I believe in the great
and universal, though in no way exclusive, mission of the Russian
people. I am not a nationalist, but a Russian patriot. For many years I
have stood in defence of the Russian East against the claims of European
man to absolute cultural supremacy. This attitude did not prevent me
from recognizing that modern mankind may yet witness an unheard-of
confrontation and conflict between Russia and the West. As the years
passed I myself came to see Russia from within the West and bore in
me the two worlds and the seeds of their possible conflict. The intense
nationalism in Europe, on the one hand, and the shattering experience
of the universal impact of present-day events, on the other, constitute
one of the fundamental contradictions of our age. Seldom did I meet
people truly conscious and in control of the movements of modern
history: as a rule people tended to surrender to nationalistic instincts
and gave the impression of being completely crushed by a kind of
aggressive provincialism in space.

French provincialism is a curious phenomenon. The French are convinced that they are the bearers of the universal principles of civilization,

[1] While still in Berlin N(ikolai) A(lexandrovich) felt the rising wave of anti-
Semitism. He wrote an article in defence of the Jews. On the day following the
publication of the article he began to receive anonymous letters full of threats and
vulgar abuse, asking him, amongst other things, how many pieces of silver the Jews
had given him.

In Paris N.A. came forward once more in a public speech in defence of Jewry. The
hall where the meeting took place was crowded. When he finished speaking a young
man began to raise objections in vulgar and abusive language: he attacked the Jews
and recited the well-known arguments from the *Protocol of the Wise Men of Zion*. His
speech was interspersed with wild applause from a group of his like-minded friends.
When N.A. began to answer him he was interrupted by hissing, whistling and shouting. I was sitting in the front row and saw how N.A. suddenly went white. I felt that
he was about to be overcome by a paroxysm of anger, such as I had occasionally
witnessed, and in which there was an almost irresistible power. 'Will you please leave
the hall at once?', his voice thundered out, 'this is not the pot-house of the Union of
the Russian People' (see footnote p. 203/Tr.). The young man was completely
dumbfounded and quickly left the hall. (Note by E. R.)

which for them is identical with Graeco-Roman civilization—of the principles of humanism, the rule of reason, freedom, equality and brotherhood. It so happened that France did in fact carry these principles into the world; but they are designed for the whole of humanity, and all people can and do share in that experience. French nationalism, however, is not aggressive or given to violence, as is German nationalism, which proceeds from a sense of national inferiority and *Geltungsbeduerfnis*. The French are, therefore, to a lesser extent victims of xenophobia and less intent on dominating others.

The Russian Orthodox in Paris, headed by the professors of the Theological Institute, held a number of annual meetings with Anglicans at the Anglo-Orthodox conferences in England. The conferences were arranged by a Fellowship working for a *rapprochement* between the Orthodox and Anglicans, the latter being represented chiefly by Anglo-Catholics. In view of its predominantly ecclesiastical and even clerical character I took no active part in the Fellowship's activities and only occasionally went to read papers at the conferences. The Anglo-Catholics struck me as genuinely alive to the issues in modern society, and this was particularly true of the 'Christendom' group, whose contribution to the study of sociology from the Christian point of view was very valuable. The response with which I met in these circles was confined to my views on social matters, since philosophically and theologically they had much more affinity with Thomism.

Of all the forms of intercourse with French and, generally-speaking, foreign circles in which I have taken part the most interesting were the *Decades* (inaccurately so-called, for we met for a bare week) at Pontigny. It was there that I really came to know French culture and French life, and not least the Frenchman's attitude to foreigners. Pontigny was an estate belonging to de Jardin, one of the most remarkable Frenchmen of his time, who died in 1940 at the age of eighty. The main house in Pontigny was originally an old monastery founded by St. Bernard. A number of historical rooms have been preserved in their original twelfth-century form. Such were the Gothic dining-hall and de Jardin's vast library. There were, however, modern and rather luxurious additions to the old abbey, which made life there extremely comfortable. Every year three 'ten days' sessions were arranged, for which the intellectual flower of France assembled. It was also attended by a great number of intellectuals from abroad: English, Germans, Italians, Spaniards, Americans, Swiss, Dutch, Swedes and Japanese. During the last years, as a result of the international situation, there were hardly any Germans, though at one time I used to meet there Max Scheler, George Curtius, and others. One *Decade* was usually devoted to a philosophical subject, the second to a literary one, and the third to a social and political one. I went to Pontigny quite often, especially during the latter years. It is there that I came to know André Gide, Georges Philippe, Fernandèz, Groethuysen, Martin Buber, Buonalotti, and many others. The only Russians who used to attend were Dimitri Svyatopolk-Mirsky (before his return to Soviet Russia) and myself.

The range of subjects was very wide indeed: romanticism; toleration and the totalitarian state; asceticism; the function of writers and intellectuals in modern society; and solitude are some of those I remember. Despite the multifariousness of the participants the atmosphere had a natural and friendly character and the intellectual level of the discussions was very high. There was even a note of elegance, largely due, no doubt, to the invariable presence of a number of beautiful and smartly-dressed women. The food and wines were excellent. The evenings were usually spent in games or in listening to orchestral music and singing. Occasionally expeditions were organized, and a *cortège* of cars would take us to look at the beauties of the surrounding country-side. The whole set-up was typical of the prosperous and cultured French *bourgeoisie*. This did not seem to prevent a number of communists and communist sympathisers from participating in the *Decades*. For my part, I could not help feeling an interloper in this world of spiritual and material well-being. Sometimes it seemed to me that beneath the fragile crust volcanic forces were seething, about to burst forth and destroy all this veneer of elegance and good manners. My own life had passed entirely in a world of volcanic eruptions, and I wondered whether it was really possible to effect a satisfactory working arrangement between the two worlds. I was also struck by a tendency, of which I have already spoken, to skate in a kind of brilliant literary or

conversational fashion round anything that could be called a real problem. And when a real one was too important to be avoided, it was
served up in a form much too pre-digested for my Russian taste. And
yet I was frankly attracted by this world.

Our hostess, Madame de Jardin, was an intelligent and pleasant
woman of a somewhat masculine appearance, candid and outspoken.
De Jardin himself was a very picturesque figure. Some people thought
he resembled a Russian peasant: for my part, I think he was more of a
French Aristarchus. He was a man of great culture, a Hellenic scholar,
and a magnificent conversationalist: his manner of arguing was delicate
and even graceful. He had worked a great deal for the establishment
of peace in Europe, for the *rapprochement* of intellectuals of all countries
and for the advancement of spiritual values, freedom and toleration.
Yet, as he was himself the first to admit, he was by nature impatient
of views opposed to his own, although he had an admirable way of
never betraying agitation. He was the heart and soul of Pontigny, apart
from being its most generous host. Despite his remarkable intellectual
gifts and a great erudition, he wrote very little: evidently his real
vocation was in the realm of cultural and social action, and the *Decades*
were a testimony to his singular success in this sphere. He also carried
on a wide correspondence with intellectuals all over the world (Leo
Tolstoy was one of his correspondents). Besides the *Decades* at Pontigny
he was also responsible for the *Union pour la Vérité*.

I remember a series of vehement, even if friendly, philosophical
arguments I had at Pontigny with Léon Brunschwicg, who was the
leading French philosopher at the *Decades*. He was typical of the
philosophical point of view represented on these occasions. There were
comparatively few participants representing the Catholic position, and
the dominant note was one of *idéalisme culturel*. Bernhard Groethuysen,
of half Dutch and half Russian origin, a *Privatdozent* at the University
of Berlin, who had spent a large part of his life in Paris, represented a
form of enlightened scepticism. A man of great intelligence and vast
knowledge, it was highly stimulating to converse with him, although
his contribution to the discussions was purely analytical, if not disintegrating. Fernandèz, a man of many gifts—he was by profession a
literary critic and also, amongst other things, an actor and a keen

sportsman—often led the discussions. He was witty, but on the whole more convincing when directing games in the evening than at the meetings by day. He was known to have been at one time near to communism, but subsequently moved to the opposite extreme. There were, as I have already said, others who had communist sympathies: this was popular at the time among intellectuals who frequented *salons*; but few took it seriously, including, unfortunately, those who were moving in that direction.

For a time, until illness prevented it, the leader at Pontigny was Charles du Bos. I had met him in 1924, together with some other Frenchmen, through Leo Shestov, and we became very friendly. Du Bos was an original man and very much unlike the usual run of Frenchmen. He did not belong to our own age, but was a true romantic in the manner of the early eighteenth century. One of his most outstanding qualities was an intense and vivid imagination. Friendship for him was the object of a romantic cult; and he had literally hundreds of close and intimate friends. When it was a question of giving his friends signed copies of a book of his, he disposed of about two hundred in this way. He was steeped in the culture not only of France, but of England and Germany, and was complete master of the English and German languages. I have seldom met a person of such candour and nobility of spirit. But he was an aesthete above everything else. He would only talk about first-class writers. His judgments and his whole attitude to life were entirely and exclusively determined by the standards of literature and art, and all problems presented themselves to him in their literary aspect. I could not help regarding this as striking evidence of cultural decadence, which, in that form, was rather widespread in France and was by no means confined to du Bos, though he was very typical. Young Frenchmen would speak of crises through which they had gone, and this generally meant that they had moved from one literary group to another: for example, from Proust and Gide to Barrès and Claudel. Russia is a country possessing a great literature, where, moreover, literature was often the only channel of cultural movements and a battlefield of politics; but we never knew of any such tendency to reduce life to literature. Du Bos had remarkable insight and, sometimes, he would make observations of amazing subtlety and discernment; but I was never able to discover what he was really driving at, or what his central concern and ideas were. His life seemed to be spent on a cult of the geniuses of human civilization. But did this provide him with resources for meeting the issues of our catastrophic age?

I met André Gide before Pontigny, after an article of mine on communism had appeared in the first issue of *Esprit*. Gide, who at that time was already attracted by communism, read the article and wanted to meet me. Our conversation was, accordingly, concerned mainly with Russian communism and with the relation between communism and Christianity. I was impressed by Gide's honest and candid way of approaching these problems. In common with some other French intellectuals he was reacting against the bourgeois capitalist environment in which he lived. He evidently longed for some radical change and renewal in the life of modern man. He was not a student of social problems, and seemed to know little of communist literature, not to speak of communist practice. I fear that during our conversation I was somewhat aggressive in my critique of arm-chair communism. Gide struck me personally as an extremely shy, unobtrusive, quiet and sensitive man. His shyness was particularly marked at large gatherings such as Pontigny, where his contribution consisted mostly of a few indifferent observations. I read Gide with avidity. I felt that he was a writer who has followed his inward bent with ardour and deliberation, not with facile hedonism, but through difficulties and dangers. I discerned in him a great religious and moral disquietude and a search for a purified Christianity. But the need for self-justification seemed to occupy a disproportionately large place in his attitude to life. He is, after all, a Puritan who wants to enjoy life and cannot do so without feeling the pricks of conscience. His *Journal* is in many respects a remarkable human document, yet there is something dreary and gloomy about it. All his life Gide struggled in vain to overcome the Protestant leaven within him. Gide fights to surmount the obstacles which bar his way to a full and unstinted life in this world; as to me, I desire nothing more than to surmount the obstacles which impede my liberation from this world into the freedom of another.

On another occasion I had the privilege of making the acquaintance of Léon Blum. Politicians, even the cleverest of them, seldom display signs of culture, intelligence, honesty and humanity. Léon Blum impressed me as possessing all these qualities. He is probably the most deserving of all the French politicians. I was very much in sympathy with his social reforms and his policy during the Popular Front period. He did not, however, seem to have great will-power, nor did he impress one as a great statesman.

Apart from those who attended the *Decades* at Pontigny I came to know another group of people, to which I have already referred, namely *Union pour la Vérité*. The two groups overlapped to some extent. The latter met in Paris every week, and at one time I was a frequent visitor to the meetings. They were usually devoted to the discussion of some book which had just come out. The main interest was in the philosophy of culture or politics and allied subjects. On such occasions experts on the respective topics were invited, as well as the authors of the works under consideration. The latter introduced the discussion. I first joined the group when asked to introduce my book, *The Destiny of Man*. *Union pour la Vérité* as the name indicates, was concerned with the free 'search for truth'. The group had a distinctly left-wing bias. The problems of communism loomed large in the discussions, and communists or near-communists, such as Nizan (who later left the Communist Party), Malraux (who also subsequently disavowed his communist sympathies), J. P. Bloch, and others took an active part in the proceedings. The room where the meetings took place was, as a rule, crammed with people and it was scarcely possible to breathe. Despite the controversial character of most of the topics, there was an air of amiability and *bienséance*; nobody ever lost his or her temper and open confrontation was definitely discouraged. Sometimes the discussion turned into a mere *questionnaire* addressed to the experts. I was at a loss to see how one could possibly get at the truth by using such methods of enquiry. The whole set-up was evidence of rationalism not run wild, as in the past, but run cool as custard. The rationalism of the past was indeed anything but cool, despite its claim to detached reasoning: it was born of a great passion. But the passion had spent itself. Here matters of vital importance for the survival of mankind were discussed in a way which suggested that they had in fact no relation whatever to the real struggle in life, and dynamite was handled as if it were a withered leaf. Only occasionally was there a faint sign of fear—fear of war, of revolution, of reaction—but a fear that was impotent and only served to prove the innate timidity of its victims.

In France, where intellectual life was commonly regarded as the touchstone of political movement, the intellectuals were, in fact, cut off from politics, which was the exclusive domain of Deputies, Ministers in the government, and possibly certain ladies behind the scenes. Hardly any Deputies, for instance, came to Pontigny or to the meetings of *Union pour la Vérité*. The intellectuals, who were discussing matters affecting the political fate of the country, were left to stew in their own juice, while the professional politicians, with rare exceptions, formed a closed circle of their own and were absorbed in the game of politics, away both from cultural life and the life of the ordinary people. This whole set-up has now come to a deserved and catastrophic end: indeed, it could scarcely have continued in its old form, for the old patterns and habits of French culture, as well as of politics, had shown unmistakable signs of decline. And yet, despite scepticism, lack of purpose and indifference to truth, there was an underlying unity in French thought. Almost everyone believed in the supremacy of reason; all were 'humanists' and stood for the universal principles of democracy derived from the French Revolution. German or Russian thought was generally regarded as 'Eastern barbarism', tenebrous, irrational and full of perils for the future of civilization. No one seemed to admit the validity of any type of culture other than their own. No wonder, therefore, that I felt myself in the *Union pour la Vérité* no less, if not more, than at Pontigny, an intruder from another world, although I had probably assimilated the French ways of thought more than was the case with other Russians. My interest in the meetings of *Union pour la Vérité* eventually spent itself; but I learnt a great deal from them.

The other opportunity of contact with the French was provided by the group associated with the 'personalist' periodical *Esprit* and by the philosophical gatherings in Gabriel Marcel's home. These contacts proved most valuable for me, and through them I met people with whom I had great affinity. I was present at the meeting at which *Esprit* was founded. This took place in the home of I., a left-wing Roman Catholic, subsequently a Deputy and a member of the Socialist Party. The enterprise owed its impetus to a group of young people, and the contributions to the journal came, at least in its initial stages, almost entirely from young men and women. I was greatly moved when at the foundation meeting it was unanimously adopted that the fundamental purpose and concern of *Esprit* should be the vindication of man. I felt that here was a place where a new spirit was blowing.

Esprit was designed not as an exclusively Roman Catholic periodical but as a forum where enlightened Catholics, Protestants, and people owing no allegiance to any organized religious body could meet and speak together. Its founder and chief editor was Emmanuel Mounier, a man of great intellectual gifts and remarkable energy. He was a Roman Catholic, but his social and political views were at variance with the accepted Roman Catholic position in these matters. The nucleus of the *Esprit* group was predominantly Roman Catholic, but the journal itself was, in the main, preoccupied not with philosophical or religious matters: it conducted studies in social, political and, to a certain extent, aesthetic problems. The aim was to work out a social programme on spiritual foundations. The professed personalism of the group, with which I was in special sympathy, was not a system but an attitude or a theme expressing a search for the transformation of the objective world into a personal universe—an attitude in which the human person is the principal object and the irreducible subject of knowledge. Inasmuch as *Esprit* had a socialistic bias, it was the case of a Proudhonian rather than a Marxist socialism, although the pages of the journal contain some important studies in the theory and practice of Marxism. The combination of socialism and personalism was expressed in the newly coined term *personalisme communautaire*. *Esprit* adopted an original method of work: there were a number of groups which dealt with different subjects. There was a philosophical group, a literary group, a group studying Marxism, and another devoted to the investigation of political problems; there was also a general group which studied the contributions of all the others and worked out the programme of the journal from the respective angles. For some years I shared in the work of these groups, which were usually attended by large numbers of people.

The movement centred in *Esprit* was deserving of the greatest sympathy. The only drawback was that it, like so many similar movements, was confined to a comparatively small group, unable to do anything which could effectively influence its environment. It could only 'endure' and try to understand the modern world, in which everything seemed to move in a direction contrary to the aims of *Esprit*. The will to evil is infinitely stronger than the will to good. One is compelled to admit that evil is productive of great talent, and that if anything progresses in this world it is evil. In the years preceding the catastrophe of the second world-war there were a number of important movements among the younger generation in France which, in contradistinction from most of the other youth movements in Europe, were born of a genuine search for truth. If only they could succeed in this evil-stricken world it would be an immense achievement indeed. For my part, I felt confident when meeting these young people, not only because I knew that they had thought deeply but because their minds had lived, too. There was a strong reaction among the thinking French of the younger generation against the world around them. Even the group of young people round *Combat* liked to call themselves revolutionary. 'Revolution', 'crisis', 'inherent struggles' became fashionable catch-words, sometimes concealing a confusion of ideas and values and exercising a subtle appeal to the divided mind and heart of a decadent intelligentsia.

I must not omit to mention the philosophical gatherings at Gabriel Marcel's home: they were, in my opinion, the only kind of meetings likely to have a permanent value. They were attended not only by the French but by Germans, Russians and Spaniards, both young and old, whose contribution had a decisive influence on the work of the group. It was probably the only place in France where problems of phenomenology and existentialist philosophy were seriously studied. The names of Husserl, Scheler, Heidegger, Jaspers, and many other foreign thinkers were constantly to be heard, and there was not the slightest sign of French or West-European cultural self-adulation.

So far as Gabriel Marcel was concerned, I felt at first a considerable degree of unanimity with him; but later on we disagreed, partly for political reasons, since he regarded me as too 'left-wing' for his taste and too much of an 'anarchist'. Existentialism was the *idée maîtresse* at his gatherings. Marcel himself had the reputation of being an existentialist philosopher, although it would, perhaps, be more accurate to describe him as a mystical empiricist. Unlike most of the other French philosophers he possesses a thorough knowledge of German thought, and has a special regard for Jaspers, to whom he has devoted an interesting essay. I valued Marcel's idea of 'the mystery', which he defined as a problem not susceptible of objectification, involving man who attempts to grasp it, and not to be reduced to external data. I was less happy with the fact that, despite his avowedly searching and questioning attitude, he always gave the impression of knowing exactly where he wanted to arrive, namely in the Catholic Church.

Marcel, however, was not the only one who represented a shift in the philosophical consciousness in France: there were a number of other philosophers, such as Le-Senne, Lavelle (the successor to Bergson and Le Roy at the Collège de France), Wahl, and others, who reacted against the ascendency of positivism over the French philosophical mind. The change found expression in the Montaigne series *Philosophie de l'esprit*, edited by Lavelle and Le-Senne. I wish I had been able to take full advantage of the frequent meetings with these thinkers, who were in so many ways congenial to me, but it was difficult to break through the conventions of ordinary human relationships and to reach out to that which mattered most to me in these encounters. My failures in this respect were a source of frequent self-condemnation.

Among the friends I made during my exile in the West I must also mention the Swiss theologian and leading socialist Lieb, of whom I think with great affection. He had a first love to which he remained for ever faithful—Russia and the Russians. He liked to be called Fyodor Ivanovich, although his real first name was Fritz! This, a certain tendency to dishevelment, and an enormous Russian library were the only Russian things about him. He had a heart of gold and a nature entirely free of conventions. I greatly valued his friendship, as well as his immense erudition and intellectual keenness. He lived on, and was torn by, the horns of a somewhat unusual dilemma: Barthianism and Russian religious ideas, for which he developed a touching attachment. I do not think I ever had such a loyal friend among non-Russians. I should also like to mention Pasteur Porret, who devoted some years of his life to writing a book on my philosophy, and I am grateful to him for his sympathetic and instructed work.

The difficulties attending intercourse with Russians are different from those experienced among Western people. The Russians, as I have already noted, are, as a rule, very sociable. They discard conventions and do not keep their fellow-men at arm's length. They have what one might call a knack of getting on with other people, whether they are, or are not, their friends or intimate acquaintances. They also like to unburden their hearts, to invade the lives of their fellow-men and to argue endlessly about ideas. They find it hard to adopt the Western habit of arranging to meet by telephone or through the post. They prefer dropping in at various times of day and night. But, in my view, they have little capacity for strong individual friendship: they are, in a general way, communicative and have a highly developed sense of fellowship. It is significant that wherever Russians find themselves (and many hundreds of thousands of them were scattered all over the world after the Revolution) they immediately and invariably form themselves into groups and fellowships and societies. Russians are disdainful of strictly defined spheres of interest and social and cultural differentiations and are incapable of living according to them. To find 'the meaning of life' is for them not a matter of abstract speculation but one of life and death, and they cannot find that meaning, unless it is in communion with others who pursue the same end.

But alongside these qualities of fellowship and solidarity there are others of a more destructive nature. No West-European is capable of inflicting such mental wounds on the person of his fellow-man, of offending, or of showing such insensibility and disrespect towards others as a Russian can; and he is himself easily wounded, offended and hurt in his self-esteem. It is almost impossible to argue with a Russian about an idea without his becoming disparaging to the person whose idea he wants to disprove, and the discussion turns into a personal indictment. Again, Russians have far less regard for thought and intellectual activity than Western people, and they easily slide from an intellectual position into a posture of moral demand and expect from you (as well as from themselves) a feat of sanctity or of revolutionary heroism. None of these qualities are typical of the French, whom I know best among the peoples of the West. Hence the difficulties and misunderstandings which arise in the relations between the French and the Russians. When a Russian talks to a Frenchman he feels irresistibly inhibited by the Frenchman's individualism, reserve, urbanity and unconcernedness. The intellect and the senses outstrip the heart. This is exemplified in the contemporary French novel, in which there is little feeling and a great deal of *intellectualité* and *sensualité*. On the other hand, the French know how to respect the personality of their fellow-men and do not encroach on their inner life; and if they discuss your ideas they do not feel moved to discuss your private life. They are more unassuming than the Russians and do not feel themselves called to be the moral judges of their fellow-men. The Russians easily admit that they are miserable sinners, and are ready to repent of their sins; but they expect others to do the same and repudiate anyone who fails to acknowledge his sinfulness. The moral passion of the Russians is duly reflected in their thought, in which ethical and metaphysical interest preponderates over the concern for the truth of logical and epistemological propositions. The latter is very characteristic of the Western mind, because it has lost touch with ultimate realities and acquired a habit of hiding from them and from those who remind it of them.

All my life I have longed to meet other men and to attain true communion, that 'deep may call to deep' and the ultimate recesses of my being be filled with the illumination which comes from true communion. But it is in this that I have failed most of all. It seemed as if there were a fundamental division within me—a division, perhaps, between the Russian and the Western elements in me. I am moved to go out to my fellow-men and, at the same time, I feel restrained and inhibited by diffidence and reserve in face of the very existence of others. It is surprising that not only social bonds but even love between man and woman fails to attain community, and man remains locked within his own solitariness, unable to understand the other or to make himself understood. Love may break the silence between lovers: but do they not speak across an impassable gulf which no intimacy can redeem? The person of every other human being must needs remain an impenetrable and untrodden mystery, which even love is unable to fathom.

Some people entertain the curious notion that the closer people are associated, the more they will like one another. I am unable to produce any evidence for this optimism from my own long experience of co-operation with other people. Thus I have worked alongside Merezh-kovsky for many years in a cause dear and important to us both. We are now living in the same town, but I hardly see and never speak to him, or he to me. So far as I remember, our only relations for some years have consisted in a series of abusive articles written by him about me. The same is true of Peter Struve and Anton Kartashov, of Boris Zaitsev and Peter Muratov. There was never any break in my relations with Father Bulgakov, but we seldom met, except on official occasions; and I fear that, had we met more often, we should have moved further apart. The only exception is Leo Shestov, with whom my friendship has grown stronger and deeper since the Kiev and Moscow days, and he is the only person with whom I can speak about matters that are of the greatest importance to us both.

One of the most remarkable people whose friendship I gained in exile was Mother Maria, who died in the gas-chamber of a German concentration-camp. Her life and tragic end seemed to reflect the fate of a whole epoch. But she also embodied all the traits characteristic of Russian women saints—above all, an all-consuming solidarity with the pain and sufferings of the world and an undaunted readiness to serve and to sacrifice herself for her fellow-men. Her death, which was an act of sheer self-immolation for the sake of a Jewish woman who would not be separated from her child and was about to be destroyed in a gas-chamber, belongs to one of the most heroic pages in the annals of this infernal war.

Among other friends I should like to mention the ex-Social Revolutionary Bunakov-Fundaminsky, a man who devoted his whole life to the idea of social and political justice and an extremely lovable person. He, together with another friend of mine, Georgii Fedotov, one of our most gifted historians and publicists, and Constantin Mochulsky, a literary critic, belonged to the same circle. Mother Maria, Fundaminsky, Fedotov and Mochulsky were constant visitors to our home, which became a resort for all kinds of people. They came whenever they liked, and they were always welcome: but if they felt happy and at ease, this was not due to me but to the other members of the family.

When we were alone in the evenings we would nearly always read aloud. Lydia was an accomplished reader, and sometimes Genia took her turn. In this way we re-read most of the Russian writers. We also read aloud the Greek tragedies, Shakespeare, Cervantes, Goethe, Dickens, Balzac, Stendhal, Proust, and other modern writers. I particularly enjoyed listening to the works of Russian writers, and these evenings were for me an occasion to re-live, again and again, the boundless humanity and understanding of the Russian genius.

I have observed a certain insincerity in the attitude of some Russians towards me. Sometimes they would display greater accord and friendliness towards me than they actually felt. Many, too, would avoid argument altogether. I wonder if it is due to my regrettable tendency to flare up in argument; or are there other reasons? Some Russians tried for a long time to keep up the pretences of unanimity, while in fact we differed fundamentally in our attitude to life.

I was frequently reproached with having moved a long way 'to the left'. I have already said what I think of such designations. The attitude taken by the majority of the *émigrés*, however, is such that to be 'left-wing' in regard to it is no more than elementary decency. I have come to the conclusion that, in the circumstances, 'left-wing' denotes a conviction concerning the supreme value of man and his pre-eminence over race, class, state, nation, economic power and ecclesiastical authority; whilst 'right-wing' denotes an outlook according to which man is subject to and enslaved by all these things. Humanity, then, and the attempt to establish social relations on the basis of humanity, I call 'left-wing'. Man ought to live according to his divine image, i.e. theocentrically; whereas society should live according to the human image, i.e. anthropocentrically. Theocentrism in society gives birth to totalitarianism, religious or secular, theocratic or ideocratic, which, as history has abundantly shown, betrays freedom.

My relations with ecclesiastical circles among the Russian *émigrés* went from bad to worse. When a conflict arose between the Patriarchal Church of Moscow, with its few representatives abroad, and the main body of the *émigré* Church headed by the Metropolitan Evlogii, I sided resolutely with the former and wrote warmly in support of it. This proved the occasion of violent abuse from the political and ecclesiastical pillars of *émigré* reaction. The conflict came to a head in the affair of Georgii Fedotov, whom the Theological Institute threatened to dismiss on account of his 'left-wing deviations'. The obvious conclusion to be drawn from the incident was that academic Orthodoxy must needs be 'right-wing'. That was hardly news to me. The ugly, slavish and prosaic countenance of official ecclesiasticism had long been a source of distress and irritation to me. On this occasion I wrote a virulent article in *Put'* under the title 'Does Orthodoxy admit Freedom of Conscience?' which finally and, it seems, irrevocably undermined my relations with the Theological Institute and its professors, and caused considerable difficulties in the publication of *Put'*. But this was only one episode among many. I never failed to denounce openly traitors to the cause of freedom. When some Russian *émigrés* charged me with unpardonable daring and temerity *vis-à-vis* 'public opinion', I used to tell them that they were paying me a compliment; all my life I have done nothing but fight public opinion and all its wretched manifestations, and I take this opportunity of reiterating that I do not care a straw for this particular opinion, and feel no greatness and no impelling force whatsoever about it.

When I was exiled to Western Europe I found myself in an intellectual climate characterized by a reaction against the nineteenth century. Such reactions against the preceding age or the preceding generations have not of course been unknown in the past. Time is a very thankless and heedless measure. But let us be 'objective'. As a matter of fact, the early twentieth century was still clearly part and parcel of the nineteenth century. Then came the period of the inter-war years, in which European mankind set itself deliberately in opposition to the preceding age. And yet it is surprising that even then the social and cultural stage was still dominated by the much despised nineteenth century and was unable to produce anything distinctly original. It was a time of few gifts, and the ideas which move modern man to react against the nineteenth century are themselves largely derived from that century. Indeed, who are the 'makers of the twentieth century?' They are: de Maistre, Hegel, Saint-Simon, Marx, Comte, Wagner, Nietzsche, Dostoevsky, Kierkegaard, Carlyle, Gobineau, Darwin. Nearly all the ideologies which loom large on the horizon of modern European civilization—communism, '*étatisme*', nationalism, racialism, individualism and anti-individualism, positivism, and the rest—were set forth in the last century. The great contribution of the twentieth century lies, as is often the case in the succession of ages, in a skilful vulgarization and falsification of these ideas. Nietzsche's legacy seems to have undergone an especially sad process of application. The nineteenth century was, indeed, much more complex and significant than its modern heirs and censors are willing to admit. Similarly, the eighteenth century was much more significant than its nineteenth century heirs were ready to acknowledge. It was an age alike of the emancipation of reason, of enlightenment and of important mystical and theosophical movements —the age not only of Voltaire and the Encyclopaedists but also of St. Martin, Swedenborg, Blake, and others. Men and history are ungrateful and terribly devoid of memory. For my part, I belong to my age, but I have reacted against my age inasmuch as it has forgotten and betrayed its heritage.

Lately I have been re-reading much of Herzen, who brought home to me the lessons of West-European history. I have lived through greater historical catastrophes than he. The events of his time seem unimportant in comparison with those of our own day. Herzen chose exile so as to escape from the servitude of mid-nineteenth century Russia into what he believed to be the freedom of democratic Europe. But he was soon disillusioned and, indeed, repulsed by the suffocating bourgeois spirit prevailing in the West. I too have reason to be 'disillusioned', though this word is an unhappy one. I feel with Constantine Leontyev the hideousness of the democratic age and share his passionate hatred of the democratic herd. Leontyev's worst enemies were those who believe in progress and want to introduce their paltry democratic perfection into this splendidly imperfect world; I too yearn for the splendour of beauty, of which there was more to be found in the past, with all its injustice, than in the present age. But, after all, Leontyev was satisfied with 'imperfection' and Herzen found comfort in the 'healthy instincts of the Russian peasant', whereas I can see an issue only in the coming of the wholly other Kingdom of God and in the apocalypse of transfiguration beyond the threshold of this world. Russia and the Russians may be particularly chosen to bear witness to this issue in view of their innate apocalyptism: the coming of the Kingdom, however, cannot be made dependent on any inborn, natural qualities; rather, it depends on the free creative act of God and man. Like Herzen, we left, or were driven to leave, Russia, hoping to find freedom in the West. We did, admittedly, find greater freedom than we would have enjoyed in the midst of the destructions and constructions of revolutionary and post-revolutionary Russia. But even this relative freedom in the West is drawing to its end: it is judged by its own betrayals, which plunge man into ever more abject servitude.

A few years ago a slight change came about in our material circumstances: a small legacy was left to me and I became the owner of a house with a garden in Clamart, near Paris. For the first time in my life since I left Russia I was a property-owner and lived in my own house. It is true that a long time before this I had inherited some iron-mines in Poland which belonged to my father. They were situated on the land which had formally been his estate. The estate was liquidated by the Polish government, but some compensation was due to me on account of the mines. In the end, however, nothing came out of it, and I was only involved in unnecessary expense. Frankly speaking, I am glad to have escaped the iniquitous burden of a shareholder. The legacy which made us the owners of the Clamart property came from a friend of ours, Florence West, an Englishwoman married to a very rich Frenchman. She was a woman of striking beauty, strong will and deep religious convictions. She was particularly devoted to Lydia. For a number of years a group met in our home for the purpose of studying the Bible, in which Florence West played the most prominent part. The house she left us made life rather easier than heretofore.

I have already spoken of my attitude to material and money matters. I have never experienced great poverty, although I was often uncertain what would happen a few months hence. But in the end something always turned up. On the whole I dislike security and well-being, except in so far as it gives independence. I am very much attached to my study in the Clamart house, with its windows opening on to the garden, and its library, which I managed to collect in the course of my years of exile.

Conditions in occupied France are strongly reminiscent of the early years in Soviet Russia. France, rich, abundant and free a short time ago, is now marred by the sight of hungry queues, empty shops, restrictions of all kinds, curfews and utter uncertainty of what the morrow will bring. The other day a servant at a friend's house said to me that our planet was reeling. I had long felt this: but the experience would be more bearable and its meaning more easily discernible at home than in a foreign land .... I have never, I think, lived such an outwardly calm and secluded life, wholly given to meditation on metaphysical problems: there is irony in the fact that such a time should be one of the most catastrophic in the destiny of Europe. I do not know, however, what ordeal awaits me to-morrow.

I have just spoken of the attraction which the past sometimes exercises for me. Is this a mere clinging to reminiscences, a form of escapism in face of an irksome present and a threatening future? 'Reminiscences' belong to museums and archaeology, not to real life. Rather, it is a matter of memory, which is creating and transfiguring—a process of selection which goes through an experience of victory over time. The beauty of the past is not a beauty of past facts recorded in the text-books of history or archaeology: it is a beauty of the real, experienced and transfigured past which has entered into the present. As likely as not the past never knew this beauty. The beauty of the ruins of the Parthenon is a beauty of the present rather than of the past. Their very antiquity is an experience of the present. Such is the paradox of time. When I remember the past I perform a creative act, whereby it is transfigured and invested with meaning. I am intent on finding a meaning in the past: but the beauty of the past, of which I am now more conscious than ever before, is not passively reflected in me; I respond to it and re-live it creatively. True life is creation and this is the only life which is worth the living.

CHAPTER XI

MY FINAL PHILOSOPHICAL OUTLOOK. CONFESSION
OF FAITH. THE DOMAIN OF ESCHATOLOGY.
TIME AND ETERNITY

The years in Paris were a time of intense philosophical activity. Apart from the books on philosophy and ethics (beginning with *Freedom and the Spirit*), which I have already mentioned, I wrote a number of social, historical and cultural essays, such as *The Fate of Man in the Modern World*, which presents a more up-to-date interpretation of the contemporary historical scene than *The New Middle Ages*, *The Origin of Russian Communism* and *The Russian Idea*. All these works express my philosophical position more adequately than any of the books I wrote before my exile, with the sole exception of *The Meaning of the Creative Act*. Nevertheless, I must repeat what I have already said on previous occasions: in the end, none of them satisfies me and none conveys my inmost idea. Thought must needs be clothed in flesh and uttered: man is compelled to speak. Yet it is incontestable that, as Tyutchev said, 'a thought once spoken is a lie'.

Throughout my long intellectual development I have from time to time acquired a new philosophical idiom; I have widened the scope of my enquiries and have gained new insights; but my work as a whole revolved round a single axis and has a number of constant dominant themes which give it an inward unity, however fragmentary and aphoristic its outward form may be. The contradictions and inconsistencies of which I am frequently accused are not, perhaps, so much due to this external disjointedness as to the fact that my thinking proceeds, as it were, on different levels, to which I have already drawn attention in previous chapters. The contradictions and inconsistencies, therefore, are inherent in the very nature of the philosophy which I profess, and they cannot and should not be eliminated.

The idea which I want to elucidate in the first instance is that of 'objectification'. This concept provided a medium for expressing one of my fundamental philosophical intuitions. My critique of objectification denotes an inability to believe in and rely on the firmness and stability of the 'objective' world, i.e., the world of our natural and historical environment. 'Objective' things are devoid of ultimate reality; they are an illusion of our consciousness; they exist only in proportion to their remoteness from the sources of being, a remoteness which in turn is dependent on a certain state or orientation of the spirit. Such remoteness is at any rate a mark of diminution in reality. The objectified world is not the true and real world, but only a condition of this true world which has come about as a result of the latter's susceptibility of change. The subject begets the object. Only the subject is ultimately real, 'existential', and only the subject is capable of knowing reality. This view should not, however, be confused with 'subjective Idealism', in the terminology of outworn and platitudinous classifications. Subjective Idealism, after all, assumes an isolated world and an isolated human mind—a world as appearance and a mind to which it appears. To adopt for the moment Dilthey's distinctions, I would call my position an 'Idealism of freedom', as opposed to 'naturalism' and 'objective Idealism'. The world truly exists in the unobjectified subject. The category of Being itself, which plays such a dominant part in the history of philosophy from the Greeks onwards, is a product of intellectual objectification: it is, in Kant's terminology, a transcendental illusion. Reality in its primordial character and originality cannot in any sense be described as undifferentiated Being or essence or *ousia*. Original reality is creative act and freedom, and the bearer of original reality is the person, the subject, spirit, rather than Being, nature or object. Objectivity signifies the enslavement of the spirit to external things: it is the product of disruption, disunion, estrangement and enmity. Knowledge, which is an activity of the subject, depends on the victory over disunion and estrangement, on the extent and intensity of spiritual communion.

Scientific knowledge deals with an objectified world and invests man with a power to master and mould this world. But it does not itself objectify: rather, it deals with a reality, namely nature, which is already in a state of objectification. Indeed, it is evidence of man's attempt to overcome the alien power of nature and to humanize it. I regard as 'object' not the subject-matter of knowledge but that which marks a certain relationship within the existential sphere, whereby man takes up a cognitive attitude *towards* something, whereas his attitude ought to *be* that something. In true knowledge man transcends the object or, rather, possesses the object creatively and, indeed, creates it himself. Reality is enriched by knowledge. Inasmuch as science and scientific method evince critically the grounds on which any given piece of knowledge is based, I am all for it; and the more I tried to clarify my philosophical position, the more I came to adopt a critical attitude and to repudiate methods of mystification. I am now particularly conscious of the value of historical science, more so than, for instance, in my early Marxist days.

I do not claim, however, to have a scientific bent either in the matter or the manner of my thinking. 'Existentialist', 'theosophist', 'historicist', or 'moralist' are more fitting labels for describing the kind of philosopher I want to be. To this may be added 'metaphysician', with all the qualifications which I have already made à *propos* of the so-called science of Being. 'Being' in isolation from the subject of Being is, existentially speaking, an unreality. The real 'object' of knowledge is not this or that Being or this or that predicate, for they do not exist in themselves, but that to which they (Being and predicate) belong or, rather, that subject to which they are related. This has been well shown by Solovyev, although in other respects he is a typical representative of ontological metaphysics in the tradition of Parmenides, Plato, Aristotle, Thomas Aquinas, Spinoza, Leibniz, Hegel and Schelling. The type of philosophy which I dislike most is naturalistic metaphysics, which is intent on objectifying and hypostatizing every idea and every process of thought and on seeing everywhere objective realities, unchangeable substances, entities and forms. The impact of such a philosophy is to freeze cold everything it touches. Man's mind may never be free from compulsion exercised by 'objective realities', but this only goes to show his fallen condition, which can be properly understood and evaluated only from the point of view of a philosophy of freedom, of creativity and of communion in love. In adopting this philosophy I find myself in the company of such different thinkers as Duns Scotus, Boehme, Kant, Maine de Biran and Dostoevsky.

My Orthodox, Roman Catholic and Protestant critics have fiercely attacked the idea of uncreated freedom, which conjured up in their minds a spectre of un-Christian dualism and gnosticism and of a presumptuous limitation of divine omnipotence. I admit that my manner of thinking, in this as in many other respects, contributed to the panic. I have already tried to explain that I am as much opposed to ontological dualism as to ontological monism, and that I regard both as rationalizations. Most of the theological and metaphysical systems are, in fact, variations on the theme of predestinarianism—the *damnosa hereditas* of monistic thought of all kinds. This is true of the traditional doctrine of divine providence as much as of Manicheanism and Calvinism. Beyond the antithesis between God and uncreated freedom, an antithesis which, in my view, is alone descriptive of the relationship between God and man as experienced in this world, there lies the divine, transcendent Mystery, in which all antithesis and all contradictions are removed, and attempts at expressing it in logical propositions become superfluous. This is the realm of the apophatic knowledge of God.

But freedom is in any case, by its very nature, not susceptible of rationalization. When I say that freedom is uncreated, and that objectification is destructive of true existence and true knowledge, I mean that man can be free only if his freedom is not determined by anything that is not himself; and that he is a subject only if he is not a 'thing' fitted in or subordinated, in a causal or any other way, to other things. 'Uncreated freedom' is a limiting notion, describing symbolically a reality which does not lend itself to logical definition. Similarly, 'objectification' is a symbolical description of the fallen state of a world in which man finds himself subservient to necessity and disunion. The objectified world is accessible to rational knowledge and conceptual definition, but the source of its objectified condition cannot be thus known and defined. I would summarize my views on this matter under the heading 'an epistemology of original sin'.

The ideas of uncreated freedom and objectification are bound up with personalism. I have come to attach supreme importance to the human person in opposition to—not by way of escape or flight or turning away from—all the impersonal and supra-personal manifestations of the objective world which constantly threaten to crush and to engulf man. This problem recalls the traditional controversy between the 'realists' and the 'nominalists'. I am, both intellectually and emotionally, opposed to realist conceptualism and do not believe in any general ideas or universals representing not particular and individual images but a supposed essence of things. I am, to that extent, an anti-Platonist, though there are other elements in Plato with which I sympathize a great deal. On the other hand, I cannot identify myself with the nominalist position, because it appears to undermine the idea of the human person, and fails to recognize the eternal image of man. I am not concerned to deny any reality to universals or to restrict philosophy to the particular: rather, I am concerned to find a universal in the particular, to understand the abstract concretely, instead of understanding the concrete abstractly. The traditional controversy between realism and nominalism seems to have been altogether based on a false 'either-or'. The realism of concepts, however, which acknowledges the primacy of the general over the individual and subjects the human mind to generalities is, in my view, a source of man's enslavement. The revolt against the domination of the 'general', therefore, is legitimate and receives its impetus from the Christian conception of God, who is neither Plato's idea of the good nor Aristotle's concept of the pure act, but the 'God of Abraham, Isaac and Jacob', the God who is made man and with whom man enters into personal relations. I am convinced that all philosophical foundations demand re-examination in the light of this Christian affirmation of the pre-eminence of the personal and the singular; and such re-examination will mark a true revolution in the consciousness of modern man.

When my critics accuse me of being a myth-maker or a 'prophet' who would do well with a drop of dullness and a little more precision in the tumultuous sea of his arbitrary assertions and intuitions, I can only repeat what I have said on other occasions, namely, that my vocation is to proclaim not a doctrine but a vision; that I work and desire to work by inspiration, fully conscious of being open to all the criticisms systematic philosophers, historians and scholars are likely to make, and, in fact, have made. Is not Nietzsche open to the same kind of criticism?

I do not think that philosophy will ever be able to speak the truth if it does not take full account of the mysterious element of inspiration. Like Nietzsche I ask about the place of creative ecstasy, vision and prophecy in man's endeavour to comprehend reality. In surrendering to these Nietzsche arrived at the conclusion that God is dead. This conclusion may, indeed, be unavoidable in the experience of human destiny, but in Nietzsche it marked not only the death of God but also the death of man in the advent of the super-man. As to me, I am concerned to show that creative ecstasy, vision, prophecy and inspiration are a pledge of the living reality of God and man.

The more I try to understand the complexity and ambiguity of human existence, the more I am brought up against the problems of eschatology. This may be partly due to my psychological make-up, to my restlessness, impatience and inability to take things for granted. When I became a Christian my first experience was one of tragic disparity between the Christian promise of ultimate fulfilment and its partial realization in this world. The eschatological interpretation of Christianity has made great headway in theology since the end of the nineteenth century, through the work of Ritschl, Schweitzer, Weiss, Blumhardt, Ragaz, and others. But my eschatological views have a metaphysical rather than a historical or biblical source. The impetus came from a vivid experience of the transitoriness of human life and of the complete lack of solid ground under men's feet. Both in my personal life and in the life and history of the world around me I tended to await and anticipate catastrophes. Many years before the outbreak of the first world-war I was living under the spell of approaching catastrophe, and spoke of this almost *ad nauseam*. I saw clearly not only the de-Christianization but also the de-humanization of man, which were gathering momentum in the modern world. My attempt to understand this human predicament brought me closer and closer to the eschatological nature of Christianity. I was unable to look to worldly standards of normal behaviour in a world of utter abnormality or to rely on the promises of natural development. It is part of our predicament that we are caught within the net of all our 'developments', and there is but one issue—the eschatological.

My predilection for the themes of eschatology did not inspire any special liking for the Book of Revelation, or any desire to indulge in interpretations and commentaries on it. If anything I recoiled at the apocalyptic literature from Enoch onwards, because of its odious elements of revenge and retributive justice and its tendency to establish a sharp division of humanity into the good and the wicked. Sadism has had a remarkable career in the history of religion, and Christian doctrine is not entirely free from it. Origen and Gregory of Nyssa are notable exceptions, and their views have made little if any headway in Christian theology. It is possible to assert the humanity of Christianity only at the risk of making oneself a fool among Christian theologians, for most of whom cruelty is an essential mark of orthodoxy. Many Christians have based their theology of vindictiveness on the Gospels. But the message of the Gospels is made known to us through human agency with all its limitations and imperfections. Man is hard and slow of heart. Christianity is the revelation of another world, and to make it conform to this world is to betray it. Eschatological Christianity has and must needs have the effect of a revolution on historical Christianity, because the latter has adapted itself to and fattened itself on the world. Even Christian asceticism proved ineffective. Indeed, no less if not more than overt secularism, it remained passively obedient to the world, and managed to combine personal austerity with an astounding servility towards the evil and injustice in the world. But eschatology is not an invitation to escape into a private heaven: it is a call to transfigure this evil and stricken world. It is a witness to the end of this world of ours with its enslaving objectifications, religious, moral, social and philosophical alike.

It has always surprised me how people can rely on the gradualness of human development, on the stability of human nature, on rational appeals to truth, on the objective standards of good, and all the other ambrosial illusions, in view of the unrelieved corruptibility and transitoriness of human life and the mortal wounds inflicted on man by every death, every parting, every betrayal, every passion. All these illusions are meant to comfort him, but, in fact, they are generalities powerless to redeem the tears of a single child. Human progress may or may not be a reality, but it is rendered meaningless if seen in the light of the dialectic which drove Ivan Karamazov to madness. One thing is certain, the trials, sufferings and storms of human existence bring men face to face with the irrational mystery of life and death.

I am not prone to the fear of death, as, for instance, Tolstoy was, but I have felt intense pain at the thought of death and a burning desire to restore to life all who have died. The conquest of death, indeed, appeared to me as the fundamental problem of life. Death is an event more significant and more fundamental to life than birth. I cannot see, as Rozanov did, the triumph of life through birth; on the contrary, I see in birth the victory of death, so far as the concrete human person is concerned: the genus lives for ever, the person dies. Christianity is a promise of life for every human individual who has passed through the gates of death, not for the abstraction 'mankind'. The Christian promise is a 'subjective', not an 'objective' promise. An 'objective' promise is no promise at all, but a counsel of Job's comforters and a mockery of man's deadly predicament. There can be no comfort in the thought that we shall be immortal in our children, or that we are helping in the making of future happiness or in the establishment of the perfect civilization and society to come, for the end calls in question all such consolations on account of the very fact that they are incommensurable with the unique destiny of each human individual. Christ was victorious over death. This victory was won not by an objective divine power acting from without, but in a divine-human act from within, in the 'subject', where original life and original reality alone reside.

To the Greeks the gods were immortal, whereas man was mortal. The virtue of immortality was recognized as appertaining to heroes, to demigods and to supermen. But this was tantamount to ascribing immortality to the divine and denying it to the human. It is significant of Nietzsche's anti-humanism that he has reverted to the Greek conception. Nietzsche substitutes the image of the new and immortal god, superman, for the divine and immortal image of man, although no one was so passionately athirst for the immortality of man as Nietzsche. Similarly, Plato had no sense of the immortal destiny of man, for the conception of immortality as set forth, e.g., in the *Phaedo* applies not to man but to the 'universal soul'. The same is true of German Idealism. Christianity alone proclaims immortality for the whole of man, for all that is truly human and truly divine in him.

Still more fundamental than the awareness of the tragedy of death and of the need to conquer it and affirm man's immortal nature is the need to free him from the 'eternal' torments of hell. I have tried to formulate this problem in *The Destiny of Man* and, on looking back, I realize that there I wanted to say something which is the touchstone of all my philosophical endeavour. But the problem is too merciless, too terrible, too dark to be susceptible of conclusive formulation. Man will have to answer before God and before humanity for what he has to say on this matter. One thing is certain: in admitting the existence of the eternal torments of hell we deny all meaning and value to man's spiritual and moral life and relegate it to the region of unrelieved and unrelievable terror. I do not deny hell: I could hardly do so, being a member of this world of ours. I admit hell for myself and, indeed, have more than once experienced its unspeakable horror, but I cannot admit it for others, and my whole being revolts against the morality which demands hell for man in the name of justice. I can conceive of no more powerful and irrefutable argument in favour of atheism than the eternal torments of hell. If hell is eternal then I am an atheist.

And yet evil, suffering and hell, as experienced in this world, cannot be invoked as evidence against the existence of God, because faith in God arises precisely in virtue of man's longing for deliverance from this evil, suffering, infernal world. The experience of evil urges man to transcend this world, and, though he be overwhelmed by the meaninglessness of his mundane existence, his very discontent and refusal to accept the conditions of life as he finds them are God's most universal witness. Nietzsche regarded the conquest of suffering, with no reward or bribes attached to it, as an act of heroism. Man, having gone through the experience of suffering, may gain new knowledge: indeed, all knowledge is painful, and the dawn of consciousness marks the end of man's elementary state of wholeness and innocence. Death is the supreme division: the division between man and God, man and man, man and the world. 'My God, my God, why hast thou forsaken me?'

No final or perfect good, and no knowledge of it, can be attained in this world at all; and unless man has passed through the division and experienced the deadliness of death he will never attain it. Dying is neither a release for the spirit, which disembarrasses itself from the body, nor is it an illusion, but a dialectical moment through which he fulfils his divine-human destiny.

Russian thought has always been preoccupied with the problems of the philosophy of history, and my own keen interest in this subject developed in accordance with the tradition of Russian thought. In setting out to understand the nature of history I had one overwhelming impression, namely, that nothing seems to succeed in history and yet all things are significant in it. The meaning of history is beyond the confines of history. History has meaning because it comes to an end. Unending history, be it as progress or as regress, is the epitome of meaninglessness. Thus I arrived at the conclusion that the true philosophy of history is eschatological in nature: that is to say, the historical process ought to be understood in the light of the end. The philosopher of history, therefore, speaks as a prophet who proceeds from the unknown to the known, not from the known to the unknown.

There is an individual eschatology and apocalypse, and there is an historical eschatology and apocalypse; but the two intertwine: history and the end are my own history and my own end, and my own history and end affect the entire course and outcome of history. But this interdependence does not lend itself to clear-cut definition, for there is a tragic conflict between history, with its complex movements and agencies, and man, with his unique and irreducible personal destiny. I have frequently found myself resisting the pressure of historical processes because of their hostility and mercilessness towards man, because they arise and grow for the sake of inhuman and impersonal aims. History must come to an end, since it is incapable of resolving the problem of personality within its limits, and leads beyond them. This is one aspect of the historiographical theme.

The other aspect is marked by an experience of man's self-identification with history: I cannot extricate myself from the world, from humanity, from the social and cultural movements in the world, from the past, present and future. History takes place within me, for I am not an isolated entity existing by itself and for itself, but a microcosmos. My sense of history, then, involves these two experiences: the experience of history's hostile and alien character and of my implication in it. The tension inherent in this twofold experience can only be resolved in the end of history, which signifies a victory over all objectification and alienation—a victory by which man ceases to be determined from without. We are, however, in danger of objectifying the end itself, and imagine it as taking place in historical time. In point of fact, what is beyond history cannot be related to history in simply historical terms. The failure to see this proves a stumbling-block in the many attempts to interpret the Apocalypse. We may not be able to dispense altogether with time when thinking of its end, and yet this end cannot be a mere part of our broken time. It belongs to another order of existence; it must be the end of time itself if it is to be an end at all, however difficult it may be for us to think of something absolutely last. Thus the Apocalyptic angel swears that there should be time no longer. The flux of time is a symptom of the disrupted, fallen state of our world: 'the new heaven and the new earth' betokens victory over this disrupting temporal flux, which splits human existence into extraneous moments and experiences, and the beginning of another time, which I have called 'existential time', and which is not open to mathematical or astronomical measurements.

The end, then, is not one among other occurrences, but each and every occurrence which derives its significance from beyond the series of disrupted moments: we experience it and live through it every time we are stirred by the eruption of transcendent forces. We are closest to it in the catastrophic moments of our personal life and of the life of peoples, in wars and revolution; in creative ecstasy; in nearness to death. In discussing this problem we encounter the same kind of difficulties which exercised Kant in his cosmological antinomies. The end of the world and of history is both within and beyond the world and history. This antinomy has no meaning if we persist in thinking 'objectively', in terms of mutually exclusive things or objects; but it becomes meaningful when we think in terms of existential subjectivity, for which

'this' world and the 'next' world co-inhere. The 'next' world signifies a
mode of life and a quality of existence which exercise a transfiguring
and illuminating power and stem the torrent of time's disintegrating
flux. This process of transfiguration cannot be expressed in terms of
cause and effect, of necessary progress and evolution, for these too are
objectifications and falsifications of the creative act of God and man.
The same must be said of theistic teleologies. In all these cases history
is regarded as something passive, shaped by a force working upon it
from without, and freedom is reduced to a pathetic illusion.

Some people may still delude themselves with the idea that men are
becoming richer and richer and are having a better and better time in
virtue of that secret force called progress, but others are not so easily
deceived. I too believe in progress, but a progress derived from the
recognition of the possibility of true creative acts in history, not from
evolutionary naturalism or determinism. But progress is, admittedly,
a misleading word. History provides the stage for a tragic struggle in
which both good and evil are engaged in an ever increasing and intense
contest. It is this which moves and presses history towards the end, in
which historic time will pass into existential time.

Man is nailed to the cross of time with its tormenting contradictions,
and he cannot bear its apparently unending, relentless course. I have
known moments of almost desperate impatience with time; I could
not absorb myself in any one instant of this relentless course.
I would fain have quickened and forestalled the end—not the end in
death, but the end beyond time in transcendence and eternity. There is
a burning, fatal antagonism between 'this' and 'the other', and it was
'this', even if my own 'this', which haunted me as an external, strange
and inimical force.

Progressives and cultural Philistines tend to be highly suspicious of
the eschatological attitude, because it is alleged to lead to inactivity and
to turn man away from his historical task. But this is true only of the
eschatological attitude as found, for instance, in ascetic monasticism or
in certain forms of apocalypticism, such as Constantine Leontiev's and
Vladimir Solovyev's later glorification of historical bankruptcy. Apocalyptic moods are undoubtedly apt to drive men into defeatism and
inertia. I am as far removed as possible from such moods and I always

combated them. Many people fall victim to eschatological panic because they cannot endure the experience of the decline of an age to which they are bound by all kinds of vested interest, fear and private commitments, which may on occasion drive them to intense activity of a very negative character.

In this matter I am more in sympathy with Fyodorov than with either Solovyev or Leontyev, because Fyodorov believed in the creative act of man and in a last judgment which is not only a divine judgment but a human judgment too: a divine-human act which would bring about a reversal of time and be effective in relation to the past as well as to the present and future. Fyodorov's philosophy is marred by an excessive naturalism and utopianism, but there is a great deal in it which ought to be retained, and above all his extraordinary sense of moral responsibility towards history. Fyodorov, little known and valued in his life-time, was indeed a true Russian prophet in search of universal salvation in whom there was one over-riding passion—unbounded solidarity with the fate of mankind and longing for the redemption of history. I am not inclined to Fyodorov's somewhat optimistic belief in the 'religous power' of science and technical knowledge, but I am at one with him in interpreting revelation in terms of divine-human creativity and in regarding the Second Coming of Christ in power and glory as dependent on the creative act of man. It may be possible to await passively the judgment of a revengeful deity, but no such attitude is compatible with the Second Coming, which is the final revelation of God-manhood. The transition from a historical Christianity, i.e. from Christianity this side of the end, to eschatological Christianity, which foreshadows the end of this spell-bound world of ours, is not a period of fear, inertia and frustration, but one of daring and creative endeavour. Historical Christianity has grown cold and intolerably prosaic; its activity consists mainly in adapting itself to the commonplace, to the bourgeois patterns and habits of life. But Christ came to send heavenly fire on earth, and what will He, if it be already kindled? That fire will not be kindled until the fire of man is set ablaze.

Elsewhere I have tried to show that the only valid morality is the eschatological one (see *The Destiny of Man*). Every moral act of love, of mercy and of sacrifice brings to pass the end of the world where

hatred, cruelty and selfishness reign supreme. Every creative act entails
the end of the kingdom of necessity, servitude and inertia and the
promise of a new, an 'other' world, where God's power is revealed in
freedom and in love. If God appears as judge punishing or rewarding
his creatures and sending them to hell or heaven, this is no more than
a projection of the laws and habits of this enslaved and objectified world
to the 'other' world of freedom and inwardness, and hence the falsification of that 'other' world. The 'last judgment' and 'eternal' damnation
are but the final stage on the road of a doomed, fallen and cringing
world this side of the end. Beyond this end there is no doom or servitude, but freedom. The world to-day is tottering to its ruin; such, indeed, may be the inexorable law of this world. But this does not mean
that man is worthy only of damnation or that the path of grace and
freedom can ever be barred to him.

None the less, the more intense the eschatological feeling the deeper
the awareness that all the middle-of-the-road positions which man
adopts in history, in societies and civilizations, are threatened by the
end, and that their precarious crust is being preserved only by deceptive
and guileful rules and conventions. In many this gives rise to a sense
of despondency and gloom. A terrible judgment hangs over history
and civilization—the imminent judgment over their human, all-too-
human pathways. History shows constant signs of a fatal lapse from the
human or divine-human to the sub-human or demonic. Out of his
idolatrous and demonolatrous instincts man conjures up real demonic
powers which in turn seize control of him. 'The beast rising out of the
sea' is a highly suggestive apocalyptic image of the last demonic attempts of the kingdom of Caesar to dominate and to enslave man and
the world. The victory of the Lamb over the Beast is the victory of
freedom and love over force and hatred. The Beast will then be cast
once more into the abyss of hell and shackled, not to eternity, but to
time: for hell is that which remains in time; that which, obsessed by
its evil nightmares, does not pass into eternity.

What a terrible irony it is that traditional Christian eschatology
should have projected the infernal nightmares of time in eternity. There
can be no vainer and no more intolerable use of God's name. But I
believe in God because he is the victor over hell, because hell disappears

in the unfathomed and inexpressible depths of God's eternity. And I pray every day for those who suffer the torments of hell; and, in so doing, I assume that these torments are not eternal.

Of late years I have been reading a great many books of biblical and historical criticism. Sometimes I had a feeling approaching exhilaration at the possibilities provided by critical methods not only for sifting the historical data of the Christian religion, but also for wrecking the balloons of religious illusions and assumed religious certainties. But these methods also pose a number of profound and serious metaphysical problems. For my part, I cannot pin down my faith to precarious, uncertain and ambiguous facts of historic time. Many a soul has lost its faith on the shifting sand of these historical facts. Divine revelation intervenes in and shines through history, but it is not strictly speaking a historical revelation: on the contrary it marks a victory over all historical revelations and all historical judgments.

I have never doubted the existence of God, even, and perhaps least of all when I denied him. Man has not succeeded in killing God. But I have often been conscious of God's absence from the world, of the world's and man's forsakenness by God. Indeed, this forsakenness by God of human societies and civilization is the basic experience of the age in which it has been my lot to live—an age of the triumph of blind and relentless fate. I have given much thought to the ways and means of combating militant atheism and of resisting its lure; and I arrived at the conviction that the current, traditional methods of apologetics only serve to support atheism and provide strong arguments in its favour. The difficulty with which traditional Christians are faced is not how to defend faith in God, but how to defend their idea of God and of his providence in the world. Sometimes I cannot help thinking that they are, in fact, endeavouring to defend and to justify not God but evil.

I have already explained the reasons which led me to the rejection of the idea of God as lord and ruler of this world. This world is ruled not by God but by the Prince of the World, and his rule is singularly successful. As to God, he reigns over another Kingdom utterly incommensurable with all the things which this world ascribes to him.

Divine providence is not an agency to be measured in naturalistic terms, but to be lived in the depths of the free human spirit. When this is realized, the chief argument of atheism, which is in effect directed against naturalistic, objectivized theology and teleology, falls to the ground.

God is not an extraneous reality, a thing or object, capable of exercising an influence from without. He is immanent in me; he is, as St. Augustine said, nearer to me than I am myself. But immanence and transcendence alike are symbolic terms. They are not meant to denote spatial relations but to surpass them and free us from the servitude to objectified thinking, for which everything is external to everything else. That is why I favour the distinction between 'esoteric' and 'exoteric' religion. The act of revelation is a twofold act, and takes place, as it were, on two levels: it issues from God, who cannot be reduced to any categories taken from this world, but it is also dependent on man, the recipient, limited and imperfect though he be. The Gospel itself reflects this twofold character of revelation. It is seen, for instance, in the striking difference between the infinite loftiness of the person of Jesus Christ and his behaviour, on the one hand, and most of his parabolic teaching, on the other, with its incredibly revengeful kings, masters, landowners, and householders, with its weeping and gnashing of teeth, and its unquenched fires and undying worms. And Christians have shown a peculiar propensity to take hold of these parables in order to bolster up their own vindictiveness.

This raises the question as to whether it is possible any more to interpret Christianity as the religion of fear and intimidation. People nowadays walk in too great a fear of the world to confess a religion of fear and terror. We must not forget, however, that the parables are addressed to the common people of that time, to whom disinterested love of God and the divine was hard of comprehension. They were spoken with reference to the limitations of the human mind and heart, and, as such, their character is exoteric. The voice of God was heard through the medium of a crude and defective human consciousness. The mass of mankind does not understand another language, and it sees truth through a glass, darkly, very darkly indeed. But the authentic image of Christ transcends the one disclosed in the Gospels, which present its refraction in the dark glass of human limitations.

I believe that the greatest revolution brought about by Christianity is the revelation of the humanity of God. This Christian truth of God-manhood is, in fact, incorporated into the Christian Creed, but its import has remained largely hidden from the mind of Christendom, which relies on a debased God-manhood, whereby God is pedagogically adapted to the requirements of fallen nature. But pedagogy suited to one age may turn out to be quite unsuitable and even harmful for another. Humanity has entered on a stage when the religious ideas, however subtle and sophisticated, of rewards and retributions, of legalistic transactions, of a moral and eschatological reign of terror are certainly quite incapable of relieving man's existence, imperilled and torn as it is by the world.

The supreme vindication of God is to be found in man himself and in the pathways of human existence. In this human world, imperfect as it is, there have yet been prophets, apostles, martyrs and saints; there have been men and women who lived in the presence of the mysteries of life and death, who sought for the truth and served it disinterestedly; men and women who created and were informed with beauty; men and women strong in spirit and free in creative exultation. Above all, this world has contained the supreme manifestation of divine truth—its crucifixion in and by the world. All this may not prove God, but it proclaims him in his divine humanity. The century-long logomachy of theology and metaphysics caused nothing but weariness in me and has not convinced me or anybody else of the truth of a single one of their religious propositions. I feel a real repulsion from the disputes and quibbles of dogmatic theologians; as to the history of Christian dogma and of the Œcumenical Councils, few things are more expressive of human pettiness, treachery and fraud.

Some of my devout and religious critics have accused me of believing in philosophy rather than religion. Strange though it may seem to them, I *am* a philosopher and, with the best intentions, can see nothing degrading to myself in calling what I say or write philosophy. I even venture to suggest that there is something more modest about philosophers than about theologians, who, in fact, strike me sometimes as extraordinarily shameless. And yet what I have written in this chapter or elsewhere certainly goes beyond the accepted limits of philosophy and represents a confession of faith: my philosophy is informed with this faith and is born of spiritual experience, rather than deduced from ascertained and assured premises. Indeed, I cannot even begin to think philosophically in the absence of that inner, spiritual experience.

The practical conclusion derived from this faith turns into an accusation of the age in which I live and into a command to be human in this most inhuman of ages, to guard the image of man, for it is the image of God. The low opinion of man which is the pre-eminent characteristic of our age cannot shake my faith in him, in the divine image and the divine idea of man. Life appears to me as the mystery of the spirit, a drama in which man strives in a constant but strangely unavailing effort to embody the creative vision of his spirit. I am conscious of my membership of the mystical Church of Christ—a bond which is stronger than all my protestations against and altercations with the Church in its outward historical and social manifestations. The meaning of life lies in a return to the mystery of the spirit in which God is born in man and man is born in God. But the return is not a relapse into some primal innocence, but a process of creation which contains in some sense all the experiences, trials and ordeals which attend the destiny of man. Eternity is beyond the conflicting 'forward' and 'backward': it contains the one and the other. But only Spirit, the Spirit of the Triune God and the spirit of man can reveal God to himself and to man.

CHAPTER XII

CONCERNING SELF-KNOWLEDGE.
THE LIMITS OF SELF-KNOWLEDGE.
AUTOBIOGRAPHICAL CONCLUSION

In the 'self' the act of knowledge and the object of knowledge, as Fichte has already tried to show, are one and the same. Human personality is not a ready-made object: man creates it especially in knowing himself, for 'self' is primarily an act. The Greeks already recognized the beginning of philosophy to lie in self-knowledge; and throughout the whole history of philosophical thinking men turned to self-knowledge as the way of knowing reality. But was this knowledge of 'self' a knowledge of the concrete, unique and unrepeatable human self or was it merely knowledge *about* man, man in general, or the species called man? It appears that the object of philosophy as currently understood was not the knowledge of that which or, rather, him who exists, but knowledge of some essence, which is apart from him in whom essence is realized. The self-knowing subject was regarded as mind or universal mind, and the object of its knowledge was man in general or the subject in general. No trace was left of the self-knowing man himself: what remained were the common features or general terms that are appropriate to all men to whom we apply them, but are not expressive of their unique characteristics. Despite the Delphic *gnothi seauton*, Greek philosophy aspired to and admitted as knowable only that which is unchangeable, objective form, and the value of knowledge consisted in the light it throws on universal and substantial entities. But on this assumption no true self-knowledge is possible.

In order to see how true self-knowledge comes about and what it is, we must leave behind Greek thought and its heirs in post-Christian philosophy and turn to the exceptions, to St. Augustine's *Confessions*, to Pascal, Dostoevsky, Kierkegaard, Amiel, and to all those who, resolutely and defiantly, exalted the subject over against the object, with

303

its inexorable and crushing determinations. But even here the human mind displayed the fatal tendency to objectify the very insights which man gained from his knowledge of himself. The only signs of the effective undoing of objectivism are seen in Confessions, diaries, autobiographies, memoirs and, more recently, in novels which do not describe types and general situations but bear witness to subjective and particular experiences, which alone are illuminating. The novel is, indeed, becoming increasingly the most significant philosophical document, and certainly the most significant form of philosophical self-knowledge. My own initiation into philosophy has been largely due to Dostoevsky, whose creative work has far-reaching anthropological and metaphysical implications.

But when the knowing subject looks at himself as the object of knowledge he is beset by a maze of difficulties, which have been a source of much criticism and much over-statement. Every attempt at looking at oneself is attended by the dangers of partiality, prejudice, vanity and pretension. I do not know if, in writing this book, I have succeeded in combining subjectivity with truthfulness, and introspection with impartiality, or whether the limits of self-knowledge have proved a stumbling-block in my own as in so many other cases. There is a danger of objectification, and hence of falsification, in the very act of regarding oneself, whether by way of self-glorification or of self-effacement, for neither the glorious nor the humble image of myself can be the truth about myself. Most autobiographies are, in fact, forms of subjective mythology, in which, beneath a crust of modesty and forthrightness, there is a thick layer of vainglory or even sentimentality made more or less innocuous on the surface. And if their authors assume the expression of the angels of innocence who tread where fools have feared to tread, they seldom, in fact, avoid the charge of not being innocent at all, but of being shrewd and calculating in a rather ingenious way. I wanted to be frank and truthful in this book, but I do not know whether I have succeeded even in this. If I make a certain claim to truthfulness, this is because of my complete inability to play the part of an actor on any stage whatsoever, even on the stage of life. Some authors of autobiographies write with a shrewd idea of what would appear interesting and impressive to them if they cared to re-read them; I have re-read this book, but the impression left on me is one of mere dissatisfaction at its uneven and ungracious manner and its inadequate matter.

Nietzsche wrote in *Beyond Good and Evil*: 'What can we describe? Alas, only that which has already begun to fade and spoil.' And Saint-Beuve says of Chateaubriand's Memoirs: '*Il a substitué plus ou moins les sentiments qu'il se donnait dans le moment où il écrivait, à ceux qu'il avait réellement aux moments qu'il raconte.*' There is a painful incommensurability between our inmost thoughts and their outward expression. Time and memory deceive us without our even noticing it. Man is a cunning creature, easily misled and even bewitched by his own unconscious intimations and assumptions. If I were consistent I would not speak or write at all. But I have the courage to be inconsistent: and I cannot be silent. No one has more poignantly expressed the tragedy of the spoken word than Tyutchev:

> Be silent, hide yourself, and let
> Your dreams and longings rise and set
> In the recesses of your heart;
> Your dearest treasures, held apart,
> Your stars, that in the deep of night
> Entrance your spirit with delight.
>
> How can the heart expression find,
> Or one man read another's mind,
> Another know what you live by?
> A thought that's spoken is a lie;
> And if you stir, you cloud the well.
> Feed on your dreams, and so be still.
>
> Live in yourself, there is a whole
> Deep world of being in your soul—
> Of thought on strange enchanted thought;
> But deafened by the noise without,
> And blinded by the daylight glare,
> Their song would cease. Oh, hush! Oh, hear![1]

---

[1] Translated by Frances Cornford in *Poems from the Russian* (Faber and Faber), quoted here with the kind permission of the publishers. (Tr.)

Of late a not very illuminating discovery has been made: namely, that writers write books, painters paint pictures and musicians compose music in order not to reveal but to conceal themselves, or even to express the exact opposite of what they think and feel and are. Nietzsche, Kierkegaard, Kafka, the 'psychological novel' and especially the school of psychoanalysis provided ammunition for the pioneers and followers of this discovery. Man is not that which he gives himself out to be. This partial truth has been much played upon and misused by Leo Shestov, who was a great and brilliant master of double meanings and paradoxes. The validity of the discovery in question cannot, however, be entirely denied, for man should be known not only 'from above' but also 'from below', in his sub-conscious and subterranean dimension. Thus it is that the Christian doctrine of the sinfulness of human nature —a doctrine which in the past easily turned into an irrelevant abstraction—was made concrete and acquired a would-be scientific character. The theories of Marx, Nietzsche, Freud and Heidegger, the disclosures of the modern novel, the experiences of war and revolution, the manifestations of known and unknown forms of cruelty together with the ubiquitous modern tendency to falsify everything—all this shattered high-falutin ideas about man. Nevertheless, I believe that Pascal and Dostoevsky were nearer to the truth and less open to illusions in showing man as a two-fold being, both mean and lofty, base and noble. I have known many blighted hopes; I have seen much meanness, falsehood, malice, cruelty and treachery; I have experienced many disappointments in men and have myself been the cause of such disappointments. And yet I have sustained my faith in man and in God's idea of man: for faith in man is the hallmark of faith in God and the divine.

For my part I do not think that, at least so far as this autobiography is concerned, I am a favourable or promising subject for psychoanalysis. For, despite my solitariness and reserve, I have neither consciously nor unconsciously aimed at concealing myself in anything I have written. There are many things in my life which I do not even attempt to disclose in this book. It is not, and it is not intended to be, a confession made before a priest or in an analyst's consulting room. My aim has been at once more modest and more comprehensive: namely, to perform an act of existential, philosophical self-knowledge, to discover the meaning of my spiritual and intellectual pathway.

André Gide wrote two books in which he speaks directly of himself: his autobiographical novel *Si le grain ne meurt* and his comparatively recent *Journal*. It is well-known that one of Gide's fundamental problems is that of sincerity: he wants to be absolutely frank and manages to be so almost to the point of obsession. To say the ugliest and most repulsive things about himself seems to him to be almost a matter of pride. Surely, this attitude is itself a rationalization: it is reflective and 'sentimental', not spontaneous and 'naïve'. Nevertheless, both the novel and the Diary undoubtedly add a great deal to our knowledge of man, particularly of man to-day.

Another example is provided by Leo Tolstoy, one of the most truthful writers in the literature of the world. But Tolstoy's *Confession*, extraordinarily illuminating though it is, is far from being a confession in the true sense of the word. He overstates his case by representing himself as a murderer, a thief, an adulterer, and so on. These self-accusatory statements, however, are no more than labels which can be attached to everybody in general and to nobody in particular. The *Confession* is of interest not as a testimony of concrete, individual sins actually committed, but as the story of a spiritual journey in search of truth. Similarly, Goethe's *Dichtung und Wahrheit* is a mixture of auto-biographical 'truth' and 'poetry', of confession and interpretation or invention. Neither is Rousseau's *Confession* entirely reliable or, indeed, important as a record of things done or left undone (on the whole, he seems to be delighted with himself, even while admitting his sins and transgressions), and yet it marked the beginning of a new attitude to the emotional life of man.

The question of frankness and sincerity as it presented itself to me in the course of writing this autobiography is not unlike that underlying all Confessions, though I am not concerned with confessing anything to anybody. I repeat, this book is an attempt to discover the meaning of life within a biographical framework. The most adequate title I could have chosen for this book is 'Dream and Reality', since it is, in the end, no more than a description of a fundamental conflict with this world and an evocation of the image of another one. Hence the emphasis on imagination, freedom and creativity which bulk large throughout these pages; hence also my predilection for Dosto-evsky's 'non-acceptance of the world' and for Ibsen's mountain-symbolism. I have minimized rather than exaggerated the gulf which divides me from the things around me, and which yawns at me wherever I turn: the commonplace, the common man, the 'we', the 'all of us', the collective mind, and so on and so forth. And yet I continued throughout life to hover between solitude and independence *vis-à-vis* the world, on the one hand, and an intense desire for communion with my fellow-men and for the establishment of just and free social relations, on the other. I do not think this paradox can be explained either in terms of individualism or in those of an impotent inclination to turn a passion for social intercourse into a philosophical asset.

I have never tried, willingly or unwillingly, to shut myself in a private world of my own; rather, I desired to find a way out into the open, to be present in the world and to make the world present within me, but to be present dangerously and freely. Man is created as a microcosmos and his vocation is to re-create the cosmos within himself. Max Stirner was right in saying that the whole world was *das Eigentum* of *der Einzige*. But the truth of this proposition was belied by Stirner's own solipsism. His solipsistic 'selfhood' was a pale, materialistic reflection and a travesty of the microcosmic spirit advocated by German mysticism. The whole universe dwells within, and is personified by, man, and nothing should be regarded as external to him. But the phenomenal, empirical world, as in fact it presents itself to me, is not my own; on the contrary, it impinges on me from without and is intent on destroying me, and I am not the microcosmos I ought to be. Man's actual condition is such as to make the intensity of his self-awareness a measure of his enslavement to an alien world; and he revolts against this world so as to stem the tide of its destructive pressures. I do not in fact possess the world, nature and society which stand over against me; what is mine is exceedingly slender and intangible in comparison with them, so slender indeed as to elude entirely the claims of nature, society and the world at large. I can only agree to submit to, and be merged with, that nature or that society which is capable of entering into me and of being my own.

Such is the aristocratism of the human spirit: an aristocratism which is the exact opposite of all those hierarchical relations which characterize the established patterns of social life. I have always been of the opinion that every social organization is plebeian in character and that the so-called aristocratic organization of society is plebeian *par excellence*. The sense of the hierarchic order is bound up with a sense of belonging to some whole, whether social or cosmic or theo-cosmic, in which each person occupies an allotted place and is subordinated to the higher stage in the hierarchic structure. The value of the human person is, accordingly, seen as determined by the whole, the general, of which he constitutes a part. I could scarcely envisage any more striking example of anti-personalism than this conception. For my part, I am entirely devoid of all hierarchic sense: I cannot even stand it when human relations are described in terms of rank; or when I hear references to someone who has achieved 'a position in society'. I have always disliked it when people referred to me as a householder, the head of a family, the editor of a journal, or the president of the Religious-Philosophical Academy. I could never put myself in the position of someone who regards men's real qualities and merits or demerits as related in any way to their position in society. Neither saints nor prophets nor geniuses have ever held such positions. And when God was made man he took the very lowest place in society and, indeed, became its victim.

When people tell me that a 'new order' is to be brought about and man is to be released by a change in the mechanism of society, I want to say to them: for God's sake refresh your memory! Your new order is as old as any other. There has never been a time when man was freed by society: he was always at its mercy, at its secular or religious mercy. So it was among the primitive tribes, so it has been ever since and, no doubt, so it will be until the end. A new 'order' will arise on the ashes of all orders and as a result of the only effective, the personalistic revolution.

I am not aware of any hierarchic order in my life, and I do not see in it the working out of some plan. All such plans and orders appeared

to me as an outward check on my freedom which I could not but reject.
I have never conformed to any fixed purposes, although I was intensely
conscious of a calling in life. In a certain sense my life always seemed to
me confused, irrational and undetermined, and I took the risks which
are necessary for living such a life. I am indebted and grateful to a great
many people who helped me in one way or another. Above all, I know
for certain that a Higher Power watched over my life and guided it
when it was most grievously imperilled. But life in its actuality often
reminded me also of a dream, sometimes of a nightmare, illumined
only by occasional flashes of daylight. And the more I let my eyes
dwell on the things around me, the more intense became my sense of
their 'objectivity' and hence their ultimate unreality. When I was
younger I was an 'idealist' in the bad as well as the good sense of the
word: I probably still am. 'Idealism' may, indeed, be a mere egotism
of the crank; but it may also spell life in that region of the spirit in
which imagination dwells like an unfettered exile in a court of shadows.
Later in life I have come to learn the terrible responsibilities which external reality, with its inexorable necessities and servitudes, impresses
on us. But I have never been able to lose a sense of the bitterness of
knowing that reality.

'Realism' may be no less false than 'idealism'. There is a realism which
betrays nothing but enslavement to this fictitious world of ours, which,
it is believed, men ought to take for granted, but which, in fact, they
idealize and rationalize in their realism. A true realism and a true
idealism issue from the recognition of Mystery beneath and beyond this
world: it is the attitude of him whose eyes do not tell what they know
or do not know. He who knows no mystery lives in a flat, insipid, one-
dimensional world. If the experience of flatness and insipidity were not
relieved by an awareness of mystery, depth and infinitude, life would
no longer be livable. In childhood all things, even a dark corner in the
room, appear as mysterious. Later the realm of mystery narrows: the
objective world around becomes more and more commonplace, and
even the infinite depth of the starry night loses its mysteriousness. But
for him who does not yield to this objectivity mystery abides and only
moves on to another sphere. Then the very emergence of the objective
world becomes a source of wonder.

I have said already that I refuse to be labelled as occupying any position in the world, be it that of a *paterfamilias*, the leader of a movement or school of thought, or a teacher of life. If I described myself as a moralist, this does not mean that I am intent on teaching or convincing anyone: the only thing I can hope to do is to provoke. I continue to regard myself as no more and no less than a youth. And even on looking into the mirror I can see behind the features of an aged and time-worn face the form of a youth. Each one has his characteristic and enduring age: I am still the dreamer, the enemy of 'reality' of my youth. I have none of the wisdom and prudence attributable to my three-score years and ten. I am more impressionable and more impetuous than ever, although physically I often feel ill and exhausted. If I were true to my age I should presumably distrust everything and take endless precautions. This I never do, except for a few eccentricities, no doubt characteristic of old age and physical decay, particularly where medicines are concerned.

Life is movement, and one of its fundamental problems is that of change, change in ourselves and in those around us. We cannot speak of human life unless its flow is measured by change, and we cannot speak of change in life except relatively to something in it that stands still. This something is the subject of life. 'All that changes remains the same, and only changes its condition', wrote Kant. Change can be a mark of ascent, advancement and enrichment; but it can equally mean degradation, perversion and betrayal. The question at issue is how to insure that change does not become betrayal, that in changing man remains true to himself. It is a commonplace that man shows his true nature in trials, catastrophes and dangers. Since it has been my lot to witness a great many historical changes and catastrophes I have observed amazing transformations in people. And there are few more painful experiences than the failure to recognize people whom one knew well and who have betrayed themselves as a result of adaptation to the changing circumstances of life. I have experienced this in Russia, I have heard of it in Germany, and I shall no doubt live to see it in France. But I have also witnessed manifestations of change in which people have shown remarkable and unexpected spiritual strength in withstanding the pressure of the changing circumstances of life. Some women particularly surprised me in this way, and I believe women have generally more stability than men.

Change plays an important part in human relationships. I have observed that change in myself and in others had a decisive effect on my intercourse with them. Sometimes it was difficult for me to keep up with the modifications in the life and outlook of my friends, because I lost the sense of their identity. But sometimes such modifications served to bring out their true character and to strengthen our relationship. And, no doubt, my friends must have known similar experiences in regard to me.

I was struck by the peculiar and rather reprehensible attitude expressed by Goethe in his *Dichtung und Wahrheit* in connection with his love-affairs, of which there were not a few. As he describes them, each of these love-affairs was, as it were, a step forward on the way to Goethe's self-fulfilment, an occasion for his emotional enrichment. But the women who, each in her own way, contributed to his advancement, were quickly forgotten and thus turned into mere tools of Goethe's development. However glorious, and pleasing to Goethe, this development may have been, it hardly redeems the personal fate of the innumerable 'Gretchens' left on the wayside of his rich and fertile life.

As I have already pointed out, I have deliberately avoided referring in this book to those most intimate relationships which are known under the heading 'love': but these relationships have been, for me too, a source of great enrichment, although they also threw a shadow over the earlier part of my life. Even if I did not wish to be elusive in this matter, I would not be able to speak, for I never spoke or speak to anyone about my intimate relations with people. It is easier for me to find words to express my feelings towards my beloved cat Muri or to my dogs now no longer alive than towards human beings. Sometimes, indeed, I feel that animals are much easier of access for me than man; and it was only to them that I was able to express myself emotionally and to drop the mask of reserve.

I have spoken earlier on of my emotional aridity; but there is one thing which is capable of dissolving my dryness of heart almost immediately, and that is music. I know, of course, that emotional shivers of this kind are an unreliable test of aesthetic value, but I do not think that such intimations can be disregarded altogether. I know little if anything about music. I have a bad ear and a poor musical memory, and the shades and subtleties of musical performance escape me. I am quite unable to keep up a conversation on the subject of music. I cannot make head or tail of the arguments used by critics and musical people in general, and I strongly suspect that such arguments prevent one from enjoying music. This may, in a sense, be applied to all art critics and art criticism. Despite my musical ineptitude, however, music does stir me to the depths of my being, and sometimes dispels moods of depression and despondency. The sensation is similar to that which I endeavoured to describe in the chapter on creativity.

Music has acquired a very unusual and prominent place in modern civilization. But this prominence is a not unmixed blessing. It makes it possible for the European bourgeois to pass quickly, without any effort and unawares, for the price of some twenty francs, into the Kingdom of Heaven, and then to return with the same speed to the world of his petty, mean and unsightly affairs. Music itself is not, admittedly, to blame for this prostitution. Beethoven did not suffer and create to while away the idle hours of the European bourgeois. Every true creative act passes into the Kingdom of God, and what remains of it on earth turns into an object at the disposal of those who are, or for the most part are not, worthy of its excellence. This is evidence of the tragedy of art which overtakes all true artists after death. Art, like all creative activity, frees man from the weight of the commonplace, even while depicting that commonplace, and carries him into another, transfigured world. But the bourgeois has no desire for such freedom or such another world: he is a mere consumer in search of a new impetus for the consolidation and expansion of his kingdom of the commonplace.

If music can be experienced as a way of liberation from triviality, the same might be said of the comic and of laughter. Laughter too may rescue us, even if for a moment, from the monotony and dreariness of existence; it may, likewise, puncture the inflated air of gravity which men are apt to assume in order to protect themselves from disturbances.

One of the privileges of man is that he can be inconsequent; he can even embody in himself conflicting or contradictory elements, and no general idea of man can reduce these inconsequences, conflicts and contradictions. This has been fully acknowledged by modern psychology. Speaking for myself, I am, for instance, conscious of the co-existence in me of a strong revolutionary bent and a tendency to form habits; an emotional and intellectual anarchism and a liking for order in my private life. These two elements, however, spring, paradoxical though it may seem, from one and the same source. I have already said more than enough about my revolutionary tendency. But how do I account for my propensity to form habits? The answer is, in the first place, that all the things associated with the organization of practical every-day life are extremely arduous for me; I have no skill in this matter and flinch from spending much of my energy on it. Consequently I try to reduce the necessary effort to the minimum by means of habit, the constant aim of which is precisely to avoid effort. In other words, I simply try to escape from the difficulty by way of habit, which creates the illusion of liberation from workaday existence. In fact, however, it only gives freedom from the effort demanded by opposition to this material world.

But there is another reason for the rôle played by habit in my life. I have frequently referred to my experience of estrangement in regard to the world as I find it. This experience imbued me with an acute sense of anguish and longing for wholeness and integration. Now habit is one way of struggling against that estrangement: I mean habit formed by oneself, not imposed from without. Every parting, with places and things no less than with people dear to one, makes the pain of estrangement more intense. If I am in the habit of doing something definite, if I have acclimatized myself in my own world, and my life is informed with a rhythm, then the sense of estrangement grows less acute. Undoubtedly this is but a palliative, perhaps even a mere anodyne, for, in the end, nothing can rescue the world from its state of estrangement except God. The revolutionary and anarchic in me are intent on subverting the whole configuration of this alien world. But I still possess bonds which give me the feeling of relative harmony, bonds which would endure even should the alien world meet with its utter and deserved destruction. But I am no master in the art of living, or in composing the differences and conflicts of which I am conscious in myself. My life has been anything but a work of art. Neither was I ever able to play with it. I have held to life with no support save a bare search for a truth wholly and utterly unlike the world, and with no other passion save the passion for freedom which dissolves the congealed and petrified modes of life and consciousness.

EPILOGUE (1940-1947)

My autobiography was broken off, and I should like now to add a few pages without which this story would be incomplete. The difficult years of the war abounded in events and experiences which were of immense importance for me. An event of such magnitude as the second world-war, the issue of which at first seemed obscure and beyond reckoning, proved a tremendous shock to the world at large as well as to every individual, and everything was thrown into the whirlpool. I awaited ever new disasters and had no faith in a peaceful future.

The horrors of war did not become apparent until the German occupation of France and the German attack on Russia. These seemed no mere external invasion, but, as it were, an insinuation from within. In June 1940 we left Paris as part of the 'exodus' for Pilat, near Arcachon. Our cat, Muri, went with us; the journey was ghastly, and he suffered no less, though with greater fortitude, than we. We hoped to escape life under German rule. But the hope proved a complete illusion: a few days after our arrival in Pilat there were more German troops there than at any time in Paris. Pilat is a heavenly but somewhat melancholy spot, situated between black pine woods and the ocean. At least we were away from Paris, which was overcharged with the emotions of a vast collapse. We settled down in a cottage in the woods. There were a number of Russian friends living not far away in Arcachon. Despite pressing invitations and repeated appeals, I refused to go to America, and I do not regret having withstood the temptation. Few experiences, however, are more bitter than foreign occupation: there is something profoundly degrading about it. I could not bear looking at the German uniforms. We remained in Pilat three months and throughout this time I went on writing my autobiography.

On returning to Paris I soon realized that my position was fraught with danger. I had attacked National Socialism and Fascism on more than one occasion, and it was well-known that I was an ideological opponent of the 'new order'. Some Russians had already been arrested. But a great number of Russian *émigrés* in France welcomed the German victories, and this became particularly apparent subsequent to Hitler's attack on Russia. Their attitude was a mixture of hope for a new Russia of their own imagination and treacherous servility towards the Germans. There were, however, notable exceptions. The invasion of the Russian land by the German armies shook me to the depths of my being. I felt that *my* Russia was exposed to mortal danger, that she might be dismembered and enslaved. The Germans advanced with incredible speed, occupied the Ukraine and reached the Caucasus. As is well-known, they lashed themselves into unheard-of atrocities against the Russian people, treating them as the scum of the earth. There was a time when many thought that Germany would win, at least in Russia. For my part, I never lost faith in the invincibility of Russia, although the dangers to which she was exposed were a source of unspeakable agony for me. My inborn patriotism, of which I have already spoken above, reached an extraordinary intensity. I felt myself one with the successes and failures of the Red Army. I even came to divide people into those who hoped for the victory of Russia and those who looked forward to the victory of Germany. I refused to meet the latter and regarded them as traitors. The fact that some Russians counted on Hitler's 'liberation' of Russia from Bolshevism aroused in me all my old feelings of repulsion against the sinister and unseemly *émigré* psychology, which I combated throughout the inter-war years and which now became particularly heinous. I have never bowed down to force, particularly to military force, but the strength displayed by the Red Army in defence of Russia was to me providential, and in Russia's ordeals I perceived a token of the fulfilment of her historic mission.

Life in Paris was very difficult. A number of our friends were arrested, and some of those who were deported to Germany as political prisoners perished there in tragic circumstances. I was visited by agents of the Gestapo (always in twos) on several occasions, and they questioned me about the nature of my activity; but they were unable to produce any definite charges against me. One day an announcement appeared in the Swiss newspapers that I had been arrested. A week or so later agents of the Gestapo arrived to make enquiries about the origin of the rumour. According to them the rumour caused some alarm in Berlin (this was undoubtedly an exaggeration), and they wanted to assure me of the authorities' 'benevolent attitude' towards me. The situation was highly embarrassing and distasteful to me. I have often asked myself why I was not arrested, considering that the Germans had not the slightest scruples in this respect, and often caught people who were quite innocent even from their point of view, whereas I had proclaimed my hostility towards National Socialism in print and in public whenever I treated of contemporary problems. Having expressed my surprise to the Gestapo agents at this bewildering omission on the part of the Nazi authorities, I added jokingly that, apparently, nothing could wipe out the Germans' respect for philosophy.

Naturally, during these troubled years I was unable to engage in any social activities. I stayed in my house in Clamart and seldom went even to Paris. Public offices and cafés (which I had always avoided even in the past) had become dangerous places. I declined to participate in any undertakings which had a connection, however remote, with the Germans. Thus I was unable to give public lectures or read papers for which an authorization from the German or German-controlled authorities would be required. My whole time was occupied with writing and reading. Nevertheless we kept up our Sunday 'at homes', at which a number of patriotically minded Russians and occasionally a few French people would appear. Our house became a kind of meeting-place for Russian patriots.

The only outside activity in which I took part was Mlle Davy's venture. In the difficult conditions prevailing in occupied Paris she managed to group around her a number of people who were in one way or another connected with the Resistance movement, mostly left-wing Catholics, and a few Protestants and Orthodox. Mlle Davy, a learned and gifted woman, was responsible for a series of conferences near Paris devoted to the study of religious and philosophical problems. It was on this occasion that I came into conflict with Gabriel Marcel, who accused me of anarchism and similar crimes of which I happen to be rather proud.

During these years I also made the acquaintance of Romain Rolland, whose wife was the widow of a nephew of mine. Tolstoy had at one time exercised a powerful influence on him (Rolland was Tolstoy's first French biographer) and he had something of Tolstoy's seriousness and search for truth. His sympathy with Bolshevism and Soviet Russia in no way issued from a materialistic conviction, but had its origin in a genuine appreciation of the spiritual significance of Russian communism. His striking appearance and expression of rare distinction were symbols of great moral and intellectual integrity.

During these years of murderous war, of bloodshed, of wholesale destruction, of concentration-camps and of indescribable human afflictions, I was pressed more and more to meditate on death and evil, on suffering, hell and eternity. The fruits of these meditations are contained in my book, which I thought would be the last, *The Divine and Human*.

In the autumn of 1942 I underwent a serious operation. I remained in a nursing-home for six weeks with our friend Tatyana Savelyevna Lampert, who looked after me with great devotion and self-denial. The issue of the operation might have been a fatal one. The pain left me comparatively unmoved: what did affect me was the ghastly experience of partial anaesthetic. I remained fully conscious, but the greater part of my body was completely benumbed. There seemed to be a wall of irresistible and inescapable necessity between my outer and inner 'self'. I experienced this as a likeness of that horror of self-estrangement which is the nightmare of human existence, the sinister dream of being always something other than I am.

At the very time of the liberation of Paris we lost our beloved Muri, who died after a painful illness. His sufferings before death were to me the sufferings and travails of the whole creation; through him I was united to the whole creation and awaited its redemption. It was extremely moving to watch Muri, on the eve of his death, make his way with difficulty to Lydia's room (she was herself already seriously ill) and jump on her bed: he had come to say good-bye. I very rarely weep, but—this may sound strange or comic or trivial—when Muri died I wept bitterly. People speculate about 'the immortality of the soul', but there I was demanding immortal, eternal life for Muri. I would not

have less than eternal life with him. A few months later I was to lose
Lydia. But of this I shall speak later.

Outwardly a new life began with the liberation of Paris. The war
was not yet over, but one could be certain of its favourable outcome.
As a consequence of the liberation an orgy of revenge was let loose,
inevitable perhaps but no less distasteful for that. Many Russians were
arrested, but now for reasons opposite to those which inspired the
German oppression. Some of these arrests were undoubtedly justified,
for many Russians had thoroughly compromised themselves by their
treacherous dealings with the German occupation authorities. But other
arrests were sheer and baseless victimization. A number of Russian
émigrés appeared to have experienced a somewhat unexpected and rapid
change of heart, and began to prostrate themselves before communism,
of which they had not the slightest understanding, and dance attendance
on the Soviet Embassy. Few displayed any sense of dignity and freedom.
    For my part, I saw no reason for changing either my attitude to the
major issues of communism or my basic 'Soviet orientation', so far as
international relations were concerned. I continued to regard the Soviet
government as the only representative national government, even
though I did not approve of its policy in some respects. No true Russian
can feel or believe the communist régime to be an alien occupation, or
will accept the view that its foreign policy is in conflict with 'national
interests'. My sympathies are at bottom with anarchism and, in the
end, I disapprove of all governments. But this does not mean that I fail
to recognise the necessity of government in the life of national com-
munities. I am, however, far more concerned with the Russian people
and with the Revolution as an inner moment in their historic destiny.
I could not even begin to evaluate post-revolutionary Russia, unless I had
lived through, or at least endeavoured to live through, this destiny and
had made it my own. I cannot look at Russia from the imaginary
heights of abstract liberal democratic principles. But neither can I agree
to make my thought and behaviour fit the directives of the Soviet
Embassy or write with my eye constantly fixed in the direction of His
Excellency the Soviet Ambassador, as some of my compatriots succeed

in doing. When the Union of Soviet (first known as Russian) Patriots, with which I was vaguely associated at the time, announced their unconditional acceptance of and devotion to the Soviet government and *régime*, I protested violently. Man ought not to accept any government whatsoever unconditionally, for that is tantamount to slavery; man ought not to bow before any power whatsoever, for that is tantamount to renouncing his freedom.

The circle of my friends changed considerably. I met now almost exclusively Russians representing the 'Soviet orientation', young writers, journalists and churchmen belonging to the Patriarchal Church. I lost all contact with the Theological Institute. But, unlike the Soviet Patriots, I did not keep running in and out of the Soviet Embassy—an activity which I regarded as highly undignified. But a number of people from the Soviet Embassy used to come and see me, and I valued these contacts as a unique opportunity of learning about life in Russia. I was particularly impressed by one young Soviet diplomat. The most fruitful and illuminating acquaintance was with a Soviet writer, a very attractive and talented man who often came to see us. I do not think I have received from anyone a more poignant impression of present-day Russia. There was not the slightest sign of the fanaticism or ideological prejudice in him. He was humane, sensitive and understanding, and he was informed with the spirit of nineteenth-century Russian literature; and yet he was a typical product of modern post-revolutionary Russia, with its unbounded and vigorous faith in man, its primitive spontaneity and its peculiar optimism. But the traditions of Russian philosophical thought had evidently not yet penetrated the thick crust of official Soviet philosophical dogma. So far as philosophical thought is concerned, people's minds were fed exclusively on Belinsky, Chernishevsky and Dobrolyubov, apart from the classics of Marxism. I could not help feeling the bitter irony of the fact that my own works should be known in Europe, America, Asia and Australia and translated into many languages, while practically no one has ever heard about me in my own country. This is evidence of a radical break in the tradition of Russian culture, although the return to the traditions of Russian literature subsequent to the Revolution is of immense importance and a token of further development in this direction.

It is possible that I shall be allowed to return to Russia. But what could I do there? The question of my return is becoming a source of increasing torment for me. Never have I felt so close to Russia, and yet there is little joy in that feeling, and my heart bleeds every time I think of her. I am faced again and again, but never so vividly as now, with the complexity and tragic nature of Russian destiny. I do not think that people in Western Europe will ever know or understand it. But nothing can prevent its being a destiny, and nothing can deprive it of its meaning. It must be lived out to the end by Russia.

I am constantly visited by foreigners and receive an innumerable quantity of letters. This vast correspondence is my misfortune and despair, since I am no good at letters, and cannot bear writing them. To my surprise and annoyance I find that I am becoming a respected and respectable 'teacher of life'. I should like to assure the readers of this autobiography that I am nothing of the sort. I am only a seeker after truth and a rebel who desires freedom from the bondage of life to things, objects, abstractions, ideologies and the fatalism of history. Whether these pursuits do, in fact, set me free I am unable to say, and I do not regard the consequences. Sometimes I think they can only lead me to the cross, where I shall find myself broken on what is enslaving and dull in life. Hence, perhaps, the melancholy which often invades my whole being, and which I try to conceal under a veneer of good humour and wit.

The war drew to its close under the cloud of great personal sorrow for me. Lydia fell seriously ill with paralysis of the throat muscles; she could hardly speak or swallow food. Her physical strength was declining with each day, but she bore this agonizing illness in a wonderful way. At the end of September 1945 she died. Her death was a source of great illumination as well as of burning pain for me. I have never known anyone inspired by such faith on the threshold of death. Her mind and consciousness remained clear until the very end, and everything she wrote (she always wrote, since she could not speak) before her death reflected her intense spiritual vision. I used to spend many hours in her room reading her pencilled notes and talking to her. Her words seemed like a direct testimony of remarkable spiritual insight and experience. I do not cease to recall what I have lost in her and what I learnt from her during those last months. I cannot be reconciled to death and the tragic finality of human existence; and my whole being resists the notion, naturalized by Heidegger, of death as the ultimate reality. There can be no life unless it restores all those we love to itself.

But this concerns one aspect of death only, death as a thief, a taker away of what is most valued; but there is another, a more luminous aspect. For death may be the triumph of self-sacrifice and love. Man finds it hard to face the mystery of death, but he also comes to know in death a unique value which is love issuing in eternal life. Life must be lost before it can be fully won. Love and death are inseparable, but love is stronger than death. That is why in death communion with those we love continues and is even intensified, for it has passed through the supreme sacrifice of love which is death. When Lydia told me on the eve of her death that she would always be with me, I knew that this was true. Death is an event in time and a token of the power of time over man; but it is also an event bringing him face to face with and issuing in eternity, in which love and kinship are victorious over estrangement and disunion.

It is said that we should speak in praise of the dead or be silent. This proverb contains a profound truth which is not, as a rule, fully realized. Why is it that dead faces bear upon them the mark of some strange beauty? I think this is because death is the moment of supreme clarification; because in death man is released from his coarse and ugly features; because death is the foreshadowing of transfiguration. Historians and biographers would do well to take note of this, lest they banish from the face of the dead the spirit which transfigures them and leave only perishable and cold monuments.

I am now left alone with Genia. She is a dear and a very special and understanding friend. I do not know how I could live were she to depart from this life.

The year 1947 has brought back to me with even greater intensity the problem of Russia. This problem is proving a source of increasing mental agony. My hopes seem to be disappointed. After a heroic war the hopeful processes and movements within Soviet Russia failed to

take the expected course. Freedom is again in danger. The affair of
Akhmatova and Zoshchenko[1] made a particularly painful impression
on me. To read the Soviet newspapers and periodicals is a no less unpleasant experience. The 'general line' is being imposed with new vigour,
and the effect is suffocating. The only redeeming feature is the radical
change in the attitude of the government to the Orthodox Church,
which enjoys considerable freedom. But the sphere of church life is, as
it were, localized, and its freedom does not extend beyond the limits of
ecclesiastical and liturgical affairs (although theological schools have
been re-opened). There can be no doubt that, as a result of the experiences of the revolution and war, the religious movement is growing
and the Christian faith is if anything stronger than ever before among
the Russian people.

The disturbing feature, however, is the unmistakable disposition
among churchmen, and especially among the hierarchy, to religious
conservatism and a tendency to re-establish the patterns of church-life
as practised in the sixteenth and seventeenth centuries. Christianity is
understood almost exclusively as a religion of private salvation within
the framework of liturgical life. There are no signs of creative thought,
or even of an intellectual disquietude. And it is just this brand of conservative religion which, on the face of it, is being encouraged by the
Soviet government. I am entirely in sympathy with the growth of
patriotic feeling among churchmen, but this should not lead, as it
appears to do, to nationalism, which is a betrayal of the true Russian
idea.

Among the *émigrés* we see the same old story: people live and think
with one question in view—do you or do you not reject post-revolutionary Russia unconditionally? The logic of this fictitious dilemma is
now proving a complete and issueless quandary for the helpless mind
and heart of the Russian *émigré*: his present state of obsession is evidence
of this. I think I have already made my own position clear. I accept the
Revolution and many changes which it has brought about in the
structure of society; I continue to believe in the great mission of the
Russian people; but, at the same time, I want to be left free to criticise

[1] When this was written Akhmatova, a poetess, and Zoshchenko, a satirist, had
fallen into disgrace and for a time lost the possibility of publishing their writings. (Tr.)

the actions of the Soviet government if and when they are, in my view, incompatible with the principle of human freedom. I find it intolerable when Orthodox Christians define their attitude to Soviet Russia on the principle that 'there is no power but of God'. This dictum of St. Paul has, in point of fact, a restricted historical meaning: it has been, I am sorry to say, a source of much servitude and servility in the Church.

My critical attitude to the ugly things that are going on in Soviet Russia is, however, complicated, though not cancelled, by the fact that in the present international situation I feel bound to defend my country. I am prepared to stand firm by the principles which govern Soviet foreign policy *vis-à-vis* an increasingly hostile world, although I do not endorse all the methods which are used in their application. Thus I am torn and see no clear-cut or black-and-white solution. Again and again I am made aware of the 'aristocratic' source and meaning of human personality and freedom, ungoverned and undetermined as they are from without; and, at the same time, of my profound implication in the pathways of history, which does not admit of a return to the past and demands a constant revision of one's attitude to Russia in the light of the far-reaching social revolution that has taken place and is still continuing there. I can endeavour to unite these two facets within myself, but can their unity be achieved on the open stage of history?

In the spring of 1947 the University of Cambridge conferred on me the degree of Doctor of Divinity. I understand that Russian recipients of an honorary Cambridge doctorate in the past have included Tchaikovsky and Turgeniev. The fact, however, that I should have been chosen for this honour struck me as somewhat ironical, for I lack all the virtues which, as a rule, qualify one for academic distinctions; moreover, I lack all the theological virtues for holding a degree in divinity. After all I am, as I have already had occasion to emphasise, no theologian, but a 'religious philosopher'—a bird rare, if not unknown, in Western Europe but, for better or for worse, rather prominent in Russia. Despite the irony of my predicament, enhanced by the fact that in Cambridge I found myself in the company of Mr. Bevin and the ex-Viceroy of India, I felt then, as on a number of previous occasions, that in no other country have I met with such sympathy and under-

standing as in England. This was a source of great encouragement for
me, especially during the difficult war years.

In the autumn I took part in the proceedings of *Les Rencontres Inter-
nationales de Genève*, devoted to the study of the problems of 'Techno-
logical and Moral Progress'. I have a special reason for noting this
occasion, since I had the unexpected experience of being thrown back
into the Russian atmosphere of fifty years ago, when Marxism was
exercising the power of attraction not primarily of a political or social
programme, but of a philosophy of life. Marxism was the point round
which the whole conference centred, although, except for my own
paper, it was no part of the agenda. There is a craving for belief in
modern man, similar to that which inspired the Russians throughout-
the nineteenth and early twentieth centuries. Faced with the futility of
his own existence the modern European finds himself stranded high
and dry. The trouble is not, of course, political in the narrow sense. It
concerns what are known as the bourgeois values of life. These values
have created an appalling vacuum in the mind and heart of modern
man. The vacuum is still there and, as it appears, historical Christianity,
no less than politicians, fails to fill it. Marxism, apart from providing
an answer to the question of improving the economic standards of
living for the working people, is intent on filling that vacuum. Christians, therefore, will have to show more than a mere taste for twentieth
century topics, and more than a mere rejection of or adaptation to
'communism', the grapes of which are so sour to them: they will have
to show a power to move men *in extremis*, without looking to the right
or to the left, coupled with a genuine sensitiveness to the issues of our
time. For my part, I can see no solution of the betrayal of the world
by Christians or the betrayal of Christianity by the world until history
is ended. Only beyond history is there victory for the spirit of God and
of man.

INDEX

329

A BRIEF OVERVIEW OF
NIKOLAI BERDYAEV'S LIFE AND WORKS

Nikolai Berdyaev (1874–1948) was one of the greatest religious thinkers of the 20th century. His adult life, led in Russia and in western European exile, spanned such cataclysmic events as the Great War, the rise of Bolshevism and the Russian Revolution, the upsurge of Nazism, and the Second World War. He produced profound commentaries on many of these events, and had many acute things to say about the role of Russia in the evolution of world history. There was sometimes almost no separation between him and these events: for example, he wrote the book on Dostoevsky while revolutionary gunfire was rattling outside his window.

Berdyaev's thought is primarily a religious metaphysics, influenced not only by philosophers like Kant, Hegel, Schopenhauer, Solovyov, and Nietzsche, but also by religious thinkers and mystics such as Meister Eckhart, Angelus Silesius, Franz van Baader, Jakob Boehme, and Dostoevsky. The most fundamental concept of this metaphysics is that of the *Ungrund* (a term taken from Boehme), which is the pure potentiality of being, the negative ground essential for the realization of the novel, creative aspects of existence. A crucial element of Berdyaev's thought is his philosophical anthropology: A human being is originally an "ego" out which a "person" must develop. Only when an ego freely acts to realize its own concrete essence, rather than abstract or arbitrary goals, does it become a person. A society that furthers the goal of the development of egos into persons is a true community, and the relation then existing among its members is a sobornost.

He showed an interest in philosophy early on, at the age of fourteen reading the works of Kant, Hegel, and Schopenhauer.

While a student at St. Vladimir's University in Kiev, he began to participate in the revolutionary Social-Democratic movement and to study Marxism. In 1898, he was sentenced to one month in a Kiev prison for his participation in an anti-government student demonstration, and was later exiled for two years (1901–02) to Vologda, in the north of Russia.

His first book, *Subjectivism and Individualism in Social Philosophy* (1901), represented the climax of his infatuation with Marxism as a methodology of social analysis, which he attempted to combine with a neo-Kantian ethics. However, as early as 1903, he took the path from "Marxism to idealism," which had already been followed by such former Marxists as Peter Struve, Sergey Bulgakov, and S. L. Frank. In 1904 Berdyaev became a contributor to the philosophical magazine *New Path*. The same year he married Lydia Trushcheva, a daughter of a Petersburg lawyer. In 1905–06, together with Sergey Bulgakov, he edited the magazine *Questions of Life*, attempting to make it the central organ of new tendencies in the domains of socio-political philosophy, religious philosophy, and art. The influence exerted upon him by the writers and philosophers Dmitry Merezhkovsy and Zinaida Gippius, during meetings with them in Paris in the winter of 1907–08, led him to embrace the Russian Orthodox faith. After his return to Russia, he joined the circle of Moscow Orthodox philosophers united around the Path publishing house (notably Bulgakov and Pavel Florensky) and took an active part in organizing the religious-philosophical Association in Memory of V. Solovyov. An important event in his life at this time was the publication of his article "Philosophical Truth and the Truth of the Intelligentsia" in the famous and controversial collection *Landmarks* (1909), which subjected to a critical examination the foundations of the world-outlook of the left-wing Russian intelligentsia. Around this time, Berdyaev published a work which inaugurated his life-long exploration of the concept of freedom in its many varieties and ramifications. In *The Philosophy of Freedom* (1911), a critique of the "pan-gnoseologism" of recent German and Russian philosophy led Berdyaev to a search for an authentically Christian ontology. The end result of this search was a philosophy of freedom, according to which human beings are rooted in a sobornost of being and thus possess true knowledge.

In 1916, Berdyaev published the most important work of his early period: *The Meaning of the Creative Act*. The originality of this work is rooted in the rejection of theodicy as a traditional problem of the Christian consciousness, as well as in a refusal to accept the view that creation and revelation have come to an end and are complete. The central element of the "meaning of the creative act" is the idea that man reveals his true essence in the course of a continuing creation realized jointly with God (a theurgy). Berdyaev's notion of "theurgy" (in contrast to those of Solovyov and Nikolai Fyodorov) is distinguished by the inclusion of the element of freedom: the creative act is a means for the positive self-definition of freedom not as the choice and self-definition of persons in the world but as a "foundationless foundation of being" over which God the creator has no power.

Berdyaev's work from 1914 to 1924 can be viewed as being largely influenced by his inner experience of the Great War and the Russian Revolution. His main themes during this period are the "cosmic collapse of humanity" and the effort to preserve the hierarchical order of being (what he called "hierarchical personalism"). Revolutionary violence and nihilism were seen to be directly opposed to the creatively spiritual transformation of "this world" into a divine "cosmos." In opposing the chaotic nihilism of the first year of the Revolution, Berdyaev looked for support in the holy ontology of the world, i.e., in the divine cosmic order. The principle of hierarchical inequality, which is rooted in this ontology, allowed him to nullify the main argument of the leveling ideology and praxis of Communism—the demand for "social justice." Berdyaev expressed this view in his *Philosophy of Inequality* (1923).

During this period, Berdyaev posed the theme of Russian

messianism in all its acuteness. Torn apart by the extremes of apocalyptic yearning and nihilism, Russia is placed into the world as the "node of universal history" (the "East-West"), in which are focused all the world's problems and the possibility of their resolution, in the eschatological sense. In the fall of the monarchy in February 1917, Berdyaev saw an opportunity to throw off the provincial Russian empire which had nothing in common with Russia's messianic mission. But the Russian people betrayed the "Russian idea" by embracing the falsehood of Bolshevism in the October Revolution. The Russian messianic idea nevertheless remains true in its ontological core despite this betrayal.

In the fall of 1919, Berdyaev organized in Moscow the Free Academy of Spiritual Culture, where he led a seminar on Dostoevsky and conducted courses on the Philosophy of Religion and the Philosophy of History. This latter course became the basis of one of his most important works: *The Meaning of History: An Essay on the Philosophy of Human Destiny* (1923). His attacks against the Bolshevik regime became increasingly intense: he called the Bolsheviks nihilists and annihilators of all spiritual values and culture in Russia. His activities and statements, which made him a notable figure in post-revolutionary Moscow, began to attract the attention of the Soviet authorities. In 1920, he was arrested in connection with the so-called "tactical center" affair, but was freed without any consequences. In 1922, he was arrested again, but this time he was expelled from Russia on the so-called "philosopher's ship" with other ideological opponents of the regime such as Bulgakov, Frank, and Struve.

Having ended up in Berlin, Berdyaev gradually entered the sphere of post-War European philosophy; he met Spengler, von Keyserling, and Scheler. His book *The New Middle Ages: Reflections on the Destiny of Russia and Europe* (1924) (English title: *The End of Our Time*) brought him European celebrity. Asserting that modern history has come to an end, and that it has been a failure, Berdyaev again claimed that Russia (now the post-revolutionary one) had a messianic mission. He wrote that "culture is now not just European; it is becoming universal. Russia, which had stood at the center of East and West, is now—even if by a terrible and catastrophic path—acquiring an increasingly palpable world significance, coming to occupy the center of the world's attention" (*The New Middle Ages*, p. 36). In 1924, Berdyaev moved to Paris, where he became a founder and professor of the Russian Religious-Philosophical Academy. In 1925, he helped to found and became the editor of the Russian religious-philosophical journal *Put'* (*The Path*), arguably the most important Russian religious journal ever published. He organized interconfessional meetings of representatives of Catholic, Protestant, and Orthodox religious-philosophical thought, with the participation of such figures as Maritain, Mounier, Marcel, and Barth.

In the émigré period, his thought was primarily directed toward what can be called a liberation from ontologism. Emigration became for him an existential experience of "rootless" extra-hierarchical existence, which can find a foundation solely in "the kingdom of the Spirit," i.e., in the person or personality. The primacy of "freedom" over "being" became the determining principle of his philosophy, a principle which found profound expression in his book *On the Destiny of Man: An Essay on Paradoxical Ethics* (1931), which he considered his "most perfect" book. This is how he expressed this principle: "creativeness is possible only if one admits freedom that is not determined by being, that is not derivable from being. Freedom is rooted not in being but in 'nothingness'; freedom is foundationless, is not determined by anything, is found outside of causal relations, to which being is subject and without which being cannot be understood" (from his autobiography, the Russian version, *Self-knowledge*, p. 231).

At around the same time, Berdyaev re-evaluated Kant's philosophy, arriving at the conclusion that only this philosophy "contains the foundations of a true metaphysics." In particular, Kant's "recognition that there is a deeper reality hidden behind the world of phenomena" helped Berdyaev formulate a key principle of his personalism: the doctrine of "objectification," which he first systematically developed in *The World of Objects: An Essay on the Philosophy of Solitude and Social Intercourse* (1934) (English title: *Solitude and Society*). This is how Berdyaev explained this doctrine: "Objectification is an epistemological interpretation of the fallenness of the world, of the state of enslavement, necessity, and disunitedness in which the world finds itself. The objectified world is subject to rational knowledge in concepts, but the objectification itself has an irrational source" (*Self-knowledge*, p. 292). Using man's creative powers, it is possible to pierce this layer of objectification, and to see the deeper reality. Man's "ego" (which knows only the objectified world) then regains its status of "person," which lives in the non-objectified, or real, world. Berdyaev had a strong sense of the unreality of the world around him, of his belonging to another—real—world.

After the Second World War, Berdyaev's reflections turned again to the role of Russia in the world. His first post-war book was *The Russian Idea: The Fundamental Problems of Russian Thought of the 19th Century and the Beginning of the 20th Century* (1946), in which he tried to discover the profound meaning of Russian thought and culture. Himself being one of the greatest representatives of this thought and culture, he saw that the meaning of his own activity was to reveal to the western world the distinctive elements of Russian philosophy, such as its existential nature, its eschatalogism, its religious anarchism, and its obsession with the idea of "Divine humanity."

Berdyaev is one of the greatest religious existentialists. His philosophy goes beyond mere thinking, mere rational conceptualization, and tries to attain authentic life itself: the profound layers of existence that touch upon God's world. He directed all of his efforts, philosophical as well as in his personal and public life, at replacing the kingdom of this world with the kingdom of God. According to him, we can all attempt to do this by tapping the divine creative powers which constitute our true nature. Our mission is to be collaborators with God in His continuing creation of the world.

Summing up his thought in one sentence, this is what Berdyaev said about himself: "Man, personality, freedom, creativeness, the eschatological-messianic resolution of the dualism of two worlds—these are my basic themes."

BORIS JAKIM

2009

BIBLIOGRAPHY OF NIKOLAI BERDYAEV'S
BOOKS IN ENGLISH TRANSLATION
(IN ALPHABETICAL ORDER)

The Beginning and the End. Russian edition 1947. First English edition 1952.

The Bourgeois Mind and Other Essays. English edition 1934.

Christian Existentialism. A Berdyaev Anthology. 1965.

Christianity and Anti-Semitism. Russian edition 1938. First English edition 1952.

Christianity and Class War. Russian edition 1931. First English edition 1933.

The Destiny of Man. Russian edition 1931. First English edition 1937.

The Divine and the Human. Russian edition 1952. First English edition 1947.

Dostoevsky: An Interpretation. Russian edition 1923. First English edition 1934.

Dream and Reality: An Essay in Autobiography. Russian edition 1949. First English edition 1950.

The End of Our Time. Russian edition 1924. First English edition 1933.

The Fate of Man in the Modern World. First Russian edition 1934. English edition 1935.

Freedom and the Spirit. Russian edition 1927. First English edition 1935.

Leontiev. Russian edition 1926. First English edition 1940.

The Meaning of History. Russian edition 1923. First English edition 1936.

The Meaning of the Creative Act. Russian edition 1916. First English edition 1955.

The Origin of Russian Communism. Russian edition 1937. First English edition 1937.

The Realm of Spirit and the Realm of Caesar. Russian edition 1949. First English edition 1952.

The Russian Idea. Russian edition 1946. First English edition 1947.

Slavery and Freedom. Russian edition 1939. First English edition 1939.

Solitude and Society. Russian edition 1934. First English edition 1938.

Spirit and Reality. Russian edition 1946. First English edition 1937.

Towards a New Epoch. Transl. from the original French edition 1949.

Truth and Revelation. English edition 1954.

www.ingramcontent.com/pod-product-compliance
Lightning Source LLC
Chambersburg PA
CBHW020336100426
42812CB00029B/3143/J